The Church in the Nineties

The Church in the Nineties
Its Legacy, Its Future

Pierre M. Hegy, Editor

A Liturgical Press Book

THE LITURGICAL PRESS
Collegeville, Minnesota

Cover design by Greg Becker

1	2	3	4	5	6	7	8	9

Library of Congress Cataloging-in-Publication Data

The Church in the nineties : its legacy, its future / Pierre
  Hegy, editor.
      p .   c m .
  "A Michael Glazier book."
  "Originally presented at the 1990 Washington Conference on the
occasion of the twenty-fifth anniversary of Vatican II"—Pref.
  Includes bibliographical references.
  ISBN 0-8146-2098-1
  1. Vatican Council (2nd : 1962–1965)—Congresses. 2. Catholic
Church—History—1965—Congresses. 3. Catholic Church—Doctrines—
History—20th century—Congresses. I. Hegy, Pierre, 1937- .
BX830 1962.I44 1993
282'.09'045—dc20   92-45242
                                                                          CIP

Contents

II. VATICAN II AND THE MODERN WORLD

The Church and Culture

Peace and Justice

Women in the Church

Marriage and Divorce

Catholic Higher Education

III. THE CHURCH AFTER VATICAN II

The Liturgy

Contributors

Rosemary BROUGHTON is program director for the Institute in Pastoral Ministries at Saint Mary's College in Winona, Minnesota. She is a frequent lecturer in the area of adult faith and spirituality and has recently authored *Praying with Teresa of Avila*.

Francis J. BUCKLEY, S.J., is professor of systematic and pastoral theology and chair of the Department of Theology and Religious Studies at the University of San Francisco. The sacraments and catechesis are his major research interests. He is the author of *Reconciling* and *I Confess: The Sacrament of Penance Today*.

James J. BUCKLEY is an associate professor at Loyola College in Baltimore. His major interests are in dogmatic and systematic theology. Among his major publications is *Seeking the Humanity of God: Practices, Doctrines on Catholic Theology*.

Walter J. BURGHARDT, S.J., long-time professor of patristic theology and for forty-five years managing editor/editor in chief of the journal *Theological Studies,* is currently a senior fellow of the Woodstock Theological Center, directing a national project, "Preaching the Just Word," to move the preaching of social justice issues more effectively into the Catholic pulpits of the country.

Charles E. CURRAN is the Elizabeth Scurlock university professor of human values at Southern Methodist University. He has served as president of the Catholic Theological Society of America, the Society of Christian Ethics, and the American Theological Society. His latest books are *Tensions in Moral Theology* and *Catholic Higher Education, Theology and Academic Freedom,* both from the University of Notre Dame Press.

Thomas F. DAILEY, O.S.F.S., is an instructor in the Philosophy-Theology Department at Allentown College of St. Francis de Sales, Pennsylvania. He has contributed to *The Bible Today, Interpretation, Biblical Theology Bulletin,* and other journals. Specializing in biblical theology and the Wisdom literature, he is preparing a book on hermeneutics and the Book of Job.

Joseph A. DiNOIA, O.P., is professor of theology at the Dominican House of Studies and editor in chief of *The Thomist.* He is the author of the forthcoming book *The Diversity of Religions: A Christian Perspective.*

Denise J. DOYLE, J.C.D., teaches in the Religious Studies Department and is director of the Peace and Justice graduate program at Incarnate Word College, San Antonio, Texas. Her areas of interest include social justice and women's issues.

Robert FASTIGGI holds a doctorate in historical theology from Fordham University. He is currently associate professor of religious studies at St. Edward's University in Austin, Texas, where he teaches courses in both Catholic theology and world religions. He has published articles in Indian journals such as *The Journal of Dharma* and *Jeevadhara* and the *Hindu-Christian Studies Bulletin.* He has recently published *The Natural Theology of Yves de Paris (1588–1678)* from Scholars Press in Atlanta.

Joseph P. FITZPATRICK, S.J., is professor emeritus of sociology at Fordham University. He is the author of *One Church, Many Cultures: The Challenge of Diversity, Paul: Saint of the Inner City,* and *Puerto Rican Americans: The Meaning of Migration to the Mainland.* He is well-known for his involvement in efforts to increase intercultural understanding and communication, especially in a religious context. For many years he has studied the experience of Hispanics in the United States and has published widely on that subject.

Zeni FOX is associate professor of pastoral theology at the Immaculate Conception Seminary School of Theology at Seton Hall University in South Orange, New Jersey. She has done extensive research on new ministries. She has just published "Preparing for Collaborative Ministry in Seminaries" and "The Need for Initiation into and Support of Ecclesial Ministers in their Roles."

James L. HEFT, S.M., is provost of the University of Dayton. Prior to this appointment, he has served as chairperson of the Department of Religious Studies. He is the author of *John XXII (1316–1334) and Papal Teaching Authority* and is published in many journals, including the *Journal of Ecumenical Studies, Commonweal, One in Christ, Archivum Historiae Pontificae, Thought,* and *Marian Studies.*

Pierre M. HEGY is associate professor of sociology at Adelphi University in Long Island. He has published *L'autorité dans le Catholicisme contemporain* on Vatican II.

Mary E. HINES, S.N.D., is associate professor of systematic theology at the Washington Theological Union where she teaches courses in ecclesiology, Christology, feminist theology, and Mariology. She is the author of *The Transformation of Dogma: An Introduction to Karl Rahner on Doctrine.*

Joe HOLLAND, currently visiting professor in ethics and society at Saint Thomas University in Miami, Florida, is president of the Warwick Institute in South Orange. He has published five books: *Varieties of Postmodern Theology, Creative Communion: Toward a Spirituality of Work, American and Catholic: The New Debate, Social Analysis: Linking Faith and Justice,* and *The American Journey.*

James R. KELLY is chairperson of the Department of Sociology at Fordham University. He is published in *Sociological Analysis,* the *Journal for the Scientific Study of Religion,* the *Review of Religious Research,* the *Journal of Ecumenical Studies, Commonweal, America,* and *The Christian Century.* He is writing a social history of the Right to Life Movement. He was born in Brooklyn and never left.

Jean Smith LIDDELL is currently assistant professor of religious studies at Saint Xavier College. She also teaches for the Archdiocese of Chicago in their lay ministry/diaconate training program. She is a doctoral candidate at Fordham University.

Joseph MARTOS is associate professor of theology at Allentown College of St. Francis de Sales. He is the author of *Doors to the Sacred, The Catholic Sacraments, The Sacraments: Seven Stories of Growth,* and many articles on the sacraments.

Carmel McENROY, R.S.M., is associate professor at St. Meinrad School of Theology. Her doctoral dissertation was *A Rahnerian Contribution Toward an Orthodox Theology of Apocatastasis.* She is currently engaged in a research project on the women of Vatican II.

John C. MERKLE is chair of the Theology Department at the College of St. Benedict in St. Joseph, Minnesota. He is the author of *The Genesis of Faith: The Depth Theology of Abraham Joshua Heschel* and the editor of *Abraham Joshua Heschel: Exploring His Life and Thought,* both published by Macmillan in 1985, and numerous articles.

Philip J. MURNION is a priest of the Archdiocese of New York and director of the National Pastoral Life Center.

Mary Kaye NEALEN, S.P., is assistant professor of religious studies at the College of Great Falls, Great Falls, Montana. While completing her Ph.D. in systematic theology at The Catholic University of America, she did five months research in South America. She has work published and in process on the Church, Latin American theology, and Providence.

Jon NILSON is associate professor of theology at Loyola University in Chicago. His articles and essays have appeared in various professional and popular publications. While pursuing his research in contemporary Catholicism, he is working on a study of the religious issues in Dostoyevsky's *The Brothers Karamazov.*

Lucien RICHARD, O.M.I., is professor of systematic theology at Weston School of Theology in Cambridge, Massachusetts. His latest books are *Is There a Christian Ethics?* and *Vatican II: The Unfinished Agenda.*

William P. ROBERTS is professor of theology at the University of Dayton. He is the author of several books including *Marriage: Sacrament of Hope and Challenge* and *Partners in Intimacy,* coauthored with his wife Challon.

Richard A. SCHOENHERR is professor of sociology at the University of Wisconsin-Madison, where he teaches and conducts research in sociology of religion and organizational analysis. Among his publications are *The Structure of Organizations* with Peter Blau, *The Catholic Priest in the United States: Sociological Investigations* with Andrew Greeley, *The Catholic Priest in the United States: Demographic Investigations* with Lawrence Young, and numerous articles.

Michael J. SCHUCK is assistant professor of theological ethics at Loyola University in Chicago. His major interests are Roman Catholic social thought and political, economic, and social theory. His book *That They Be One: The Social Teaching of the Papal Encyclicals 1740–1989* was published in 1991 by Georgetown University Press.

William M. SHEA is a professor in the Department of Religious Studies at the University of South Florida. He authored *The Naturalists and the Supernatural* and published essays in journals such as *The Journal of Religion, The American Journal of Education,* and *Commonweal.* From 1984 to 1986 he was president of the College Theology Society.

Mary Ellen SHEEHAN, I.H.M., S.T.D., is associate professor of theology at the University of St. Michael's College, Toronto, Canada, and director of the Doctor of Ministry Program for the Toronto School of Theology. She has published articles recently on feminist theory and theory-practice correlation in theology. She chairs the C.T.S.A. Seminar on Practical Theology.

Krister STENDAHL is the Robert and Myria Kraft and Jacob Hiatt Distinguished Professor of Christian Studies at Brandeis University. Born, educated, and ordained in Sweden, he taught at Harvard Divinity School for twenty years and was dean from 1968 to 1979. He served as bishop of Stockholm, Sweden, from 1984 to 1988. Jewish-Christian relations have been one persistent focus of his work for twenty years.

Paul SURLIS is associate professor of moral theology and social ethics at St. John's University, New York. Recent publications have dealt with capitalism, social justice, and inculturation in papal teaching, and challenges of liberation theologies. In 1990, Fr. Surlis was awarded the Thomas Hoar Justice Incentive Award for his social justice activities at the university.

Patrick D. VISCUSO is a priest of the Greek Orthodox Archdiocese of North and South America. He holds a Ph.D. in historical theology from The Catholic University of America. His publications have concentrated on the theology of marriage and Oriental canon law. A forthcoming book will deal with Byzantine thought on sexuality.

Rembert G. WEAKLAND, O.S.B., is archbishop of Milwaukee, having been appointed to that See in 1977 by Paul VI. Before being named archbishop, he was abbot primate of the Benedictine Confederation. His major work has been done in music and liturgy.

Lawrence A. YOUNG is assistant professor of sociology at Brigham Young University. Currently he is studying issues of organizational power and clergy decline in the post-Vatican II Roman Catholic Church. He also is investigating how ethnicity, especially for Hispanics, interacts with other social and demographic characteristics to produce patterns of religious disaffiliation.

Preface

Pierre M. Hegy

The papers in this volume were originally presented at the 1990 Washington Conference on the occasion of the twenty-fifth anniversary of Vatican II. Out of about 150 papers presented at this conference, only a few could be included in this volume.

The Washington Conference was made possible thanks to the collaborative effort of the Organizing Committee. Most supportive from the very beginning was Joseph Fitzpatrick, S.J., from Fordham University. The wisdom and experience of Walter Burghardt, S.J., helped overcome difficult times. Joan Chittister, prioress of Mount St. Benedict, was also of great encouragement. Special thanks also to the other members of the Organizing Committee, Brian Daley, S.J., then dean of the Weston School of Theology, and Dean Hoge, from The Catholic University of America.

Now a word about how the idea of the 1990 Conference came about. For that, I would like to go back to 1177 when a shepherd boy, Benezet, suggested building a bridge over the Rhone in Avignon, France, the city of the popes. Everybody thought he was crazy, but soon help and funds flowed in. The Benezet bridge was completed in 1190, and a few arches are still left today. I had the idea of a conference for the twenty- fifth anniversary of Vatican II in 1987; what a strange idea on the part of a sociologist from a local university! But what is so strange on the part of a shepherd to build a bridge when there was none? The Washington Conference was also supposed to build bridges between fields, and between the Vatican Council and the burning issues of the 1990s. In any case, help and funds flew in, thanks to the Organizing Committee.

Very special thanks to Archbishop Weakland for providing this volume with both an introduction and a conclusion, hence providing a bridge, maybe not the easiest to build, between pastors and scholars. Hopefully in distant years a few arches will still be left of this common endeavor.

I think I speak for all of us when I say that we look upon the Conference of 1990 and the coming volume as a beginning. We hope that it has started to link together a network of pastors and scholars that will continue in the future, and help bring a little more light to all of us who are struggling to understand the relationship of the Church to our modern world.

Introduction

From Dream to Reality to Vision*

Rembert G. Weakland, O.S.B.

In 1985, twenty years after the closing of Vatican Council II, bishops from around the world assembled in Rome for an extraordinary synod to study the impact of that council on the history of the Church. They sent a message to the people of God; and I want to begin by citing one sentence from that message, in which they summed up the whole purpose of Vatican Council II as they saw it: "The council in effect had been convoked in order to promote renewal of the church with a view to evangelizing a radically changed world" (Message to the People of God, Sec. IV).

It will be noted that there are two aspects to that concept of why Vatican Council II was called, the first being the renewal of the Church itself, but it is to be remembered, in relationship to a new engagement of the Church with a radically changed world. It was recognized by the bishops that the world had indeed changed much when the bishops had assembled for Vatican Council II and that any renewal, any transformation within the Church had to recognize that similar changes had also taken place within the world. For some time Pope John XXIII had been talking about signs of the times which had characterized that radically changed new world.

A New Engagement with the World

When one thinks back to one's own personal experiences during the council, one could indeed say that the idea of renewal within the Church was uppermost. John XXIII had used the concept *aggiornamento* to mean that the Church had to be updated. Some may have felt a little bit embarrassed by such terminology because it seemed to imply that the Church was in need of a reform and that would simply concede that the Protestants had been right all along.

The attitude that the council projected was that the Church was fallible, had its warts and human weaknesses, and was always in need of being

*Reprinted with permission from *Origins,* vol. 20, no., 18, October 11, 1990.

reformed. That our Church was a Church of sinners had to be accepted before one could begin to read Vatican Council II documents. With this new attitude, humble and searching, came also the end of the baroque triumphalism that had characterized the Church since the Council of Trent. The Church would not be considered then as a perfect society to be emulated by the rest of the world; but rather the Church was *in via,* always searching for truth and willing, in its humility, to engage the world in that same kind of struggle.

Perhaps more than anything else, the council saw the action of the Holy Spirit not only within the Church, but also outside the Church, pulling the Church on to greater holiness as well as engagement toward those values that should characterize the preaching of the kingdom of God.

No other document sums up this attitude of the Church toward the world better than The Pastoral Constitution on the Church in the Modern World. It was finalized toward the end of the council and thus is not just the result of an initial statement of humility before one gets down to work at the material at hand; it is, rather, a mature judgment on how the Church should continue its dialogue with the rest of humanity.

That attitude of being an imperfect society struggling on pilgrimage became a favorite topic for all of us as we preached or taught in the 60s. No one seemed to mind that somehow or another it may have given in to the Protestant contention that the Church was constantly in need of a reformation.

In keeping with that same humble attitude, a new way of looking at holiness evolved. It may seem like a platitude today to speak of the fact that all are called equally to holiness, but in those days it seemed almost like a discovery. No longer did we talk of degrees or states of perfection within the Church. Rather, we accepted that holiness can no longer be compared, that each person is called to the fullness of life in Christ in and through each one's particular calling in the Church and in the world.

This kind of spiritual egalitarianism may not have been easy to swallow by some, but for many of us it was liberating as well as innovative and creative. Till then the Church had been canonizing mostly religious priests and bishops, but now one sensed that the future models of holiness would come from all the people of God and especially from the laity and would be held up as examples for the laity.

It may have been unfortunate, hindsight could tell us this, that the renewal within the Church began in Vatican Council II with the renewal of the public worship of the Church, namely, the liturgy. Since liturgy is so culturally bound, so integral to the life of every Christian, any change in liturgy was bound to affect people in unpredictable ways. The Church may have been a good theologian at that time but was not a wise anthropologist.

One could also say that, as good as the document on liturgy is, it seems to ignore the pastoral implications of the changes demanded. Underneath the document on liturgy is a concept of community, or assembly, that simply had not been realized in our own Catholic piety up to that time. The communal demands placed upon the people of God by the liturgical reform did not seem to synchronize with the personal devotional attitudes that had been theirs, especially during the Eucharist. One could also say that the Church had not heard itself called a reconciling and healing Church, and so renewal in that area demanded a new reawakening of the value of community.

Liturgical renewal, though, had been prepared for for decades, but that preparation had remained rather peripheral and had been a part mostly of scholarly groups and done within monastic enclosures. The whole Church was not quite ready for it. Wisdom would have dictated to have made those changes very gradually so that the new signs and symbols would evolve from the culture of the people and not be superimposed upon them.

This same renewal presupposed that there would be a return to the great tradition of Roman liturgy, with its sobriety and rationality unlike the Byzantine tradition. But no one asked if the people of God wanted or needed such a liturgy. There is no wonder, then, that the next decades were to prove difficult in terms of implementation.

Vatican Council II also awakened in all of us a new sense of the role of the laity. Perhaps no other area gave such a sense of hope as the documents on the laity. Suddenly it was seen that baptism was the important sacrament and that baptism gave to the individual a whole new vocation both within Church and with regard to the world. Suddenly it seemed so commonplace to see the Church as the laity, sustained by the clergy, but not somehow relegated to a second place. Even the fact that the great document on the Church began with a chapter on the people of God indicated that the laity were indeed the Church.

Vatican Council II also balanced the concepts of Vatican Council I on the role of the pope with an extended theology of the role of the bishop as well as the role of the particular and local churches. This new concept of ecclesiology seemed also like a fresh air within the Church itself. Perhaps one of the hopes at that time was that both the renewal of the laity as well as the renewal of the concept of collegiality would create whole new mechanisms and organisms within the Church so that the Spirit could speak through all of these as the Church moved ahead in its new engagement with the world.

The role of the bishop as well as the concept of the local church harkened back to the theology of St. Ignatius of Antioch, and it was hoped that such a theology would become a closer link with the Orthodox

Churches. The whole concept of collegiality in the minds of many extended beyond the relationship between the pope and the body of bishops or the relationship among the bishops themselves to include ways in which other groups within the Church could participate in renewal. The idea that conferences of bishops would become more important in the whole of Church governance seemed like a welcome answer to the rising question of racial differences as well as new cultural manifestations of catholicity itself. The creative minds within the Church worked hard during those years to fathom the depth of these new intuitions and their extent.

It must also be said that one of the great achievements of Vatican Council II that was a sign of tremendous hope for all of us was the ecumenical renewal. As one looks back at the document on ecumenism, one can see the working of the Holy Spirit among the bishops. It is indeed an incredible achievement and opened up all kinds of new vistas. Such a renewal could not have happened without the first renewal of attitude on the part of the Church itself, namely, to see itself in a new, humble way as imperfect and growing through its encounter with others, both with the world and with other Churches and faiths. This new and positive judgment on the part of the Church did away with the biases built up through years, if not centuries. A new euphoria seemed to be upon all of us.

Perhaps the two areas that were the least satisfactory in Vatican Council II in terms of renewal were the documents on religious life and those on priesthood. Somehow or other the bishops did not seem comfortable in either defining or talking about renewal within religious life. The document produced, *Perfectae caritatis,* is weak compared to the other documents and lacking in the kind of inspiration that was needed. Perhaps it is because the religious did not have a strong voice at the council in order to express their own positions or perhaps it was that within the Church itself the prophetic role was not properly esteemed in the 60s.

My own feeling is that a whole new concept had arisen, namely, secular institutes, that were to be instruments of engaging the Church precisely in the world. To develop this whole concept of secular institutes and permit them the space for growth, the concept of religious life had to be confined to a kind of other-worldly existence, one that did not engage the world. But religious took up willingly the vision of Vatican Council II with regard to the world and did not hesitate to move ahead in new directions of engagement with it on their own.

The role of priest was also poorly developed even though the documents wanted to be encouraging. Between the expanded role of the laity and the exalted sense of the position of the bishop, the priest gets a bit shortchanged. That deficiency in the documents of Vatican Council II has stayed with us to this day.

A Single History

All of this renewal of people within the Church was, of course, in order to engage the Church in a new way with the world. The Church was to become a sacrament to the world, that is, a sign to the world of certain values that pertain to the kingdom of God and that could be easily overlooked by that world. On the other hand, the world was not seen as intrinsically evil, as the kingdom of Satan, but rather as a mixed arena that also had its own search for truth and its own contribution to make to history.

Some have said that the document, The Pastoral Constitution on the Church in the Modern World, put an end to the whole Augustinian theory of the two kingdoms. Rather than see the world divided into two camps in a kind of Johannine fashion, one now would rather see good and evil in all camps and that the lines were not carefully drawn.

Vatican II calls this a single history and a model of compenetration. Biblical concepts such as the kingdom of God and the people of God, also a new sense of the role of the Holy Spirit, permeated this attitude toward the world. The Holy Spirit was seen as active not only within the Catholic Church but also outside the Church, drawing the Church on to a new realization of the kingdom. The people of God were not seen as somehow receiving the Spirit from the hierarchy, but rather through their baptism they brought the life of that Spirit to Church and world.

Perhaps one of the greatest contributions of Vatican Council II to the dialogue of the Church with the world was its emphasis on the value of the human person. One could say that the emphasis of Catholic social teaching on the value of the human person that began 100 years ago with *Rerum novarum* found its expression in The Pastoral Constitution on the Church in the Modern World. Here it was seen that what the Church can contribute to the world is indeed an insistence on the intrinsic worth of each person regardless of gender, race, or personal achievements.

To understand also the documents on education and communications, one has to see them in the light of this new attitude of the Church toward the world. Communications should no longer be seen as an evil but, when used properly that they could work for the advancement of the values of the kingdom.

There is no doubt that this new attitude of Vatican II toward the world came at an opportune moment for the Church in the United States. That Church had just opened up to the world in a new way. It was no longer to be a ghetto group defending its own positions and rights, but rather it could begin to take now a new place in American society. That positive attitude toward the world coincided with the teaching that all of us had received in Catholic schools and that had given us the incentive to move ahead to higher education and to take up willingly the challenges of our society.

Many have stated that Vatican Council II was too optimistic with regard to the world. There is some truth in that assertion. The somewhat naive attitudes then seemed to be characteristic of an adolescent rather than of a mature person. The world was perhaps a little less ready to receive those values of the kingdom than the bishops had supposed. Also, the bishops in Vatican Council II had no real theology of the Cross. In that optimism they had somewhat neglected the role of Good Friday or suffering as a necessity for any kind of renewal and also before any kind of Passover can be complete. This naive optimism and also this lack of an approach to suffering became more evident as the implementation began to take place in the following decades.

What Has Happened in Twenty-Five Years?

If one were to ask what has changed the most in the last twenty-five years, that is, what would characterize our day today within the Church as distinct from 1965 in terms of the documents of Vatican Council II, I would have to say that somehow the enthusiasm has spun itself out. All of the optimism and enthusiasm that characterized the termination of the council seem now to have dissipated.

In the mid-60s I remember in my own monastery working through so many difficulties, but always with the feeling that somehow, although we disagreed among ourselves on many issues, we would come to a solution that would be ecclesially correct and benefit all. There was a certain élan within the Church that accompanied that enthusiasm. Although there were marked differences of opinion, there was not polarization, because we were forced to continue to engage in the dialogue that was necessary at the time.

Now I would have to admit that polarization is much more common than the willingness to work toward a common solution. Part of that polarization has come about through a return to a pre-Vatican Council II concept of the perfect Church, some claiming to already possess that Church or at least wanting to restore it. All of the humility in the approach to the world seems to be gone, and it is rare today that one hears anyone in authority talk, as Pope John XXIII did, of a Church that was constantly in need of reform.

Polarization simply means that people no longer dialogue. This can be so clearly seen with regard to the periodicals that appear in our church vestibules each Sunday. People can pick according to their present ecclesiology and feel fairly certain that the periodical that they pick up will have only the point of view that they already agree with. Letters to the editors in these magazines are totally predictable as well as every review of every book. One could tell you immediately by looking at the periodical how the book will be reviewed or how any delicate issue will be tackled.

That polarization was not found in those early years; and in so many ways it was much easier then to be a superior in the Church and probably also just to be among the people of God than it is today. In the twenty-seven years that I have been a major superior in the Church I can honestly say that the lack of enthusiasm now and the polarization have made life so much more difficult in the Church and in so many ways so much more un-Catholic.

Polarization also leads to a certain amount of bitterness and can induce much rash judgment. The media thrives on such polarizations, and concepts that are in any way more subtle or nuanced soon get whittled down so that they can be pitted against another group. The whole Catholic tradition of both/and almost always ends up being either/or. That polarization makes life within the Church not only difficult, but at times almost totally unbearable. Unfortunately, the opinion sometimes circulates that the authorities within the Church like to keep that polarization alive because it seems to be a check and balance against any kind of liberal aberrations. On the contrary, it usually leads only to discouragement and apathy. Loyalty and disloyalty become the politicized terms used, and words such as dissent become the common jargon for disagreement.

Unresolved Issues

But there are aspects of Vatican Council II that remained unresolved at the closing of the council. I think it is very important to admit that there are these loose ends that were never totally drawn to their fullest conclusions and thus could give birth to various interpretations. I do not think it is helpful to make the distinction between the "spirit" and the "letter" of the council with regard to these unresolved issues. One should simply say that they were enunciated by the council but not totally clarified.

I would like to name some of these in passing. First of all, the extent of the principle of collegiality is not clear. By admitting that special role within the Church of each person through baptism, one begins to ask how far people should and can participate also in the decisions that touch their lives without falling into congregationalism. Tensions have arisen between the role of the clergy and the role of the laity. One simply has to admit that these tensions do exist and that the aspirations created by the Vatican II documents are not going to go away simply by edicts that reinforce the power of the hierarchy.

One also has to admit that Vatican Council II and subsequent documents did not do justice to the concept of religious life. Perhaps the last document that was encouraging and clear was *Evangelica testificatio*. Much of this confusion revolves around the question of what is the "world" in Vatican Council II. One simply cannot define religious life, and never could, as a withdrawal from the world; but in the light of Vatican Council II it becomes even more difficult to say that religious should not be involved in that world when they have been doing so for centuries in ways that touch the very heart of the world itself. I still cannot help but feel that this ambiguity on religious life was kept that way so that the whole concept of secular institutes as a kind of consecrated life in the world could be opened up and given full sway. New terminology was invented, but it is not clear if it came out of experience and corresponds to reality or was superimposed.

The priesthood, as mentioned, remains full of ambiguities, and priests have rebelled against being restricted to just the cultic or the therapeutic models. That identity must continue to be worked out in the light of the role of both bishop and laity.

Ecumenism, too, has not worked as people had thought it might. There seems to be no attempt on the part of the Churches to come to a true hierarchy of truth. Often what seems to be most important to theologians takes on a whole different weight with regard to the faithful themselves. Perhaps, too, the documents of Vatican Council II were a bit naive with regard to the political aspects of ecumenical dialogue on the larger scale and have faltered in terms of prophetic witness. Recently one could say that there is a certain apathy with regard to ecumenism, and there exists a real need right now for a clear breakthrough.

It has already been mentioned that the liturgical renewal was fine but seemed not to get at the roots of the concept of society that permeates our cultures. There is always the fear that there will be the return now to a new kind of rubricism; the permissions granted to the Tridentine groups have left everyone a bit disillusioned. The message that seems to be sent out is that the reforms of Vatican Council II were not to be taken seriously in the area of liturgy. The Holy Father has said the opposite in his document on the anniversary of the document on liturgy of Vatican Council II, but the fear does remain that there is a certain inconsistency between teaching and practice, with the result that a certain malaise exists in our midst.

There is also a fear that the liturgical reforms of Vatican Council II were stopped in midair in order to regain a certain stability and that they are indeed quite irregular, if not inconsistent, at times. So, for example, the whole Rite of Christian Initiation of Adults ritual does not seem always to be consistent with the individual rituals for baptism and confirmation. Strangely enough, the whole theology of the sacraments and the whole question of sacramentality seem to be profound crises in the Church today, and yet these issues have not been dealt with in any serious form.

If there is a scarcity of priests and we move ahead to a non-sacramental Church, what will that mean? Is the reception of Communion to be equated with the celebration of Mass? Already some of the difficult questions of signs and symbols in our day were approached by Romano Guardini, but the substantial questions he asked about our modern culture and these signs and symbols have never been answered.

Positive Results

Next, however, I would like to be positive and name some of the fine results of Vatican Council II, where even though the concepts were not too developed they have produced excellent results. So, for example, the synod in 1971 worked on the whole question of justice in the modern world and produced one of the finest documents that we have had in postconciliar thinking. It seemed of itself to justify the whole question of synods of bishops. One could also say that the document on evangelization which Pope Paul VI prepared as a result of the synod on that topic is a masterpiece and a great help in pulling together all of the ideas that had emerged through the various documents of Vatican Council II.

Another highlight of postconciliar reform would have to be, of course, the biblical renewal among us that has for so many of us changed our prayer life as well as our lifestyle. I would also like to enumerate here the major works of the U.S. conference of bishops, in particular the documents on peace and economic justice, as part of the working out of concepts of The Pastoral Constitution on the Church in the Modern World of Vatican Council II.

But there are also new signs of the times and challenges that have arisen in these twenty-five years. One cannot ignore them as if somehow the world stopped in 1965. I list here four of these, as they seem to me to be so important in our day.

The Church is now much more aware of its racial diversity than it was when Vatican Council II opened. That moment was a new moment in its history, but it has not yet come to terms with that racial diversity and what it means to be truly *catholic*. In our own country racial diversity must be respected and be seen as truly a sign of our times.

Perhaps, however, no other area has been so highlighted of late as that of ecology or the care of this earth. Vatican Council II did not really approach the issue of cosmology or, rather, how the human person, with all the dignity that human person has, should relate then to this whole planet. One could say that those issues are going to be the issues for the next decades, and Vatican Council II is not of much help in solving them. It is more than just a question of not polluting the earth; it becomes a whole question of what lifestyle we must live as followers of Christ in order that the earth can be constantly regenerating itself and, as it were, renewing itself from our waste and pollution. A kind of Christian cosmology has to accompany a Christian anthropology.

It is also quite evident that Vatican Council II did not really give us any new insights with regard to human sexuality. In fact, that subject was avoided. Approaches to sexuality, though, divide us most in this day and age and seem to leave us as Church in a most ambiguous situation. It will be important for us to realize how humble we must be with regard to human knowledge in that area and perhaps accept to do just the best we can without pretense of full knowledge as we move ahead to assist the human sciences in analyzing more accurately and more carefully what human sexuality is all about.

Perhaps, however, more than anything else that intuition of John XXIII that women are playing a whole new role in Church and society has become now a commonplace. The Church simply must see that sign of the times as reflective of where the Holy Spirit wishes to guide us and courageously take up that challenge even though Vatican Council II only laid the groundwork for the role of laity as such.

Last of all, I would have to say that one of the new signs of our times is, of course, the whole crisis of authority both within the Church and within our society. Vatican Council II had raised high expectations for a whole new style of exercising authority within the Church. That style simply has not come about. And yet we as a people see changes everywhere on this globe where we thought changes in authority were absolutely impossible. But those changes have only highlighted the fact that the Catholic Church has not changed and remains somehow isolated. It leaves the Church very defensive, then, in terms of its exercise of authority.

This was pointed out so accurately by Andrew Greeley in his comments on *Humanae vitae,* where the whole question of sexuality, the role of women, and now the crisis of authority have all come together. All of these issues relate to the credibility of Church authority for the future, and one could say that the enthusiasm of Vatican Council II has given way to a certain amount of skepticism on the part of some or even fear on the part of others.

And What about the Future?

I would like to name a few issues that I feel are important for us at this juncture, twenty-five years after Vatican Council II, as we face the future.

Needless to say, I would want to begin, first, with a recapturing of that attitude that the Church is but a humble partner, an imperfect society, engaging this world in dialogue. We must avoid any kind of veering toward fundamentalism or integralism that could follow from that fundamentalism. We must recapture the courage that is needed to be prophetic toward a world that is waiting for the values of the kingdom. But, most of all, we must recapture also the hope that was ours twenty-five years ago. If it was naive then, now it can be the mature hope that has come from experience and a certain amount of disillusionment. I realize that this new humble attitude must be accompanied by deeds, and that means a new simplicity of lifestyle based on the gospel and the Beatitudes, a lifestyle that might at times seem to be countercultural to the hopes and ambitions of many in the world.

Second, I would like to stress the need for the Church today to be aware of its duty to bring to the world a sense of the sacred and the transcendent. There is a need for a new God-language that our people can understand. Here I would call for a renewal of our mystical and contemplative traditions that have been so much a part of our past. One should not see that renewal as contradictory to the liturgical renewal; rather, the two go hand in hand. The sense of the sacred and the transcendent must be very much a part of our liturgy and not something that is divorced from our daily life. In this way we can show to the world that we are a sign of something which is more meaningful and more complete than just the daily tragedies that all of us must face.

Third, we also must learn to deal with and live with differences that might seem at first to be threatening and not immediately reject everything as somehow heretical. Recently Father Marlé, in the magazine Civiltà Catolica, spoke again of the pluralism of theologies that has always been a part of our Church. Those theologies come out of our cultural and racial differences, and they are the ways in which so often the Spirit today is speaking to us and drawing us to a whole new level of existence within the kingdom.

Fourth, we must continue our consistency in teaching about justice and especially enlarge this now to the whole area of ecology. These are the problems that we must face, and the new vision must contain them even though the issues of natural resources and their regeneration have not been a part of Vatican Council II thinking. Vatican Council II spurred us on to a kind of new global attitude but that now must become truly ''catholic'' in the best sense of the term.

Fifth, it would come as no surprise if I say that at a certain point we have to begin to be courageous with regard to the role of women. I think I have said enough on this in other areas, but I sense that the whole credibility of our Church and its future will rest on our ability to face up to this issue. Moreover, I expect that we will have to continue to be humble with regard to all sexual issues that face us in the next decades. Human science simply does not have the answers, and it is very difficult to base our moral judgments on imperfect knowledge. In such a case we have to realize the imperfection of the whole process. We have indeed so much to learn.

Sixth, I also would wish that we could integrate more clearly the question of suffering and the Cross into our spirituality and not see that it is in any way contradictory to Christian hope. We live in a period where few people have signs of hope for the future. So many are a bit disillusioned with both world and Church. So many are suffering in ways that we have not known in the past because they involve instability and uprootedness. Hope and suffering are but two sides of the same expression of a deep and enlivened faith. I would like to quote a Brazilian author, Rubem Alves, in this regard:

"The two, suffering and hope, live from each other. Suffering without hope produces resentment and despair. Hope without suffering creates illusions, naiveté, and drunkenness. Let us plant dates, even though those who plant them will never eat them—we must live by the love of what we will never see. This is the secret discipline. It is a refusal to let the creative act be dissolved away in immediate sense experience and a stubborn commitment to the future of our grandchildren. Such disciplined love is what has given prophets, revolutionaries and saints the courage to die for the future they envisaged. They make their own bodies the seed of their highest hope."

I would like to end by reiterating the need to accept that if the future is going to be hopeful for all of us, then we have to indeed accept the Cross right now and suffering. It means that we have to accept the fact that prophets are never truly accepted among their own. It means that often we have to speak a word that neither Church nor world wants to hear. More than anything else, it means that we have to remain hopeful and faithful through those challenges. The future is not in the hands of those who give up, but only in the hands of those who within their hearts remain faithful to the gospel values as they see them.

The world today needs to take again that attitude of Vatican Council II which was indeed one of enthusiasm and hope for the kingdom and renew it today in a more mature and realistic way after twenty-five years of much sacrifice and stumbling. It means that we say within our hearts that it was the Holy Spirit that brought about and brought to conclusion Vatican Council II and gave so many new insights and so many sources of renewed inspiration. That same Holy Spirit is with us today in our generation, in our day. That same Holy Spirit will continue to guide us in a truly creative and expansive way.

A global Church that is concerned about every individual and every aspect of this planet awaits us. The Spirit pulls us on to an even greater involvement if we have the courage to say yes.

Part I

The Theology of Vatican II

Ecclesiology

Mary E. Hines

Vatican II initiated an intense period of reflection on the mission, nature, and structures of the Church. Often referred to as the council on the Church, Vatican II produced two major constitutions, *Lumen gentium* and *Gaudium et spes,* devoted entirely to the Church, while most of the other documents deal with issues that have ecclesiological dimensions. The theological reflection which grew out of the council was accompanied by significant changes in Church practice, initially experienced most dramatically in increased participation by the laity in the liturgy and a gradually developing awareness that the Church's mission in the world required a concrete commitment to action on behalf of justice.

The more than twenty-five years following the council have been years of excitement and enthusiasm for many as well as fear and hesitation by others about the Church's new direction. There continues to be some debate concerning interpretation of the council fathers' intentions. Was continuity, particularly with the directions of Vatican Council I, their primary concern, or did they truly wish to set the Church on a new course within the modern world?

The German theologian, Karl Rahner, arguably the most influential Catholic theologian of the twentieth century, was present at the council and took the latter view. He interprets the council as the first great act of the coming *world-Church* which represents only the second great caesura in the Church's history. While the first move, very early in the Church's history, was accommodation to the Greek world, this new leap in ecclesial understanding sees the Church as coming to be authentically within each unique culture in which it is incarnated. His *world-Church* thus envisions the Church as a communion of local indigenous Churches.[1]

Central to the theology and ecclesiology of Vatican II is its changed understanding of the proper relationship of Church and world. While earlier

---

[1] Karl Rahner, "Basic Theological Interpretation of the Second Vatican Council," *Theological Investigations XX,* trans. Edward Quinn (New York: Crossroad, 1981) 77–89.

3

ecclesiologies had often pictured the Church as refuge from an evil world, Vatican II firmly fixes the vocation of the ecclesial Christian and indeed the mission of the Church itself within the world which it sees as a place of both sin and grace. The history of the world is coterminous with salvation history. In a development of this idea, Edward Schillebeeckx reverses the old adage "no salvation outside the Church," to read "no salvation outside the world."[2] Christians may find positive elements in the world or may find it necessary to be prophetically critical of much that is *worldly,* but flight from the world is no longer viewed as an authentic Christian option.

This very central insight has ramifications in all other aspects of Church life. Laity, who live their lives in the world, are no longer viewed as secondary citizens of the Church, at least theoretically. Since the council laity have been struggling to claim, in practice, their rights and responsibilities as full members of the people of God by baptism.

Perhaps the second major paradigm shift at the council, to which both of the following essays allude, is the move from viewing the Church primarily in its institutional aspects to an emphasis on its communal dimensions. The Church is thus understood as a communion of baptized and participating members, all of whom are called in various ways to share in the ministry and mission of the Church. The hierarchy as well as the laity and members of religious communities are seen in the first instance as members of the holy and sinful people of God journeying together toward God's realm. The Church is not an end in itself, but a means to the final eschatological fulfillment of God's promise of justice, peace, and freedom from human oppression. Here again the past twenty-five years have involved a good deal of struggle toward realizing this insight.

The Church understood as communion has ecumenical implications as well, for the Church of Jesus Christ is understood to be a much wider reality than the institutional Roman Catholic Church. The *communio* includes all those who believe and confess Jesus as savior. People of God is understood to include all persons of good will. How the Church is actually related to the other historical religions, however, remains a matter of considerable discussion.[3]

Also implied in understanding the Church as communion is the retrieval of the theological notion of reception with which both of the following essays deal in different ways. Reception as more than a juridical concept refers to the incorporation of conciliar or doctrinal Church declarations into the actual life of the local Churches. If the Church is truly a community

---

[2]Edward Schillebeeckx, *Church: The Human Story of God,* trans. John Bowden (New York: Crossroad, 1990) 5–15.

[3]See for example, John Hick and Paul F. Knitter, eds., *The Myth of Christian Uniqueness* (New York: Orbis, 1987).

of participation and dialogue[4] then all voices must be heard in bringing the new theological vision articulated at Vatican II to reality. As the first of the following essays points out, in the process of reception voices of opposition play an important part. The silencing of such voices by Church authorities is a serious impediment to the authentic dialogue needed to realize a truly communal ecclesial vision. The voices of those traditionally marginalized in the Church, women and the poor,[5] must also be heard and incorporated before the Church can speak a credible, liberating word in today's world. Twenty-five years later, then, Vatican II remains an enormous challenge. Whether its vision will transform the Church or remain largely unrealized depends on the outcome of the process of reception in which we are now engaged.

[4]See Paul Lakeland, *Theology and Critical Theory: The Discourse of the Church* (Nashville: Abingdon, 1990).

[5]See for example, Anne Carr, *Transforming Grace* (New York: Harper and Row, 1988); Rosemary Ruether, *Sexism and God-Talk* (Boston: Beacon Press, 1983); Gustavo Gutiérrez, *A Theology of Liberation* (New York: Orbis, 1973); Jon Sobrino, *The True Church and the Poor* (New York: Orbis, 1984).

Chapter 1

Reflections on Dissent and Reception

Lucien Richard, O.M.I.

I. Reception as an Ecclesial Process

Derived from the ecclesial practice of the early Church, the concept of reception refers to the process through which an ecclesial community incorporates into its own life a particular custom, decision, liturgical practice, or teaching. Today the term is used in two distinct but related contexts. The classical or historical sense of the term refers to the acceptance by local Churches of particular ecclesiastical or conciliar decisions. A more contemporary, ecumenical use of the term refers to the acceptance by one Church of a theological consensus arrived at with another Church and ultimately the recognition of the other Church's faith and ecclesial life as authentically Christian.

The renewal of interest in the concept and reality of reception is due to many factors. The emphasis of Vatican II on the nature of the Church as a traditionary process is clearly one of them. The renewed interests in the *sensus fidelium,* i.e., the role of the whole Church in grasping Christian truth, in the relation between evangelization and inculturation, and in the relation of local Churches to the Universal Church, are also factors. What is of crucial importance for us in this paper is the fact that such a renewal of interest carries with it fundamental options on the nature of the Church that affect our understanding of dissent.

It is important for our case to note that the practice of reception emerged as an ecclesiological reality during the first millennium when the Church was understood as a communion of Churches. It somehow disappeared when the excessively hierarchical concerns of the Church developed and emphasized the centralization of ecclesiastical authority. In an exclusively hierarchical concept of Church, reception is reduced to a purely juridical category.

II. Reception as a Theological Reality

Over the past twenty years the phenomenon of reception has increasingly captured the attention of Western scholars, especially in the history of law. As a legal reality, reception has its roots in Roman law. While the concept of reception was first clearly articulated in a legal context, it is much more than a legal theory: it is a theological reality that flows from the very nature of the Church. Reception is a process of ecclesial life, a process of the "we" which hands on the Christian tradition—a corporate process. Reception flows from the fact that human beings are essentially social. They are formed in community via communication; they seek truth communally via dialogue. In short, communion is the law of life, and reception, as a group process, flows from this communion. Reception in its complex theological meaning is well described by Henry Chadwick:

> We take it, I think, that it is a technical term for that process by which in the Church of God we digest and assimilate a definition of doctrine in the making of which we ourselves may not have participated except indirectly. And yet if the definition presented to us, perhaps received from those who have faithfully transmitted to us the faith, if that definition which is presented to us truly belongs to the authentic deposit of faith or to what the Church sees that it needs for the safeguarding of the clarifying of that, then our receiving has a positive, vital effect. It is in that sense, I take it, that reception is distinct from the submission of obedience to duly constituted authority. It is totally unlike my normal response to the tax inspector's demands or even to my respect for the highway code. It implies not a passive acquiescence but an active exercise of the trained, critical judgment; it is a consent of the believing mind and heart which, perhaps slowly but surely, comes to see that through that definition, whether it was of a synod or a primate, the authentic, living voice of faith has been spoken in the Church, to the Church, by God.[1]

III. Reception and the Church *Koinonia*

To grasp the particular ecclesiological foundation for reception one must perceive that reception only makes sense when the Church is understood as a *koinonia,* i.e., as a communion. Ecclesiologically speaking, reception flows from the Church perceived as communion. The renewed vision of the Church as a communion has been essential in the resurrection of meaningful talk about reception.

The concept of the Church as a communion harmonizes with several biblical images: those of the body of Christ and the people of God. The

---

[1]Henry Chadwick, General Synod, *Report of Proceedings* 16/1 (February 1985) 75.

image of the body of Christ is organic rather than sociological. The Church is seen on the analogy of a human body equipped with various organs. It has an in-built vital principle thanks to which it can grow, repair itself, and adapt itself to its changing needs. The principal image of the Church in the documents of Vatican II is that of the people of God. The people of God is a biblical concept having deep roots in the Old Testament, where Israel is constantly referred to as the nation of God's special predilection. Both images emphasize the immediate relationship of all believers to the Holy Spirit; both focus attention on the mutual service of the members toward one another and on the subordination of the particular good of any group to that of the whole body of people. Both images are more democratic in tendency than the so-called institutional model of the Church. The image of the people of God differs from that of the body of Christ in that it allows for a greater distance between the Church and its divine head. The Church is seen as a community of persons each of whom is individually free. But both images illuminate from different angles the notion of the Church as communion or community.

Both communion and community derive from the Greek *koinonia*. *Koinonia* in turn comes from *koinos*, "common," and the verb *koinoun* means "to put together." *Koinonia* and its Latin cognates *communion* or *communicatio* indicate the action of having in common, of sharing in and participating in. Yves Congar pointed out that the real sense of these two words is that of participation.[2]

The Church from the point of view of participation is not in the first instance an institution or a visibly organized society. Rather it is a communion of women and men, primarily interior, but also expressed by external bonds of creed, worship, and ecclesiastical fellowship. Reception is a concrete manifestation of the *koinonia* in the Church—the *koinonia* which *is* the Church. It is within the understanding of the Church as communion that the concept and reality of the *sensus fidelium* can best be understood. Reception itself is intrinsically connected with the affirmation of the *sensus fidelium*, and an integral element of the Church understood as "communion." For Newman the *sensus fidelium* was viewed as one element of the *sensus ecclesiae*, and he put the emphasis on its active and dynamic aspects.[3] The term later took on a more passive connotation: a source to be tapped for doctrinal definition by the magisterium. In its more active sense, the *sensus fidelium* merges with consensus and reception in the Church. Vatican

[2]Cf. Yves Congar, *Le Concile de Vatican II: Son Église, peuple de Dieu et corps du Christ* (Théologie Historique 71; Paris, 1984) 34; see also *Sainte Église: Études et approches ecclésiologiques* (Paris, 1963) 37–40.

[3]Cf. J. H. Newman, "On Consulting the Faithful in Matters of Doctrine," ed. J. Colson (London, 1961) 63–65.

II seems to have preferred a more active meaning for the word. "Thanks to a supernatural sense of the faith which characterizes the people as a whole, it manifests this unerring quality when 'from the bishops down to the last member of the laity' it shows a universal agreement in matters of faith and morals."[4] This seems to suggest a vision of the Church as a community of wisdom.

The *sensus fidelium* must be related to a doctrine of the Holy Spirit. It cannot be understood without situating it within an understanding of the action of the Holy Spirit in the midst of the people of God. Because of the relation of the Spirit to the body of the Church, "simple Christians" do not participate in the knowledge of the Christian mystery simply through the hierarchy. Rather, the Holy Spirit leads each believer to a knowledge of the mystery of Christ in such a way as to benefit the whole body of believers. Tillard states:

> Even at the level of the understanding of the content of Revelation and of the rendering explicit of its elements, those faithful who have no hierarchical responsibility cannot be seen as simply receiving what is determined by the heads of the Church enlightened by the research of theologians, or other specialists in "educated faith"; the faithful have a specific part to play in this knowledge by the whole Church of the truth given in Jesus Christ.[5]

This is a point that Congar also stresses strongly:

> It is one thing to say: the believing and loving Church is only infallible when it listens to the teaching Church and thereby receives the communication of infallibility *from the latter;* it is another thing to say: the believing and loving Church is infallible through the animation which it receives from the Holy Spirit in its quality as the believing and loving Church, a quality which involves an organic reference and submission to the Magisterium. In the first case, the Holy Spirit gives infallibility to the hierarchy which, in subjecting the faithful to itself, communicates to them the benefit of its infallibility; in the second case, the Holy Spirit gives infallibility to the whole Church as such and, in it, each organic part according to what it is: the whole body, in order to believe and live, the hierarchical apostolate or Magisterium, in order to transmit to the body the apostolic deposit and to declare the authentic meaning of this deposit.[6]

Congar also emphasizes that a believer does not receive tradition as some kind of passive object; rather, what is passed on is received by a living, active subject. He writes: "If faith, the initial reality of salvation, is transmit-

---

[4]*Lumen gentium*, no. 12.
[5]J.M.R. Tillard, "Sensus Fidelium," *One in Christ* II (1975) 11–12.
[6]Y. Congar, *Jalons Pour Une Théologie du Laïcat* (Unam Sanctam 23, Paris, 1953) 402.

ted, it must also be *received*, actively received. 'Actively' that is, there exists a *subject* who receives (saving) faith, and this subject is in turn active in receiving it. Thus tradition will not be merely a transmission followed by a passive, mechanical reception; it entails the making present in a human consciousness of a saving truth.'"[7]

The nineteenth-century distinction between active and passive tradition and the distinction between an active infallibility for the magisterium and a passive infallibility for the laity tends to neglect the acting subject. This distinction turns members of the Church into things, hardly recognizing them as living subjects. The *sensus fidelium* implies that not only the magisterium, but the whole ecclesial body is an organ of tradition. It is interesting to note here that one key concept used by John Paul II, especially in *Laborem exercens* (1981) and *Sollicitudo rei socialis* (1987), is that of the human being as "subject", i.e., responsible agents of their society. Subjects have the right to participate in the decisions that affect their lives. The pope emphasizes the true subjectivity of society.

The *sensus fidelium* in the Church is an intrinsic element of the Church as communion. It also emphasizes two basic elements that are essential for the Church to be communion: communication and participation. Without true communication communion does not occur. Communion as a reality underlines the rule of conscious intentions of human agents; it emphasizes that the nexus of relations which unites us in a human society is not organic but personal. Personal unity is possible only through communication.

Besides communication, communion demands participation. As L. Vischer wrote:

> Reception is another aspect of participation. To the degree in which teaching has been arrived at through the participation of the entire body of Christ, reception will be facilitated. Structures of participation at all levels of the Church prepare the way of reception.[8]

Participation implies some degree of equality. Equality does not mean that all people are similarly endowed or that everyone is capable of doing everything. But in the Church equality must at least mean that all individuals have certain rights that have not been received from other members of the Church and that flow simply from the fact of their being created to the image of God and having been baptized.

[7]Y. Congar, *Tradition and Traditions*, trans. N. Nasebi and Rainborough (London, 1966) 253.

[8]L. Vischer, "How Does the Church Teach Authoritatively Today?" *Concilium 148: Who Has the Say in the Church?*, eds. Hans Küng and J. Moltmann (Edinburgh: T. & T. Clark, 1981) 7.

Authentic reception demands communication and participation. To the degree in which teaching has been arrived at through the communication and participation of the entire Church, reception has played its proper role. Structures of participation and communication at all levels of the Church prepare the way of reception. In his classification of reception as an essential part of the principle of verification of orthodoxy in the Church, E. Schillebeeckx also emphasizes this implication of communication:

> Christian faith is the faith of a community which has a history in time and space and which interprets this in the light of the need to act consistently in a Christian manner and in the light of changing (philosophical and social) assumptions. Christian proclamation takes place in a specific situation of discourse, which of course has a context of communication. The world of faith is a communal world, with a sphere of shared interest and also a world of shared speech and understanding—a "universe of discourse."[9]

For example, people do not confirm a doctrine juridically by a majority vote or some similar political mechanism; rather, they approve and therefore "receive" a doctrine insofar as they manifest in their life and attitudes that they recognize in it the right expression of their faith.

Reception functions within an ecclesial reality where communication and participation are effective realities. Yet reception implies authority. It implies an authority, however, that is not *above* the Church, but *within* it. Reception, then, is a direct threat to the Western tendency to isolate authority from the community. Reception is at home in a more wholistic, organic context. The whole Church is anointed with the Holy Spirit; its mode of existence is dialogical. Authentic dialogue always allows people to be themselves. It leaves room for the other person's identity, modes of expression, and values. True dialogue does not invade; it does not manipulate. For there can be no such thing as dialogical manipulation. The primary dimension of true dialogue is intersubjectivity, or intercommunication, which cannot be reduced to a simple relation between a knowing subject and a knowable object. Just as there is no such thing as an isolated human being, there is also no such thing as isolated thinking. Dialogue is simply the co-participation of persons in the very act of thinking and speaking. In this dialogue the object is not simply the goal of the act of thinking, but the mediator of communication. Dialogue achieves a communion of horizons which leads to self-disclosure and self-understanding.

It is a dialogical understanding of the search for truth which seems to be the context for the following statement found in "The Declaration on Religious Freedom":

[9]E. Schillebeeckx, *The Understanding of Faith: Interpretation and Criticism* (London, 1974) 70–72.

> Wherefore every man [sic] has the duty, and therefore the right, to seek the truth in matters religious in order that he may with prudence form for himself right and true judgments of conscience, under use of all suitable means.
>
> Truth, however, is to be sought in a manner proper to the dignity of the human person and his social nature. The inquiry is to be free, carried on with the aid of teaching or instruction, communication and dialogue, in the course of which men explain to one another the truth they have discovered, or think they have discovered, in order thus to assist one another in the quest for truth.
>
> Moreover, as the truth is discovered, it is by a personal assent that men are able to adhere to it.[10]

A Church in dialogue will certainly not be a smooth-running, frictionless body. Schillebeeckx recognizes this when, speaking of the process of the acceptance by the community of a new theological interpretation, he writes:

> History teaches us that centuries may pass before the community of the church comes to recognize itself in a given interpretation of faith. To begin with, a new interpretation is more likely to be disputed and even declared heretical by the community than to be accepted, because of its surprising newness. So long as the church permits and encourages scientific freedom and openness and does not make a theologian suffer harm because of juridical regulations—in which case all theological discussion comes to an end—scientific criticism and counter-criticism arise. A new interpretation of this kind is often accepted by a considerable number in the community of the church, while another section of the community rejects it. In my opinion, the official church should respect this tested dialectical process within the community of faith. It is only after a great deal of friction that a new interpretation can be either accepted or rejected. In the course of this debate, naturally, all kinds of new problems will have arisen.[11]

To emphasize reception as an essential element of the Church's reality is to accept simultaneously the possibility of non-reception. Either there is a "Yes" of acceptance or a "No" of rejection. These two alternatives are healthy expressions of a dialogical community. Leading to the death of such a community would be "the deafening silence of the total indifference of the majority of the faithful." If reception is an essential element of the Church, then the possibility of non-reception is built into the structure of the Church. And that is because the Church itself as a communion is characterized by communication and participation.

John Paul II's book *The Acting Person* can serve to illustrate the intrin-

---

[10]"Declaration on Religious Freedom," no. 3.
[11]E. Schilllebeeckx, *The Understanding of Faith: Interpretation and Criticism,* 70–71.

sic relation between community and dialogue. In his discussion on authentic community, the Pope points to three characteristics that distinguish authentic community: solidarity, opposition, and dialogue. Solidarity is the attitude of a community in which the common good properly conditions and initiates participation. It refers to a readiness to accept and realize one's share in the community. The author sees *opposition* as "essentially an attitude of solidarity."[12] It is the attitude of those who because they are deeply devoted to the common good disagree with official ideas and policies. Of such opposition, the then Cardinal of Krakow makes several statements: "The one who voices his opposition in the general or particular rules or regulations of the community does *not* thereby reject his/her membership. Indeed, such opposition is vital to the community's growth and well-being. It is essentially constructive. . . . "[13] He continues, "In order for opposition to be constructive, the structure and beyond it the system of communities of a given society must be such as to allow opposition that emerges from the soil of solidarity not only to *express* itself within the framework of the given community but also to *operate* for its benefit. The structure of a human community is correct only if it admits not just the presence of a justified opposition but also that practical effectiveness of opposition required by the common good and the right of participation."[14]

Dialogue allows us to "select and bring to light what in controversial situations is right and true." Wojtyla admits that dialogue involves strains and difficulties and is sometimes messy. But a "constructive communal life" cannot exist without it. Opposed to solidarity and opposition are "inauthentic" attitudes of "servile conformism" and "non-involvement." For example, "conformism brings uniformity rather than unity."

Opposition is not opposed to communion; it can be essentially constructive, a sign of health and vitality. One of the many questions emerging relative to the non-reception within the Church and to the possibility of public dissent is the nature of the assent given to the non-infallible teachings of the magisterium. This assent is described in the new canon law as *obsequium religiosum* (Canon 752). What is religious submission? For some it is obedience; for others it is religious respect. Respect is due the teacher and this is possible even when one dissents relative to some teachings. The emergence of an attitude of indifference or apathy toward the magisterium could not be reconciled with religious respect. The proper response to teachings is such respect but not obedience.

---

[12] Cardinal Karol Wojtyla, *The Acting Person*, trans. Andrzei Putocki (London: D. Reidel Publishing Co., 1979) 286.

[13] Ibid.

[14] Ibid., 287.

Truth as understood within the Christian community by necessity refers to the Christ-event, a reality that happens. The paradigm of dialogical communication is central for setting the conditions for the adequate search of such a truth. My point of view is governed by the vision of the Church as a pilgrim community renewing itself by creative interaction with its changing environment. From the Lord it has received a vision, a vision expressed and communicated in parabolic language.

Thus the Church may in some sense be called a "society of explorers." Not map readers. The Church, like any other society, needs outside criticism and depends on all the help that its reflective members can provide in the task of discerning the real meaning of the gospel for our time. Faith, then, is not simply a matter of accepting a fixed body of doctrine. More fundamentally, it is a committed and trustful participation in an ongoing process, marked by a situation of "not yet" and "already."

Chapter 2

Models of the Church
and *Baptism, Eucharist and Ministry*

Mary Kaye Nealen, S.P.

Today, in many parts of the world, under the influence of the grace of the
Holy Spirit, many efforts are being made in prayer, word and action to attain
that fullness of unity which Jesus Christ desires. The sacred Council exhorts,
therefore, all the Catholic faithful to recognize the signs of the times and to
take an active and intelligent part in the work of ecumenism.[1]

These words from the *Decree on Ecumenism* of Vatican Council II speak
loudly of new understandings of Church which have emerged in the past
twenty-five years. " . . . To attain that fullness of unity which Jesus Christ
desires" is a great cry of longing which issues from the mouths of Catholics
and non-Catholics alike. In this anniversary year of Vatican II, it is appropriate to explore anew the meaning of the Church. The search to be undertaken here is not a purely theoretical one. Rather, it is a delving into the
results of over fifty years of ecumenical dialogue, to which Roman Catholics are relative newcomers, about topics very closely related to the meaning of the Church.

The subject chosen here is the document *Baptism, Eucharist and Ministry,* commonly known as the "Lima text." Adopted by the Faith and Order
Commission general meeting January 3–15, 1982, in Lima, Peru, the document was then judged ready to send to the Churches for their responses.
The first of four questions directed to the Churches asked them to reply
to "the extent to which your church can recognize in this text the faith
of the Church throughout the ages."[2]

Against the horizon of the invitation extended by the conference at
Lima, and under the impetus of the Vatican *Decree on Ecumenism,* this paper

---

[1]"Decree on Ecumenism" *Vatican Council II: The Conciliar and Post Conciliar Documents,*
ed. Austin Flannery (Northport, N.Y.: Costello Publishing Co., 1975) art. 4.

[2]Faith and Order Paper 111 (Geneva: World Council of Churches, 1982); the four questions appear in the Preface.

will explore the Lima document in respect to models of the Church recognizable in its content and in its method. It will argue the thesis that the 1982 World Council of Churches document, *Baptism, Eucharist and Ministry* (B.E.M.), projects a community model of Church as conciliar fellowship. It will further maintain, in support of this thesis, that conciliar fellowship exemplifies important aspects of all the ecclesiological models described by Dr. Avery Dulles in *Models of the Church*.[3]

The paper will first summarize Dulles' five basic models as they apply to B.E.M. and as they are reflected in the official Catholic response.[4] It will then outline Dulles' sixth model, the community of disciples, as a key to the model most representative of the World Council of Churches document. It will examine in greater detail the paradigm to which community of disciples points, conciliar fellowship. It will, further, explore reception both as concomitant with conciliar fellowship and as integral to its method or *praxis*. Finally, it will propose implications of the foregoing reflection for movement into the future.

I. Five Perspectives on the Church in B.E.M.

While essentially positive and supportive of the progress toward Christian unity represented by B.E.M., the response by the Vatican Secretariat for Promoting Christian Unity made abundantly clear the need for a thorough ecclesiology to ground the understanding and practice of baptism, Eucharist, and ministry. Yet even within the preliminary theology of Church in the Faith and Order document, certain emphases are apparent. A brief discussion of Church models may illuminate these beginnings.

Dulles' five basic models of Church—institution, mystical communion, sacrament, herald, and servant—serve as lenses through which to view the Church as presented in the Lima document and in the official Catholic response. The five models do not stand out equally in the Lima text. In the order of increasing prominence, the herald and servant models are visible but not highly so—yet both are more salient in B.E.M. than in the Vatican response. The sacrament model, although nominally more obvious because of the subject matter of B.E.M., is present only inchoately. In B.E.M. the institution model appears in terms of the necessary structural dimension of ecclesial action, undertaken within the diversity of participating fellowships. In the Catholic response, by contrast, the institution model acquires more prominence through the aspects chosen for comment. Even more sig-

[3]Expanded edition (Garden City, N.Y.: Doubleday, 1987).

[4]Secretariat for Promoting Christian Unity, "Roman Catholic Church," *Churches Respond to BEM*, vol. 6, Faith and Order Paper 144, ed. Max Thurian (Geneva: World Council of Churches, 1988) 1–40.

nificantly, the official Catholic stress on the institution represents the high value placed on Church order. The mystical communion model, finally, stands out in the emphasis of both B.E.M. and the Vatican response upon the saving work of the triune God carried out through the Church.

The last mentioned of Dulles' five basic models brings this inquiry to the central affirmation that communion is the foundational model of Church in *Baptism, Eucharist and Ministry*. At the same time, let it be said that communion is a highly complex model in both the World Council and the Roman Catholic faith understandings.[5] How this is true will become clearer in the following discussions, first of Dulles' synthetic model of a community of disciples and then of the World Council model of conciliar fellowship.

II. A Synthetic Model: Community of Disciples

Dulles sets forth his idea of "community of disciples" with the reservation that "there can be no supermodel that does full justice to all aspects of the Church" (206). Nevertheless, while he deliberately draws sharp lines of demarcation for the first five models, here he unites complementary aspects of Church and makes connections among the diverse models previously described.

A model which emphasizes discipleship harmonizes closely with B.E.M. The unquestionable center of the Lima text is Jesus Christ. Discipleship stems from Jesus' call to his followers and his forming them to share his mission. After his death, resurrection, and gift of the Spirit, discipleship expanded to include all those who follow his way. Disciples continue to gather to hear his word proclaimed and to celebrate his sacraments, especially the memorial of his Body and Blood. Within the rhythm of community and mission, they reach out to the world in evangelization and service.[6]

Thus the model of community of disciples, with its scriptural and Christological focus, can be of great assistance in understanding the Church and appreciating B.E.M. It can, in particular, help to integrate understandings of Church and of sacrament. Dulles identifies four traditional elements of sacrament and shows how the elements are true also of the community of disciples:

[5]Much valuable work on communion and community has been done within the various traditions which enriches this discussion. To mention only two: Jerome Hamer's *The Church Is a Communion* (New York: Sheed and Ward, 1964) is a classic presentation of biblical, historical, and theological insights on the concept. In Lukas Vischer and Harding Meyer, eds., *Growth in Agreement* (Faith and Order Paper 108; Geneva: World Council of Churches; New York: Paulist Press, n.d.) are a number of documents dealing specifically with community. The Lutheran-Roman Catholic statement "Ways to Community, 1980," 215–39, is one of these.

[6]See Dulles' exposition of the discipleship model in relation to the other five in *Models*, 204–26.

In the first place, this community unquestionably has its origins in Christ, who instituted it in his earthly ministry and later energized it by the gift of his Spirit. Second, the disciples visibly represent Christ. . . . Third, Jesus is really present in the community of the disciples, as in a sacrament. . . . Finally, Christ's presence in the community of disciples is dynamic and effective. . . . Thus the two models of Church, while resting on different analogies, express much the same reality.[7]

The author demonstrates well how this community model incorporates the essential elements of the other five. The communion of grace (mystical communion) is structured as a society (institution). It offers worship to God (sacrament), proclaims the good news (herald), and serves the needs of the world (servant; 204). Without discussing the models specifically, Thaddeus Horgan describes in almost these same words the *koinonia* ecclesiology which he holds up as a highly significant outcome of Vatican Council II: "That appreciation of the church that sees it as a communion of persons gathered in the body of Christ, a visible praying, worshipping, and serving community of believers, has become the ecclesiology of the ecumenical movement."[8]

III. Conciliar Fellowship: Called to Unity

How, then, does the preceding overview of models, and particularly of the community of disciples, help to understand conciliar fellowship and its relationship to B.E.M.? First of all, the Fifth World Assembly in Nairobi in 1975 used the term "conciliar fellowship" officially to specify the goal of unity. The Nairobi Assembly described the main purpose of the World Council, which is also the singular aim of the Faith and Order Commission, as "a conciliar fellowship of local churches which are themselves truly united."[9] The official Catholic response to B.E.M. specifically underlined this goal within the "broader ecumenical perspective" (6).

Horgan identifies "conciliar fellowship" as one of three terms frequently used to refer to *koinonia* ecclesiology. According to it, "local churches retain their identity but are joined locally in a communion, with each local communion belonging to a larger worldwide communion."[10] Jeffrey Gros brings additional elements into his definition:

[7]*Models*, 223–24. Scripture references given by the author in the portion quoted have been omitted.

[8]Thaddeus D. Horgan, "The Second Vatican Council's Decree on Ecumenism—25 Years Old," *America* 162 (June 2, 1990) 550.

[9]William H. Lazareth quotes this Nairobi formulation in "1987: Lima and Beyond," *Ecumenical Perspectives on Baptism, Eucharist and Ministry,* Faith and Order Paper 116, ed. Max Thurian (Geneva: World Council of Churches, 1985) 185.

[10]Horgan, 550.

The B.E.M. document follows an affirmation of a view of the church as a conciliar fellowship united in each place and in all places, looking forward to the day when a General Council of the church recognized as such by Orthodox, Catholic and Protestant can be convened to celebrate the fullness of eucharistic unity and witness with one voice to a suffering and divided world plagued by injustice, hostility, war, and ignorance.[11]

Historically, the conciliar approach reaches back to the past and forward to the future. John Deschner points out that the participation of the Roman Catholic Church and the increased involvement of the Orthodox Churches in the World Council of Churches has helped to produce an "historical deepening" in the ecumenical movement. The Churches are now revisiting not only sixteenth-century questions, but also those of the fourth century.[12] These early centuries were times of Church councils which bear major significance to this day. Such councils spark the hope that the Christian Churches may see a future council in which Protestants, Orthodox, and Roman Catholics may act together to express the meaning and the power of Christ's message for the world today.

"Conciliar fellowship" implies a theological as well as an historical depth. A Faith and Order study that grew out of the Nairobi Assembly points out that the root of "conciliarity" and "conciliar" is the Latin verb *conciliare,* which means "to call together." While the usages of "council" and its derivatives over many years are far from univocal and the linguistic history of the terms complex, the World Council holds to a core meaning of being called together by Christ in the name of the gospel.[13]

The same study spells out three theological dimensions of the concept of conciliarity as used by the W.C.C. First, the notion is used here as ecclesiological and theological. Second, it expresses the sacramental and eschatological aspects of the Church of Jesus Christ, which points to and makes effective the mission of Christ. Third, the concept refers to the unity of the Church and, more specifically, its *visible* unity (245–46).

Deschner emphasizes that the term is more than a concept or a theory. It is a structural principle, integral to the unity being effected. Even more, it is "an ecclesial principle with profound roots in the nature of the divine triune life in which we share and profound implications for the future of

---

[11]Jeffrey Gros, "Baptism, Eucharist and Ministry: Introduction," *Journal of Ecumenical Studies* 21 (Winter 1984) 5.

[12]See John Deschner, "The Unity of the Church and the Renewal of Human Community," *Toward Visible Unity: Commission on Faith and Order, Lima, 1982,* vol. 2, *Study Papers and Reports,* Faith and Order Paper 113, ed. Michael Kinnamon (Geneva: World Council of Churches, 1982) 184–92.

[13]Faith and Order Commission, *Conciliar Fellowship* (1982) 247.

our Churches' life together.''[14] He continues, " 'Conciliar fellowship' must be a fellowship of both ecclesial and situational integrity among churches which are facing and making the 'preferential options' demanded by God in our time—and for whom controversy concerns not whether but how such options are to be actualized" (196–97).

Questions which arise at this point are, for one, what basic elements of "conciliar fellowship" are found in the discussion above? Can this description of Christian unity be considered a model of the Church? What relationship does "conciliar fellowship" bear to the Lima document?

Conciliar Fellowship as a Form of Communion

First, some of the common elements found in the definitions are: (1) local faith communities which retain their distinctiveness, (2) a larger unity which participates in God's own unity and within which each finds a place, (3) concerted action which addresses the serious needs of the world, and (4) the anticipation of a fuller unity yet to come. These elements as concretely lived by the various local Churches give particular shape to the reality of communion. In *The Church Is a Communion*, Jerome Hamer nuances the way that "communion" can be attributed to the Church, "only on condition that it is not shorn of any of the components it has acquired during its long history" (173–74). The distinct ways of being, relationships, levels of unity, and forms of organization in the participating Churches are all dimensions of that communion which takes the form of conciliar fellowship in the last quarter of the twentieth century.

Does "conciliar fellowship" qualify to be a model of the Church? As an image which functions paradigmatically both to integrate and to stimulate thought about the meaning of the Church, this more-than-a-concept does serve as a model in the ecumenical arena. Concerning the use of models in ecclesiology, Dulles notes that "each paradigm brings with it its own favorite set of images, its own rhetoric, its own values, certitudes, commitments, and priorities. It even brings with it a particular set of preferred problems" (31). Even this brief exposition indicates the type of coherence that each model possesses.

All this may be true, yet one might argue that the term "conciliar fellowship" never appears in B.E.M. At first glance the substance of the notion does not even appear in the Lima document in the way that "institution," "mystical communion," "sacrament," "herald," "servant," and "community of disciples" do. Nevertheless, the conciliar fellowship model does pertain to B.E.M., if in a different though real manner than the six models pertain that Dulles proposes.

[14]Deschner, 196; see also 194.

This relevance appears in two ways. The first is the context of B.E.M. within the whole Faith and Order process. Recall that the World Council at Nairobi, Kenya, in 1975 interpreted the goal of the W.C.C. as conciliar fellowship. The 1978 Faith and Order meeting in Bangalore, India, listed three basic requirements for reaching the desired visible unity. They were: "(1) full mutual recognition of baptism, the eucharist and the ministry; (2) common understanding of the apostolic faith; and (3) agreement on common ways of teaching and decision-making."[15] Study subsequent to the Bangalore gathering was to focus on these three requirements. *Baptism, Eucharist and Ministry* was a direct response to the program outlined in Bangalore and an important step toward conciliar fellowship and full visible unity.

The second point of connection between conciliar fellowship and B.E.M. is the method by which the text was formulated and the means by which its acceptance is being sought. The text represents more than fifty years of effort by Faith and Order, the World Council, and bilateral and multilateral dialogues among the Churches. It stems from the work that more than one hundred theologians and pastors from nearly every major Church group accomplished in Lima in January 1982.

Just as significantly, the Lima document initiated a process of study and official response by the Churches. In this process the common elements in the definition of "conciliar fellowship" are identifiable. The Churches could respond (1) according to their own distinctiveness. They focused their responses around questions which (2) reflected a larger unity, not only the awareness of belonging to a worldwide fellowship, but also a loyalty to "the faith of the Church through the ages." They replied (3) in a spirit of service to the world to whom they desire to witness effectively. And they gave voice to their faith that (4) the unity they seek is the unity which God gives in Jesus Christ. Varied as they are, the responses published in seven volumes by the World Council impressively signify a new way of being Church today, a respectful, multiform, participative mode called "conciliar fellowship."

IV. Reception as Conciliar Action

While the immediate period of official response is now over, the time of study and reception has only begun. Jeffrey Gros states succinctly that *"reception* is a theologically defined process by which a community sees in a text or formulation an authentic witness to the biblical faith."[16] William

---

[15]Quoted in Lazareth, "1987: Lima and Beyond," 185.

[16]"Reception of the Ecumenical Movement in the Roman Catholic Church, with Special Reference to *Baptism, Eucharist and Ministry,*" *American Baptist Quarterly* 7 (March 1988) 40.

G. Rusch holds the ecclesial reality of reception "to include all the phases and aspects of a process by which a Church makes the result of a bilateral or multilateral conversation a part of its faith and life."[17]

This process is familiar in substance, if not in vocabulary, to Roman Catholics. The steady growth in familiarity with the *Rite of Christian Initiation of Adults* on the part of parishioners is an example. As congregations gain experience welcoming candidates formally for baptism, or watching the candidates leave the church after the prayers of the faithful to continue sharing the Word of God, people's understanding of the whole life of faith is slowly changing. The reception of this aspect of the renewed liturgy of initiation is taking place.

What will happen to Catholics' perception of the life of faith when parish and diocesan groups use the questions posed by Faith and Order about the Lima document? What will be the significance of deciding "the extent to which your church can recognize in this text the faith of the Church throughout the ages" (Preface)? What will change in hearts and habits when Catholics, along with Methodists and Russian Orthodox and Pentecostals, determine "the guidance [their] church can take from this text for its worship, educational, ethical, and spiritual life and witness"? When local Churches, particularly in ecumenical settings, grapple with these and related questions, reception is occurring.

In addition to the conversion of hearts and the intra Church processes which occur in reception, the inter-Church dynamics are important. Geoffrey Wainright draws attention to the report on "Steps Towards Unity" from the Sixth World Council Assembly in Vancouver, B.C., in 1983:

> The ways in which the churches respond to B.E.M. and the ways in which they engage in a longer process of reception provide an ecumenical context within which the churches can learn to understand and encounter each other's ways of making decisions about church teaching. The significance of this opportunity needs to be emphasized, for common agreement about ways of teaching and decision-making is one of the fundamental marks of church unity.[18]

Therefore, to return to the question at hand, the reception process underway for B.E.M. is conciliar fellowship at work. In terms of models, con-

[17] " 'Baptism, Eucharist and Ministry'—and Reception," *Journal of Ecumenical Studies* 21 (Winter 1984) 140.

[18] Geoffrey Wainright quotes this passage in "Reception of 'Baptism, Eucharist and Ministry' and the Apostolic Faith Study," *Journal of Ecumenical Studies* 21 (1984) 78. This article is one in an excellent series on the theme of reception which appeared in this issue of the *Journal*. They represent the fruits of a symposium on the Lima document and reception, held in Chicago a few months prior to the issue.

ciliar fellowship exemplifies important aspects of the ecclesiological models described by Dulles. While it takes the approach largely of a partnership of communities, equally disciples of Jesus Christ, it does not ignore questions of authority and decision-making. It looks to the inner life of the participating communities which they receive from Christ and celebrate particularly in his memorial meal. It seeks to be more faithful to the Word of God so that this Word may be believed in a world which longs for healing and hope. In brief, essential elements of all six of Dulles' models are present in the model of conciliar fellowship which B.E.M. helps to make vital.

V. Movement into the Future

In Respect to B.E.M.

ECCLESIOLOGY. As encouraging as the response to the Lima text has been, much remains to be done. Some challenges pertain directly to the ecclesiology of B.E.M. Not only Catholic theologians and Church officials urge further study of Church and sacrament. The Faith and Order study on conciliar fellowship says frankly, "Without a common understanding of the nature, notes, authority, and mission of the Church, there will be no genuine visible unity. At the same time, we learn more about the Church in the struggle for visible unity and in working together" (258).

The Sixth Assembly of the World Council in Vancouver, 1983, also

> affirms that it will be impossible to take this common step [toward an expression of the apostolic faith today] if in this study of the apostolic faith we do not give special attention to the nature and mystery of the Church of God, since the confession of the one, holy, catholic, and apostolic Church belongs to the apostolic faith.[19]

The many commentaries and official responses indicate areas calling for further study in common. Serious inquiries into some of these areas are already underway through the continuing bilateral and multilateral dialogues.

INCLUSIVENESS. A second concern is the issue of who will be heard in the reception process. The fact that Faith and Order and the World Council characteristically locate their assemblies in varied parts of the world helps ensure that not only northern hemisphere Christians will have a voice. The official responses from Churches of many countries contribute to a pluralistic reading of the text. At the same time, both Protestant and Catholic women

---

[19]Quoted by William H. Lazareth in "Baptism, Eucharist and Ministry Update," *Journal of Ecumenical Studies* 21 (Winter 1984) 18.

have urged more extensive participation by women in the reception of B.E.M. Francine Cardman considers this involvement imperative. She asserts also that "the aim of relating the goal of ecumenism—the unity of the church—to the renewal of the human community cannot be realized without seriously confronting the obstacles to both unity and community presented by the systematic subordination of women in the church and beyond it."[20] Authentic reception requires participation by all, especially those who might most easily be excluded, in this process.

In Respect to Christian Unity

Yet the challenges posed by B.E.M. unfold onto the whole horizon of Christian unity. They involve the process of reception; this means not only reception of the Lima document, but—specifically for Catholics— reception of the new understandings of Church articulated in the *Decree on Ecumenism*. In Dulles' framework of models, the prevailing model in the Roman Church prior to Vatican II was the institutional, with significant consideration of mystical communion and sacrament. Influenced by such factors as the liturgical renewal, the greater prominence of Churches in the southern hemisphere, and the ecumenical movement, the Catholic Church has manifested more of the herald and servant models. Catholics are being moved to live Church in a different way.

This invitation to newness of perception and practice is, in fact, a call to conversion. It is the profound renewal urged in the *Decree:* "There can be no ecumenism worthy of the name without interior conversion" (art. 7). It acknowledges sinfulness, which "holds good for sins against unity. Thus, in humble prayer we beg pardon of God and of our separated brethren, just as we forgive them that offend us" (7). In his commentary on the *Decree*, Johannes Feiner states strongly the implications of this conversion:

> With its powerful emphasis on self-denial and humility, the text is a clear rejection of all self-righteousness and superiority, every kind of "triumphalism," and also of the self-assured and opinionated apologetics which says nothing about the deficiencies and failings in its own church but expatiates all the more on those of other Churches. The spirit of brotherly love and service . . . creates a new climate in Christianity . . . , produces a desire for unity, and

---

[20]"BEM and the Community of Women and Men," *Journal of Ecumenical Studies* 21 (Winter 1984) 93. In the same issue appears Victoria Chandran's "Reception and Women in the Third World," 125–28. Lorna Shoemaker provides a Protestant view in "Feminist Symposium on *Baptism, Eucharist and Ministry,*" *Ecumenical Trends* 13 (November 1984) 155–58. This symposium comprised nine Presbyterian women theologians, both lay and clergy, February 13–14, 1984, at San Francisco Theological Seminary.

alone makes possible a true encounter and fruitful dialogue among Christians of different denominations.[21]

The new vision of Church—or rather, a willingness to envision Church newly—is a powerful challenge posed by the Lima document and the process of its reception. Since the Catholic Church had fully functioning participants at the Lima meeting, this document offers the opportunity for serious attention by Catholic people and local Churches. If it receives such attention, a more humble, cooperative, enthusiastic understanding of the Church will surely result. If women and men alike have the opportunity to examine the Lima text in light of the apostolic tradition of faith, and to examine Catholic doctrine and practice in light of this same tradition, a new model of Church will certainly emerge. Catholics will come more fully to recognize Christians in other Churches as companion disciples of Jesus Christ. New and important steps will be taken toward the unity desired by Christ and expressed in the gospel. In this spirit the words of the *Decree on Ecumenism* will be more fully realized and "all believers in Christ [will be] able to learn easily how they can understand each other better and understand each other more, and how the road to the unity of Christians may be made smooth" (art. 12).

---

[21]"Commentary on the Decree," *Commentary on the Documents of Vatican II,* vol. 2, ed. Herbert Vorgrimler (Freiburg: Herder, 1967; Montreal: Palm, 1968) 99.

Introduction to Systematic Theology

Dogmatics after Vatican II

Joseph A. DiNoia, O.P.

In the twenty-five years since Vatican Council II, nearly every doctrinal topic has been the object of vigorous theological inquiry. Leaving aside topics addressed elsewhere in this volume, the following brief sketch considers in turn the Trinity, creation and providence, theological anthropology, Christology, soteriology, pneumatology, mariology, sacramental theology, revelation, and theological method. My purpose is to identify the principal issues central to discussions of each topic and the chief figures whose contribution in this area is either seminal or representative. In the course of this frankly selective survey, there will be occasion to note the impact of both broad twentieth-century theological concerns as well as distinctive conciliar emphases.[1]

A concern to supplement and indeed to surmount neoscholastic textbook approaches to Catholic dogmatics has prevailed everywhere in postconciliar theology.[2] This is particularly evident in the theology of the Trinity. Following the lead of the greatest twentieth-century Catholic theologians—Karl Rahner (1904–1984) and Hans Urs von Balthasar (1905–1988)—others have sought to recover the center field in Catholic dogmatics for the doctrine of the Trinity.[3] When separated from consideration of the existence and nature of God (a procedure canonized in the textbook disjunction of the tracts *De Deo Uno* and *De Deo Trino*), the doctrine of the Trinity seemed to be marginalized. Recent theologians have sought to restore the doctrine's

[1]For extensive discussion of the council's impact on theology, see René Latourelle, ed., *Vatican II: Assessment and Perspectives*, 3 vols. (New York: Paulist Press, 1989). For an interpretation of postconciliar theology within the context of broad trends in twentieth-century theology, see J. A. DiNoia, "American Theology at Century's End: Postconciliar, Postmodern, Post-Thomistic," *The Thomist* 54 (1990) 499–518. For another perspective, see David Tracy, "The Uneasy Alliance Reconceived: Catholic Theological Method, Modernity and Postmodernity," *Theological Studies* 50 (1989) 548–70.

[2]See Walter Kasper, *Theology and Church*, trans. Margaret Kohl (New York: Crossroad, 1989) 1–16.

[3]Karl Rahner, *The Trinity*, trans. Joseph Donceel (New York: Herder and Herder, 1970); for an entré to the corpus of H. U. von Balthasar's works, see his "A Resume of My Thought," *Communio* 15 (1988) 468–73.

significance for Catholic thought and life by exhibiting the Trinitarian structure of the whole economy of salvation and centering theological explication on this mystery. Notable postconciliar contributions to this discussion are works by the Tübingen theologian Walter Kasper (1933–) and by Thomists William J. Hill (1924–) and Jean-Herve Nicolas (1909–).[4]

In contrast to the doctrine of the Trinity, the doctrine of creation has not been the subject of a major work by a Catholic theologian in the postconciliar period. But this is not to say that the doctrine has been neglected. Several issues have surfaced in recent theology of creation. Debate has centered on the consistency of the notion of *creatio ex nihilo* with the scriptural account of creation. Also, increasing attention has focused on the appropriation of rapidly developing scientific findings concerning the origin of the universe—particularly as represented by the prevalence of a modified Big Bang theory among astrophysicists in combination with inflationary theory among particle physicists. The bearing of these findings and theories on explication of the doctrine of creation is widely debated among theologians who can boast at least a modicum of scientific literacy. Creation and evolution are at the center of a related debate, particularly since disputes about this issue consistently gain a high media profile in the United States. Another set of issues clusters around the plausibility of Christian claims about the providential guidance of a universe viewed increasingly in the perspective of chaos theory and of the operation of chance.[5]

But the cosmocentrism basic to science-theology debates has not been a typical feature of recent theology. In this sense, postconciliar theology has been resolutely modern: it has tended to be anthropocentric rather than cosmocentric in its concerns. To be sure, the scientifically well-informed theological anthropology of Benedict Ashley (1915–) shows that these concerns are by no means mutually exclusive.[6] But in much recent theology, theological anthropology has retained its longstanding ordering role. No theologian in this period exemplifies this more clearly or more influentially than Karl Rahner.[7] Typical of theology in this vein is the endeavor to frame

---

[4]Kasper, *The God of Jesus Christ*, trans. Matthew J. O'Connell (New York: Crossroad, 1984); W. J. Hill, *The Three-Personed God* (Washington, D.C.: The Catholic University of America Press, 1982); J.-H. Nicolas, *Synthèse dogmatique: De la Trinité à la Trinité* (Paris: Beauchesne, 1985).

[5]For discussion of these issues, see Ernan McMullin, ed., *Evolution and Creation* (Notre Dame, Ind.: University of Notre Dame Press, 1985); David B. Burrell and Bernard McGinn, eds., *God and Creation* (Notre Dame, Ind.: University of Notre Dame Press, 1990); Robert John Russell, William R. Stoeger, and George V. Coyne, eds., *Physics, Philosophy and Theology* (Vatican City State: Vatican Observatory Press, 1988).

[6]Benedict Ashley, *Theologies of the Body* (Braintree, Mass.: Pope John XXIII Center, 1985).

[7]Rahner, "Theology and Anthropology," *Theological Investigations*, vol. 9, trans. Graham Harrison (London: Darton, Longman and Todd, 1972) 28–45.

theological affirmation in categories drawn from analysis of the structures of human consciousness, experience, or existence. Powerful nineteenth-century currents feed this enterprise and sustain postconciliar theology's continuing efforts to appropriate constructively the diverse agendas of modernity.

Within theological anthropology itself, no topic has been more hotly debated than that of the relation of nature and grace. The issues have been framed chiefly in terms of the relation of the supernatural order to the natural order. Controversy about this topic—already well underway in the preconciliar period—reflected the attempt of progressive theologians to recover the prescholastic sources of the tradition (*ressourcement*) and to deploy them in all areas of Catholic dogmatics. Against baroque Scholasticism and post-Reformation polemical theology, Henri de Lubac (1896–1991) and Karl Rahner argued in different ways for a unified conception of the economy of salvation in which the natural order is seen to be embraced within the supernatural order and ordained to the single end of fellowship with God.[8] Although this debate waned somewhat in the immediate postconciliar period, it shows signs of gathering renewed momentum in current theology.

The impact of *ressourcement* has been felt in Christology and soteriology as well. Theologians who specialize in these topics have sought to appropriate the results of historical-critical study of the Scriptures. Here the names of Edward Schillebeeckx (1914–) and Walter Kasper stand out.[9] Reflecting long-term trends in this area, theologians continue to be challenged to explicate the universal soteriological significance of Jesus Christ. Disagreement about how best to tackle this issue sharply divided Rahner and von Balthasar in this period. Rahner favored a soteriology subsumed under a universal Christology, conceived as the ontological culmination of the divine self-giving to the human race. Von Balthasar, on the other hand, insisted that soteriology—as dramatically enacted in the Cross of Christ—is the clue to Christology.[10]

The council itself provided the basis for robust theological renewal in the areas of pneumatology, mariology, and sacramental theology. By plac-

---

[8]Henri de Lubac, *The Mystery of the Supernatural*, trans. Rosemary Sheed (New York: Sheed and Ward, 1967); Rahner, "Concerning the Relationship between Nature and Grace" and "Some Implications of the Scholastic Concept of Uncreated Grace," *Theological Investigations*, vol. 1, trans. Cornelius Ernst (Baltimore: Helicon Press, 1961) 297–346.

[9]Edward Schillebeeckx, *Jesus: An Experiment in Christology*, trans. Hubert Hoskins (New York: Seabury Press, 1979) and *Christ: The Experience of Jesus as Lord*, trans. John Bowden (New York: Crossroad, 1981); Kasper, *Jesus the Christ*, trans. V. Green (New York: Paulist Press, 1976).

[10]See Rahner, "On the Theology of the Incarnation," *Theological Investigations*, vol. 4, trans. Kevin Smyth (Baltimore: Helicon Press, 1966): 105–20; von Balthasar, *The Moment of Christian Witness*, trans. Richard Beckley (New York: Newman Press, 1969).

ing the work of the council under the "patronage" of the Holy Spirit, Pope John XXIII was popularly viewed as having ushered in a new Pentecost. The great stimulus this has entailed for theology of the Spirit is perhaps best exemplified in the work of Yves Congar (1909–).[11] As it turned out, the role of the Blessed Virgin Mary became one of the great themes of the council. Here earlier works of Rahner and Schillebeeckx were influential.[12] These two theologians also contributed significantly to the renewal of sacramental theology.[13] The renewal of Catholic sacramental practice prompted by the council—itself the fruit of decades of theological work—supplied the impetus for a vast outpouring of energy in this area in the post-conciliar period.[14]

Postconciliar theology of revelation has for the most part sought to consolidate the results of earlier work on this doctrine. In the period under review here, works by Avery Dulles (1918–) and René Latourelle (1918–) stand out.[15] Debate has centered on the issues of the relationship of experience to revelation, and the role of propositions as vehicles of revelation. Here, the prevailing explication of revelation in personalist categories has favored the widespread adoption among theologians of the notion of "divine self-communication."

A typically modern feature of postconciliar theology has been its preoccupation with fundamental theology and theological method. Bernard Lonergan (1903–1984) and Karl Rahner have provided the lead in this area.[16] In the following generation, several theologians have addressed various aspects of the nature and method of theology from different perspectives, notably David Tracy (1939–), Joseph Ratzinger (1927–), Francis Fiorenza (1941–), and Aidan Nichols (1948–).[17] Pressing challenges for all these

[11]Yves Congar, *I Believe in the Holy Spirit*, 3 vols., trans. David Smith (New York: Seabury Press, 1983).

[12]Rahner, *Mary, Mother of the Lord* (New York: Herder and Herder, 1964); Schillebeeckx, *Mary, Mother of the Redeemer* (New York: Sheed and Ward, 1964).

[13]Rahner, *The Church and the Sacraments,* trans. W. J. O'Hara (New York: Herder and Herder, 1963); Schillebeeckx, *Christ the Sacrament of the Encounter with God* (New York: Sheed and Ward, 1963).

[14]See Kevin W. Irwin, "Recent Sacramental Theology," *The Thomist* 47 (1983) 592–608; 52 (1988) 124–47; 53 (1989) 281–313; and "Sacramental Theology: A Methodological Proposal," 54 (1990) 311–42.

[15]Avery Dulles, *Models of Revelation* (Garden City, N.Y.: Doubleday, 1983); René Latourelle, *Theology of Revelation* (New York: Alba House, 1966).

[16]Bernard Lonergan, *Method in Theology* (New York: Herder and Herder, 1972); Rahner, *Foundations of Christian Faith,* trans. William V. Dych (New York: Crossroad, 1978).

[17]David Tracy, *The Analogical Imagination* (New York: Crossroad, 1981); Joseph Ratzinger, *Principles of Catholic Theology,* trans. M. F. McCarthy (San Francisco: Ignatius Press, 1987); Francis Schüssler Fiorenza, *Foundational Theology* (New York: Crossroad, 1984); Aidan Nichols, *The Shape of Theology* (Collegeville: The Liturgical Press, 1991).

thinkers are the endeavor to secure the unity of theology in the midst of increasing philosophical pluralism and to exhibit the rational basis for Christian theology. In connection with the latter, but on a more popular front, several apologetic works by Hans Küng (1928–) have had wide appeal and won a vast readership.[18]

[18]Hans Küng, *On Being a Christian,* trans. Edward Quinn (Garden City, N.Y.: Doubleday, 1976); *Does God Exist?,* trans. Edward Quinn (Garden City, N.Y.: Doubleday, 1980).

Chapter 3

The Doctrine of God
in the Postconciliar Church

James J. Buckley

The notion of "postconciliar" has all the ambiguities of the notions of "post-liberal" theology outside the Catholic community and "post-modern" postures outside the Christian community. That is, on the one hand such notions point to something *new* post-wherever-many-of-us-are-now, *avant garde*. On the other hand, it is less clear what notions such as "postconciliar" (post-liberal, post-modern) refer to than what they do *not* refer to; the liberal or conservative cynic might argue that postconciliar theology will always be parasitic on that council which it claims to transcend. I shall presume that "the postconciliar Church" is the community of Christians in various neighborhoods and nation-states—reading their Scriptures, worshipping in Word and sacraments, contributing to the common goods of the Church and their churches, sent on a mission to a world of many religions and unbeliefs, in solidarity with the joys and griefs of that world, saintly and sinful characters.

Among many other activities, this community will teach each other and others about God. Indeed, by "the doctrine of God" I mean the set of teachings about God which are articulated by the Christian community. What does Vatican II teach us about God and the doctrine of God? The goal of the following remarks is to answer this question in four steps. Needless to say, limits of space and time will prevent developing each point in detail.

I. The doctrine of God has played what Jaroslav Pelikan calls a "largely implicit role" in the history of Christian doctrine.[1]

When Christians hear "the doctrine of God," they may think that we are dealing with something well-established that must either be conserved

[1]Jaroslav Pelikan, *Christian Doctrine and Modern Culture (since 1700)*, The Christian Tradi-

or revised. But this is not true. Admittedly, theologians will be familar with doctrines like the Nicaean *homoousion* or Vatican I's chapter "On God" in *Dei Filius*. But these constitute the exception rather than the rule. Neither Pelikan nor I, of course, would deny that Christians have taught many things about God in their homes and from the pulpit and in various classrooms. Claiming that the doctrine of God has been largely implicit is not denying this truism but only affirming that such teachings have not become teachings of the whole Church in contrast to one individual or group within the Church.

II. Vatican II continues the tradition of offering an implicit rather than explicit doctrine of God.

In one of his important articles on Vatican II, John O'Malley has proposed that one of the ways Vatican II differed from previous reforming councils was "the lack of a single 'focused issue' "—including (and perhaps particularly) a doctrine of God.[2] The emphasis ought to go, I believe, on "single." Vatican II took up a range of issues: the sources of revelation, the reform of our liturgy, the nature and mission of the Church and the churches, Judaism and other religions, and the joys and griefs of modernity (particularly those of the poor and afflicted). But postconciliar debates are shaped by debates over which of these issues are crucial for our times. And this means that we are frequently—certainly in the case of the doctrine of God—left with "implicit" rather than "explicit" guidance.

III. In a world which as a whole (if not in all its parts) does not any longer know roughly (as Aquinas puts it at the conclusion of each of his five ways) what "God" signifies, it is crucial that Christians learn to make the "largely implicit" doctrine of God explicit.

One reason Christians have been able to afford a "largely implicit" doctrine of God, I think, is that our forebears lived in largely theistic cultures—cultures which bore the marks of Judaism or polytheism, Islam or deism.

tion. A History of the Development of Doctrine, vol. 5 (Chicago and London: University of Chicago Press, 1989) 182–83. In context, it is clear that Pelikan thinks that this implicitness is not good in "modern culture," but he does not address the range of reasons with the directness necessary to clarify *why* we need to make the implicit explicit.

   [2]John O'Malley, "Developments, Reforms, and Two Great Reformations: Towards a Historical Assessment of Vatican II," *Theological Studies* 44 (1983) 373–406, now reprinted in John W. O'Malley, S.J., *Tradition and Transition: Historical Perspectives on Vatican II* (Wilmington, Del.: Michael Glazier, Inc., 1989) 82–125.

This suggests, I think, three reasons why we need to learn to make our doctrine of God "explicit." First, what John Courtney Murray called the godless persons of the Academy or the Marketplace, of political Revolution or the Theatre did not formerly play the sort of role they play today.[3] Second, neither did what Vatican II calls the "Non-Christian Religions"—ways of living which include claims about "the ultimate . . . mystery" of our lives but which propose competing candidates for such unrestricted importance—formerly come in the massive varieties we find in our world. A third and more important reason for articulating our teachings about God is that our doctrine of God is the set of teachings about God the Christian community articulates as we engage in various activities before and with God: as we read our Scriptures, worship in Word and sacrament, contribute to the common goods of the Church and the churches, undertake our mission to a world of many religions and unbeliefs, in solidarity with the joys and griefs of that world, saintly and sinful characters. In other words, we need to make our implicit doctrine of God explicit not only because strangers and enemies call us to do so but also and primarily because we need to be truthful about who the God is whom we seek and celebrate, preach and teach.

IV. Against this background, Vatican II's contribution to our postconciliar doctrine of God is twofold. First, Vatican II's main contribution to the doctrine of God in a postconciliar Church is its implicit teaching that God, who is the ultimate mystery of our lives, is with us in each and every occasion of our lives.

At this stage, what students of Vatican II would demand is a journey through the details of the actual texts of Vatican II, making the case that God is thus with us. I will spare you these details in favor of posing a question. Is it not the case that, in decrees of Vatican II with which we are all familar, Vatican II variously teaches that God is with us in the joys and griefs of modernity (especially those of the poor and afflicted) [*Gaudium et spes*], in non-Christian religions and Judaism [*Nostra aetate*], in the Roman Catholic Church and other Christian Churches [*Lumen gentium, Unitatis redintegratio,* etc.], in our liturgical life [*Sacrosanctum concilium*] and our Scriptures [*Dei Verbum*], and most particularly in Jesus Christ and the mission of the Spirit to Church and world [*Ad gentes divinitus*]? If so, there are two

---

[3]John Courtney Murray, S.J., *The Problem of God Yesterday and Today* (New Haven and London: Yale University Press, 1964) ch. 3. On how "atheism" is ambiguous and parasitic, see Michael J. Buckley, S.J., *At the Origins of Modern Atheism* (New Haven and London: Yale University Press, 1987) esp. 337f.

crucial implications. (1) God is (to use a description from the decrees on the Church as well as non-Christian religions) the *ultimate mystery* of our lives—the One of unrestricted holiness and grace, not to be identified with the world or any part of the world; (2) and yet, in Word and Spirit, this God is with us in each and every occasion of our lives—our private and public joys and griefs, our engagement with the ways of living and the teachings of those in other religions, our contributions to the common goods of the Church and the churches, our worship of this God and use of Scriptures.[4]

I am, of course, not suggesting that Vatican II provides us with a systematically complete account of how God is with us in our lives as individuals and communities, in our activity throughout the cosmos and our activity in the Church, in our worship and our lives of faith and hope and love. The history of the texts of Vatican II after Vatican II all but proves that no such systematic account is offered. But far from a reason for under- or overestimating Vatican II, this subsequent history teaches us a second, more formal lesson. If Vatican II's main contribution to the doctrine of God in a postconciliar Church is its confession that God is with us (*Dominus nobiscum,* we might say), Vatican II also teaches us a second and more formal lesson, namely . . .

V. It is very important to distinguish "dogmatic" and "systematic" theology with regard to our doctrine of God.

Let me briefly explain. By "dogmatic" theology I mean the activity of articulating what we, the Christian community, ought to teach about God in our families and schools, in our various neighborhoods and nation-states. By "systematic" theology I mean the activity of relating what the Christian community teaches about God to the particularities of our selves and our circumstances, the politics our our various nation-states, and the philosophies of our various educational institutions.

Now there is a large unresolved controversy among theologians over the relationship between these two activities. What we might call neo-Augustinians or neo-Thomists relate these two in the complex ways we relate "natural" and "revealed" theology. What we might call neo-liberal, correlationalists relate these to the ways we correlate a Christian tradition and the contemporary situation (Tracy, Schillebeeckx, Küng, and others). Those whom the correlationalist David Tracy calls "neo-Barthian anticorrelational theologians"[5] focus on the way dogmatic theology deals with the

---

[4]The phrase "not to be identified with the world or any part of the world" is borrowed from Kathryn Tanner, *God and Creation in Christian Theology* (Basil Blackwell, 1988), although I have reservations about some features of Tanner's proposal.

[5]David Tracy, "The Uneasy Alliance Reconceived: Catholic Theological Method, Modernity, and Postmodernity," *Theological Studies* 50 (1989) 548–70.

internal logic of the faith, and claim that this can only be related to the culture in *ad hoc* (rather than systematic) ways.

This is not the place to explore the details of the battle between these and other theological options. (Suffice to say that I think the nub of this issue would be various views of the nature, tests, and relationships between truths of various sorts.) But let me suggest how Vatican II might address these theological options with its central material claim that God is with us. (1) The subject of this teaching is God, the Trinitarian God whose identity is enacted in creation and the election of Israel, in the life and death and resurrection of Jesus Christ, and in the promise of the Spirit for Church and world. (2) The predicate of this teaching is "us" in our multilayered individualities, in our various social and historical circumstances.

If this is so, there are two major mistakes postconciliar doctrines of God can make—mistakes which each of the above theological options are tempted to make. (1) One temptation is to speak about God, but a God who is not with us. Such is the risk of dogmatic theology as well as the anti-correlational theologies, whether they be neo-Augustinian, neo-Thomist, or neo-Barthian; (2) another temptation is to speak about us, but not about the ways we are constituted by the God who is with us. Such is the risk of neo-liberal correlational theologies (whether the cultural correlate is modern philosophies, nation-states, or deconstructive suspicion of all modern ideologies and institutions)—the risk of speaking to ourselves about ourselves (instead of about God).

Now I am not claiming that neo-Augustinian, neo-Liberal, or neo-Barthian theologies succumb to these temptations; in fact, I believe their more sophisticated representatives do not make such simple mistakes. And I am not claiming that Vatican II resolves their theological debate. What I am proposing is that, if we view Vatican II as an exercise in dogmatic theology, we can say that Vatican II's confession that "God is with us" provides a way of holding together (2) the *relationship* between God and us without (1) reducing that relationship to any sort of identity. It is a large mistake, on Vatican II's terms, to reduce what we teach about God to what we teach about our Scriptures or our liturgy, our Church or our churches, various religions or the joys and griefs of modernity. To teach that *"God is with us"* is to teach that God who is with us is of unrestricted love and freedom, holiness and grace. This, I take it, is what Vatican II is suggesting in describing God as "ultimate mystery." That is, to conclude with a quote from Gerard Manley Hopkins, "a Catholic by mystery means an incomprehensible certainty: without certainty, without formulation there is not interest. . . . ; [but] the clearer the formulation the greater the interest. . . . [for example, y]ou know there are some solutions to, say, chess problems so beautifully ingenious, some resolutions of suspensions so lovely in music that even the feeling of interest is keenest when they are known and over, and for some time survives the discovery. . . . Therefore we speak of the events of Christ's life as the mystery of the Nativity, the mystery of the Crucifixion and so on of a host; the mystery being always the same, that the child in the manger is God, the culprit on the gallows God, and so on. Otherwise birth and death are not mysteries, nor is it any great mystery that a just man should be crucified, but that God should fascinate—with the interest of awe, of pity, of shame, of every harrowing feeling. But I have said enough,'' said Hopkins.[6] And so have I.

[6] *A Hopkins Reader.* Rev. and Enlarged Ed. Selections from the *Writings of Gerard Manley Hopkins,* ed. John Pick (Garden City, N.Y.: Doubleday, 1966) 408–09.

Introduction to Moral Theology

Moral Theology since Vatican II

Charles E. Curran

Enormous changes have occurred in Catholic moral theology since Vatican II. The council document on priestly formation (*Optatam totius*) maintained that special attention should be given to the development and perfection of moral theology (n. 16). I feel confident that those making the call for the renewal of moral theology had only a vague idea of what might emerge in the ensuing twenty-five years. Looking back from the present vantage point one can more readily assess what has taken place. It is impossible in a short space of time to discuss all the issues and questions that moral theology has faced in the twenty-five years since the Second Vatican Council. This short introduction will try to give a perspective on what has occurred in Catholic moral theology by touching on the following areas—the scope, the contexts, and the method of moral theology.

The scope of pre-Vatican II moral theology was to train confessors as judges in the sacrament of penance. The primary concern involved an analysis of particular actions to determine if they were sinful or not and the degree of gravity connected with them. Contemporary Catholic moral theology has a much broader aim and scope in studying the full Christian moral life with all its dimensions and in trying to develop in a systematic and scientific way all the various aspects of morality.

The contexts in which moral theology is done have also changed to a great degree. Before Vatican II the Catholic seminary or theologate was the primary place in which moral theology was done. Within Catholic colleges or universities theology was at best derivative from seminary textbooks. Catholic theology in general and moral theology in particular are flourishing today in Catholic colleges and universities and even in non-Catholic institutions of higher learning. As a result moral theology has taken on many of the characteristics of an academic subject with a great interest in developing the discipline of moral theology as such. The changing nature of the professoriate in moral theology well illustrates this academic nature of the discipline today. Before Vatican II, the professionals in the subject were one hundred percent male and clerical. Today many women and men who are not clerics are working in the area.

The ecclesial context is bound to influence moral theology, which is ultimately connected with the understanding and ongoing life of the Church. Ecumenism has become significant in the last few decades, and the contemporary state of moral theology reflects this ecumenical dimension. Catholics and Protestants, for example, have joined together in a professional society—the Society of Christian Ethics. Moral theology today is done ecumenically. Catholic authors are in constant dialogue and discussion with their Protestant colleagues and vice versa.

Perhaps the biggest ecclesial impact on moral theology has been the question about the legitimacy of dissent in theory and in practice from official Catholic moral teaching as proposed by the hierarchical magisterium. The question came to the fore in the response to *Humanae vitae*, the 1968 encyclical letter of Pope Paul VI condemning artificial contraception for spouses. Many Catholic moral theologians (but by no means all) recognize the legitimacy of dissent from specific moral teachings that are remote from the core of faith. In the midst of specificity and complexity one cannot claim a certitude that excludes the possibility of error. However, the hierarchical magisterium itself appears reluctant to affirm the legitimacy of such dissent. The tensions between many theologians and the hierarchical magisterium are most evident in sexual and medical issues.

The world itself forms an important context, since moral theology reflects on what one should do and how one should live in the years since Vatican II. Catholic moral theology has had to deal with questions raised by the so-called sexual revolution. Before Vatican II Catholic moral theologians were practically the only people interested in medical ethics. Today an entirely new discipline in bioethics has arisen to deal with the moral dilemmas brought about by the burgeoning biomedical technology.

Political and economic questions have arisen in the light of the issues that have come to the surface all over the globe—the fear of nuclear war, the economic problems of the Third World, the growth and decline of the cold war, and the struggles for independence and nationhood in many parts of the world. In this connection official Catholic social teaching as enunciated by the pope and the bishops has played a very influential role. Throughout the world the cry of the poor has been heard and liberation theologies, beginning in Latin America, have come to the fore. The changing role of women has occasioned the rise of feminist theologies which challenge many positions accepted in the past.

The method of moral theology has also seen significant development. Before Vatican II the pioneering work of Bernard Häring was beginning to have some influence in Catholicism, but for the most part pre-Vatican

II moral theology employed the neoscholasticism of the manuals of moral theology. The natural law methodology of the manuals has been criticized for neglecting Jesus Christ, grace, the Bible, as well as sin. The natural law has also been criticized for being ahistorical, too identified with the physical and biological structure of the human act, too rationalistic, and too *a priori*. Today there exists a variety of different methodologies being employed in moral theology. This pluralism of methodologies is evident in all parts of the world and in dealing with all different issues. However, there also are continuities with the method of the past—a careful and reasoned approach to morality, the basic acceptance of the goodness of the human despite human sinfulness, and a properly casuistic concern with what one must do in concrete actions in our changing and complex world.

In the light of these significant changes in the scope, contexts, and method of moral theology one would rightly expect some significant new issues have arisen and some revision of older positions has taken place. It is impossible to discuss in the short space available all the substantiative questions that have been addressed. The two essays in this section illustrate a few of the issues involved.

Looking back over the history of moral theology since Vatican II, one is struck by the development that has taken place as well as the continuities within the Catholic theological tradition. Moral theology is truly part of a living tradition. Hindsight always affords us a generally clear picture of what has occurred. However, in 1965, I do not think anyone could have predicted very accurately what would happen in the twenty-five-year span after the council. This reminder can be both consoling and challenging as we come to the end of the second millennium.

Chapter 4

Moral Theology: A Tradition to Be Rejected?

Toward a New Paradigm in Moral Argument

Paul Surlis

For purposes of raising tough questions for discussion and debate, the title I have given this paper is blunt and uncompromising. I am not, of course, talking about rejecting moral theology as such. I am concerned with what the pope, the Vatican, and some conservative Catholics are making the litmus test of what it is to be an authentic Catholic today. They are busy creating a "tradition" (*paradosis,* the New Testament Greek word for "tradition," means also "betrayal") which is, I believe, a false tradition; its logic entails betrayal of gospel values and therefore it should be rejected.

I wish to argue that the correct response to a false tradition is rejection, not contestation; in other words, to accept what Rome is presenting as the test of being Catholic but to argue some of the details is to place oneself in a losing position. Many theologians and other Catholics do this arguing for more exceptions while continuing to concede that the issues as presented do indeed count decisively in determining Catholic— and hence Christian— fidelity.

I argue for rejection of a circumscribed agenda for a number of reasons: principally because I believe that Rome has not only got the wrong issues. It has also got the issues wrong.

Everyone who follows what Pope John Paul says, especially on his trips abroad, knows that he demands absolute fidelity to his teaching on the evil— no exceptions—of birth control by artificial means, abortion, homosexuality, and remarriage after divorce, where no annulment was obtained. Not only is no dissent tolerated, e.g., on the issue of birth control by artificial means, but the teaching of numerous episcopal conferences from the seventies— on the propriety of following conscience if after serious study and prayer the papal position was found untenable—is suppressed and infallible status is, at times implicitly, claimed for the papal position.

While strong positions cannot be based on an argument from silence, it is still noteworthy that there is no explicit biblical teaching that is decisive for settling the issues of abortion and birth control. Both practices were known in the wider culture even if perhaps not widely practiced within Judaism when the traditions in the Scriptures were being formed. Surely, though, if these were to be issues decisive of what it is to be Christian one would expect them to have figured in the discourses of Jesus and in foundational, revealed Christian Scriptures.

It is not from Judaism or from Jesus that the teaching that the act of intercourse must always be open to procreation derives. Rather, it is from Stoicism with its emphasis on nature and biological function, and its rejection of pleasure and erotic love as valid purposes for sexuality in marriage. Passion experienced in intercourse took away the prized Stoic apatheia or detachment, a loss so grave that it would be compensated for only by an intention to procreate each time intercourse was had.[1] All this is already well known.

Condemnations of homosexuality in Scripture are to be evaluated in terms of the contemporary cultural devaluation of women, the sexual exploitation of slaves and the poor, the belief that all homosexual behavior was freely chosen perversion, and perhaps pervasive but unconscious socio-economic concerns over providing an army and the workforce necessary for tribal survival.[2] To argue from selected Scripture passages to intrinsic evil is to ignore historical and cultural conditioning of human understanding and it is to negate the empirical evidence afforded today by faithful, committed, same-sex relationships.

Concerning remarriage after divorce where no annulment is forthcoming, the position that this constitutes until death a barrier to receiving the sacraments of reconciliation and the Eucharist is simply untenable as is recognized by the Greek Orthodox and mainline Christian Churches.

Making Jesus's prohibition of divorce a universal, exceptionless law for all time has the effect of turning him into an authoritarian, punitive, moralis-

[1]See J. T. Noonan, *Contraception* (Cambridge: Harvard University Press, 1965) 46ff.; P. Brown, *The Body and Society* (Columbia University Press, 1988) 120ff. This latter is a superlative account of the tension and attitudes in early Christian thinkers on marriage and sexuality as they responded to a complex variety of positions adopted by pagan and heterodox Christian groups.

[2]See J. Boswell, *Christianity, Social Tolerance and Homosexuality* (Chicago and London: University of Chicago Press, 1980). Professor Boswell has announced that he is preparing for publication a critical edition of a same-sex marriage ritual (copies of which he found in the Vatican Library!) which has been in continual use in Mediterranean countries since about the sixth century. For the best recent analysis of homosexuality from a liberationist (not liberal) perspective, see D. C. Maguire, "The Shadow Side of the Homosexuality Debate" in *Homosexuality in the Priesthood and Religious Life*, ed. J. Gramic (New York: Crossroad, 1989) 36–55.

tic legislator contrary to his repudiation of these very traits in the religious leaders of his time in favor of mercy and compassion. The heavy and insupportable burden which official intransigence on this issue represents, especially for the poor and less well-instructed, is only partially alleviated by the whole tribunal apparatus which is not unfairly accused of sometimes using smoke and mirrors to make marriages disappear. Having marriage tribunals which mainly specialize in annulments is not unlike having a medical system which specializes in autopsies while neglecting disease prevention and health care.

It is sometimes argued that this sexual ethic is pro-life and that universality of application and rigid enforcement of a discipline of no exceptions is essential in defense of the sacredness of life. The fact is, however, that both in theory and in practice Catholic moral teaching is tolerant of moral rules and behavior which permits the taking of human life. But one is not allowed to argue that any motive, intention, or circumstances justify masturbation, homosexual or artificial contraceptive intercourse, or remarriage after divorce. Processes in sexuality associated with the generation of human life are inviolable while in theory and practice persons' lives are not inviolable, even though the proportionalist and consequentialist arguments used by all who justify taking human life in certain circumstances are not permitted to be invoked where non-procreative use of sexual intercourse is concerned, as in the cases listed. One who *murders* his wife can be absolved, remarry, and receive the Eucharist. One who *divorces* his wife and remarries may not be absolved or receive the Eucharist unless he agrees to live with the latter in a "brother-sister" relationship, a condition which when imposed appears to be inspired by Manicheistic repudiation of sex as evil and has the effect of making religious leaders who impose such a condition appear ludicrous. This raises the question of whether or not sexual teaching is being instrumentalized to serve political purposes related to institutional maintenance or control—something to which we shall return. So much for my assertion that many conservatives including the Vatican have got the issues wrong. Now briefly I wish to address the fact that the wrong issues are being made the litmus test of Christian, or Catholic, orthodoxy.

It is clear from the Gospels that the thrust of Jesus's message, ministry, table-fellowship, and prayer was the inauguration of the rule, reign, or kingdom of God. The poor, disease-ridden, oppressed, and marginalized, especially children, slaves, and women, were the focus of his efforts. Jesus was concerned with abuses of religion, of power and prestige which allowed affluence and privileged status to some while consigning others to poverty, hunger, disease, and loss of human dignity and status at the bottom of the social pyramid. Jesus is reported as having declared that *mammon*, or reliance on and relentless *service* of wealth, was incompatible with true *service* of God (Matt 6:24). And this because of a real connection between relentless pursuit of ever-increasing wealth and the creation in others of poverty and need. The kingdom of God entailed personal conversion and whatever larger changes were needed to achieve an inclusive society where solidarity, service, fellowship, mercy, truth, justice, and right relationships to others and to God would prevail—shalom through justice.

And these were also the concerns of the early Jesus movement[3] until by degrees a process of accommodation to the values of the Empire set in so that by the early fourth century (313 C.E.) the Christian religion having lost its social-critical bite is declared a public religion and is recognized by the Emperor Constantine. Professor Samuel Laeuchli's thesis, first argued almost twenty years ago, is, I believe, still valid and more relevant today than ever. Professor Laeuchli argues that at the beginning of the fourth century a process already in place for a long time culminated in the Council of Elvira in Spain (309 C.E.) which made sexual conduct the center of the Christian Church's moral and pastoral concerns. By focussing on the production of a morality devoted to restricting and at times vetoing sexual behavior—even when it would be legitimate as in the case of priests who were forbidden to have sexual relations the night before offering Mass; this is abstinence not celibacy—church authorities simultaneously consolidated a power system that was hierarchical and patriarchal.[4] And it is essentially this power system with its twin pillars of hierarchy and patriarchy that the Vatican fears is under attack today and whose buttressing it seeks through the instrumentalizing of sex and through the rules and regulations it has formulated to govern the behavior of Church members.

It is difficult to understand the allegiance demanded by the Vatican to the sexual code unless one takes into account the desire to boost allegiance to the papacy which has invested so much of its authority in maintaining this ethic as an absolute from which no one may dissent, much less depart. In this respect control is aimed at in the universal Church, but, as we can see every day, it is in fact rapidly being eroded, as is the legitimate authority vested in the papal office which is jeopardized through over-commitment to an outmoded sexual discipline. At present Rome's power—modelled on that of the ancient emperor's—is universal, producing doctrine, appointing nuncios and bishops, and aligning itself at will with power and wealth even while maintaining verbally aspects of an option for the poor and marginalized. Conservative bishops and clergy utilize hierarchical and patriarchal control over women when they make abortion the single issue dominating the political, moral, and pastoral spheres. Today patriarchal control

[3]See E. S. Fiorenza, *In Memory of Her* (New York: Crossroad, 1985).
[4]S. Laeuchli, *Power and Sexuality,* (Philadelphia: Temple University Press, 1972).

is recognized as insidious because it contributes to the reduction of women—half the human race—to second-class status or worse. Women's labor, so necessary for human nurturing and subsistence, is neither fully recognized nor valued; women and children are everywhere the poorest of the poor and subject to various forms of institutionalized violence in all societies globally, including our own with its extremes of affluence and degrading poverty.

I am not in any way arguing that sexual issues are unimportant or that they should not receive sustained moral evaluation. What I am saying is that the Vatican sexual code misconstrues these issues and creates a false sense of what Christian morality is. Following the value system of the gospel entails, I believe, that the issues claiming moral priority today are planetary and socio-political. They include: global warming and destruction of the ozone layer by toxic gases released into the atmosphere; poisoning and befoulment of air, earth, and water. Global issues include spreading poverty, especially in Central and South America, in Asia and Africa where hunger, disease, underemployment, unemployment, scarcity of housing, and absence of health care and educational facilities are endemic and pandemic. These problems all affect the unemployed and increasingly unemployable segments of inner cities and rural areas in super-developed countries including the U.S.A. Everywhere there is an increase in rape, violence against women, homophobia, and sexual abuse of children. Structurally these problems are related to economic insecurity and a harshly competitive, individualistic public sphere, which is the shadow side inseparable from capitalism and so-called "socialist" modes of production.

Globally, today, capitalism with its logic of exploitative production, is becoming the unchallenged, dominant, economic system with three principal focal points.[5] Japan dominates in the Pacific, the United States, Canada, and to a lesser extent Mexico dominate in this hemisphere, and the European Economic Community (EEC) in Europe. This capitalism continues to exploit cheap labor and resources in Africa, Central and South America, and part of Asia. More than once Paul VI asserted that the contemporary world is sick. He also taught that "both for nations and for individuals avarice is the most evident form of moral underdevelopment" [*Populorum Progressio* par. 19, par. 66]. Production everywhere exploits the labor of women, especially women of color. A sexual code that is blind to economic, social and political exploitation, and violence not only makes social justice and peace issues invisible, it actually supports the *status quo* and gives the illusion that morality is about restricted forms of sexual conduct but not

[5]For one account of this see Walden Bellow, *Brave New Third World? Strategies for Survival in the Global Economy* (San Francisco: Institute for Food and Development Policy, 1989).

about public, socio-economic affairs, even though these latter keep the majority of the human race in states of marginalization and suffering.

In conclusion, I wish to argue that the task facing moral theology today must and should be reformulated. We need a Copernican revolution, a new paradigm; it is not primarily a question of creating more exceptions in a sphere where Vatican discipline allows none. To accept that as the issue is to fight a losing battle; but worse still, it is to continue to endorse what is fundamentally a flawed view not just of sexual morality but of morality itself.

Along with the weaknesses I have already sketched, a major, fundamental error in much contemporary moral (secular as well as religious) theory is the dichotomy that is created between *personal* and *social* morality. In practice this amounts to morality being identified with a narrow range of sexual issues that are torn from their social, cultural, political, and economic contexts. Traditionally, fundamental treatises in ethics, moral theology, and Christian ethics have been elaborated in individualistic categories. Then later social topics are introduced and discussed in what has to be an extrinsicist fashion. One cannot build a skyscraper on the foundation prepared for a single-family dwelling.

The dichotomy I am referring to reflects within moral theory the larger separation of public and private which has been exacerbated by the rise of capitalism and which has been legitimated and mystified by some forms of liberal thought which, in this, serves as the ideology of capitalism. This accounts for the tendency to think of morality with reference to so-called personal and private issues which confront persons in their individual lives and in interpersonal relationships. Ana Maria Bidegain, concurring with aspects of the analysis developed here, writes, " . . . in the pastoral activity of the Catholic church since the sixteenth century, sexual morality has moved from the peripheral, secondary status it had in the Middle Ages with an Albertus Magnus or a Thomas Aquinas, to constitute for all practical purposes the principal focus of that activity. The resultant polarization of sexual morality has meant the relegation of politico-social concerns to a secondary status . . . ."[6]

Today, all too frequently, economic, social, and environmental issues are thought of and treated as beyond moral evaluation and—as we see in the Mideast crisis—a mentality of *realpolitik* prevails. If a policy serves the economic and power-related interests of ruling classes then it is regarded as being correct even if—as in Nicaragua, El Salvador, and Guatemala—it involves breaches of international law, murder, torture, oppression, and

[6]A. M. Bidegain, "Women and the Theology of Liberation," *Through Her Eyes* (New York: Orbis, 1989) 19.

overall deflection of resources into excessive military expenditures at the cost of the survival needs of the poor and the genuine human needs of other classes.

Racism, oppression of women, covert and overt military expenditure, and maintenance of war economies to control access to cheap labor, to exploit other peoples' resources, and to fight and destroy groups who are struggling for jobs, houses, land, education, and health-care—all these activities tend not to arouse widespread moral indignation or even evaluation. Meanwhile, an individual act of sexual indiscretion is major news in the media for months.

All significant sexual issues are also social issues when properly regarded. Issues which affect women's reproductive rights must first be approached in terms of justice for women and children: day care, employment with equal pay for comparable work, adequate health care and pre-natal care, education in responsible parenthood, especially for men, and provision of effective means to practice it. Rape, compulsory heterosexism (itself a form of social control of behavior), and homophobia are all rooted in socio-economic, cultural, political contexts marked by injustice, violence, and exploitation of women, especially women of color, of children, and in different ways of undereducated, unemployed males, especially men of color. Bringing these issues to the forefront of personal and public consciousness is part of the task of renewed moral theology and Christian ethics. What must be recognized is that *all morality is social-political;* within this we may and should determine individual, personalist concerns but always keeping them in dialectical relationship to the wider and weightier matters involving economic structures, institutionalized violence, militarism, political intrigue, murder of people fighting for justice, racism, manipulation of religion, justice, mercy, truth, peace-keeping, and local and planetary environmental concerns.

This reordering of priorities is clearly called for by the Second Vatican Council when it states: "Profound and rapid changes make it particularly urgent that no one, ignoring the trend of events or drugged by laziness, content himself [or herself] with a merely individualistic morality. It grows increasingly true that the obligations of justice and love are fulfilled only if each person, contributing to the common good, according to his [or her] own abilities and the needs of others, also promotes and assists the public and private institutions, dedicated to bettering the conditions of human life." The challenges envisioned twenty-five years ago by the council, though more narrowly focused than the ones presented here, cannot be met, according to the council, "unless men [and women] and their associations cultivate in themselves the moral and social virtues, and promote them in society" (Pastoral Constitution on the Church in the Modern World, par. 30).

Paul VI in his repeated calls for "an international morality based on justice and equity" was responding to the council's intentions. Unfortunately, Catholics in general have not caught up with his social teaching with its radical perspectives and global vision. Unless Catholics study deeply the social teaching of Paul VI, they will not recognize the continuity that exists in the themes lifted up for in-depth analysis and consciousness-raising by John Paul II, especially in his encyclicals on Labor and on Social Concerns. Especially in Social Concerns John Paul II can be seen to work for the most part with the understanding of social morality sketched in this paper. One notes how often in that letter he refers to economics, labor-related and socio-political issues as *moral* issues thereby enlarging the Catholic moral agenda and setting a program for Catholic moralists who are challenged to do what I have attempted here. Of course, all Catholic teaching is social teaching or has social dimensions and implications: this is true of doctrine, spirituality, liturgy; it is especially true of teaching on marriage, sexuality, women, and related issues. Together with the Copernican revolution and paradigm shift called for in this paper must come institutional and structural reformations so that the people of God, the Church, especially women, the poor, people of color, and the marginalized, have input based on their experience, their suffering, and God's love of predilection for them, input into the production or formation of Catholic teaching. Hitherto, the preserve of a small group of celibate, white, affluent males, Catholic moral teaching must welcome enrichment from the Spirit-guided people of God. Thus, the "tradition" for whose rejection I have called will be rediscovered, enlarged, and purified, and as such it will enhance, not retard, the Church's task to be "the universal sacrament of salvation" (Dogmatic Constitution on the Church, 48), a task which the council tells us also entails a process of "continual reformation" (Decree on Ecumenism, 6).

Chapter 5

In Praise of God's Word:
Biblical Studies since Vatican II

Thomas F. Dailey, O.S.F.S.

In 1985 the bishops of the world met in extraordinary synod to celebrate the twentieth anniversary of the Second Vatican Council. The theme of this synod, as introduced by Godfried Cardinal Daneels, focused on how "The Church, obedient to the Word of God, celebrates the mysteries of Christ for the salvation of the world." In the formulation of this theme, two specific responses relative to the role of Scripture in the life of the Church were noted. Positively, Vatican II has led to the renewal of spirituality among many groups in the Church, for "the richness of the Word of God . . . has penetrated into the consciousness of the faithful." Negatively, "the accentuation of the Word of God" has sometimes occasioned an isolation of the Bible from the "living Tradition" which is its context "by a subjectivism which is substituted for the ecclesial comprehension and authentic interpretation of the Magisterium."[1]

While these generalizations served to introduce the anniversary synod, few interventions at this assembly dealt specifically with *Dei Verbum,* the Dogmatic Constitution on Divine Revelation. The place and function of Scripture seems to have been treated only in its relation to the threefold font of revelation in Scripture, Tradition, and the Magisterium.[2] Though such a focus may be attributed to the limitations of time and scope by which this assembly was burdened, the field of biblical studies has actually enjoyed a much greater renewal and impact since that celebrated council.

[1]Godfried Daneels, "La Chiesa nella Parola di Dio celebra i misteri di Cristo per la salvezza del mondo," *L'Osservatore Romano* (November 26, 1985) 5.

[2]In the only intervention specifically addressed to biblical studies, William Cardinal Baum spoke to the need of an exegesis that is "truly in symphony with the prescriptions given by the Constitution, particularly as it concerns the relation among Sacred Scripture, Tradition, and the ecclesiastical Magisterium." To this end, the cardinal wished for "a biblical renewal which puts into relief that Sacred Scripture is the Word of God, a living Word which comes to be read in the Church" ("Per una esegesi non critica ma teologica ed ecclesiale," *L'Osservatore Romano* [November 29, 1985] 4).

Hence, this present study, on the occasion of Vatican II's twenty-fifth anniversary, attempts to bring together some reflections on the import of *Dei Verbum* and some suggestions for a further development by which the "biblical and liturgical" theology exhorted by the 1985 synod[3] may become a living reality in the Church of the twenty-first century. To achieve this objective, a theological nexus must be realized whereby the praise of God's Word in the liturgy is established as the interpretive horizon for the actualization of Sacred Scripture.

To explicate this thesis, we will integrate a threefold analysis of biblical studies since Vatican II. We will summarize, in very broad strokes, the novel teachings of *Dei Verbum*.[4] This document, unlike its predecessor *Divino Afflante Spiritu*,[5] "emphasized a very different aspect of the Church's ongoing task of becoming ever more responsive to the Word of God whose privileged witness in the historical community of faith is the Sacred Scriptures."[6] It speaks to the issue of the Bible in an inclusive manner: first, by situating the Word of God in its fundamental context (i.e., revelation); then by outlining and encouraging its scientific study (i.e., critical exegesis); and finally, by exhorting its renewal in and for the life of the Church. Both the structure and the content of *Dei Verbum* thus witness to the compromising achievement of this council, which seeks to balance a theology which is "traditional, essentialist, and heavily supernatural and static" with one that is "historically sensitive, immanentistic, dialectical, and process-oriented."[7]

We will also report, though briefly, on the contemporary developments in biblical studies which have been occasioned by the conciliar teachings.

---

[3]In the section of the synod's final report which dealt with "the sources by which the Church lives," the bishops suggested that "the presentation of doctrine must be biblical and liturgical. It must treat of a healthy doctrine adapted to the actual life of Christians" (*L'Osservatore Romano* [December 10, 1985] 6).

[4]*AAS* 58 (1966) 817–35. English translation in Austin Flannery, ed., *Vatican Council II: The Conciliar and Post Conciliar Documents* (Collegeville, Minn.: The Liturgical Press, 1975) 750–65. There have been several well-written commentaries on this document, among which in English are: J. Ratzinger, A. Grillmeier, and B. Rigaux, *Commentary on the Documents of Vatican II*, ed. H. Vorgrimler (New York: Herder and Herder, 1969) vol. 3, 155–272, and René Latourelle, *Theology of Revelation* (New York: Alba House, 1968) 453–88.

[5]*AAS* 35 (1943) 297–326. English translation in J. J. McGivern, ed., *Bible Interpretation: Official Catholic Teachings* (Wilmington, N.C.: McGrath, 1978) 316–42. For an historical summary of the period between these documents, see T. A. Collins and R. E. Brown, "Church Pronouncements," *The New Jerome Biblical Commentary,* eds. R. E. Brown, J. A. Fitzmyer, and R. E. Murphy (Englewood Cliffs: Prentice-Hall, 1990) 1167–74.

[6]S. Schneiders, "From Exegesis to Hermeneutics: The Problem of the Contemporary Meaning of Scripture," *Horizons* 8:1 (1981) 24.

[7]Donald Senior, "Dogmatic Constitution on Divine Revelation—*Dei Verbum,*" *Vatican II and Its Documents: An American Reappraisal, Theology and Life,* 5, ed. T. E. O'Connell (Wilmington, Del.: Michael Glazier, Inc., 1986) 123.

Here we will see what advances have been made in twenty-five years and what business has been left unfinished.

Finally, we will offer a prospective on biblical studies in the twenty-first-century Church. This will include some suggestions for future tasks in the areas of both theological inquiry and magisterial administration.

I. The Horizon of Revelation

As the title of the document suggests, *Dei Verbum* is concerned not simply with biblical studies but with the broader reality of divine revelation. This "horizon" is the totality of understanding which conditions and determines the content of Scripture and within which the biblical texts are continuously and progressively known.

An understanding of revelation, then, is the starting point for comprehending Scripture, and the opening chapter of *Dei Verbum* describes this horizon as the sacramental self-communication of God for the purpose of fellowship with humans. Emphasizing the Trinitarian character of the economy of revelation, the document highlights its concrete disposition (in "deeds and words") as well as its mediation in and through Jesus Christ, who brings revelation to fulfillment. The enlightenment brought by Christ to humans calls forth in them a response of faith, whose character is theological (involving "submission" and "assent"), graced (through the "interior helps of the Holy Spirit"), and progressive (bringing about an ever deeper understanding).

This revelation of the truth of God is transmitted (ch. 2) through the heralds of the gospel—the apostles and their successors. Hereby elucidating the horizontal dimension of revelation, *Dei Verbum* proffers a notion of Sacred Tradition which is at once dynamic (where there is "growth in insight into the realities and the words that are being passed on") and progressive (since "the Church is always advancing towards the plentitude of divine truth"). Without prejudice to the polemical question of the number of sources of revelation or their respective sufficiency, the document seeks to justify the mutual relation between Scripture and tradition and the common relation of these to the Church as a whole, a relationship that is mediated through the magisterium.

The notion of revelation as divine truth revealed in and through the Church issues from its inspired character (ch. 3, no. 11). Balancing both the divine and human contributions to the authorship of Scripture, *Dei Verbum* invokes the key text of 2 Timothy 3:16-17 to substantiate its claim to inspiration. But without further elaboration, the document simply adopts an *a posteriori* approach to the biblical text and demands an acknowledgment of the salvific truth contained and expressed in the written Word of God.

Thus situated within the horizon of an inspired communication of the divine through the human, Scripture holds pride of place in the Church's living tradition. Since the time of Vatican II, however, this horizon has not been adequately explained or developed.

From the perspective of official pronouncements, the magisterium has given no further indication of the nature of the relationship between Scripture and tradition. While the magisterium is acknowledged as having the capacity to reformulate its teachings due to the difficulties in expressing revelation which arise from their historical conditioning,[8] the question of how the Bible may be adopted to critique the Church and the multiplicity of traditions remains an issue to be confronted.[9]

Moreover, a theological exposition on the nature and function of inspiration has yet to be set forth in any systematic fashion. Both Raymond Brown and Bruce Vawter note the inadequacies of current theories of inspiration,[10] and some other scholars have even attempted at least partial clarifications.[11] But the period since Vatican II has not seen the "new heyday of creative speculation on biblical inspiration" that could have originated from the council's pastoral viewpoint on the issue.[12]

Hence, in the prospective of future studies, the theological elaboration of this horizon remains a task to be completed. Contrary to some opinions,[13] a more precise comprehension of the inspired nature of revelation

[8]*Mysterium Ecclesiae* (June 24, 1973) *AAS* 65 (1973) 394–408. English translation in A. Flannery, ed., *Vatican II: More Post Conciliar Documents* (Grand Rapids, Mich.: Wm. B. Eerdmans, 1982) 428–40. See also R. E. Brown, *Biblical Reflections on Crises Facing the Church* (New York: Paulist Press, 1975) 116–17.

[9]This issue is raised by R. E. Murphy, "Vatican III—Problems and Opportunities of the Future: The Bible," *Toward Vatican III: The Work that Needs to Be Done,* ed. D. Tracy (New York: Seabury Press, 1978) 23.

[10]R. E. Brown, "The Meaning of the Bible," *TDig* 28 (1980) 319. B. Vawter, *Biblical Inspiration* (Philadelphia: Westminster, 1972).

[11]Proposing a threefold influence of traditions, situations, and compilers is P. Achtemeier, *The Inspiration of Scripture: Problems and Proposals* (Philadelphia: Westminster, 1980). Suggesting the possibility of basing a theory on charisms is R. F. Collins, *Introduction to the New Testament* (Garden City, N.Y.: Doubleday, 1983) 343–54. Relying on linguistic rather than historical-critical input is W. Vogels,, "Inspiration in a Linguistic Mode," *BTB* 15 (1985) 87–93.

[12]J. T. Burtchaell, *Catholic Theories of Inspiration since 1810: A Review and Critique* (Cambridge: Cambridge University Press, 1969) 276–77. See also C. M. Martini, "Parola di Dio e parola umana: il problema dell'ispirazione e della verita biblica in prospettive pastorale," *Incontro con la Bibbia: leggere, pregare, annunciare,* ed. G. Zevini (Rome: Libreria Ateneo Salesiano, 1978) 41–53.

[13]A. R. Greeley, "The Failure of Vatican II after Twenty Years," *America* 146:5 (June 2, 1982) 87: "One hates to say it, but the precise definition of the nature of revelation will not affect much either the Sunday homily . . . or the individual reading of the Bible." This same author proceeds to say that the religious impact of revelation "is long term, at best, very long term."

is critical for a deeper understanding of the relationship between the sacred text and the community of faith. Perhaps the continuing research in tradition history, which "views the bible as 'historical' memory accompanied by those interpretations through which the community found meaning in its expressions,"[14] may shed light on this subject. A more promising source of illumination, however, seems to be the relationship between semiotics and the Bible. Recently introduced by James Reese,[15] a sociosemiotic definition of inspiration, which emphasizes the role of the mediating community, sees Scripture as a corpus of writings provided for the divinely-protected community as a continuous source of nourishment for its faith and growth. Whichever avenue of research is followed in these theological inquiries, it would seem advantageous, as James Swetnam suggests,[16] to dedicate a synod of bishops to the theme of the fundamental nature and consequences of revelation in the written, taught, and lived Word of God.

II. The Actualization of Scripture

While detailed treatments of the fundamental horizon of revelation may require further development, the same is less true for the study of Scripture in terms of its interpretation. In this realm, which concerns the historical and human aspects of revelation, the discipline of biblical studies "is probably more healthy than at any other point in its history" since "more worthwhile research is being carried out by more scholars in more areas than ever before."[17] Yet, as we shall argue, this proclivity toward and propensity for exegesis has resulted in a concern for the lack of actualization of such studies.

In its third chapter, *Dei Verbum* gives no formal definition of exegesis, yet its teachings have opened the way for critical biblical scholarship as we know it. Explaining how Sacred Scripture is to be interpreted (no. 12), the document gives official recognition to, and encouragement of, several avenues of research: in literary forms and styles and in historical variants and their time-conditioned situations. The document also acknowledges the spiritual sense of the sacred writings and the process-oriented nature of its interpretation. In this way it accounts for both the divine wisdom in the text and the human language by and through which it is to be appropriated.

[14]P. Perkins, "Biblical Studies: Looking toward the Future," *A Companion to the Bible,* ed. M. Ward (New York: Alba House, 1985) 415.

[15]J. M. Reese, "Toward a Sociosemiotic Definition of Inspiration," *BTB* 21:1 (1991) 4–12.

[16]J. Swetnam, "Parola di Dio e teologia pastorale nella Chiesa contemporanea," *Vaticano II: bilancio e prospettive,* venticinque anni dopo 1962/1987, ed. René Latourelle (Assisi: Cittadella Editrice, 1987) 1:339, n. 35.

[17]P. J. Achtemeier and G. M. Tucker, "Biblical Studies: The State of the Discipline," *BCSR* 11 (1980) 73.

With regard to the Old Testament (ch. 4), *Dei Verbum* speaks very little; nevertheless, the document clearly affirms the importance of the Hebrew Scriptures for Christians. Surveying the divine plan of salvation, this chapter highlights the lasting elements of soteriology in the Old Testament economy with the themes of election and covenant. This economy, and the sacred books which express it, remains permanently valid for Christians due to its prophetic nature—as an announcement of, and preparation for, the coming Messiah. While the typological manner in which the document presents the Old Testament is a limitation to be superseded in further investigations,[18] yet *Dei Verbum* preserves and emphasizes the importance of the Old Testament notion of God, "whose word lasts forever."

With regard to the New Testament (ch. 5), *Dei Verbum* proceeds according to the methodology of critical research. It outlines the process of formation which the New Testament as a whole underwent, with specific attention being given to the excellence and apostolic origin of the Gospels as well as their historicity and particular formation. These processes serve to validate, maintain, and further the mission of Jesus Christ and the pneumatological truth entrusted to the Church by him and encoded in the language of the New Testament.

In order to interpret this truth of Scripture, biblical scholars since Vatican II have engaged wholeheartedly in the historical-critical method of study. Now sanctioned for all by the official teaching of the Church,[19] this approach to the Bible investigates as objectively as possible the persons, situations, and expressions found in the sacred text. In this format, what is requested of the biblical scholar is "the general attention to history, the exigency of an accurate determination of literary genres, (and) the confrontation with other texts even profane ones."[20] With its positivistic approach, this technique of interpretation "has had undisputed methodological hegemony in the field of scientific biblical studies" and has enabled the Catholic community to bridge the gap in biblical studies with its Protestant counterparts.[21]

Owing to the popularity and the success of this historical-critical meth-

---

[18]Murphy, 25.

[19]J. H. Neyrey, "Interpretation of Scripture in the Life of the Church," *Vatican II: The Unfinished Agenda*, ed. L. Richard (New York: Paulist Press, 1987) 38: "What had been the provenance of scholars and the Biblical Commission became the heritage and the future of the pastoral Church at large."

[20]U. Vanni, "Esegesi e attualizzazione alla luce della *'Dei Verbum*,'" *Vaticano II: bilancio e prospettive*, venticinque anni dopo 1962/1987, ed. R. Latourelle (Assisi: Cittadella Editrice, 1987) 1:313.

[21]Schneiders, "From Exegesis to Hermeneutics," 26–27. One outstanding result of this methodology is the production of scholarly results compiled in *The New Jerome Biblical Commentary*.

odology, several specific approaches ("criticisms") and emphases in biblical studies have evolved.[22] From an historical perspective, tradition criticism examines the "pre-history" of the text and attempts to elucidate the stages through which the text has undergone development. Redaction and canonical criticisms, on the other hand, emphasize the viewpoint and theology expressed in the final form of the canonical work.

From a more literary viewpoint, biblical texts have been analyzed in successively larger units. Textual criticism seeks to establish the original wording of a particular passage among various possible alternatives. Grammatical criticism analyzes its language in terms of the words themselves and their syntax.[23] Form criticism concerns itself with an entire passage and gives specific attention to its genre and the meaning which derives from the way such forms are employed by the author. Finally, literary criticism considers the context of a biblical passage and focuses on questions of composition, structure, style, and mood.

Moreover, allied approaches to these standard criticisms have begun to emerge. A concern for structuralism sees the text synchronically in its totality of significant and signifying signs.[24] Reader-response criticism, equally synchronic but more subjective, stresses the reciprocal relation between the literary work and the creativity of the reader, the interrelationship of which can produce multiple interpretations of a text.[25] Finally, the narrative criticism of story theology, with its differentiation among real and implied authors and readers, analyzes the multiple factors which contribute to the meaning effect of a text.[26]

Beyond these focused "criticisms" there have also arisen newer and varied "readings" of the Bible. Flowing from particular theories about the text, these modes of interpretation seek a more "practical" exegesis in contrast with the prevailing scientific criticisms. Materialist readings take into account

---

[22]For an excellent introduction to the major "criticisms" and a representative bibliography, see J. H. Hayes and C. R. Holladay, *Biblical Exegesis: A Beginner's Handbook* (Atlanta: John Knox Press, 1982). See also O. Kaiser and W. G. Kummel, *Exegetical Method: A Student's Handbook,* rev. ed. (New York: Seabury Press, 1981) and the collection of monographs in the "Guides to Biblical Scholarship" series published by Fortress Press (Philadelphia).

[23]A noteworthy contribution in this regard is the revolutionary, two-volume work *Greek-English Lexicon of the New Testament Based on Semantic Domains,* eds. J. Louw and E. Nida (New York: United Bible Societies, 1988).

[24]For a methodological survey and bibliography, see D. and A. Patte, *Pour une exégèse structurale* (Paris, 1978); for applications of this method in exegesis, consult the journal *Semiotique et Bible* published in Lyon.

[25]See, for example, S. Brown, "Reader Response: Demythologizing the Text," NTS 34 (1988) 232–37, and S. D. Moore, "Doing Gospel Criticism as/with a 'Reader'," BTB 19 (1989) 85–93.

[26]See M. J. Valdés and O. J. Miller, eds., *Interpretation of Narrative* (Toronto, 1978).

the economic, political, and ideological concerns encoded in a text so as to engage these with contemporary situations.[27] Psychoanalytical readings attend to the significant discordances in the message of a text and the symbolic representations which contribute to and emerge from it.[28] Feminist readings concern themselves with uncovering and disarming the patriarchal bias in biblical concepts, thereby allowing for a more equitably dignified reflection.[29] And, in the midst of these contemporary readings, there resounds the call for a return to a patristic mode of reading, in which the "spiritual sense" of the writing is coupled with the personal co-involvement and subjectifying input of the reader.[30]

In addition to these exegetical investigations, biblical scholarship has also begun to benefit from the contributions of other fields of study. From philosophical quarters which study the phenomenon of human communication through language, biblical scholars have garnered a better understanding, appreciation, and application of notions such as syntactics, semantics, and pragmatics in order to explicate a theory of meaning.[31] So, too, biblical scholars have profited from studies in the history of Israel and the archaeology of the Ancient Near East; excavations have unearthed significant finds, though several projects still suffer from an acute problem of delayed publication.[32] Finally, the emergence of the social sciences has given a new orientation to exegetical methodology; by noting that particular cultures may influence one's experience of reality, this approach provides insightful theories and models for a cross-cultural reading of the biblical texts.[33]

[27]See F. Belo, "Why a Materialist Reading?" *Conc* 138 (1980) 17–23.

[28]See A. Vergote, "Psychanalyse et interprétation biblique," *DBS* 9 (1973–1975) 252–60; M. Sales, "Possibilités et limites d'une lecture psych-analytique de la Bible," *NRT* (1979) 699; D. Stein, "Is a Psycho-Analytical Reading of the Bible Possible?" *Conc* 138 (1980) 24–32.

[29]See E. S. Fiorenza, "To Set the Record Straight: Biblical Women's Studies," *Horizons* 10 (1983) 111–21.

[30]See I. de la Potterie, "La lettura della Sacra Scrittura 'nello Spirito': il modo patristico di leggere la Bibbia è possibile oggi?" *CivCatt* 137:3 (1986) 209–23, and M. Gilbert, "Prospettive e istanze nell'esegesi dopo il Vaticano II," *Vaticano II: bilancio e prospettive,* venticinque anni dopo 1962/1987, ed. R. Latourelle (Assisi: Cittadella Editrice, 1987) 1:289–307, esp. 301–06.

[31]See J. Louw, "A Semiotic Approach to Discourse Analysis with Reference to Translation Theory," *BT* 36 (1985) 101–07, and M. Bertram, "Semiotics: The Structural Approach," *TBT* 23 (1988) 26–30. Publications dedicated to this area include the journal *Semeia* and the Society of Biblical Literature's "Semeia Studies" series.

[32]Achtemeier and Tucker, 74. See also M. Dahood, "Ebla Discoveries and Biblical Research," *Month* 13 (1980) 275–81, and P. J. King, "The Contribution of Archaeology to Biblical Studies," *CBQ* 45 (1983) 1–16.

[33]See T. F. Best, "The Sociological Study of the New Testament: Promise and Peril of a New Discipline," *SJT* 36 (1983) 181–94; J. Pilch, "Interpreting Scripture: The Social Science Method," *TBT* 23 (1988) 13–19; C. Osiek, "The New Handmaid: The Bible and the Social Sciences," *TS* 50 (1989) 260–78. A comprehensive bibliography, in a journal influenced by

These many and varied developments in the area of biblical interpretation have certainly unlocked for contemporary readers many of the mysteries encoded in the biblical texts. Historical and literary criticisms allow for an appreciation of the coming-to-be of the sacred writings and their inner workings. The allied approaches provide for a subjective input in the reading process and offer particular vantage points from which the myriad of biblical passages may be seen and variously understood. Finally, the encounter with other fields of study affords biblical scholarship the opportunity to dialogue with valued disciplines about the human and historical issues in Scripture.

However, while these developments in historical-critical scholarship have flourished since Vatican II and continue to remain valid and necessary,[34] it is recognized that "we are at a turning point concerning our fundamental methodologies for interpreting biblical texts."[35] Looming in the not-too-distant future is a major paradigm shift,[36] which will decrease the current emphasis on the objective results of historical criticism in favor of the theological meaningfulness of biblical truth. This change in focus accords with the epistemological stance of our contemporary culture, in which "All knowledge is present knowledge, and the only truth which humanity has time left to pursue is that which means something to us either individually or collectively."[37] The future prospective of biblical studies, then, must concern itself not simply with analysis but with "actualization."

Rather than seeing the Bible "as theological source book with its implied theory of historical-critical exegesis," biblical studies in the future should consider Scripture's resourcefulness for the spiritual life through a multidisciplinary theory of hermeneutics. Such an approach incorporates "both a global theory of human understanding and a special theory of the understanding of texts" evident in such philosophers as Gadamer and Ricoeur.[38] Such interpretations will necessarily blend both dimensions of

this approach, is given by D. J. Harrington, "Second Testament Exegesis and the Social Sciences: A Bibliography," *BTB* 18 (1988) 77–84.

[34]J. A. Fitzmyer, "Historical Criticism: Its Role in Biblical Interpretation and Church Life," *TS* 50 (1989) 244–59.

[35]Achtemeier and Tucker, 73.

[36]See W. Wink, *The Bible in Human Transformation: Toward a New Paradigm for Biblical Study* (Philadelphia: Fortress Press, 1973); P. Stuhlmacher, *Historical Criticism and Theological Interpretation of Scripture: Towards a Hermeneutic of Consent* (Philadelphia: Fortress Press, 1977); B. P. Robinson, "Biblical Authority: Is It Time for Another Paradigm Shift?", *ScriptB* 18 (1988) 34–41.

[37]S. Schneiders, "Freedom: Response and Responsibility: The Vocation of the Biblical Scholar in the Church," *Wither Creativity, Freedom, Suffering?: Humanity, Cosmos, God*, proceedings of the Theology Institute, ed. F. A. Eigo (Villanova, Penn.: Villanova Theology Institute, 1981) 34.

[38]Schneiders, "From Exegesis to Hermeneutics," 31, 32.

biblical reading—the historical-critical and the pneumatic[39]—by which Sacred Scripture continues to be the communication of God to the believing community spoken in the actuality of the present day.

From a practical viewpoint, this paradigm shift will affect both the biblical scholar and the official teaching authority. For the exegete, this demands that he/she be "both spiritually mature believer and adequately trained theologian." For the magisterium, it demands respect for biblical scholarship "in the exercise of ecclesially responsible theological and pastoral initiative within the common tradition."[40] In this mutual interaction, which conceivably could be fostered by a more public and active functioning of the Pontifical Biblical Commission,[41] both theological publications[42] and magisterial pronouncements[43] will enhance the Church's ability to actualize fully its inherited tradition.

III. The Liturgy of the Word

The actualization of Scripture concerns, ultimately, the living and enduring significance of the Bible in the Church. That the Salvific Word of God may be brought to life in all believers is, no doubt, the purpose of the sacred writings. Thus, the "liturgical" effect of the Word, understood in the broad sense of being beneficial for its readers, should be the culmination of all biblical studies.

In its final chapter, entitled "Sacred Scripture in the Life of the Church," *Dei Verbum* highlights the Church's mutual attraction to the Bible: on the one hand, a holy reverence and veneration of the inspired Word and, on the other, a practical and functional concern for the sacred text. As Scripture is the force-filled meeting ground with God, so it should extend its influence to all realms of the Church's life (prayer, theology, preaching, etc.) and to all believers in the ecclesial community (clergy, laity, even non-Christians).

This existential reality of the Word has found much receptivity after Vatican II. Flowing from the council's pastoral directives, the Word of God

---

[39]Vanni, esp. 313–14.

[40]Schneiders, "From Exegesis to Hermeneutics," 39.

[41]This is a recommendation of Murphy, 22–23. Similarly, in his keynote address at the conference, Archbishop Rembert Weakland pointed to the need for cooperation and dialogue so as to overcome the polarization that reigns within the Church.

[42]Some publications already emphasizing this theological approach include the commentaries in the "New Testament Message" and "Old Testament Message" series and the "Message of Biblical Spirituality" series, all published by Michael Glazier, Inc. (Wilmington, Del.). See also the "Overtures to Biblical Theology" series published by Fortress Press (Philadelphia).

[43]Recent documents from the Pontifical Biblical Commission include a study on Women Priests (April 1976) and a study on Christology (April 1983).

is now more readily available to peoples than ever before. Moved by the renewed interest in Scripture generated by the council, the Secretariat for Christian Unity in 1969 instituted the World Catholic Federation for the Biblical Apostolate, which "concentrates its own efforts in the promotion of the Bible as the animating force of catholic life in the liturgy, in catechesis, and in evangelization."[44] Moreover, fellowships of biblical scholars, such as the Catholic Biblical Association and the Society of Biblical Literature, have not only stimulated ongoing discussion about Scripture but, through their publication of journals and monographs, have greatly advanced and enhanced biblical research.

In addition, by capitalizing on the cooperative spirit engendered by the council's teachings, biblical scholars of many denominations have collaborated in providing new translations of the original texts. The New American Bible, the New International Version, the New Revised Standard Version, Today's English Version, the Jerusalem Bible—many of which have undergone even further revision—have provided both better and more critical versions for the faithful's reading of the divine Word. Even within the Roman Rite, one advantage of the liturgical reform has been to open up the treasures of the Bible (SC no. 51), so that virtually all of the Gospels are heard, along with most of the New Testament letters and a significant portion of the Old Testament.

In the years since the council, this greater access to and knowledge of Scripture has enlivened several "life" issues within the Church, among the believing communities, and in various cultures of the world. On the home front, all means and methods of teaching are to be rooted in the Word:[45] theology, homiletics, catechesis—these and other such ministries constitute the practical application and adaptation of the Word of God, inspired and interpreted, in the life of believers.

In ecumenical circles, the greater availability of the Bible and the greater freedom with which it may be studied have led to a greater cooperation with others, Catholic and non-Catholic alike, in the pursuit of sacred truth.[46]

---

[44] See the panoramic summary of the role of the Bible in various nations given in the article by Swetnam (see n. 16 above). On the WCFBA, see also L. Feldkamper, "A Season for Everything. Today's Bible Consciousness Demands Intensified Cooperation," *World Events* 58 (January 15, 1985) 28–31.

[45] On the "Ministry of the Word" in Vatican II, see S. Marrow, "Vatican II: Scripture and Preaching," *Vatican II: The Unfinished Agenda*, ed. L. Richard (New York: Paulist Press, 1987) 82–92, esp. 85–88.

[46] L. Boadt, "Biblical Studies on the Fifteenth Anniversary of Nostra Aetate," *Biblical Studies: Meeting Ground of Jews and Christians*, eds. L. Boadt, H. Croner, and L. Klenicki (New York: Paulist Press, 1980) 3: "In all these decrees and guidelines of Vatican offices . . . the dominant note has continually been the call to Christian scholars to explore the Scriptures more deeply in a spirit of dialogue and collaboration with their Jewish peers."

Certainly this ecumenical task is far from being completed,[47] but the mutual interest in and dependence on the Word by the various believing communities offers one common foundation on which to build an ever closer relationship.

Reaching outward, biblical scholars have concerned themselves with the question of "culture" in terms of Scripture. While the sacred text is one and universal, and its exegesis fundamentally similar in all cultures, yet the depth of truth expressed in Scripture allows for and encourages inquiries and investigations proper to the particular concerns of a given world-view. Thus, the renewed attempts at inculturating and acculturating the biblical message cannot help but contribute to "a real enrichment in the whole Church, just as the different cultures which have established themselves in Europe for two thousand years have enriched the reading of Scripture and its very life."[48]

Granted that this development in making the sacred text available, known and assimilated by all is worthy of further extension, the primary concern for the Word of God in any future prospective must not remain simply linguistic or purely functional or merely cultural. Rather, as it is intended to be the living Word of God spoken continuously in the midst of the community,[49] the place of Scripture must be accorded a greater status, as existentially necessary for sustaining the life of the Church. It must assume that place, both in understanding and practice, where the horizon of God's self-revelation will be actualized. To this end, the Bible must be "intra- culturated" in the liturgy, for in Scripture we possess "the consecration of the history of salvation under the species of the human word, inseparable from the eucharistic celebration which recapitulates the whole of history in the body of Christ."[50]

The future vitality of Scripture in the life of the Church requires, therefore, a greater awareness of and attention to its role in the Sunday liturgy.

---

[47]This is noted particularly in the article by Senior (see n. 7 above).

[48]Gilbert, 307. See also the work of the Pontifical Biblical Commission entitled *Foi et culture à la lumière de la Bible* (1981), and P. Beauchamp and others, *Bible and Inculturation*, Inculturation, 3 (Rome: Gregorian University Press, 1983).

[49]This ever-present sense of actualization is emphasized by Vanni, 315: "Scripture is presented in the preceding chapters (of *Dei Verbum*) as a communication of God made to humans, but mentioned normally with verbs in the past tense. . . . In this chapter (6) Scripture is taken up again as a literary fact already completed, but the verbs which refer to the communication between God and humans are all in the present tense."

[50]This forms part of the intervention at Vatican II by Msgr. Edelby, a representative of an Eastern Church (cited in L. Alonso-Schoekel, *Celebrating the Eucharist: Biblical Meditations* [New York: Crossroad, 1989] 38). Similarly, in his major address at the conference, Lucien Deiss described the Liturgy of the Word in the new lectionary as the "greatest opportunity for the renewal of the Church" in its local settings.

There, where the greatest number of the faithful encounter the biblical texts, the experience of God's Word is to be found, for "the whole purpose of the liturgy of the Word is to illuminate for us the mystery of Christ—what it represents for us, what it offers us, what it demands of us."[51] There, where the interactive process of proclamation, commentary, and participative attentiveness unfolds, the realization of God's Word takes place, for the experience of the community is transformed and enlivened through the impulse of the Spirit.

Thus the Liturgy of the Word, as the privileged place of encountering the sacred text from which all other readings extend and towards which they also converge,[52] is the locus of the Spirit's inspiring consecration of the Bible and, in turn, of the Church's life. More than just another rite or ceremony, the Liturgy of the Word must regain and retain its fruitfulness, so that the Word of God may be for us not simply a source of information but a powerful means of personal and communal transformation. Only when this dynamic of the Word is perceived and understood will the concluding statement of Vatican II in *Dei Verbum* be fully realized,[53] that "Just as from constant attendance at the eucharistic mystery the life of the Church draws increase, so a new impulse of spiritual life may be expected from increased veneration of the Word of God, which 'stands forever.'"

[51] Alonso-Schoekel, 38.

[52] Alonso-Schoekel, 52.

[53] This unfulfilled potential of Vatican II is noted by G. P. Fogarty, "American Catholic Biblical Scholarship: A Review," *TS* 50 (1989) 243: "Vatican II was an important moment in the Church's history, but it was only a moment."

Part II

Vatican II and the Modern World

Introduction to the Church and Culture

Religion and Culture

Joseph P. Fitzpatrick, S.J.

These three articles present three different types of religious response to cultural situations: one, a general response of rejection or collaboration, depending on the way a particular culture is evaluated; the second, an analysis of the way important cultural values become complicated by the political process in moral judgments around the issue of abortion; and a third, discussion of the way cultural changes in our ways of thinking result in noticeable modifications in theological concepts and terminology.

The objective of this introduction is not to summarize the articles but to note the insights the articles give to our understanding of the relationship of religion to culture. Culture, simply defined, is the sum total of the ways of thinking, feeling, believing, acting, and interacting which constitute what we call the way of life of one group of people in contrast to another; in brief, the difference of the way of life of Italians in contrast to that of Japanese; of the people of India in contrast to that of the people of Mexico. Critical to every culture is the framework of meanings—the ultimate meaning of existence as well as the meaning of language and behavior. These important aspects of meaning constitute the values of the life of a people. In every society, people must express their values in some tangible or visible form. In this way a particular form of behavior is understood to mean respect or disrespect, praise or insult, approval or disapproval. In other words the forms of behavior which identify a culture (a bow, for example, rather than a kiss) become the symbols of the meaning they have for the members of a cultural group.

In the first article, it is clear that the critical item is the meaning that persons find in forms of behavior. The very same aspect of the culture of the United States, the emphasis on personal freedom, has an unfavorable meaning for one group of critics (it opens the way to unrestrained license) while to another group it has a favorable meaning (it has released people from oppressive historical restrictions and enables them to fulfill in themselves many of our religious ideals).

Thus any religious belief faces two problems: one, if the belief is to be proclaimed in an already established society, those who proclaim it must determine what forms of behavior in that society can adequately carry the meaning of the religious belief(s), that is, whether a form of economic activity, such as the taking of interest, means virtuous conduct or immoral exploitation. The proponents of a religious faith, by their judgment of the meaning of the behavior, will be guided in their decision to accept or to oppose the practice. The first Gentile Christians had to decide whether the eating of food that had been offered to idols was acceptable behavior for a Christian.

The second problem a religion must face is to determine what forms of behavior they will cultivate to convey the meaning of the religious belief, e.g., whether circumcision and the observance of the Mosaic Law were necessary for Gentiles who sought to live a Christian life.

These determinations are very complex. In evaluating the meaning of social institutions, it must be remembered that every social function involves a dysfunction. Thus the free selection of the marriage partner provides great satisfaction to many persons, in fact, provides the opportunity for a mature spirituality by placing this great responsibility into the hands of young people. It has the dysfunction of resulting in a weaker family life and tends to leave the family of the young people socially unsupported. Thus in evaluating a culture, the functional advantages must be weighed against the dysfunctions, and a decision made whether the cost (in dysfunctions) is too great for the enjoyment of the functional advantages.

Thus it is understandable that a culture so new in human history as that of the United States, and so dynamically changing, could be judged so differently by persons who hold the same religious beliefs. There are numerous dysfunctions and, if brought together, they reveal the plausibility of those who challenge the culture of the United States as evil. At the same time, a congeries of the advantages reveal why others would judge United States culture as a favorable environment for the expression of Catholic values. Keeping both advantages and disadvantages in clear focus indicates that those who see great possibilities for the expression of religious values must also consistently challenge and seek to minimize the dysfunctions which are contrary to Christian values.

The second paper is much more subtle, but it reveals how members of a society can promote, as a fulfillment of cultural values, forms of behavior which actually contradict those values. Polls reveal that the great majority of the citizens of the United States are opposed to abortion on demand, while the practice is legally protected because it has been represented as the fulfillment of the civil rights of citizens, namely, the right of each woman to control her own reproductive activity. Kelly clearly describes this as a series of rights in conflict or values in conflict. More accurately he points out the way one value will or will not be supported depending on its relation to a distinct value. In other words, right wing capitalist advocates have supported restrictions on abortion, but when the possibility of greater population increase comes to be seen as a threat to the prosperity of the wealthy, this support may weaken or vanish. On the other hand, citizens of socialist orientation who now favor abortion because they see pro-life as favorable to capitalist leaders, may have to face more clearly the issue of the rights of the fetus if it is no longer seen as a class issue in support of capitalist interests.

On another level, when the right of mothers versus the right of the fetus is represented as a "conflict of interest," there is a tendency to favor the "interest" of the mother. Thus the appeal to the rights of the unborn as a right with preference over that of the mother has never prevailed in the pro-choice/pro-life argument. However, Kelly points out that if it becomes clear that the choice of abortion by poor women is often not a free choice at all, but a decision forced on her by economic circumstances, there could be a decided shift in favor of the protection of her freedom to choose to bear the child.

What Kelly's paper illustrates clearly is the political context in which the conflict of values plays out. Politics is the process of accommodating conflicting interests, that is, accommodating conflicting values. The clear perception of a basic value is often clouded in the conflict of political interests. If some shift suddenly occurs, the full meaning of the basic value (the right to life of the unborn) may shine clearly forth and result in important political shifts. Briefly, Kelly's paper provides the evidence that culture is continually intertwined with the political process.

The third paper is really an epistemological rather than a cultural analysis. However, the way we think is certainly an essential feature of our culture. The essay is really the application of the creative insights of Thomas Kuhn, *The Structure of Scientific Revolutions,* to the theology and canon law of the sacraments. Martos points out clearly that the development of a theology of the sacraments has passed through a series of "paradigm" changes very much like the radical changes in scientific theory. He explains that the theology of the sacraments became tightly fixed in the conceptual framework of scholastic philosophy, which was considered the "philosophia perennis," the eternal philosophy, until recent years. But developments in the psychological and social sciences resulted in perceptions of reality quite different from that of scholastic philosophy. Traditional concepts were no longer convincing in the presence of our emerging knowledge. New perspectives emphasize the existential rather than the essential; are the result of inductive rather than deductive reasoning; and are influenced by "ecclesial praxis" such as in liberation theology. This results, according to Martos, in a pluralism of theories or explanations rather than a fixed systematic theology of sacraments.

This affects culture directly because it gives the appearance of undermining the ultimate meaning of life and human behavior which was communicated in the traditional theology, whereas it is simply a new perspective of the sacrament in a new conceptual framework. As a result, Catholics speak of sacraments using the old vocabulary, just as we speak of the sun rising when we know that is not what is happening. And ecclesiastic authorities still oppose giving wide publicity to the new explanations and new vocabulary lest it shake the faith of the people.

Thus the theology of sacraments is another example of the problem religion has in determining what features of a culture (in this case, a way of knowing) are or are not compatible with the essentials of faith. Martos does not fully address this problem. A pluralism of theologies is easy enough to assert. But eventually some discrimination must be made between those that provide a better explanation of the meaning of essential beliefs in contrast to those that do not. It is true that this discriminating consensus often emerges after long years of patient searching by sincerely believing scholars together with years of experience among the faithful. The only recommendation Martos suggests is the advice of Niels Bohr to hold out "until the old professors die off and the new professors take their place." History suggests that much more than that is needed.

Chapter 6

The Divided Mind of American Catholicism

Jon Nilson

Introduction

> Numerous priests and religious announced, during the postconciliar crisis, that they no longer wished to play a special role, that the burdens of living up to what the Church expected of them were now intolerable. Humanly such feelings were quite understandable. Yet unnoticed was an implication of the most profound theological significance—no longer was the religious vocation treated as a call from God that might or might not coincide with the individual's own wishes. The possibility that God might will certain people to assume tasks they would rather shirk was implicitly denied. The entire Judaeo-Christian understanding of the ways in which God deals with man was being silently rejected.[1]

> Authority has been put at risk in Catholicism by many of the very officials who claim to be defending it. There is no mistaking their real intentions when they seek the unconscious erotic rewards of domination over other persons as a substitute for healthy heterosexual relationships in their own lives . . . they communicate their real inner authoritarian desires in what are, in truth, sacrilegious forays into the most intimate and sensitive facets of individual lives.[2]

These opinions of two prominent and knowledgeable Catholics indicate the bases and bitterness of the conflicts boiling in the Roman Catholic Church in the United States since Vatican II.

In October 1983, a "visitation" to the Archdiocese of Seattle and its archbishop, Raymond Hunthausen, was ordered by the Vatican. In September 1984, Hunthausen reported that he had been directed to cede authority in five major areas of his episcopal responsibilities to his newly named auxiliary bishop, Donald Wuerl. In November 1986, the United

---

[1]James Hitchcock, *Catholicism and Modernity* (New York: Seabury Press, 1979) 7.

[2]Eugene Kennedy, *Tomorrow's Catholics, Yesterday's Church* (New York: Harper and Row, 1988) 134.

69

States bishops met in executive session for over four hours to seek a solution to the mounting controversy over these actions and to offer their help to Hunthausen and the Vatican. Their official statement spoke of the "deeply troubling pain," the "dismay and confusion" that attended the Seattle case.[3]

On September 13, 1984, Governor Mario Cuomo of New York delivered an address at the University of Notre Dame in which he argued that Catholic politicians should not seek legal restraints on abortion under the present circumstances.[4] Eleven days later, Representative Henry Hyde of Illinois appeared at Notre Dame, too. He argued that Cuomo's view opened the way to Dachau, Auschwitz, and the Gulag.[5]

On November 12, 1984, Bishop Thomas Grady of Orlando expressed his concern about Catholics who were "becoming increasingly aggressive in condemning their opposite numbers" and urged his fellow bishops to decry this divisiveness as a "wound on the body of Christ."[6]

In June 1986, the Catholic Theological Society of America overwhelmingly (one hundred seventy-one yeses, fourteen noes, four abstentions) adopted a resolution, saying " . . . that for the good of Roman Catholic theology, Catholic higher education, and the Catholic Church in North America, we strongly urge that no action be taken against Charles Curran that would prohibit him from teaching on the theological faculty at The Catholic University of America." The September 1986 *Fellowship of Catholic Scholars Newsletter* carried a statement, "The Church and Father Curran," which expressed the diametrically opposite position. A list of thirty-six signers was appended.

Disagreements like these do not create problems. The problems stem from the way we deal with them. Seldom does serious disagreement lead to genuine debate within the Church. There is little of the open discussion we claim to cherish as Americans. Instead of the cooperative inquiry urged by Vatican II,[7] we American Catholics are locked in what Walter Burghardt calls "our intramural internecine hostility."[8]

This article offers a typology of the three dominant forms of contemporary American Catholicism in the hope of making greater mutual under-

[3]*Origins* 16:23 (November 20, 1986) 400. A chronology of the Seattle case is given in *Origins* 17:3 (June 4, 1987) 39.

[4]"Religious Belief and Public Morality," *Origins* 14:5 (September 27, 1984) 234–40.

[5]"Religious Values and Public Life," *Origins* 14:17 (October 11, 1984) 266–72.

[6]*Origins* 14:24 (November 29, 1984) 396–97.

[7]"They should always try to enlighten one another through honest discussion, preserving mutual charity and caring above all for the common good." *Pastoral Constitution on the Church in the Modern World*, 43, trans. Abbot and Gallagher.

[8]"Intellectual and Catholic? Or Catholic Intellectual?" *America* 160:17 (May 6, 1989) 425.

standing and respect—if not agreement—possible. H. Richard Niebuhr's classic, *Christ and Culture,* and Avery Dulles' soon-to-be-if-not-already classic, *Models of the Church,* are the inspiration for this typological approach.

Niebuhr wrote *Christ and Culture* "to set forth typical Christian answers to the problem of Christ and culture and so to contribute to the mutual understanding of variant and often conflicting Christian groups."[9] Dulles argued that many of the Church's intramural disputes could be traced to conflicts between different understandings or "models" of the Church.[10] Perhaps, then, a typology of American Catholicism may promote toleration and charity in the Church.

This typology will identify the central convictions, values, and judgments which divide American Catholics. Each of the three types has a particular interpretation of American culture and of the Roman Catholic Church's role in that culture. Each has a different perception of which Catholic values need to be defended and promoted today. Each has a distinctive view of the main tasks facing the Church in this country at this moment in history.

No typology fully captures the complexity of any individual or group. Nor does it support predictions. As Niebuhr remarks, "When one returns from the hypothetical scheme to the rich complexity of individual events, it is evident at once that no person or group ever conforms completely to a type."[11] To turn a type into a reductive, simplistic label is to misunderstand and misuse it.

Across the spectrum of current interpretations of American Catholicism, whether scholarly or journalistic, a dualistic view prevails. The Church is supposedly split into two opposing camps, tagged as Right vs. Left, liberal vs. conservative, preservationist vs. transformationist, Roman Catholic vs. American Catholic. This dualism suggests that the late nineteenth-century Americanist controversy still furnishes the interpretive paradigm for the Roman Catholic Church in the United States. In fact, however, it no longer fits.

I. The Church as Adversary of American Culture

1. The Adversary View of American Culture

The Adversary type of American Catholic considers United States culture as fundamentally antagonistic to Catholic truths and values. The his-

[9]H. Richard Niebuhr, *Christ and Culture* (New York: Harper and Row, 1956 [orig. ed., 1951] 2.

[10]Avery Dulles, "The Use of Models in Ecclesiology," ch. 1 of his *Models of the Church,* expanded ed. (Garden City, N.Y.: Doubleday, 1987).

[11]Niebuhr, *Christ and Culture,* 43–44.

tory of the country and the philosophy that shaped its political system suggest that the prospects for a happy marriage between Catholicism and American culture are very slim.

This nation has always been hostile to Catholicism. The forms of that hostility have merely changed over time. In the early period, the antagonism was blatant and often violent; witness the burning of the Charleston convent in 1834 and the "Know Nothing" movement. Today the hostility is more subtle. Convictions and values for which the Church stands and by which it lives are portrayed as benighted and outdated. Good Catholics, therefore, maintain and strengthen their Church. It is the only sure bulwark against the modern spirit which seeks freedom from ecclesiastical authority, from divine authority, and from the obligations arising from human interdependence and community. If modernity should triumph, nothing will keep humankind from the path which leads to its self-destruction.

In the Adversary's analysis, modernity originates in the Reformation. While reform of the Church was certainly necessary, Luther went too far when he placed the authority of his own private conscience above the divinely established authority of the Church. In effect, Luther inverted the proper order. In saying "Here I stand; I can do no other," he declared that his own individual reason was no longer subordinate to the faith taught and maintained by the authority Christ gave to his Church. Now authentic Christian faith would include only those truths which met the norms of his individual reason. The subordination of reason to faith in a cooperative harmony which produced the great medieval syntheses of faith and culture was sundered.

To the Adversary, American culture is essentially a branch on modernity's tree. It is largely part a product of the same spirit and ideology that spawned the French Revolution. It is a culture impatient of every restraint upon human impulse. It cloaks its anarchism in pseudo-philosophical speech about human dignity. Only the values and teachings of Roman Catholicism (and of those Protestant denominations untainted by liberalism) keep American culture from the war of all against all. Where the influence of the Church is not felt (e.g., the "subcultures" of drugs, cults, sexual promiscuity; reliance upon nuclear weapons for defense), we can glimpse the horrors of the future that awaits us all if we are not vigilant.

In a culture which is misguided at best, individually and socially destructive at worst, what should the Church do? Adversary types agree that the Church, not the nation, must be the shining "city on a hill," the light which shows the way out of the threatening darkness. They want the Church to oppose American culture not out of enmity or envy but out of love for the people seduced by it. The Church must be "against the world for the world"[12] just as a wise, loving parent must oppose a wantonly self-destructive child.

Within the Adversary type, however, there is disagreement about priorities. One group, the Evangelicals,[13] say that the Church's main task is greater and greater fidelity to Jesus' radical demands. That fidelity would make the Church a "counterculture" whose inner life was incontrovertible evidence of the gospel's truth. If Catholics were only faithful enough, the Church would be the sign of the reign of God on earth. From those millions of intensely committed followers would inevitably spring the cultural transformation of America. Now, however, the Church falls far short of what Jesus asks of his followers. So Evangelicals appeal to their fellow Catholics to take their baptismal commitment radically, since personal conversion and commitment are the keys to ecclesiastical and social reformation.

The second group within the Adversary type, the Conservers, admit the need for reformation in theory. But they are wary of reformation in practice. It is one thing to call oneself and one's fellow Catholics to truer discipleship in every facet of daily life. It is quite another to call for structural change in the Church under the banner of "Ecclesia semper reformanda." Institutional reform can easily be subverted by the spirit of modernity. It may begin with the best intentions, but it may end by making the Roman Catholic Church virtually indistinguishable from American culture. Instead of opposing American culture's convictions and values, it would become its mirror image. In other words, it would travel the road of liberal Protestantism.

Moreover, the Conservers are not convinced that the Church needs major reforms now. They regard many calls for Church reform as pseudo-religious echoes of modernist ideologies opposed to the spirit of authentic Catholicism. For example, Conservers often counter proposals for more participatory governance in the Church by saying that the Church is not a democracy. If it became one, Catholic doctrines and moral norms would soon be watered down to the bland religiosity still acceptable in American culture.

To Conservers, the main task of the Church is to conserve and reinvigorate the divinely-revealed and time-tested principles of authentic Roman Catholicism by teaching them clearly, insistently, and constantly. The threats posed by American culture are so strong that clarity and uniformity in teaching are critical. Church leaders should clearly mark the boundaries between its teachings and the dangerous half-truths of modernity. If they do not,

---

[12]See Peter L. Berger and Richard John Neuhaus, eds., *Against the World for the World: The Hartford Appeal and the Future of American Religion* (New York: Seabury Press, 1976).

[13]This is David O'Brien's term. See his *Public Catholicism* (New York: Macmillan, 1989).

they let ambiguity cloud the credibility and cohesion of Catholic principles.

This was the reasoning behind Cardinal Ratzinger's statement to Fr. Charles Curran that the Church could not tolerate the "inherent contradiction" in which someone who taught in the name of the Church in fact disagreed with certain points of the Church's teaching. To allow Curran to remain on a Vatican-chartered faculty would suggest that Roman Catholicism permits public dissent from its official teaching or that its teaching was incoherent since it included diametrically opposed positions within it.

2. How the Adversary Types Interpret Vatican II

Evangelicals see the demonic character of modernity manifested nowhere so clearly and so horrifyingly as in nuclear weaponry and the deterrence strategy of the superpowers. The prospect of "mutually assured destruction" demonstrates the madness of rejecting the gospel. Nuclear weapons make Catholicism's traditional "just war" ethic completely irrelevant in the contemporary world. Only radical discipleship, only full fidelity to Jesus' command to love our enemies and trust in his word, can save the world from nuclear suicide.

Consequently, Evangelicals consider *Gaudium et spes,* the Pastoral Constitution on the Church in the Modern World, as the most important document of Vatican II and, in particular, its final chapter on peace among nations (nos. 77–90). They stress that this council had decided to forego *anathemas,* yet had condemned the indiscriminate destruction wrought by nuclear weapons in the strongest, most uncompromising terms. They see the council as a major step in Roman Catholicism's turning into a "peace church," one which finally embraces "Love your enemies" as the paradoxical but sole path to true life.[14]

In the Conservers' vision, the Church in the United States is limping in weakened disarray. Gone is the vigor and confidence it enjoyed just prior to Vatican II. Conservers do not blame the council for crippling the Church but, rather, the news media and the new "knowledge class" of bureaucrats within the Church. These exploited the council for their own purposes. Today's chaos and confusion prove how successful they have been.

To the average Catholic, Vatican II came to mean simply: "Out with the old, in with the new!" To be a contemporary Catholic now meant turning away from the Tridentine Mass in Latin and long-treasured private devotions (e.g., the Nine First Fridays) and embracing new ways of worship, no matter how untried and bland and mistaken they might be. It meant

---

[14]See., e.g., James Douglass, "Toward a New Perspective on War: The Vision of Vatican II," in his *The Non-Violent Cross: A Theology of Revolution and Peace* (London: Macmillan, 1968) 100–36.

judging the fundamental principles and doctrines of Catholicism in light of modern values and philosophies. Soon "traditional" became synonymous with "irrelevant" and "outdated." Portraying the council as a battle where the forces of progress triumphed over the forces of reaction was, therefore, the way by which modernity's real agenda, freedom from all the restraints of the past, was advanced within the Church itself.[15]

Vatican II was further exploited by a new, postconciliar bureaucratic elite within Catholicism. This elite included theologians, religious education specialists, and heads of newly created diocesan offices for liturgy, peace and justice, youth ministry, etc. They took advantage of widespread interest in what the council meant to promote their own agenda for radical change in the Church. Unable to bear the burden of teaching and living the difficult, counter-cultural Roman Catholic doctrines and morality any longer, they portrayed the council as an historic, authoritative mandate to bring the Church "up to date." What they really wanted, however, was to reduce authentic Catholicism to a bland secularism.

Conservers look mainly to *Lumen gentium,* the Dogmatic Constitution on the Church, for support. Since they consider teaching the divinely-revealed and time-tested doctrines and values of authentic Roman Catholicism with clarity and constancy to be the Church's main task, they emphasize section twenty-five of the Constitution which sets forth the authority of pope and bishops. Characteristically, their interpretation of this passage is consistent with a particular understanding of nature and grace.

"Nature" is the order of creation flawed by original sin. "Grace," however, is the order of redemption. No created being can do anything that lies beyond the powers of its nature. A bush cannot move ten feet to get out of the shadow of an oak. A dog cannot give a speech or draw a picture. Human beings unaided by grace cannot accept what God has revealed since human nature cannot verify or falsify truths which transcend the human intellect.

Baptismal grace empowers a person to believe what God has revealed, though it remains opaque to mere human reason. The baptized can now trust in God for the help necessary to lead a virtuous life and to be saved. They can now love God above all things. Without sanctifying grace, they could do none of these.

In the sacrament of orders, God gives graces to enable men to meet the responsibilities of leadership in the Church. This sacramental grace is not limited by the nature and abililities of the men who receive it.[16] Thus,

---

[15]See Hitchcock, *Catholicism and Modernity,* 7.

[16]See Kenneth Baker, "Reflections on the Morale of Priests," *Fellowship of Catholic Scholars Newsletter* 12:2 (March 1989) 9.

for example, a pope's talent may fall far short of the demands of his office. Yet grace so compensates that with good will he can perform his duties effectively.

Since God provides special help to the pope and the bishops in their teaching and governing the Church, the Catholic should accept their teachings and directives. The teachings may seem problematic and the directives imprudent, but the Catholic may rely on God's grace, even when the teaching troubles reason and the directives seem unwise. To dissent from the teaching or to withhold obedience is tantamount to turning one's back on God.

Grace does not make every official word and action of a pope or bishop correct and appropriate for the situation. Nor is complete assent and obedience required of Catholics to every teaching and directive. Nonetheless, the pope and the bishops do receive special graces for leadership in the Church which other Catholics do not. Dissent is a theoretical possibility but a practical impossibility.[17]

Since God bestows special graces on the pope and bishops and modernity poses a serious threat to the Church and the world today, it would be foolish (to say the very least) to question official teaching or to withhold obedience.[18] A Church whose voices are not "symphonic" (von Balthasar) but discordant cannot witness to the supreme beauty and harmony of the divine truths.

II. The Church as the Pupil of American Culture

1. The Pupil View of Culture

While Adversary types consider it fundamentally demonic (despite its glittering technological accomplishments), Pupil types consider modernity as "liberation writ large." They accept the Enlightenment's self-understanding as a movement to free human potential from the shackles of the past.

The essence of modernity, then, is not a demonic struggle for absolute human autonomy. Rather, it is a thrust towards freedom in order to realize humanity's full potential. Throughout history this thrust has been resisted by self-appointed defenders of tradition. They oppose change because they are blind. They do not realize that the wisdom of the past is inadequate for the demands of the present. They keep trying to cram the genie of free-

---

[17]See the letters from the Congregation for the Doctrine of the Faith to Charles Curran reprinted in his *Faithful Dissent* (Kansas City: Sheed and Ward, 1986).

[18]See William E. May, "Bishops, Scholars, and the Church," *Fellowship of Catholic Scholars Newsletter* 12:2 (March 1989) 1–2, esp. his refusal to distinguish levels of teaching.

dom back into the bottle of tradition, often using religion to do it, because freedom leads to changes that will take away their power and privilege.

The "American experiment" was designed precisely to escape from the outmoded political and religious straitjackets of the past. The experiment was aimed at generating a new kind of civilization where all humanly fabricated barriers to human potential would be removed. From the past would be kept only what could pass through the mesh of reason. From debate among free, well-informed, and thoughtful people, truth would emerge. A Bill of Rights would put the necessary freedoms beyond the reach of political meddling.

American political philosophy and its resultant culture certainly have blemishes and defects. Still, Pupil types of Catholics see much to praise and to learn from, little to condemn or blame in American culture. Pupil types enthusiastically embrace American ideals, like participatory democracy, upward mobility, pragmatism, and freedom from those constraints that may have been necessary in other times and places but now are obstacles to full human development.

Pupil types also think that Church leaders need to change their theological outlook to realize that American culture, like every culture, is already "graced." The Church does not bring God to culture; God is already there, healing, loving, and saving people. Since God is already present and working in the textures of American life, the Church must discern, support, and celebrate those grace-filled social and individual experiences which permeate life in the United States.

They find theological support for their positive view of American culture in the implications of the incarnation. If God became human in Jesus, all that is human is truly God's very own. The humanity of Jesus, organically united with the whole of material and spiritual creation, makes all creation belong to God intimately and indissolubly. The incarnation reveals not only that nothing in creation is alien to God but also that God is intimately present to it through the Logos' everlasting bond with human nature.

The Pupil type, therefore, wants the Roman Catholic Church to reform itself according to the implications of this view. This means, first of all, a major shift in the Church's self-understanding. Its purpose is not to mediate grace to a God-less culture. Instead, it must help people to discern, celebrate, and immerse themselves more deeply into the holy mystery which already pervades their individual and communal lives.

The Church loses its credibility—and members—by clinging to a vocabulary, a world-view, a set of rituals, and a governing structure suited for the past but no longer corresponding to people's experience of the sacred today. Church leaders who say the ordination of women is impossible, who refuse even to permit them to serve at the altar, who keep celibacy as a condition for priesthood, who require full adherence to the entire range of Church teaching (no matter how far from the core of Catholic Christian faith some of these teachings may be) betray an understanding of God and grace which is no longer viable in American culture.

The Church must learn from the world even in the realm of morality. Pupil types acknowledge the constancy in the Church's prohibitions of, e.g., artificial contraception, divorce and remarriage after a valid marriage, and genital expression of homosexual love. Yet, they say, these prohibitions were developed to safeguard human and Christian values in other ages and circumstances. But times and circumstances do change and have changed radically. Now the Church must heed and be guided by the testimony of thousands of its own members who say that what was long forbidden by the Church can be (and often is) nurturing and life-giving.[19]

The traditional prohibitions express ideals which the Church should teach and strive to realize. "Till death do us part" and "genital expressions of love are proper only within marrage" contain important values. Yet the Church must understand that many people today find these ideals impossible to meet. Further, they often discover God's loving, healing presence in officially prohibited relationships, like a second marriage without benefit of annulment. Until the Church recognizes and acts upon this discovery, it ignores the call of God in today's new human experiences. It will alienate people whose experiences of the holy fall outside of the narrow boundaries which the Church has drawn in the past.

2. How Pupil Types Interpret Vatican II

Pupil types think that their view of the Church-world relationship is precisely the one that Vatican II intended to inculcate in the Church. They argue that John XXIII convoked the council and Paul VI continued it because the council was the most effective way to reverse the Church's isolation from the modern world.

The "counter-cultural" Church began in the early nineteenth century when Rome perceived the strong anti-ecclesiastical thrust of the European revolutions. The Church fell under siege philosophically, theologically, politically, and socially. Thus, its leaders, beginning with Gregory XVI, began building fortress walls to protect it. Leo XIII's encyclical *Aeterni Patris* made the thought of Aquinas the philosophical and theological foundations of the bulwark. Ecclesial governance became more and more centralized in the Vatican to make bishops less vulnerable to political pressures. Wherever possible, the Church developed parallel institutions, such as

---

[19]See, e.g., Anthony Kosnik and others, *Human Sexuality: New Directions in American Catholic Thought* (New York: Paulist Press, 1977).

schools, hospitals, and orphanages, so that Catholics could be sheltered as much as possible from the world's anti-Christian barrages.

John XXIII terminated this policy. His own broad experience of the "world" taught him that it was not thoroughly and irremediably evil. Instead, he saw that much good had been accomplished in modern times and great potential good was still to be realized. So John set out to dismantle the walls of the fortress and effect a happy marriage between the modern world and the Church.

To the Pupil type, then, the most important document of the council is *Gaudium et spes,* the Pastoral Constitution on the Church in the Modern World. Its most important words are its opening lines: "The joys and the hopes, the griefs and anxieties of the people ["hominum"] of this age, especially those who are poor or in any way afflicted, these too are the joys and hopes, the griefs and anxieties of the followers of Christ."

Since reversing the Church's self-imposed isolation from the modern world was the main purpose of Vatican II, Pupil types stress the discontinuity between preconciliar and postconciliar Catholicism. They automatically suspect preconciliar theological axioms, devotional practices, styles of Church governance, etc., of maintaining that isolation which must now be completely abandoned.

For example, the Church may have needed the autocratic style of leadership prior to the council. Autocracy made for a uniformity in Catholic thought, policy, and action which seemed necessary in a Church that felt besieged. Today, however, autocratic styles make the Church look antiquarian at best and oppressive at worst. Autocracy estranges people from the Church now. It betrays the new spirit mandated by the council.

Pupil types thus prefer egalitarian models and images for the Church. To them, the Church is primarily the "people of God" and a parish is a "community of believers." Some Pupil types use the "family" image for the Church since it differentiates roles without implying that some are subordinate to others. The family image also relativizes the importance of necessary but distasteful elements of the Church like the Code of Canon Law, marriage tribunal procedures, and ecclesiastical finances.

III. The Church as the Critical Partner of Culture

1. The Partner View of Culture

The Church can be the partner of culture because American culture is not fundamentally evil or antagonistic to Christian truths and values.[20] Yet

---

[20]As Pope John Paul himself indicated in the speeches he delivered during his 1989 visit to the United States.

it must be a critical partner, since every culture is an intricate mix of good and evil, sin and grace. For instance, the Church may welcome and encourage the development of new communication technologies which can make information more accessible, widen the range of human choice, and so contribute to human fulfillment. Yet the Church should warn against abusing these technologies when they become means of violating the right to privacy, glorifying violence, or degrading women.[21]

From the Critical Partner perspective, the Church and culture are inescapably symbiotic. The Church can never be hermetically sealed off from cultural influences, even when it used Latin for its official language and medieval thought for its world-view. In fact, preconciliar Latin and fondness for the Middle Ages[22] concealed a massive irony. Church leaders assumed that they were preserving the pure, ahistorical essence of the Church from the contaminations of modernity. In fact, they were trying to maintain only the medieval form of Church-culture symbiosis, just one of the many forms which the Church-culture relationship has assumed throughout the Church's history. The Partner type concludes that the Church cannot choose whether or not to relate to its cultural environment and to be shaped by it. The Church can only try to make the symbiosis mutually beneficial.

In the Partner type's view, the Reformation and the French and American Revolutions ultimately helped the Church to realize more fully the implications of the gospel it preaches. Human dignity and rights figured prominently in the movements of 1776 and 1789. Even John Paul II has pointed to the Christian origins of these revolutionary ideals.[23] Yet Partner types also acknowledge the decades of virulent Church opposition to these same ideals[24] and suspect that the Church finally embraced them for two reasons. First, if it continued opposing these ideals, millions of Catholics would leave the Church. Second, the authentic congruence of these values with the gospel became more and more apparent.

Once the Church embraced human dignity and rights at Vatican II, it came quickly to see them as central to its mission in the contemporary world. Notions rejected by Pius VI, Pius VII, Gregory XVI, Pius IX, Pius X, Benedict XV, Pius XI, and Pius XII have become the cornerstone of John Paul II's message in his worldwide travels and in his major development of the Church's social teaching in *Laborem exercens* and *Solicitudo rei socialis*. On this score alone the Church owes much to modernity.

---

[21]See Vatican II's Decree on the Instruments of Social Communication, 2.

[22]As indicated in the very title of a perennial Catholic "best seller," James J. Walsh's *The Thirteenth, Greatest of Centuries* (New York: Catholic Summer School Press, 1913).

[23]See "Human Rights and the Church," *The Tablet* 243:7773 (July 8, 1989) 775.

[24]Pius IX's "Syllabus of Errors" remains the locus classicus.

Its ethic of personal responsibility has also contributed much to the Church. Kant distilled the essence of the Enlightenment when he said, "Enlightenment is man's release from his self-incurred tutelage. Tutelage is man's inability to make use of his understanding without direction from another."[25] As this ideal pervaded Western culture, it purified the meaning of personal faith. Authenticity became essential to faith. Then faith no longer meant primarily reliance upon Church authorities as divinely guaranteed in their teaching and official decisions. Rather, faith became a way of life rooted in a personal relationship with God. Thus, personal autonomy and religious pluralism have a legitimate place in the Church. A post-Enlightenment faith no longer supports devotional or theological conformity in the Church.

Dialogue makes demands on the Church. Besides discernment, dialogue requires the Church to eliminate its triumphalism, the attitude which suggests that the Church has nothing to learn from culture. Dialogue calls for real mutuality. It is not a subterfuge for the Church to tell the culture how to organize and run itself. Instead, the Church must enter into dialogue with culture in the awareness that it has some things to learn—and not all of them may be pleasant! Monarchical styles and attitudes in the Church are out.

The Church must also find a language to use in its dialogue with culture. From Leo XIII to Pius XII, Catholic social teaching had employed the language of "natural law," purportedly derived from reason alone, to facilitate acceptance of that teaching by the wider culture. With the collapse of neo-Scholasticism, that language became so problematic that it could no longer serve as the bridge between culture and the Church.

The United States bishops are well aware of this difficulty. Their effort to contribute to a more just and peaceful world demands that they find a language which speaks to American culture. If the natural law tradition can no longer provide it, what will? This question has not been answered fully. Yet the discussion and debate which *The Challenge of Peace* and *Economic Justice for All* stimulated outside the Church shows that these two initiatives constitute the beginning of an answer.

2. How the Partner Type Interprets Vatican II

Like the other types, Partner types see Vatican II providing the mandate and the theological foundations for their understanding of the Church and its mission. They argue that the council's main purpose was to end the isolation from the modern world in which the Church had enclosed itself for 150 years and to forge a new relationship to that world.

---

[25]"What is Enlightenment?" trans. and ed. L. W. Beck (Chicago, 1955) 286.

To insure uniformity of Church teaching and freedom from hostile interference, Vatican I in 1870 put full, immediate, and supreme jurisdiction over the Church in the hands of the pope. This council also struck back at intellectual trends (like rationalism, fideism, and traditionalism) thought to be the main reasons for modernity's defection from Catholic Christianity. Those with opinions contrary to the council's teachings about faith and reason were treated in the customary fashion: *Anathema sit!*

John XXIII envisioned a different kind of Church for the contemporary world; not an enclave of the smugly certain saved nor an ark floating safely above the floodwaters of modernity. He wanted the Church to be renewed so that it might proclaim the gospel to the world most effectively by its loving service. John's vision was embraced by the council Fathers most decisively in the Pastoral Consititution on the Church in the Modern World, *Gaudium et spes.*

They became convinced that the main obstacles to belief today were not so much theoretical as practical. Intellectual challenges had largely been met by theologians like Rahner, Lonergan, Schillebeeckx, and Congar. Instead, the main obstacle to faith now is the contradiction between the massive sufferings and injustices in the world and God's unconquerable love proclaimed and embodied by Jesus. Thus, the Church's social mission and presence are the most necessary and effective ways to proclaim the gospel in the world today.

So *Gaudium et spes* is the pivotal document of the council for the Partner type. Vatican II's fifteen other documents have to be understood in light of this one. It lays the groundwork for the Church's social mission in two ways. First, it offers a biblical and doctrinal framework for the developing tradition of the Church's social teaching, from Leo XIII's *Rerum novarum* to John Paul II's *Solicitudo rei socialis.* Second, it establishes the social mission as the Church's task today, whose specific demands have to be discerned through dialogue with culture.[26]

The four short years of Vatican II thus set in motion massive changes in the Roman Catholic Church's self-understanding and direction. It signified the Church's acceptance of the modern world as justifiably secular. Vatican II marks the end of the Church's old hope of re-establishing "Christendom," a culture where every aspect of life would be understood and lived out in explicitly Christian terms. The dream of a body politic with a brain, skeleton, and heart furnished by the Church died at Vatican II. The council summons the Church out of its isolation into critical partnership with the world.

[26]J. Bryan Hehir, "American Catholics and Public Policy," transcript of address to Chicago Call to Action Conference, November 17, 1984.

IV. Toward a Different Future for American Catholicism

As long as Adversary, Pupil, and Critical Partner types of Catholics think that theological agreement and a common interpretation of American culture are necessary for conversation and collaboration, Catholics in this country will remain seriously divided. Intellectual resources which could be devoted to evangelizing culture will be directed to internal wrangling. Funds will be allocated to projects that advance one type's agenda, not spent according to priorities determined by consensus. Bishops and priests will have to spend valuble time and energy simply keeping intramural peace.

Two promising efforts to overcome this divisiveness and lack of communication between the major types of American Catholicism are now underway.

In the Fall of 1987, a Commission of Bishops and Scholars was formed to encourage communication and foster collaboration between American bishops and Catholic scholars in fields bearing upon American Catholicism. The Commission pursues this goal by sponsoring colloquies between bishops and scholars in a particular region (October 1988: Los Altos, California; October 1989: Mobile, Alabama; September 1990: Mundelein, Illinois) on issues of academic and pastoral importance. Thus, the Los Altos meeting was devoted to the history of episcopal ministry, the Mobile meeting to fundamentalism, and the Mundelein meeting to reception.[27]

The Leadership Council of Catholic Laity (LCCL) is an outgrowth of the broad consultation used to prepare the American bishops for the 1987 Synod on the Laity in Rome. After the Synod, certain lay leaders saw the need for an organization to continue to articulate lay Catholic concerns and needs to the bishops and other groups in the United States Church. This organization would have to be as inclusive as possible to be effective. It could not be the mouthpiece of one or another of the dominant types.

So representatives from Catholic associations across the ideological spectrum ("from the Cardinal Mindszenty Foundation to Pax Christi," as one observer put it) were invited to a meeting at Belleville, Illinois, in January 1989. This gathering provided sufficient impetus for follow-up organizing efforts, which include searching for common concerns and convictions beneath ideological differences and finding issues that transcend the disagreements, such as the poisoning of the environment. Though it is still in its infancy, LCCL offers great hope to a seriously divided Church.

Liturgy, the public worship of the Church, mainly the Mass and the sacraments, has always been the common ground for all Catholics. Together they hear the Word of God, recite the Creed, and share in the Lord's Sup-

---

[27]I am grateful to Donald Buggert, O.Carm., Secretary of the Commission, for this information.

per. Yet it would be naive to say that the liturgy alone can heal the divisions within American Catholicism.

Vatican II's Constitution on the Liturgy affirms that the liturgy cannot produce its full effect if those who participate do not have the proper attitudes and commitments.[28] As the number of priests declines and their average age increases, will Catholics experience liturgy that expresses and fosters the authentic unity of the Church?

Furthermore, elements of American culture seem to diminish or even nullify effects of the liturgy. For instance, most Masses are offered in and for a particular parish whose boundaries are geographically defined. Since income and race largely determine one's place of residence and, thus, one's parish, most Catholics worship with Catholics very like themselves. A suburban white lawyer never shares the Eucharist with an inner city black nurse. The Catholic unity between them is well nigh invisible.[29]

What can overcome the divisions within American Catholicism and allow its authentic unity to emerge? Only a common, untiring commitment to the discipline of dialogue. To paraphrase the late A. J. Muste, there is no path to dialogue; dialogue is the path. Continuing and respectful conversation among Catholics concerning the most important issues facing the Church locally, nationally, and internationally is the only way to a future different from the polarizations of the postconciliar past.

The dignity and vocation that come with full membership in the Church call for this dialogue. No one's views and opinions are *a priori* less worthy of a full and respectful hearing. Inner-Church dialogue is sustained by Jesus' words, "Do not judge lest you be judged" and by the perennial Catholic conviction that no one can know another's standing before God. Good will, Christian commitment, and love for the Church must be presumed by all for all.

If dialogue remains a vague ideal, it is useless. It must become concrete and ongoing to be fully productive. Perhaps people with special responsibilities for the Church's intramural life (like bishops, priests, religious, theologians, deacons, parish administrators) should commit themselves to regularly read a periodical associated with a type with whom they disagree. An Adversary type might read *Commonweal* or the *National Catholic Reporter;* the Pupil or Critical Partner type could read *Crisis* or *The Wanderer*. When teeth stop gnashing and blood pressure subsides, one begins to discern the convictions and motivations that underlie another type's initiatives. Areas

---

[28]See *Sacrosanctum Concilium*, 11.

[29]See M. Francis Mannion, "Liturgy and the Present Crisis of Culture," *Worship* 62:2 (March 1988) 98–123, for a more extensive analysis of American culture's negative impact on the liturgical experience.

of common concern can start to emerge. Possibilities for collaboration can become visible.

Bishops and pastors can foster dialogue by inviting Catholics of different types to work together on efforts important to the local Church. A shared concern for the vitality of Catholicism in the area brings these Catholics together. Then personal interactions can destroy stereotypes, so that mutual respect and understanding becomes possible.

Yet the peace, harmony, and consensus we seek are not, ultimately, the results of organizational techniques. Authentic Catholic unity is another term for what Paul calls the gifts of the Holy Spirit. Happily, we need not wait until they are given. We can ask for them now and in the asking itself receive a foretaste of their plentitude.

Chapter 7

Learning Consistency:
Catholicism and Abortion

James R. Kelly

The movement to make abortion legal took Roman Catholicism by surprise. The term "abortion" did not even make the forty-five-page index of the American edition of The Documents of Vatican Two (1966). All Christians were surprised. Abortion also failed to make the index (or agenda) of the published proceedings of the March 27–31, 1963, Harvard-sponsored "Roman Catholic-Protestant Colloquium," even though one of the seminars dealt explicitly with questions of morality and pluralism. In fact, everyone was surprised. One of the founders of the National Association for the Repeal of Abortion Laws straightforwardly acknowledged (Lader, 1973: vii) that until the late 1960s abortion reformers were part of a "lonely" movement that could claim "only a few clusters in a few states." Because the movement to legalize abortion was unexpected and initially weak, abortion opponents were entirely reactive. Early abortion opponents had no plans other than to persuade (by the data of biology) their legislators to leave intact the laws restricting non-medically necessary abortions passed by every state since at least 1900.

The Roman Catholic Church played a central but far from solitary role in the anti-abortion countermovement. Scholarly observers (Leahy, 1982; Luker, 1984; Francome, 1984; Cuneo, 1990; Kelly, 1979; 1989) report that the earliest abortion opponents, though disproportionately Catholic, were ecumenical, largely self-recruited, and autonomous. Although abortion activists, often successfully, characterized their opponents as financed and controlled by the Catholic Church (Noonan, 1979:56; Nathanson, 1983), right to life activists were self-financed and often complained about the lack of Church involvement. Since the Catholic Church became the only national entity opposing any changes in the abortion law, it soon became a communication center for the hundreds of state right to life groups. Protestant recruitment was impeded by the initially limited reform goals proclaimed by abortion reformers (by defining "health" to include psychological and even economic factors, Roe made all abortions legal throughout pregnancy), although by the late 1970s all denominations had antiabortion organizations and evangelical Protestantism became a distinct presence in the movement. In 1966 Rev. (now Bishop) James McHugh, the director of the Family Life Bureau of the United States Catholic Conference, invited a small number of already active abortion opponents to serve as advisors to a "national Right to Life Committee" (legally incorporated after Roe and now the dominant social movement organization). McHugh had begun to monitor abortion law activity in all the states and the NRLC became a central information bank about laws and tactics. In 1967 California, Colorado, and North Carolina legislatures altered their laws to permit abortions performed before viability for reasons such as rape, incest, and maternal health. But it was not until November 15, 1968, that the National Conference of Catholic Bishops made a collective statement about legal abortion.

In terms of the evolution of the Church's role in the abortion controversy, it is worth noting that in their first collective statement[1] the bishops, as had the Second Vatican Council, characterized abortion as an issue of social justice and human rights, not as a matter of sexual ethics. Their first statement dealing with abortion acknowledged that the retention of the traditional moral teaching about abortion required something more than opposition to abortion reform. The still evolving understanding of what this "something more" required is an important aspect of the Catholic Church's involvement in abortion politics and of increasing moral significance to the movement sparked by abortion reform.

The first NCCB reference to abortion is the November 15, 1968, statement entitled "Human Life in Our Day" (Benestad and Butler, 1981). By its title, we might think that the statement dealt with abortion. In fact, abortion comprised but a section of a statement concerned about the problem of militarism generally and the war in Vietnam more specifically. Perhaps in retrospect the most striking detail in this letter is the bishops' first use of what later became a favorite pejorative used by abortion opponents

---

[1]In his explanation of the role of national conferences of bishops, Dulles (1988) explains that only the Universal College of Bishops with the pope, or the pope speaking "ex cathedra," can issue teaching on faith or morals that is binding on the Catholic conscience. No statement of policy can form the matter for such pronouncements. The Second Vatican Council recommended the return of national and regional conferences of bishops (they had been common in the history of the Church until European nationalism—and imperialism—blurred their value) as a way of "inculturating" or adapting Church teaching to specific cultural contexts. But the council left unspecified the nature of their authority. In any case, the authority of documents on public policy and law—such as abortion—rests entirely on the persuasiveness of their arguments and the agreement they enlist from their various audiences.

to describe abortion supporters—"antilife." But here the bishops use the phrase to describe the "neutron bomb," elsewhere called the perfect capitalist weapon because it preserved buildings as it killed populations.

One year later (on April 17, 1969) the bishops issued a letter directly dealing with legal abortion. There they note that legal abortion activists now frankly admit that their goal is unrestricted abortion. They made three major points in this statement: (1) that unrestricted abortion will not solve the deeper problems that cause women to seek abortions; (2) that the implicit premise of legal abortion—that personal and social problems can be solved by deliberately terminating human life—will affect how society deals with other forms of unwanted life, such as the incurably ill; (3) that opponents of legal abortion must adopt an ethic of "social responsibility" supporting efforts to "provide to all women adequate education and material sustenance to choose motherhood responsibly and freely."

It's clear from the very first statements issued by the National Conference of Catholic Bishops that their moral critique of abortion was always placed in a larger social and economic context. They linked resistance to easier abortion laws with community assistance to women burdened with unwanted pregnancies. But these early descriptions of community aid seemed to promote mostly a kind of "social work" assistance (such as that provided now by the more than three thousand emergency pregnancy centers staffed by "Birthright," "Alternatives to Abortion, International," the Christian Action Council, and others) which did not directly raise questions about the very structuring of society that might itself be a major factor in the high abortion rate.

I. From Benevolence to Justice

The first unambiguous break by a Catholic bishop with a "social work" response to abortion that I can locate is a July 4, 1971, sermon by the late Archbishop of Boston, Humberto S. Medeiros, entitled "A Call to a Consistent Ethic of Life and the Law" given at St. Patrick's Cathedral, New York City, at a special Mass for Catholic judges, lawyers, and public officials. He told them that "a strong stand on abortion demands a consistently strong stand on social issues . . . If we support the right of every fetus to be born, consistency demands that we equally support every man's (sic) continuing right to a truly human existence."

Since they argued in "slippery-slope" fashion that legal abortion would in time erode the moral taboos against infanticide and euthanasia, all segments of the right to life movement assumed at least a kind of "partial" consistency which researchers have corroborated (Blake, 1971; Singh, 1979; Ostheimer and Moore, 1981; Granberg and Denny, 1982). But Madeiros preached a comprehensive "consistency" that required a concern for the "quality of life" that embraced issues of poverty, militarism, and capital punishment. Medeiros invited a societal analysis of abortion that looks far beyond a solitary woman's decision to terminate her pregnancy. After the January 22, 1973, Supreme Court Decision "Roe vs. Wade," the National Conference of Catholic Bishops added to their "social work" response to abortion a more searching critique of American society itself, especially of its dominant economic assumptions and practices. In a November 13, 1973, statement entitled "Resolution on the Pro-Life Constitutional Amendment," the NCCB pointed out that Roe means that for the Court "the right of privacy takes precedence over the right to life," and they pledged themselves to support efforts to seek a reversal of Roe. They explicitly linked their antiabortion efforts with a "determination to uphold the dignity of the human being after as well as before birth."

Two years later (in the interim the United States Catholic Conference declared its opposition to capital punishment) on November 20, 1975, the bishops announced a three-part plan for restoring legal protection to the unborn. The first part described an educational program called "Respect Life" and the second promoted pastoral and governmental assistance for women and children. The third part, more controversial, called for the promotion of parish and diocesan pro-life committees to assist in the formation of "independent, bipartisan, political action committees" in each congressional district. In their "Respect Life Program" the bishops explicitly encouraged a comprehensive approach linking abortion opposition to the issues of poverty, help for the mentally retarded, the aging, and reduced military spending. "The program must extend to other issues that involve support of human life: There must be internal consistency in the pro-life commitment." Throughout its involvement in the right to life movement the bishops have resisted strenuous efforts by some activists to declare that support for a human life amendment reversing Roe should be the sole criteria (assuming that the candidate is otherwise qualified for public office) for evaluating candidates.

Undoubtedly the bishops' teaching that opposition to abortion required a "Consistency" received its most prominent phrasing in Joseph Cardinal Bernardin's December 6, 1983, address at Fordham University entitled "A Consistent Ethic of Life: An American Catholic Dialogue." Bernardin was well positioned to speak authoritatively on this approach. He was then the chairman of the Bishops' Committee on Pro-Life Activities, and he had chaired the committee which drafted the bishops' highly publicized and controversial 1983 pastoral letter "The Challenge of Peace." This letter had been interpreted as a criticism of the Reagan escalation of military spending and especially of its policies of "nuclear superiority" and possible "first-use" of nuclear weapons. Reporters covering Bernardin's address had expected that he would respond to the charges that the bishops' had made themselves unreliable allies against communism. Instead, Bernardin developed a largely ignored point in "The Challenge of Peace." There the bishops had explained that the moral principle underlying their opposition to any conceivable use of nuclear weapons (even in retaliation) was also the reason they opposed abortion. Bernardin expanded this point: "It is because the fetus is judged to be both human and not an aggressor that Catholic teaching concludes that direct attack on fetal life is always wrong. This is also why we insist that legal protection be given to the unborn. The same principle yields the most stringent, binding, and radical conclusion of the pastoral letter: that directly intended attacks on civilian centers are always wrong . . . such attacks would be wrong even if our cities had been hit first; second, anyone asked to execute such attacks should refuse orders." In Bernardin's 1983 address it was especially clear that the Church had conjoined its defense of traditional moral teaching about abortion with what Bernardin conceded were radical criticisms of long-standing American military policy. This approach guaranteed that the authoritative Catholic approach to abortion could not easily be characterized by the usual labels of "conservative," "liberal," and "radical." This labeling problem also signaled that there was no immediately recognizable political location for such a "consistent ethic" approach to abortion.

Few American politicians can be called supporters of a consistent ethic approach to abortion. In the Spring of 1986 a consistent ethic of life political action committee was formed to evaluate voting records of congresspersons by the criterion of a consistent ethic of life. In their first analysis of congressional voting records for the year 1985, JustLife² was able to identify only eighty members of congress—less than fifteen percent—as "consistently pro-life." Their analysis of the 1987–1989 Congress found no increase in the number of congresspersons voting consistently prolife.

Nor have the more dominant parts of the anti-abortion movement (the National Right to Life Committee, the Christian Action Committee, the March on Washington Committee, the American Life League, the Ad Hoc Committee for the Defense of Life, the Pro-Life Action League) welcomed

²JustLife rated Senators on twelve votes, four each from the three categories of economic justice, opposition to the arms race, and abortion. The economic justice votes dealt with increasing the minimum wage, stopping military aid to El Salvador, supporting higher welfare support, and parental medical leave and child care. Opposition to the arms race was measured by votes against funding for the "Strategic Defense Initiative" and for the Salt 11 Treaty Observance, nuclear testing limits, and the dismantling of select nuclear submarines. Congresspersons were evaluated by the same categories, but the votes were not always the same. For example, pro-life congresspersons were partially determined by votes against funding the "stealth" bomber.

Bernardin's forceful attempt to redirect opposition to abortion into wider channels of social criticism.

But it cannot be said that there were no potential constituencies for a "consistent ethic of life" linking positions ordinarily thought to divide political parties and voters into "conservative" and "liberal" wings. Empirical studies of American Catholic laity showed that while few Catholics support a legal prohibition on all abortions, there already exists a general readiness to view the issue of abortion in a social justice context. The Notre Dame study of parish affiliated Catholics (Gremillion and Castelli, 1987: 42–43) found that while only about fifteen percent say they oppose all legal abortions not necessary to save the mother's life, they overwhelmingly "reject abortion on demand or as a form of birth control." D'Antonio and others (1989:135) found that less than one-fifth of a randomly drawn sample of Catholics said that their faith was weakened by the teaching "that abortion is morally wrong" and almost half said that this teaching had actually strengthened their faith. No researcher has yet asked a national sample if they have heard of the "consistent ethic of life" and whether they agreed with it. After reviewing decades of polls, Gallup and Castelli (1987: ch. 7, "The Seamless Garment") inferentially conclude that Catholics do. Moreover, in their summary of decades of polling, Gallup and Castelli show that because Protestants from liberal denominations are more likely to favor nonrestrictive abortion laws, and Evangelical and Fundamentalist Protestants more likely to favor the most restrictive laws, on balance Catholic and Protestant attitudes toward legal abortion are (at least in the statistical aggregate) rather similar. As late as 1989, a *Los Angeles Times* poll (July 1, 1990:1) found that fifty-seven percent of the American public still described abortion as "murder."

Despite the media stereotype, there is surprisingly little evidence linking the deeply rooted moral repugnance to abortion with inegalitarian notions of class or gender, even among the rank and file of the movement. Jelen (1984:220–31) found that among Catholics opposition to euthanasia was a better predictor of abortion opposition than was sexual conservatism, and among mainline Protestants there were no systematic relationships (though there were some among Fundamentalists). Cleghorn (1986) found that educated Catholics largely affirmed a consistent ethic approach and, more generally, no evidence that abortion opponents fit "new right" stereotypes. Wilcox and Gomez (1990:380–89) show that few self-identified abortion opponents supported the "Moral Majority" and, indeed, "a sizeable bloc of pro-life support adopted fairly liberal positions on other issues . . . (especially) equality values, including gender equality." No group of right to life activists (as opposed to groups already formed who add abortion opposition to their agenda) has ever advocated social welfare cuts, increased military spending, or capital punishment. The first book written by grassroots leaders of the right to life movement was the 1972 edition of *Abortion and Social Justice,* co-edited by the founder of Americans United for Life and the founder of the Pro-Life Youth Committee. From its beginning, abortion opponents described themselves as populists battling economic elites. In the September 1974 issue of the NRLNews, editor Janet Grant described pro-choice supporters as mostly wealthy and mostly upper class: "The rich want to 'share' abortion with the poor. But 'sharing' stops when it comes to wealth, clubs, and neighborhoods." The initial post-Roe right to life analyses were not at all conservative. In the February 1973 NRLNews, Donna M. Sullivan asked, "Are social pressures now geared more to getting rid of poor babies than assisting their mothers with their economic problems?" She added, "When pro-life people object to the use of tax money for abortions, we are really saying that even if it costs us more to help those who cannot help themselves, we are willing to spend more, if necessary, so long as it is spent to foster and sustain life." The March 1974 NRLNews editorial noted the irony in the pro-abortion argument that it would lower welfare costs when Congress has spent "billions to wage a war in Indochina." Among the first congresspersons supporting an amendment to reverse Roe were two prominent critics of the Vietnam War, Senators Harold Hughes and Mark Hatfield. In the first years after Roe an alliance with the fiscally conservative Republican party seemed unlikely. Ellen McCormick initiated the first direct right to life political effort by quixotically seeking the Democratic nomination for president in 1975. The August 17, 1981, issue of the Christian Action Council's "ActionLine" cautioned that Republican elites feared that Reagan's support for a Human Life Amendment "would jeopardize their plans to scuttle New Deal welfare programs . . . (and) have viewed the influx of moderate-to-liberal anti-abortionists into the Republican Party with great apprehension."

Still, the consistent ethic of life has been adopted only by a small and media-ignored part of the movement. But it should be noted that the linkage of opposition to abortion with traditional "left" issues of peace and social justice preceded Cardinal Bernardin's 1983 address "A Consistent Ethic of Life." Interestingly enough, "consistent ethic" group began in the late 1970s as the right to life movement was, in large part, successfully courted by Ronald Reagan and the Republican Party. In 1979 Judy Loesch began "Prolifers for Survival" (PS) which attracted a few thousand activists who opposed both abortion and American nuclear strategy. Other religious groups on the Left, such as the Catholic pacifist group "Pax Christi" (at its October 1980 convention) and the evangelical Protestant "Sojourners" (November 1980) extended their commitment to pacifism to include opposition to abortion.

At its last March 13–15, 1987, convention (attended by representatives from "Feminists for Life," "Pax Christi," "the Catholic Worker," "the Leadership Conference of Women Religious," "the Conference of Major Superiors of Men," "the Association for Public Justice," "the Christian Life Commission of the Southern Baptist Convention," and "Evangelicals for Social Action") "Prolifers for Survival" disbanded and became part of a larger interreligious network called "A Seamless Garment Network" which promoted the consistent ethic of life. The Network's June 1990 publication *Consistent Ethic Resources* (San Francisco, Calif.: Harmony) listed fifty-five member organizations, eleven pages of available speakers, and the titles of five consistent ethic journals/newsletters (*Harmony, Sisterlife* [by Feminists for Life], *JustLife, Salt,* and *Sojourners*).

The religious left's attempt to frame support for laws protecting fetal life as a social justice issue has found little sympathy from American liberals and the diffuse secular left. But the Webster decision—which I argue will soon detach the movement from its conservative political base—might alter this somewhat. If the increasingly explicit differentiation among morality, law, and policy by the American bishops becomes better known, this might also invite a more searching look at the evolving "consistent ethic of life" and its significance in opposition to abortion.[3]

II. Webster Weakens Anti-Abortionists' Political Support

On July 3, 1989, the Supreme Court in "Webster vs. Reproductive Health Services" returned to the states at least some authority to pass laws restricting abortion. This decision meant that politicians could no longer expect to be shielded by the Supreme Court from the responsibilities of passing or opposing abortion legislation. The immediate effect of Webster was a loosening of support from anti-abortion officeholders and seekers.

[3]Anti-abortion pressures on the bishops against even the appearance of any compromise of principle are strong. A campaign by several independent anti-abortion groups headed by Roman Catholics (Judie Brown of The American Life League and Joseph Scheidler of the Pro-Life Action League) began soon after Webster to have the bishops excommunicate pro-choice Catholic officeholders such as Senator Ted Kennedy and Governors Mario Cuomo and Jim Florio. In 1982 the Christian Action Council, the Ad Hoc Committee in Defense of Life, the American Life League, and the March on Washington Committee publicly criticized the American bishops because they endorsed the "Hatch Amendment" which by itself would have prohibited no abortion but restored to the states (more completely than Webster later did) their pre-Roe authority to pass abortion laws. Since some states would retain permissive abortion laws, these critics said that a vote for Hatch (which was easily defeated in the Senate) meant a vote for permissive abortion laws that killed the unborn. The May 1983 Christian Action Council newsletter agreed with James McFadden that the Hatch amendment was a deal to help Catholic congressmen "get rid of the issue of abortion."

As we have seen from *JustLife's* analysis of voting records, the congressional political support for the right to life movement was not located in any sizeable "consistent ethic" voting bloc but rather in the far larger number of fiscal conservatives who opposed federal funding of abortions and who often declared themselves supporters of more restrictive abortion laws. The alliance between major segments of the right to life movement and the Republican Party began to unravel after Webster. Soon after the 1989 elections, Lee Atwater, then the chairman of the National Republican Committee, announced that the "Republican umbrella" now extended to all Republicans regardless of whether they supported the Party platform's support for a Human Life Amendment and restrictions on government funding for abortion. Six months after Webster, three distinct Republican Political Action Committees formed specifically to raise funds for pro-choice candidates. At the same time, the Catholic hierarchy tried to find ways of honoring the traditional teaching that directly intended abortion was immoral with the realities of politics in pluralist secular societies.

Between October 1989 and June 1990 at least twenty bishops from at least seven states wrote twelve separate pastoral letters on abortion (some were signed by several bishops). Both the outgoing and a past president of the National Conference of Catholic Bishops issued separate statements on abortion. And the NCCB on November 7, 1989, passed still another resolution on abortion. The substantial agreement found in the post-Webster documents permit us to sketch, though roughly, the general approach to legal abortion taken by the American hierarchy after the Webster decision. It might read as follows:

Abortion is a human rights issue. But besides the "right to life" abortion involves social justice, and thus opposition to legal abortion must be consistent. Consistency includes not only other "life" issues such as euthanasia, infanticide, and capital punishment, but also social justice issues of medical care, employment, and poverty. No return to the pre-Roe era when only medically necessary abortions were legal can be expected. Good laws require social consensus. A consensus prohibiting all non-medically necessary abortions is highly unlikely. The hope for both a consensus supporting more protective abortion laws and for actually lowering abortion rates rests largely on the application of a consistent ethic of life to abortion. There should not be a single-issue approach to abortion and there is no single acceptable approach to framing abortion laws and policies in modern secular states. The bishops' legal focus is laws that stop as much abortion as possible.[4] Catholics themselves will legitimately disagree about which laws

[4]Dr. Jack C. Willke, long-time president of the NRLC, has described ("Unity or Divisiveness?", NRLNews, August 16, 1990:3) a Winter 1989 meeting called by Cardinal O'Connor to deal with the internecine conflict between "No-compromise" groups (represented by Judie

might best accomplish this. The only proscribed political course for Catholic officeholders and seekers is a self-description as personally opposed to abortion but publicly pro-choice. This sharp dichotomy between morality and politics corrupts political as well as personal integrity.

This description of Catholic abortion policy is entirely derived from the documents of the National Conference of Catholic Bishops and the available post-Webster statements of more than a dozen bishops. But it is unlikely than most Americans would recognize it as the emergent consensus of the authoritative teachers of the American Catholic Church. It sounds too modest, too accommodating, too open, too close to the position of the majority of American voters. The minimum requirement of this teaching is that laws acknowledge that abortion stops a developing human life and that laws reflect this core community value to the degree supported by an educated public consensus. But very little of the moral nuances abundantly clear in all these documents has found its way into the American media or into the debate over abortion. Right to Life activists have long complained that the media is biased against them. This is increasingly acknowledged as a legitimate complaint. In his July 1–4, 1990, *Los Angeles Times* series on media coverage of abortion, David Shaw found that major print and television media almost always reported abortion in the terms favored by pro-choice advocates. He cited a 1985 *Los Angeles Times* nationwide poll of reporters which found that more than eighty percent favored legal abortion. Ethan Bronner of the Boston Globe told Shaw that "opposing abortion, in the eyes of most journalists, is not a legitimate, civilized position in our society."

But the media pro-choice bias should be viewed in the larger context of support for elective abortion among the affluent and the professional. Surveys (Blake, 1971, 1973, 1977, 1980; Ademik, 1982) have consistently found that abortion support is strongest among the wealthiest and most educated (especially among men and the religiously unaffiliated) and weakest among less affluent and less educated Americans (especially among religiously affiliated women). If there were two inclines measuring support for abortion and elite status, the two curves would largely overlap. A comparison of those organizations who signed briefs opposing and favoring the Web-

Brown, Nellie Gray, and Joseph Scheidler) and the National Right to Life Committee (represented by Willke) and the Bishops' Committee for Prolife Activities (represented by Richard Doerflinger). The meeting failed. Willke reported that Brown insisted "the most important thing is not whether we win (some legal restrictions) but whether we are right." Soon after Brown publicly opposed a NRLC endorsed Idaho law that would have restricted abortion for "birth control" but permitted it in "hard" cases, such as rape, incest, and fetal deformity. The bill passed the Idaho legislature but was vetoed by Governor Andrus. Brown opposed the bill in paid ads and testimony before the legislature because "the bill did not go far enough. It should have tried to stop all abortions."

ster brief is fully illustrative of this great status gap between pro-choice and pro-life supporters. Professional organizations signing anti-Webster briefs included: The American Medical Association, the National Association of Public Hospitals, the American Psychological Association, 281 American Historians, the American Library Association, 167 Distinguished Scientists and Physicians, the American Nurses Association, 885 American Law Professionals, the American Association of Social Workers, the American Academy of Child and Adolescent Psychiatry, the American Academy of Pediatricians, the American College of Obstetricians and Gynecologists, the American Psychiatric Association, the American Fertility Society, the American Society of Human Genetics, the American Civil Liberties Union, the National Education Association, the Newspaper Guild, the National Writers Union, the League of Women Voters, the American Federation of State, County and Municipal Employees, the American Association of University Women, Center for Women's Policy Studies, National Women's Studies Association, and the National Urban League.

Besides the great number of elite professional organizations signing anti-Webster briefs, and thus opposing any restrictions on elective abortion, were those organizations more directly concerned with abortion: The National Abortion Rights Action League, Planned Parenthood, NOW, and about thirty population control organizations, such as the Pathfinder Fund, the Population Council, World Population Society, and Zero Population Fund. The over 1.5 million annual abortions yield yearly fees of over 600 million dollars a year and population organizations can count on substantial foundation support (Hartman, 1987: ch. 6).

Those groups signing briefs in support of Webster are far less prestigious, far less professional, far less affluent, and far less mainstream. The anti-abortion briefs included no women's studies academic associations and no coalitions of scientists, deans, or academicians. Moreover, the professional sounding groups that signed pro-Webster briefs were mostly formed in opposition to the acceptance of Roe by their larger parent professional groups. These dissenting splinter groups include the American Academy of Medical Ethics, the American Association of Prolife Obstetricians and Gynecologists, and the American Association of Pro-Life Pediatricians. The women's groups that signed pro-Webster briefs also owe their existence to the legalization of abortion: Birthright, Feminists for Life, Women Exploited by Abortion, and the National Association of Pro-Life Nurses. Pro-Webster briefs were signed by a variety of religious organizations, including: Agudath Israel, the National Organization of Episcopalians for Life, Presbyterians Pro-Life, American Baptists Friends of Life, Southern Baptists for Life, Moravians for Life, United Church of Christ Friends for Life, the Task Force of United Methodists on Abortion and Sexuality, and the Christian Action Council. But among the numerous groups submitting pro-Webster briefs, the Catholic Church was almost singular in that its opposition to abortion was not a defining reason for its existence.

Any systematic comparison of the sources of pro-choice and pro-life support, whether in terms of surveys of individuals or analysis of organizational support, shows at least the partial pertinence of a class analysis. Elites and their organizations are far more likely than non-elites to support elective abortion. On almost any other issue, this cleavage would spark critical thoughts. So too would the distrust of legislative debate and voting on the local level found in the anti-Webster briefs.

In the face of such overwhelming elite and professional support for unrestricted abortion, there should be no surprise that the National Right to Life News (August 16, 1990:1) described as right to life victories the August 1, 1990, decision by the Executive Council of the AFL-CIO and the August 8, 1990, decision by the House of Delegates of the American Bar Association to remain neutral on abortion. But not for long. At their next vote the ABA dropped its neutrality and it too became an advocacy group for abortion rights.

The evolving role of the Catholic Church in the abortion controversy is best seen in terms of massive elite and professional support for unrestricted abortion and the increasingly public cleavages in the movement opposing abortion. The movement (with some overlap, of course) is comprised of an anti-abortion wing, a pro-life component, and the larger National Right to Life Committee and its hundreds of state affiliates. The anti-abortion group has had strong ties with the fiscal conservatives who dominate Republican politics and who have included opposition to Medicaid funded abortions within its individualist ideology of limited government. Since the Reagan era, the National Right to Life Committee has made tactical alliances with the Republican Party but has continued to adhere to a "single-issue" appraisal of officeseekers and supported many Democrats on the local level. The pro-life wing has pushed beyond the critique of abortion in terms of a "human rights" issue characteristic of liberal philosophy to the more comprehensive analyses characteristic of religious socialism more generally.

After the July 3, 1989, Webster decision the fragmentation of the alliances between fiscal conservatives and the anti-abortion and the National Right to Life wings became more apparent. Arguments based on equality have never been appealing to political conservatives, and the central philosophical argument of the right to life movement is that each human life has substantial claims on the community.[5] Even more important, op-

---

[5]Largely unnoticed by its critics, a large amount of right to life writing, when it presses

posing abortion is too costly for fiscal conservatives. By the end of 1989 New York State Health officials were predicting that the cost of the medical intensive care for babies born to crack-addicted mothers in the state (ten percent of all non-white births by 1987) would exceed one billion dollars by 1995. Since these babies often suffer lifelong handicaps, the welfare costs would exceed the initial medical costs. Henshaw and Silverman (1988: 158–60) report that while fourteen percent of all American women fall beneath the poverty line, one-third of abortion patients do. Torres and Forrest (1988:169–79) found that among the more than a dozen reasons women give for aborting, the second was "she couldn't afford the child." Before Webster, when they thought the Court would continue to keep the elective abortion permitted by Roe intact, fiscal conservatives could ally with anti-abortion activists without fearing their success and the huge economic costs that more protective abortion laws would bring. The vast majority of abortion opponents are moral conservatives, not necessarily fiscal conservatives. In the case of abortion especially, moral conservatism and ideological fiscal conservatism are in the long run incompatible. With Webster, the anti-abortion wing of the right to life movement began its slow decline. The National Right to Life movement, tied to a liberal conception of rights extended to fetal life, the handicapped, and the non-productive sick and elderly, will continue but cannot succeed on its own terms. The pro-life movement, firmly supported by the institutional resources of the Catholic Church and inter-religiously secure in many autonomous groups, will slowly grow as a cultural presence, especially where religious sentiment remains. In short, the alliance between abortion opponents and ideological fiscal conservatives during the Reagan era will increasingly appear as entirely tactical.

The steady pro-life criticism of elective abortion will probably continue to find an undenying but unwilling ear among the American public. Every new medical advance in fetology and every new advance in microscopic photography reaffirm the pro-life claim that even very early fetal life is patently one of our human family (Lennert Nilson, "The First Days of Creation," *Life,* August, 1990:26–49). Powerful elite groups will continue to define abortion as contraception and define overpopulation as a chief cause of pov-

towards its political underpinnings, is decidedly egalitarian, pushing beyond a legal equality towards substantive equality. See for example the February 14 and May 2, 1985, NRLNews editorials by Dave Andrusko: "To appreciate the inner dynamics of the issue, we must appreciate that abortion should be seen as the port of entry into the popular and legal imagination of the idea of 'conditional personhood' where the term personhood is a widely used shorthand to denote that segment of the human community which is to receive legal protection." His May 2 editorial even cited the quintessential philosopher of political elites, Hobbes. Andrusko concluded: "What could be more obvious than that abortion and infanticide have established deep roots in the same anti-life 'You're protected-if-you're-strong-enough soil'?"

erty and international instability. Dominant feminist groups, still mostly attentive to issues of women's equality defined in the context of elite males, have continued to define abortion as a necessary aspect of personal autonomy. Juli Loesch, who started PS, found that among the secular left "abortion rights had become so nearly an absolute that discussion itself was taken for treason" (1990, ch. 3). But as the loss of the support of ideological fiscal conservatives makes more unlikely any major removal of legal protection for abortion, liberals and the secular left will be less likely to overlook the association between elites and support for abortion and begin to question whether all abortions, especially those by the poor, are freely chosen. There has always been some skepticism on the feminist left that the promotion of "abortion rights" abstracted from critiques of poverty would in practice lead to coercive pressures to abort. Hartman (1987:120) has noted the class basis for construing population problems as "management problems" and the willingness to use force or coercive incentives to control births that destabilize existing wealth and power distributions. She notes (1987:97) the historical tendency expressed by dominant figures in the eugenics movement to view poverty in Social Darwinian terms and to have no principled objection to compulsory sterilization. Shaw (1977:7) explicitly includes family income as a factor in computing whether doctors should perform surgery on handicapped children that would be performed on "normal" children, and certainly liberals and the Left will come to pay more attention to the use of criteria derived more from social class than from medicine to determine treatment availability (Kelly, 1989:101). When advocacy groups for the handicapped (The Association for Retarded Citizens, The Down's Syndrome Congress, The Spina Bifidia Association, and The American Coalition of Citizens with Disability) learned that doctors were using Shaw's criteria they formed a coalition with abortion opponents such as the National Right to Life Committee to lobby successfully for the passage of the Child Abuse Amendments of 1984 which requires that handicapped neonates receive the same standard of care as other infants (U.S. Commission of Civil Rights, 1989:7). The 1990 Annual Conference of Black Lawyers listed as a program highlight a panel called "Beyond Reproductive Freedom."

Left/liberal fears that "abortion rights" can lead to coercion and mask social inequalities have not been entirely absent. The editor noted that the reader response to the article by Mary Meehan entitled "Abortion: The Left Has Betrayed the Sanctity of Life" in the December 4, 1980, edition of *The Progressive* was "unusually heavy in volume." Such misgivings can more commonly be found in *Religious Socialism,* the quarterly newsletter of The Religion and Socialism Committee of the Democratic Socialist Organizing Committee.

In time, opposition to elective abortion will more clearly join those continuous, and not always subterranean, religious and humanist counterforces that confront the competitive individualism that both fuels and results from acquisitive capitalism and the dominance of instrumental reason. As both American political parties practice a politics of scarcity and narrowly define equality in the meritocratic terms of equal opportunity, more on the Left will confront the coercive nature of many abortions by poor and not-so-affluent women.

Opponents of legal abortion, however, are likely to succeed only where restrictions on abortion can be justified in terms other than protecting fetal life. Americans are used to viewing life as a conflict of interests and where women's rights are pitted against developing human life, past experience suggests public opinion will favor the woman's claims against claims made on behalf on the fetus. But abortion restrictions that can be framed as providing more real "choice" to women, such as information about abortion alternatives, available community help, and the health aspects of abortion, will have strong chances for public support. So too will restrictions that require more adult participation in the abortion decisions of adolescents. Restrictions on late-term abortions already have strong public support.

The powerful role that the "consistent ethic of life" now plays in the Catholic Church's protection of traditional morality of abortion will continue to evolve and affect other aspects of the Church's inner and public life. Increasingly the Church's social thought will criticize the largely privatizing and inegalitarian aspects of America's "democratic-capitalism," using the democratic component to critique the capitalist component. Deeper introspection (Weakland, 1990) into the equality of women will also affect Church life and practice, straining any authority that seems to incorporate views of gender that subordinate women.

The argument here is that the fear that the movement sparked by legal abortion might achieve the political strength to again make all non-medically necessary abortions illegal has obscured its cultural significance. In time, the erosion of the alliances between ideological fiscal conservatives and major components of the movement will considerably lessen these fears. Then the "consistent ethic" component of the movement opposing abortion will grow in importance, publicly guarding the foundational principle of all socialisms and humanisms that each human life, with no regard to its talent or potential achievements, has intrinsic worth and claims on the community. This moral insight, dramatically and energetically present in the right to life movement, resists all conceptions of a social order based on meritocracy or economic efficiency. The protection of fetal life against the claims of autonomy and the efficient ordering of economic life is so profoundly pre-modern that only the naive would predict any significant victory. Among other things, the collapse of state dominated planned economies in Russia and elsewhere and the ascendancy of economic liberalism have furthered weakened socialism's egalitarian aspirations. Once again, liberty and equality seem contrary moral values. Principled defense of an equality deeper than the formal equality of an equal opportunity for the meritorious to achieve (and others to lose) now resides with any public vitality mostly in segments of the movement sparked by legal abortion, and there in largely underdeveloped ways. The mainstream movement so far has represented mostly a "liberalism" applied to fetuses, defining its goal as protecting the most fundamental right of all—the right to life. The consistent ethic of life significantly broadens this moral conviction and carries its political dimension to more organicist conceptions of political responsibility animated by radical views of equality that collide with the premises of both political and economic liberalism. Webster has weakened the political power of the movement, but by disengaging it from its alliance with fiscal conservatives, it will strengthen its cultural presence. It will be many, many decades before the full meaning of abortion opposition is morally clear.

REFERENCES

Abbott, Walter M. *The Documents of Vatican II*. New York: Guild Press, 1966.

Adamek, Raymond J. "Abortion and Public Opinion in the United States." National Right to Life Educational Trust Fund. Washington, D.C., 1982.

Benestad, J. Brian, and Francis J. Butler, eds. *Quest For Justice: A Compendium of Statements of the USCC on the Political and Social Order, 1966–1980*. Washington, D.C.: United States Catholic Conference, 1981.

Bernardin, Cardinal Joseph. "A Consistent Ethic of Life: An American Catholic Dialogue." *Thought* 59:4 (March 1984).

———. "The Consistent Ethic of Life after Webster." *Origins* 19 (April 12, 1990) 741–48.

Bishops of Ohio. Statement on Abortion and Public Office. *Origins* (December 28, 1989).

Bishops of Pennsylvania, Latin and Eastern Rites. "The Church, Public Policy and Abortion." *Origins* (April 6, 1990).

Blake, Judith. "Abortion and Public Opinion: The 1960–1970 Decade." *Science* 171 (February 1970) 540–49.

———. "Elective Abortion and Our Reluctant Citizenry: Research on Public Opinion in the United States." Howard J. Osofsky and Joy D. Osofsky, eds., *The Abortion Experience: Psychological and Medical Impact*. Hagerstown, Md.: Harper and Row, 1973, 447–67.

———. "The Supreme Court's Abortion Decisions and Public Opinion in the United States." *Population and Development Review* 3 (March/June 1977) 45–62.

Blake, Judith, and Jorge H. Del Pinal. "Predicting Polar Attitudes toward Abortion in the United States." James Tunstead Burtchaell, ed., *Abortion Parley*. New York: Andrews and McMeel, 1979.

Cleghorn, J. Stephen. "Respect for Life: Research Notes on Cardinal Bernardin's Seamless Garment." *Review of Religious Research* 28:2 (December 1986) 124–42.

Cuneo, Michael W. *Catholics against the Church: Anti-Abortion Protest in Toronto, 1969–1985*. Toronto: University of Toronto Press, 1989.

D'Antonio, William, James Davidson, Dean Hoge, and Ruth Wallace. *American Catholic Laity*. Kansas City, Mo.: Sheed and Ward, 1989.

Dulles, Avery, S.J. "What Is the Role of a Bishops' Conference?" *Origins* 17:46 (April 28, 1988) 789–96.

Feuchtman, Thomas G. *Consistent Ethic of Life*. Kansas City, Mo.: Sheed and Ward, 1988.

Francome, Colin. *Abortion Freedom: A Worldwide Movement*. London: George Allen and Unwin, 1984.

French, Howard W. "Rise in Babies Hurt by Drugs Is Predicted." *New York Times* (October 1989).

Gallup, George, and Jim Castelli. *The American Catholic People*. Garden City, N.Y.: Doubleday, 1987.

Glendon, Mary Ann. *Divorce and Abortion in Western Law*. Cambridge: Harvard University Press, 1988.

Granberg, Donald, and Donald Denny. "The Coathanger and the Rose: Comparison of Pro-Choice and Pro-Life Activists in the U.S." *Transaction/Society* (May 1982).

Gremillion, Joseph, and Jim Castelli. *The Emerging Parish: The Notre Dame Study of Catholic Life*. San Francisco: Harper and Row, 1987.

Hartmann, Betsy. *Reproductive Rights and Wrongs*. New York: Harper and Row, 1987.

Henshaw, Stanley K., and Jane Silverman. "The Characteristics and Prior Contraceptive Use of the U.S. Abortion Patients." *Family Planning Perspectives* 20:4 (July/August 1988) 158–68.

Horan, Dennis J., and Thomas W. Hilgers. *Abortion and Social Justice*. New York: Sheed and Ward, 1972.

Hubbard, Bishop Howard. "Bishops and Catholic Officeholders after Webster." *The Evangelist*. Diocese of Albany (November 30, 1989).

Jelen, Ted G. "Respect for Life, Sexual Morality, and Opposition to Abortion." *Review of Religious Research* 25:3 (1984) 220–31.

Kelly, James R. "Beyond the Stereotypes: Interviews with Right to Life Pioneers." *Commonweal* (November 1981) 654–59.

———. "Aids and the Death Penalty as Consistency Tests for the Pro-life Movement." *America* (September 1987) 151–55.

———. "Toward Complexity: The Right-to-Life Movement." *Research in the Social Scientific Study of Religion* 1, Calif.: Jai Press, 1989, 83–107.

———. "Abortion: What Americans Really Think and the Catholic Challenge." *America* (November 1991).

Lader, Lawrence. *Abortion 11: Making the Revolution*. Boston: Beacon, 1973.

Leahy, Peter J. "The Anti-Abortion Movement." Unpub. Ph.D thesis, Syracuse University, 1982.

Luker, Kristin. *Abortion and the Politics of Motherhood*. Berkeley: University of California Press, 1984.

Malone, Bishop James. *Catholic Trends* (October 28, 1989).

May, Archbishop John. "Faith and Moral Teaching in a Democratic Nation." *Origins* (November 16, 1989).

McHugh, Bishop James. "Abortion and the Officeholder." *Origins* (May 31, 1990) 40–42.

Morrison, Robert G. "Choice in Washington: The Politics of Liberalized Abortion." University of Virginia, MA thesis, 1982.

Myers, Bishop John. "The Obligations of Catholics and the Rights of Unborn Children." *Origins* (June 14, 1990) 65–72.

Nathanson, Bernard N. *The Abortion Papers*. New York: Frederick Fell, 1983.

National Conference of Catholic Bishops. *Pastoral Plan for Pro-Life Activities*. Washington, D.C.: United States Catholic Conference, 1975.

_____. *Pastoral Plan for Pro-Life Activities: A Reaffirmation*. Washington, D.C.: United States Catholic Conference, 1985.

_____. "Resolution on Abortion." *Origins* (November 16, 1989).

Nilson, Lennert. "The First Days of Creation," *Life* (August 1990) 26–49.

Noonan, John T., Jr., *A Private Choice*. New York: The Free Press, 1979.

O'Connor, Cardinal Joseph J. "Abortion: Questions and Answers." *Catholic New York* (June 14, 1990).

Ostheimer, J. M., and C. L. Moore, Jr. "Correlates of Attitudes toward Euthanasia Revisited." *Social Biology* 28 (1981) 145–49.

Shaw, A. "Defining the Quality of Life." Hastings Report 7 (1977).

Shaw, David. Three-part series on abortion reportage. *Los Angeles Times* (July 1–4, 1990).

Singh, B. K. "Correlates of Attitudes toward Euthanasia." *Social Biology* 26 (1979) 247–53.

Torres, Ada, and Jacqueline Darroch Forrest. "Why Do Women Have Abortions?" *Family Planning Perspectives* 20:4 (July/August 1988) 158–68.

United States Catholic Conference. *Documentation on Abortion and the Right to Life* 11. Washington, D.C.: United States Catholic Conference, 1976.

Weakland, Archbishop Rembert. "Listening Sessions with Women on Abortion." *Origins* (May 31, 1990) 33–39.

Wilcox, Clyde, and Lepoldo Gomez. "The Christian Right and the Pro-Life Movement." *Review of Religious Research* 31:4 (June 1990) 380–89.

Wiley, Juli Loesch. "Solidarity and Shalom." *Confessing Conscience: Churched Women on Abortion*. Phyllis Tickle, ed. Nashville: Abingdon, 1990.

Chapter 8

The Copernican Revolution in Sacramental Theology

Joseph Martos

In the second century of the Christian era, the Egyptian mathematician and astronomer, Ptolemy, devised a geometric system to account for the movement of the seven known heavenly bodies which traversed the firmament of the fixed stars, and for over a thousand years his system stood unchallenged. Not until the sixteenth century did any astronomer suggest that a better way to "save the appearances" or account for the motions would be to devise a completely different system, one which put the sun at its center and made the Earth one of the planets rather than the focal point of all heavenly radii. The scientist who first proposed this new system was Nicholas Copernicus and, since then, the term "Copernican revolution" has come to stand for a change in thinking in which the fundamental assumptions of specialists and ordinary folk alike are turned on end, and in which the old way of looking at reality is turned upside down.

In the twentieth century, philosophers occasionally reflected upon the phenomenon of periodic revolutions in thinking. However, it was only when Thomas Kuhn published *The Structure of Scientific Revolutions* (University of Chicago Press, 1970) that English speaking intellectuals widely acknowledged the pervasiveness of what Kuhn referred to as "paradigm shifts" not only in the natural sciences but in other theoretical pursuits as well.

Such paradigm shifts occur in three phases. In the first phase, what Kuhn calls "normal science" is done by those who accept the prevailing paradigm and understand the data of their discipline within the mental framework that the paradigm prescribes for them. The second phase is introduced with the discovery of anomalies, or new data which do not fit the old paradigm. In the absence of a better explanation, however, anomalies continue to be treated within the boundaries of normal science. Finally, the third phase is the introduction of a new paradigm or a new theoretical framework for interpreting the data, which includes not only the traditional data which were satisfactorily accounted for under the old paradigm but also the anomalous data.

Although this displacement is easy to understand after the fact, it initially encounters intellectual and social resistance. Anticipating such resistance, Copernicus postponed publishing his theory until he was lying on his deathbed. Galileo more naively assumed that men of science would be pursuaded by the facts, but when he used his telescope to show that Jupiter had moons (an anomaly that ran counter to the Ptolemaic assumption that there had to be only seven moving bodies in the heavens), he was rebuffed with the comment that his instrument was obviously bewitched. Undaunted, Galileo published his version of the heliocentric theory, only to be tried and convicted of heresy.

I. Theology in the Mid-Twentieth Century

The analogy between astronomy in the sixteenth century and theology in the twentieth century can be drawn by anyone who is conversant with the history of theology prior to and following the Second Vatican Council.

As early as the turn of the century, Catholic intellectuals who were familiar with developments in the natural and human sciences saw that some of these advances were incongruous with the Aristotelian paradigm within which Catholic thinking had been proceeding since the Middle Ages. From the viewpoint of Scholasticism, incompatable data provided by geology and biology, history and literary criticism were anomalies. The philosophers and theologians who attempted to suggest a new paradigm for Catholic thought, however, were branded as modernists and condemned by the hierarchy.

Gradually, however, even data which supposedly should fit within the scholastic paradigm were providing anomalies that suggested a need for some revision. Historical data on the liturgy, for example, demonstrated that not only had liturgical forms evolved over the centuries before the Council of Trent but also that sacramental theology had tolerated diversity of thought during the patristic era. In addition, biblical data gathered with the Vatican's approval since *Divino Afflante Spiritu* in 1943 suggested that the simple distinction between the literal and figurative meanings of a text was no longer adequate to accommodate the range of potential interpretations made possible by modern biblical scholarship. Like the Ptolemaic system before it, the scholastic system was straining at the seams.

Very prudently, the bishops at the Second Vatican Council did not attempt to develop a new theoretical paradigm for Catholic thinking. Instead, using a combination of biblical and secular terminology, they described the data for which any new system would have to account and pastorally prescribed the direction toward which the Church should move. The very fact that the council did not overtly endorse the scholastic system, however, gave Catholic thinkers permission to search for other paradigms in their analysis of theoretical and practical problems.

At the beginning of the third phase of the most recent paradigm shift in Catholic thinking (which is to say, from the middle to late 1960s), the emerging new paradigm seemed to be the critical Thomism of Rahner, Lonergan, Schillebeeckx, and other rather weighty intellectuals. By the end of the 1970s, however, it was becoming clearer that this neo-Scholasticism was in competition with other new thought systems which were then beginning to emerge. Biblical and liturgical studies were developing languages of their own, ecumenical dialogue and the charismatic movement prompted borrowings from Protestant thought, philosophical interfaces gave rise to existential and process theology, pastoral concerns led to thinking within psychological and sociological frameworks, and sensitivity toward the poor and the marginalized led to the development of a new method of theologizing which expressed itself as liberation theology.

At first, this proliferation of explanatory paradigms seemed to belie the interpretation that what was occurring was a shift from the "normal science" of scholastic theology to another system which would eventually replace it. In the 1980s, however, it became clearer that the new system was indeed emerging, but that it was very different than anticipated. Instead of being a new, comprehensive synthesis, it was a paradigm of simultaneous pluralism, or a plurality of co-existing systems.

For those familiar with contemporary developments in the human or social sciences, this ought not to be surprising. There was a time in the emerging human sciences of the mid-twentieth century that the goal of research was assumed to be a single overarching theory which would prove to be the truest among competing hypotheses. In psychology, for example, Freudians competed with neo-Freudians, existentialists, behaviorists, and other schools for the honor of revealing the ultimate truth about the human psyche. But now in the latter decades of this century, except for a few die-hards and ideologues, few psychologists accept this description of their field. The new goal seems to be the simltaneous development of multiple models of psychic activity in order to understand a human reality which is too complex to be completely comprehended within a single model.

Arguably, a parallel development has been occurring in theology. Whereas, prior to the recent ecumenical council, theologians and their schools sought to prove themselves correct to the exclusion of their rivals (especially their rivals in other Churches), the majority of theologians today seek to contribute to an ongoing collaborative attempt to understand faith and religion from viewpoints that are not necessarily mutually exclusive even if they cannot be simultaneously employed. Again, the assumption seems to be that the divine and human realities probed by theology are too complex and variegated to be simply subsumed within a single set of categories, and that therefore multiple theological models are required.

Needless to say, not all contemporary thinkers appreciate the necessary pluralism of contemporary theology. Some still yearn for the "good old days" when truth was one and error multiple. And since some of these hold positions of ecclesiastical power, they claim the authority to pontificate about debatable issues, and they use their authority to stifle those who point out anomalies in the once-reigning paradigm or who choose to work completely within alternative models. One might as well try to stop the motion of the earth by condemning it as heretical—though, of course, this too was once tried.

II. The Situation in Sacramental Theology

Applying Kuhn's developmental schema now to recent developments in sacramental theology, we can again discern the three phases of normal science, the uncovering of anomalies, and the emergence of an altogether new paradigm.

The normal science of the sacraments from the Middle Ages to the mid-twentieth century was, of course, scholastic theology. Interestingly, although this branch of theology was developed in the *Sententiae* and *Summae* as part of dogmatics or systematics, it was eventually treated in nineteenth- and early twentieth-century manuals as part of canon law since the main problems with the sacraments had to do not with understanding them correctly but with administering and receiving them correctly. This coincides completely with the prevalent concern of any normal science, which is solving problems that arise within an already accepted paradigm.

The anomalies which eventually challenged the scholastic paradigm were at first not perceived as anomalies since they appeared in historical investigations and the scholastic system was conceptually ahistorical. As time went on, though, the system had to be adjusted to account for the new data. Liturgical studies uncovered developments in the early and medieval history of the sacraments and their theology, and these developments were accounted for as steps leading up to the fullness of the Tridentine sacramental system and the perfection of scholastic theology.

In a similar manner, biblical studies increasingly suggested that many of the proof texts used by the scholastics to buttress Catholic interpretations of the sacraments had been taken out of context, but these anomalies were dismissed by employing a distinction between scriptural and dogmatic theology.

Insurmountable anomalies did not emerge until the Second Vatican Council called for a revision of the sacramental rites and a restoration of a style and understanding of liturgical celebration more reminiscent of the patristic age than the Middle Ages. At the same time, the council pointed out the desirability of people worshipping in their own language and in forms appropriate to their own culture. If that were not enough, at the very same time, widespread social changes were accompanied by revolutions in people's ways of thinking and behaving. Within a few years, altars were turned around, everyone was going to Communion, no one was going to confession, marriage was becoming statistically less permanent, anointing was not just for the dying, ministry was not just for priests, baptism was supposed to be for adults, and no one knew for certain what to do with confirmation.

Clearly, the scholastic paradigm was no longer adequate to explain the sacraments as practiced, and the time had passed when the system could be patched up with the theological equivalent of a few more epicycles. A new paradigm had to be found.

Concomitant with the experimentation that was characterizing the introduction of the revised liturgical rites, a noticeable amount of exploration characterized the theological attempt to explain the revised liturgy and sacraments. As indicated earlier, the initial leaders in the new theology were primarily variants of neo-Thomism, since the writings of Rahner and Schillebeeckx had been instrumental even before the council in convincing the bishops that change did not necessarily entail a betrayal of tradition. Within a short time, however, additional contenders made their own attempts to explain the Catholic sacramental rites within other philosophical and theological frameworks, the more noteworthy of which were existentialism and phenomenology, process thought, charismatic theology, and liberation theology.

These initial attempts to discover an alternative to the scholastic paradigm were traditionally oriented in the sense that they each proposed a system of thought which purported to be able to eventually provide a complete explanation of all the data on the sacraments. Even if individual authors are somewhat more modest in their claims, the implication of a systematic approach is that eventually, if the system is adequate to the task at hand, it can and should replace less adequate competitors. Attempts such as these were typical of most of the sacramental theology done through the 1970s.[1]

A quite different and nontraditional approach also made its first appear-

---

[1]For a summary treatment of these sacramental theologies, see my books *The Catholic Sacraments* (Wilmington, Del.: Michael Glazier, Inc., 1984) ch. 4, and *Doors to the Sacred* (second ed., Tarrytown, N.Y.: Triumph Books, 1991) ch. 5, in which I sketch theologies developed within phenomenological, existential, sociological, process, liberation, and charismatic frameworks.

ance in the 1970s, when some Catholic thinkers began to employ categories from the social or human sciences to understand and analyze Christian sacramental rituals. Anthropologists had long analyzed non-Christian rituals in terms of their symbolism and meaning, their internal structure and their social function, but now their tools of conceptual analysis began to be turned on Christian rituals as well. In addition, works on the psychology and sociology of religion began to be mined by Catholic theologians for further insights into the effects of ritual on the individuals and groups who participate in them.[2]

The fuller fruits of this interface between theology and the human sciences did not begin to appear, however, until the 1980s. In *From Magic to Metaphor* (Paulist Press, 1980), George Worgul collected much that had been done in the sciences during the two preceding decades and applied it to the sacraments. In *Sacraments and Sacramentality* (Twenty-Third, 1983), Bernard Cooke produced a theological synthesis in large measure grounded in reflection on the human experience of friendship and the transforming power of ritualized symbols. Most of the volumes in the Michael Glazier series "Message of the Sacraments" included insights drawn from psychology and sociology as well as history to better understand the individual sacraments in their contemporary setting. The Liturgical Press series entitled *Alternative Futures for Worship* (7 vols., 1987) went even further in envisioning possible developments in sacramental practice based on knowledge gleaned from the human sciences. And the collection by Mary Collins which appeared as *Worship: Renewal to Practice* (Pastoral, 1987) contained a number of articles analyzing the concrete performance of rituals in order to discover what they actually mean for those who participate in them.[3]

The above works and others which were published in the 1980s represent the emergence of a new genre in the literature of sacramental theology. In terms of Thomas Kuhn's *Structure of Scientific Revolutions,* they point towards a new paradigm for understanding liturgy and the sacraments; that is, they indicate the development of a new frame of reference for interpreting Catholic worship as it is experienced and practiced in the Church today.

---

[2]For a discussion of these developments, see *The Catholic Sacraments,* chs. 1 and 2, and my article, "Sacraments and the Human Sciences," in Peter Fink, ed., *The New Dictionary of Sacramental Worship* (Collegeville, Minn.: The Liturgical Press, A Michael Glazier Book, 1990) in which I summarize contributions from psychology, sociology, history, philosophy, anthropology, and linguistics which have been incorporated by theologians into their reflections on the sacraments.

[3]These and other works are described more fully in "Sacraments in the 1980s: A Review of Books in Print," *Horizons* 18 (Spring 1991).

III. The New Paradigm in Sacramental Theology

Just as Ptolemy's and Copernicus' systems can be most easily contrasted in terms of obvious differences such as geocentrism versus heliocentrism, the new paradigm in sacramental theology can best be summarized in terms of contrasts between itself and its "normal science" predecessor, scholastic theology.

Although much more could be said, the major contrasts between the two paradigms can be summarized under three headings: differences in approach, differences in presentation, and differences in application.

First, the differences in approach to the subject matter, which is the liturgy and the sacraments.

If scholastic theology can be characterized as systematic in its approach to topics, the new paradigm could be characterized as non-systematic. This should not be taken to imply that the new approach is unmethodical, but only that its method does not proceed within the parameters of a single conceptual system. Scholasticism consciously confined itself to concepts contained within or congruent with Aristotelian metaphysics, including concepts that could be generated from a reading of the Scriptures and the doctrines of the Church, both those found in ecclesiastical statements and those found in the writings of non-magisterial authorities such as orthodox theologians. The new paradigm, on the other hand, accepts categories that can be found within or generated from any of the human sciences, including history, philosophy (which encompasses many schools of thought), psychology (both experimental and clinical), sociology and anthropology, linguistics, semantics, literary criticism, exegesis, and hermeneutics.[4]

In a word, whereas the previous approach was unified within a single philosophical framework, the emerging approach is radically pluralistic. There is no longer a single Catholic sacramental theology but a sometimes competing and sometimes complementary set of sacramental theologies simultaneously in use in the Church today. Moreover, since Scholasticism as developed by the time of the Thomistic revival in the nineteenth century

---

[4]In addition to examples given above notes, see Patrick Collins, *More Than Meets the Eye: Ritual and Parish Liturgy* (Mahwah, N.J., Paulist Press, 1983) for philosophy, psychology, poetry, and music; Alexander Ganoczy, *An Introduction to Catholic Sacramental Theology* (Mahwah, N.J.: Paulist Press, 1984) for communications theory; David Power, *Unsearchable Riches: The Symbolic Nature of Liturgy* (New York: Pueblo Publishing Co., 1984) for philosophy, psychology, sociology, and anthropology; Robin Green, *Intimate Mystery* (Boston: Cowley, 1988) for Jungian psychology; Lawrence Hoffman, *The Art of Public Prayer* (Washington, D.C.: Pastoral, 1988) for systems thinking and linguistics; David Newman, *Worship as Praise and Empowerment* (Cleveland: Pilgrim, 1988) for a psychosociological approach inspired by liberation theology. In addition to these on liturgy and worship in general, many others could be cited with reference to particular sacraments.

had achieved the status of a mature discipline or normal science, it was essentially a closed system; it did not and could not allow for the emergence of questions nor the possibility of answers which did not fall within its purview. In contrast, the new approach is open to as many types of questions and answers as can be formulated within the thought systems that it utilizes as bases for reflection. Whereas scholastic sacramental theology could view itself as fundamentally complete and self-contained, therefore, the new paradigm necessarily views its task as perennially incomplete and ongoing. New insights from the human sciences are always raising new possibilities for interrogating and explaining the liturgy and sacraments.

Secondly, there are differences with regard to presentation, that is, with regard to the ways that the Church's rituals are talked about.

If Scholasticism can be characterized as being essentialistic in its manner of presentation, the new paradigm can be said to favor a more existential mode of speaking. To say it in another way, whereas traditional sacramental theology was doctrinal and deductive, beginning with doctrinal statements about the nature and number of the sacraments and reasoning to their necessary effects, the new paradigm is experiential and inductive, beginning with liturgical and ecclesial praxis and arguing either to a confirmation or, at times, a disconfirmation of traditional doctrinal formulations about the sacraments. Needless to say, this manner of presentation is somewhat disconcerting to theological traditionalists who understandably regard the conclusions of contemporary theologians as undermining the very foundations of faith. However, proponents of the new paradigm, inasmuch as they are consciously utilizing the methodology of the human sciences, usually recognize that their conclusions are limited and tentative, which contrasts sharply with results achieved within the scholastic paradigm, which could usually be regarded as dogmatic and definitive, even when the definitive conclusion was that a particular opinion was not *de fide* but only *certa* or *probabilior,* for example.

A closely related contrast in the manner of presentation is between abstractness and concreteness. Theologians working within the scholastic paradigm could begin with definitions of sacraments (abstractly considered) and deduce effects of sacraments (again, abstractly considered) without ever having to verify their inferences experientially. The easily misunderstood principle of *ex opere operato* readily led to conclusions in the spiritual realm such as the remission of sins or infusions of grace which had no observable effects and hence could be imputed to have occurred automatically and magically. Theologians working within the new paradigm, on the other hand, often begin with concrete observations or recollections of the performance of sacramental rituals and then try to analyze what is effectively occurring. They also have a strong tendency to contrast actual performance and actual effects with the abstract religious ideals explicit in the text and with doctrinal generalities propounded about the rite and its intended effects.[5]

Because the scholastic approach was systematic, and given the fact that there was fundamentally only one system, scholastic presentations on the sacraments could be systematically descriptive. That is, traditional theologians could work with the self-understanding that they were describing the sacramental system objectively and in the only way that it could be described without falling into heresy. From the perspective of the contemporary paradigm, however, those theologians were utilizing one particular model for understanding ritual events and they were assuming that the model was providing them with a picture of reality as it was. Contemporary theologians acknowledge the existence of a variety of models, some mutually exclusive and some not, some at least verbally congruent with the scholastic model and some not.

Within the new paradigm, therefore, the only assignable meaning of heresy is a statement which is made within the scholastic model or within the general context of Catholic dogmas (which is still basically scholastic), but which is contrary to one or more statements of dogma. Statements made outside the traditional Catholic language game cannot, strictly speaking, be contrary to scholastically formulated dogmas any more than statements made in behavioral psychology can contradict statements made in clinical psychology, even though on the face of it they may seem to be in conflict. Since the same complex reality—whether it be a religious ritual or a secular activity—is being observed and anyalyzed from the perspective of two different models, statements made within each model can be correct even though their verbalized expressions can appear to be at variance with one another.

Note, however, that the emerging paradigm in sacramental theology (as in all areas of theology) is not one model among others but an overarching, open-ended set of working models or interpretive frameworks borrowed from the various human sciences. The paradigmatic assumption is

[5]For example, see Rafael Avila, *Worship and Politics* (New York: Orbis Books, 1977) and almost anything on sacraments and liturgy written by liberation theologians; Regis Duffy, *Real Presence: Worship, Sacraments, and Commitment* (San Francisco: Harper and Row, 1982) for contrasting ritual and praxis in contemporary America; Gerard Fourez, *Sacraments and Passages* (Notre Dame, Ind.: Ave Maria Press, 1983) for a phenomenological critique of liturgical practices; William Willimon, *The Service of God* (Nashville: Abingdon, 1983) on the impact that Church rituals ought to have on Christian living; Michael Downey, *Clothed in Christ: Sacraments and Christian Living* (New York: Crossroad, 1987) for the praxis implications of sacramental symbols; Timothy Sedgwick, *Sacramental Ethics* (Philadelphia: Fortress Press, 1987) for the moral implications of liturgical structure; James Empereur and Christopher Kiesling, *The Liturgy that Does Justice* (Collegeville, Minn.: The Liturgical Press, 1990) for the social justice implications of sacramental rituals. Again, other books specifically related to particular sacraments could be added.

that the human reality of liturgical worship as well as the transcendent realities symbolized and spoken of in ritual are too complex on the one hand and too mysterious on the other to be completely subsumed within a single system or neatly comprehended within the concepts of a single model.

Third, and last, there are the differences in the manner of application, that is, in the way that the results of conceptual analysis are applied to sacramental performances.

In a narrow sense, it can be said that scholastic sacramental theology was not at all concerned with performance, since that was the province of canon law. In a wider sense, though, both because the Church's canons were often cast in scholastic terminology and because the manual tradition in theology dealt with the sacraments within the framework of canon law, traditional theology can be said to have been concerned with the performance of the sacraments. Nonetheless, this concern was minimalistic and legalistic, that is, there was concern for the minimum that had to be done in order for a sacrament to be valid, and that concern was expressed in terms of canonical legalities.

Although sacramental performance today is more the concern of liturgists than theologians, liturgists do engage in theologizing and theologians do make inferences about what constitutes good and bad liturgy. When either group does this, however, they tend to be maximalistic rather than minimalistic, that is, they encourage more to be done rather than less in the celebration of the sacraments, in order that the rituals might have their greatest possible symbolic impact. In addition, while not being totally antinomian, liturgists tend to look beyond the letter of the law in the interest of enhancing the ritual drama and heightening its effect on the participants. The standard by which such performance is measured thus tends to be not legalistic but pragmatic; the concern is not whether it is valid but whether it works.[6]

To say it in another way, while those who operate within the scholastic paradigm are concerned about sacramental *products,* those who operate within the contemporary paradigm are more concerned with sacramental *processes.* This is to some extent due to the fact that in Scholasticism the focus was

[6]See Kevin Seasoltz, *New Liturgy, New Laws* (Collegeville, Minn.: The Liturgical Press, 1980) on full and active participation in the liturgy; Thomas and Sharon Neufer Emswiler, *Wholeness in Worship* (San Francisco: Harper and Row, 1980) on the need for expansive and inclusive liturgy; John Burkhart, *Worship* (Louisville, Ky.: Westminster, 1982) for the liturgical implications of a theology of worship; Ralph Martin, *The Worship of God* (Grand Rapids, Mich.: Wm B. Eerdmans Publishing Co., 1982) for an application of scriptural theology to Christian worship; Aidan Kavanagh, *On Liturgical Theology* (New York: Pueblo Publishing Co., 1984) for a theological critique of liturgical spirituality. Many other illustrations could be gleaned from the literature on the practical implementation of liturgical rites.

on the *sacramentum et res,* the sacramental reality that was bestowed through the ritual and received by the recipient. Like being pregnant or not, this was a binary possibility: either one received the sacrament or one did not. The *sacramentum et res,* however, as a hypothetical entity, is not found in other models than the scholastic, just as epicycles are not found in systems other than the Ptolemaic. Because of contemporary theologians' interest in experience and concreteness, therefore, their focus is much broader, ranging from concern for the communal and personal situations antecedent to the sacramental celebration to concern for the immediate and long-term consequences, if any, wrought by preparation for, participation in, and commitments following such a celebration.[7]

IV. Copernican Implications and Ptolemaic Residues

The primary implication of the shift from traditional to contemporary paradigms in sacramental theology is precisely this shift in focus. Deleting the imputed sacramental reality from the vocabulary and conceptuality of theoretical models simultaneously deletes talk and thought about administering and receiving sacraments as metaphysical entities. Although one still finds these phrases in popular and ecclesiastical usage, they are becoming increasingly scarce and increasingly inoperative in theological literature. That is, they no longer function as explanatory concepts; they are atavistic remnants of an earlier use of language, just as one still speaks of the sun rising and setting even though one knows that the sun is stationary relative to the spinning earth.

---

[7]Many examples of concern with sacramental processes and their effects can be found in works devoted to the Rite of Christian Initiation of Adults, such as Thomas Morris, *The RCIA: Transforming the Church* (Mahwah, N.J.: Paulist Press, 1989). On baptism and confirmation, see Regis Duffy, *On Becoming a Catholic* (San Francisco: Harper and Row, 1984) and Henri Bourgeois, *On Becoming Christian* (Mystic, Conn.: Twenty-Third, 1985). On Eucharist, see Ralph Keifer, *Blessed and Broken* (Wilmington, Del.: Michael Glazier, Inc., 1982) and Kenneth Stevenson, *Eucharist Offering* (New York: Pueblo Publishing Co., 1986). On penance, see Monika Hellwig, *Signs of Reconciliation and Conversion* (Wilmington, Del.: Michael Glazier, Inc., 1982) and Bernard Cooke, *Reconciled Sinners* (Mystic, Conn.: Twenty-Third, 1986). On anointing of the sick, see James Empereur, *Prophetic Anointing* (Wilmington, Del.: Michael Glazier, Inc., 1982) and Charles Gusmer, *And You Visited Me* (New York: Pueblo Publishing Co., 1984). On marriage, see David Thomas, *Christian Marriage* (Wilmington, Del.: Michael Glazier, Inc., 1983) and William Roberts, ed., *Commitment to Partnership* (Mahwah, N.J.: Paulist Press, 1987). On ordination, see Thomas O'Meara, *Theology of Ministry* (Mahwah, N.J.: Paulist Press, 1983) and Edward Schillebeeckx, *The Church with a Human Face* (New York: Crossroad, 1985). With regard to the priesthood, however, the field is still rather polarized, with those embracing the new paradigm discussing ministry rather than holy orders, and those defending the old paradigm insisting on the reality of the sacramental character bestowed by the rite of ordination.

Properly speaking, therefore, outside the scholastic paradigm, sacraments are neither given nor received. There is simply nothing that corresponds to the *sacramentum et res* in many contemporary sacramental theologies, just as there is nothing that corresponds to the four humours in contemporary psychology. Nor is it the most felicitous use of words to say that sacraments are celebrated, even though that phraseology has become increasingly popular during the past twenty-five years. Properly speaking, the sacraments *are* the celebrations, or what were called in the scholastic system *sacramentum tantum*. What is celebrated in and through a sacramental ritual is not itself but something other than itself which is symbolized by the words and gestures of the rite. Just as a birthday party celebrates a person's completion of a year of life, and just as a national holiday celebrates some cultural reality in the nation's life, so the sacraments celebrate the Christian mysteries that are being lived by individuals and communities.[8]

In a period of transition such as ours is, however, one cannot expect that old language and thought patterns would instantaneously transmute into the new. In fact, one weighty reason why the old language lingers with such tenacity is that it is enshrined in the Code of Canon Law. Even though the Code was substantially revised in 1983, and even though the sections on the sacraments reflect the many changes in the liturgy mandated by the Second Vatican Council, the theology implicit in those sections remains substantively scholastic. In canons 842 and following, one repeatedly finds such phrases as administering or conferring the sacraments, as well as receiving the sacraments. Moreover, the Code explicitly refers to the imprinting of a character (which is a species of sacramental reality) by baptism, confirmation, and orders. Until the language and conceptuality of the Code are changed, one cannot expect the hierarchy and the Roman magisterium to change their thinking.

Additional Ptolemaic residues can be discerned in certain magisterial attempts to "save the appearances," which in this case means preserving the integrity of the scholastic sacramental system, sometimes at the expense of pastoral needs within the Church. The insistence on confession before first Communion, the strictures placed on the conferring of general absolution, the prohibition against women's ordination, the necessity of an annulment

---

[8]Almost all of the authors mentioned who use the contemporary human sciences to understand the sacraments simply assume (as a matter of scientific methodology) that what is to be understood is the visible rite and not an invisible sacrament that is received into the soul of the recipient, even though the traditional language of "receiving the sacraments" still sometimes lingers in Catholic usage. Among the works not yet mentioned in this chapter which make a clean break with the traditional language are Robert Browning and Roy Reed, *The Sacraments in Religious Education and Liturgy* (Birmingham, Ala.: Religious Education, 1985) and Leonardo Boff, *Sacraments of Life, Life of the Sacraments* (Washington, D.C.: Pastoral, 1987).

before a second marriage, and the restriction of the anointing of the sick to administration by presbyters are all, to a greater or lesser extent, related to constrictions placed on the magisterium's thinking by the limitations of the scholastic paradigm.

One of the pervasive consequences of the current revolution in sacramental theology is the inability of parties operating within the mutually exclusive paradigms to communicate with one another. As an intellectual state of affairs, this does not disturb thinkers who work with models in the pluralistic, open-ended paradigm, but it is of some significant concern to thinkers who use the scholastic model either primarily or exclusively. As a practical state of affairs, therefore, this inability to communicate due to the mutual exclusivity of explanatory language games can have disturbing results when theologians who have less political power are verbally harassed or academically attacked by the politically more powerful hierarchy.

One practical implication of recognizing this reality is that the majority of contemporary theologians have to be cautious about their language and have to avoid making statements which would appear to contradict accepted dogmas. Also, by publishing in esoteric journals and academic presses they can usually escape the attention of those guardians of orthodoxy who vigilantly peruse the more popular media for wanderings from the straight and narrow. If theologians choose to confront the traditional paradigm or, as is more frequently the case, if they find themselves confronted by its proponents, they should not expect to persuade traditionalists of the validity of non-traditional thinking. Rather, they should heed the advice implicit in the observation attributed to Niels Bohr, that revolutions in science do not succeed by being more explanatory or more precise or more comprehensive, but by holding their own until the old professors die off and the new professors take their chairs.

Peace and Justice

Michael J. Schuck

The period since the Second Vatican Council has been a watershed in modern Catholic social thought. Renewed attention to Scripture and patristic studies, greater openness to modern philosophical movements, and serious interest in the social sciences has inspired a new moment in Catholic social thought.

Scholars like Johannes B. Metz have developed a "political theology" informed not by natural law but by the theological concept of the kingdom of God. In the United States, heirs to the legacy of John Courtney Murray have continued exploring the positive meaning of democracy and human rights not only for Catholic political thought, but also for the order and operation of the Church. The work of Bryan Hehir, David Hollenbach, and John Coleman exemplifies this trend.

New developments in Catholic social thought also include liberation and feminist theology. Through attention to human "praxis" and a commitment to liberation of the oppressed, Latin American scholars such as Gustavo Gutiérrez and Juan Luis Segundo have challenged the sources, methods, and conclusions of previous Catholic social thought. So too has feminist social ethics. Thinkers like Margaret A. Farley, Christine E. Gudorf, and Rosemary Radford Ruether have criticized the longstanding link in Catholic thought between a human being's reproductive biology and their social role.

Thinkers critical of these liberation and feminist developments have created a sizable social literature of their own. Michael Novak has insisted on the merits of the capitalist market economy for Christian social life. Roger Charles has reasserted the value of neo-Thomism for modern Catholic social thought, while James Shall has questioned the naive optimism of much contemporary Christian political thought by recovering an Augustinian sense of the human limits of social reform.

Since Vatican II, the social writings of the Church hierarchy have expanded beyond papal pronouncements and conciliar documents to include social statements of bishops around the world. Together, these writings have covered a wide variety of social concerns.

The conciliar document *Dignitatis humanae* presented a forthright endorsement of freedom of conscience in religion (thereby reversing earlier papal teaching). In their 1971 statement *Justice in the World,* the General Assembly of bishops declared "action on behalf of justice" a "constitutive dimension of the preaching of the Gospel." As such, Paul VI insisted the same year that "it is up to the Christian communities to analyze with objectivity the situation which is proper to their own country" (apostolic letter *Octogesima adveniens*).

The central political statement of the Church hierarchy during this period has been John XXIII's *Pacem in terris.* Here, the pope endorsed a wide range of political and economic rights within the context of promoting peace and condemning the arms race. On the last issue, the United States bishops' pastoral letter *The Challenge of Peace* noted the importance of both pacifism and just war theory for resolving the problem of war in the nuclear age.

The popes have also sustained an interest in the morality of economic life. John XXIII's *Mater et magistra* emphasized the global dimensions of economic ethics, focusing particularly on the crisis of world agriculture. The structural links between Third World poverty and First World patterns of investment and consumption were explored by the Latin American bishops in their *Medellin* and *Puebla* documents. In *Laborem exercens,* John Paul II focused on the meaning and experience of work in contemporary society, seeing here "a key, probably the essential key, to the whole social question." As a creative dimension of work, he has also supported a "right to freedom of economic initiative" (*Sollicitudo rei socialis*). At the same time, both the Canadian bishops (*Ethical Reflection of the Economic Crisis*) and American bishops (*Economic Justice For All*) have come to quite distinct conclusions on the moral propriety of capitalist initiative.

A sweeping moral analysis of Western culture occurs in the conciliar document *Gaudiem et spes.* Unlike earlier hierarchical writings, this text sought to understand "the joys and the hopes, the griefs and the anxieties" of modern people. In a similar spirit, Paul VI insisted in *Populorum progressio* that because no single culture enjoys "a monopoly of valuable elements," people must be open to knowledge from other cultures.

The period since Vatican II has also witnessed many grass-roots social movements inspired by Catholic leaders. In the United States, people such as Thomas Merton, Gordon Zahn, James W. Douglass, and the Berrigan brothers crystallized a Catholic peace movement. As older links between the Church and organized labor began weakening in the United States, Cesar Chavez mobilized successful grape and lettuce boycotts in support for his United Farm Workers Union.

On a less conspicuous, but no less meaningful level, Canadian Jean Vanier organized the L'Arche movement for enhancing the lives of handicapped and nonhandicapped people around the world. And though sometimes dismissed in academic discussions of Catholic social thought, the work of Mother Theresa has also had a deep influence on social thinking at the grass-roots level.

The following two chapters focus on social teaching in the hierarchical writings of the Church since Vatican II. In the first discussion, Denise J. Doyle analyzes how social justice concerns are reflected in the revised Code of Canon Law. In chapter ten, Michael J. Schuck investigates whether encyclical social teaching as a whole remains coherent after the momentous changes of Vatican II.

Chapter 9

Social Justice and Canon Law:
The Legacy of the Second Vatican Council and the Future of the Church

Denise J. Doyle, J.C.D.

Introduction

The purpose of this paper is to explore what canon law may contribute to the pursuit of social justice. The influence of the Second Vatican Council will be important for understanding both canon law and social justice as they are perceived today. It provided the impetus for a shift away from the predominance of law in Catholicism and initiated the revision of the Code of Canon Law. Moreover, the council has been a primary inspiration for furthering Roman Catholic understanding of and action for justice within the Church's own structures and in the larger political and economic realities. This paper will consider some of the connections between these two aspects of Church life by looking at the juridical and legislative tradition of the Catholic Church both as a strength and a weakness in the journey toward full commitment to social transformation and justice primarily within the ecclesiastical system.

Some might wonder if law and justice are even on speaking terms in the Church. Despite claims to the contrary, I believe that they are and that canon law is at least a second cousin to social justice. My own experience as a student and a teacher of ecclesiastical law has shaped my sense of justice and awareness of injustice, gradually developing in me a conviction that within the field of canon law (which I shall define shortly) there are tools beneficial to the creation of social justice in general, and, specifically, justice within the institutional Roman Church.

In discussing canon law I will be referring to the legal system or structure which has a place and function within the Roman Catholic Church, and also to a mentality or way of thinking which has influence within this Church. In the most narrow sense, canon law refers to that collection of individual laws and norms which is codified within the recently revised Code of Canon Law, 1983.

Social justice, even though it is used commonly, is a more difficult term to define or limit. One may say in a general way that social justice is the creation of right relationships on the systemic or structured level. The synodal document "Justice in the World" called social justice (perhaps somewhat anthropomorphically) love of neighbor put into practice through the recognition of the dignity and rights of one's neighbor.[1] Social justice is working to reveal and eliminate any situation of injustice, and more narrowly, situations characterized by the diminution of or denial of human rights and inherent dignity of the person. Social justice is both the goal, in the sense of a just world, and the strategy, in the sense of the actions and commitments necessary to arrive at the goal.

I. The Influence of the Second Vatican Council

Many authors have reflected upon the significance of Vatican II for the Church as a whole and for a plethora of individual topics and concerns.[2] Certainly the Constitution on the Church in the Modern World (*Gaudium et spes*) and the Declaration on Religious Freedom (*Dignitatis humanae*) contain teachings which are fundamental to the emergence of a conscious sense of social justice in the past twenty-five years. In the area of canon law, the Constitution on the Church (*Lumen gentium*) presented ecclesiological shifts which in turn engendered significant legal shifts. While one must necessarily recognize that every change trails with it a long history, both canon lawyers and social justice activists point decisively to the Second Vatican Council as the *raison d'être* for the newness of their endeavors.

Vatican II and Canon Law

Prior to the Second Vatican Council, canon law had dominated the structure of the Roman Catholic Church with the *Codex Iuris Canonici* of 1917 accurately reflecting the ecclesiology of Vatican Council I. A completely centralized Church with all power in the hands of the pope, except for that power which he conceded to bishops, was the Church of the Code of Canon Law. The static quality of the Church, the complete dependence on Rome for everything, and the a-cultural style of Catholicism inspired

---

[1]1971 Synod of Bishops, "Justice in the World," *The Gospel of Peace and Justice*, ed. Joseph Gremillion (New York: Orbis Books, 1976) no. 34.

[2]See Dom Alberic Stacpoole, O.S.B., ed., *Vatican II Revisited by Those Who Were There* (New York: Harper and Row, 1986); Timothy E. O'Connell, ed., *Vatican II and Its Documents* (Wilmington, Del.: Michael Glazier, Inc., 1986).

Pope John XXIII to want to air out the Church, seek the signs of the time, and bring Catholicism into the twentieth century.

The recent history of canon law has been reviewed often enough and has become quite familiar.[3] Pope John XXIII, at the very time when he revealed his plan to reform the Church with an ecumenical council, also announced his intention to create a commission to revise the Code of Canon Law. Underlying the Pope's Church-shaking design is a very simple equation: law follows doctrine. The renewal of the Church anticipated in the Second Vatican Council would only further accent those elements of the 1917 Code of Canon Law which were already obsolete in 1959. *Aggiornamento* in the Church's life would necessitate revision of Church law as well.

There was a period of relative fluidity after the Vatican Council while the Code of Canon Law was being revised. The reforms of the council were being interpreted and put into law in a variety of postconciliar documents,[4] and they were being appropriated at the level of the local Church. After a number of years of revision and a number of draft presentations had been circulated worldwide, the revised Code was promulgated on February 3, 1983, and became law on November 27, 1983.

The link between the revised Code of Canon Law and the documents of the Vatican Council was made clear by Pope John Paul II in the Apostolic Constitution "Sacrae Disciplinae Leges," January 25, 1983.[5] In presenting the revision to the Church the Pope reflected on how it was intended to be an expression of conciliar doctrine.

> In fact, in a certain sense, this new Code can be viewed as a great effort to translate the conciliar ecclesiological teaching into canonical terms. If it is impossible perfectly to transpose the image of the Church described by conciliar doctrine into canonical language, nevertheless the Code must always be related to that image as to its primary pattern, whose outlines, given its nature, the Code must express as far as is possible.[6]

Indeed, more than a reflection of the council, the Pope describes the Code as a "complement to the authentic teaching proposed by the Second Vatican Council and particularly to its Dogmatic and Pastoral Constitutions."[7]

[3]John A. Alesandro, "General Introduction," *The Code of Canon Law A Text and Commentary,* eds. James A. Coriden, Thomas J. Green, and Donald E. Heintschel (New York: Paulist Press, 1985) 1–22.

[4]See Austin P. Flannery, ed., *Vatican Council II: The Conciliar and Post Conciliar Documents* (Collegeville, Minn.: The Liturgical Press, 1975).

[5]John Paul II, Apostolic Constitution, "Sacrae Disciplinae Leges," *The Code of Canon Law* (London: Collins Liturgical Publications, 1983) xi–xv.

[6]Ibid., xiii–xiv.

[7]Ibid., xiv.

Vatican II and Social Justice

Certain key themes of the council are directly related to social justice. The dignity of the human person, the role of the Church vis-à-vis the state, and the ministry of the Church within the world are foundational doctrine in the development of the social ministry of the Church.[8] Social justice ministry is properly concerned for the human dignity of the individual, particularly the poor and powerless. Human dignity is promoted through the protection of human rights. This ministry required the Church to articulate a positive role for the Church in relation to the here and now modern world, while denying any special status in its relationship to the modern state.

The Church's social ministry is what Bryan Hehir has called "a religiously rooted but politically significant style of ministry."[9] The Church essentially preaches the gospel, with the growing recognition that the gospel's message is one which has practical and immediate consequences in the political arena. This was how *Gaudium et spes* described the Church's mission:

> Christ did not bequeath to the Church a mission in the political, economic, or social order: the purpose he assigned to it was a religious one. But this religious mission can be the source of commitment, direction, and vigor to establish and consolidate the human community according to the law of God. In fact, the Church is able, indeed it is obliged, if times and circumstances require it, to initiate action for the benefit of all, especially of those in need, like works of mercy and similar undertakings.[10]

In addition to a newly defined mission, the ecclesiology initiated by the council has significantly altered the participants in social ministry. The involvement of the local Church and the voice of episcopal conferences have brought social justice to bear upon the problems within individual countries or regions and has engendered activism at the grass-roots level. This is different from the preconciliar body of social teaching, which was largely a product of papal authority.[11]

The documents of the Second Vatican Council are a theme which run through subsequent ecclesial social documentation. Papal teaching continued strong after the council and can be traced through the works of Paul VI and John Paul II. The General Council of Latin American Bishops held in Medellin, Columbia, translated the message of Vatican II into the lan-

---

[8] J. Bryan Hehir, "Church-State and Church-World: The Ecclesiological Implications," *The Catholic Theological Society of America Proceedings* 41 (1986) 54–74.

[9] Ibid., 59.

[10] *Gaudium et spes,* no. 42.

[11] See Bryan Hehir, "Church-State and Church-World" and *Catholic Social Teaching: Our Best Kept Secret,* ed. Peter J. Henriot and others (New York: Orbis Books, 1988).

guage and diverse realities of Latin America, extending the meaning of justice. This was followed by the second general assembly of the Synod of Bishops and the document *Justice in the World*.[12] Episcopal conferences worldwide have given specificity to these teachings by applying them to their national economic and political realities. From beginning to end, pastoral letters, such as the United States bishops' *The Challenge of Peace* and *Economic Justice for All*, are woven through with references to conciliar and postconciliar social teachings.

These documents and the ensuing activities they have fostered are examples of how the Church has attempted to remain true to its responsibility "of reading the signs of the time and of interpreting them in the light of the Gospel."[13] This mandate of *Gaudium et spes*, basic as it is to the Church's social justice engagement, was taken up and reaffirmed by the participants in the 1985 extraordinary session of the world Synod of Bishops which was called to commemorate the Second Vatican Council. In the final report of that synod the following was recorded in regard to *Gaudium et spes:*

> In this context we affirm the great importance and timeliness of the pastoral constitution *Gaudium et spes*. At the same time, however, we perceive that the signs of our time are in part different from those of the time of the council, with greater problems and anguish. Today, in fact, everywhere in the world we witness an increase in hunger, oppression, injustice and war, sufferings, terrorism and other forms of violence of every sort. This requires a new and more profound theological reflection in order to interpret these signs in the light of the Gospel.[14]

Conclusion

Both canon law and social justice, as they function within the Roman Catholic Church today, are heavily indebted to the Second Vatican Council. Before considering their roles in the Church of the twenty-first century and questioning what if any tie they may have with each other, it is important to recognize that there are differing opinions about the exact influence of Vatican II. There are authors who have raised questions, for example, about how accurately the teaching of the Second Vatican Council has been incorporated into the revised Code of Canon Law.[15] They suggest that some

[12]"Justice in the World," *The Gospel of Peace and Justice*, 513–29.

[13]*Gaudium et spes*, no. 4.

[14]1985 Extraordinary Synod of Bishops, "The Final Report," *Origins* 15 (December 19, 1985) 449.

[15]See, for example, Thomas J. Green's comprehensive works which touch on this theme: "The Use of Vatican II Texts in the Draft 'De Populo Dei," *Concilium* 147 (1981) 45–53; "Persons and Structures in the Church: Reflections on Selected Issues in Book Two," *The*

ideas of Vatican II have been altered in the process of transposing them into law. They point out that compromise was a part of the revision process.[16] Some of the controversies of the council became controversies of the Code, with solutions being legislated without agreement. They warn that some aspects of the council, perhaps the spirit of the council, has been compromised in the Code of Canon Law.

Similarly, some question exactly what Vatican II proposed in regard to social justice. Avery Dulles has suggested that many assertions about the role of Vatican II in the area of social justice are distorted.[17] He is concerned with the tendency to use passages of documents as proof texts to bolster certain current ideas. Inaccurate claims are made about the council, according to Dulles, while ignoring contradictory statements and, thus, creating ''a certain myth regarding the achievement of Vatican II.'' It is important to recognize, both in the area of canon law and social justice, the absence of one, unified teaching or even tendency in the many documents of the council. The truth is that there was no single, clear vision then and there isn't one now.

II. The Church of the Twenty-First Century

There is little doubt that the Second Vatican Council will continue to have a dynamic impact on the Church of the next century. After all, Vatican Council I, through the Code of Canon Law, had a tremendous impact on the major portion of this century. While one may not honestly attribute every new vision of the future on the foresight of Vatican II, it is true that the council began processes which are continuing to evolve. Codification is not, of course, evolutionary in nature. But the social concern of the Church and the duty to cast new light on doctrine are both new and constant tendencies.[18] My task, however, is to suggest where Roman Catholicism may be directed, in the sense of ''fashioned,'' and where social justice and canon law may contribute to this direction.

The past twenty-five years of prolific social teaching certainly give us reason to expect that the Church of the twenty-first century will continue to grow in commitment to seeking unity between faith and action on behalf of justice. And here liberation theologians have been instrumental in

Jurist 45 (1985) 24–94; ''The Revised Code of Canon Law: Some Theological Issues,'' *Theological Studies* 47 (1986) 617–52.

[16]James H. Provost, ''Approaching the Revised Code,'' *Code, Community and Ministry*, ed. James H. Provost (Washington, D.C.: Canon Law Society of America, 1983) 13.

[17]Avery Dulles, ''Vatican II and the Church's Purpose,'' *Theology Digest* 32 (1985) 341–52.

[18]John Paul II, ''Sollicitudo Rei Socialis,'' *The Logic of Solidarity*, ed. Gregory Baum and Robert Ellsberg (New York: Orbis Books, 1989), no. 3.

placing the emphasis on action, since it is not merely the task of the Church to point out injustice but to actively engage in the transformation of society.[19] Again, social justice, or social ministry, is both an image of justice and a methodology for achieving justice. Social justice is both vision and action. Both notions, with constant tending, do seem to be growing in the Church.

While the Church's continued commitment to world justice may be predicted, commitment to justice within the Church itself has not so clearly been established. We could not so freely assert the continuance of efforts for ecclesial justice in the next century. Here is a serious problem. The prophecy of the 1971 synodal document *Justice in the World,* " . . . anyone who ventures to speak to people about justice must first be just in their eyes,"[20] has a hollow ring within the Church itself and within societies which hear the Church call for justice in the economic and political realm.

Social Justice within the Church: Problems

While social justice may be defined at least partially in terms of human dignity protected through the recognition of human rights,[21] lack of justice within the Church has been defined specifically in terms of the lack of human rights. Leonardo Boff, basing his reflections upon the words of *Justice in the World,* has outlined a now familiar list of grievances within the Roman Catholic Church. Failure to grant moral legitimacy to the conscience decisions of priests leaving ministry, discrimination against women, restrictions placed on information and control of the Catholic means of communications, restrictions on the free expression of ideas, the process of accusations and denunciations made by the Sacred Congregation for the Doctrine of the Faith against theologians, and problems of academic freedom within Catholic institutions of higher learning are continuing examples of human rights violations.[22]

However, it is significant that Boff begins his litany by pointing to the centralization of decision-making within the Church as a violation of human rights.[23] Here he is pointing to not just one of many examples of the lack

[19]See Richard A. McCormick, S.J., "Moral Theology 1940–1989: An Overview," *Theological Studies* 50 (1989) 15.

[20]"Justice in the World," no. 40.

[21]See, e.g., *Catholic Social Teaching: Our Best Kept Secret,* 20, and "Church-State and Church-World," 73.

[22] Leonardo Boff, *Church: Charism and Power: Liberation Theology and the Institutional Church* (New York: Crossroad, 1988) 32–46. Also, James A. Coriden, "A Challenge: Make the Rights Real," *The Jurist* 45 (1985) 1–23.

[23]Boff, *Charism and Power,* 34.

of human rights within the Church but toward the root of the gap between what the Church teaches about human rights and what is practiced within its own structure. And it is precisely here that the project of fashioning a Church for the twenty-first century meets social justice. It is also here that it meets canon law. For the centralization of decision-making within the Church is very precisely articulated in Book 2 of the Code, called "The People of God." Part 2 of that book is "The Hierarchical Constitution of the Church," and here one may find the legal description and definition of "the pole [which] runs from the Pope to the bishop, to the priests—excluding religious and laity."[24]

Boff digs deeper into the problematic nature of hierarchy, but let me clarify the link between injustice and canon law in the effort to shape a Church which would both teach justice and be just. In all of the aforementioned abuses of human rights in the Church, the Code of Canon Law may be counted upon to supply the law necessary to justify the violations. The law itself is frequently perceived as the cause of injustice in the Church. However, one must insist that injustice within the Church does not occur because the law dictates injustice, but rather injustice occurs because behind the structure of the Church is the theological and doctrinal support for decision-making based on systemic exclusion. What lies behind this structure is not canon law, but as expressed in cc. 330, 375, and 1008, divine law, as this is understood in Roman Catholicism.

It is not my intention to tackle "divine law," but such a term does suggest the difficulty of fashioning a socially just Church. The understanding of authority within the Church is heavily shaped by presuppositions which are not particularly malleable—even for the twenty-first century. The problem of what canon law calls "divine law" is what Boff tackles as the problem of "revelation":

> What self-concept forms ecclesiastical authority? It considers itself to be the principal if not exclusive bearer of God's revelation to the world, with the mission of proclaiming it, explaining it, and defending it. This revelation is found in the sacred Scriptures and interpretation is given by the magisterium of the Church. . . . This is the crux of the problem: the doctrinal understanding of revelation. God reveals necessary truths, some unattainable by reason, to facilitate the road to salvation. The magisterium possesses a collection of absolute, infallible, and divine truths. The magisterium presents an absolute doctrine, free from any doubt. Any inquiry that is born of life and that calls into question a given doctrine is mistaken. Doctrine substitutes for life, experience, and everything from below.[25]

[24]Ibid., 40.
[25]Ibid., 41–42.

So what we experience is injustice. Consider, for example, the exclusion of women from full participation in the Roman Catholic Church. Canon 1024 ("Only a baptized man can validly receive sacred ordination.") implies, but by no means exhausts, the exclusion of women from leadership. The situation continues despite a variety of appeals on behalf of the rights of women that may be traced back through magisterial documents from *Pacem in terris*, 1963,[26] to the yet problematic United States bishops' attempts at what was once called *Partners in the Mystery of Redemption* and in the second draft is called *One in Christ Jesus: A Pastoral Response to the Concerns of Women for Church and Society*.[27] And this leads to one difficulty that Peter Henriot describes with promoting modern Church social teaching: "Someone inevitably asks how we can—or why we should believe the teaching when it is so poorly practiced by the teacher, the church which proclaims it."[28] The failure of the Church to implement its own teaching does not necessarily lessen the intrinsic value of the message proclaimed. It is, however, creating a serious credibility gap.

Injustice within the Church: A Comparison

Magisterial recourse to "divine will" in the form of divine law or divine revelation, in response to human rights abuses within the Church, invites comparisons to national security claims. The need to diminish the rights of individuals for the sake of the state, called the doctrine of national security, has been denounced, especially by the Catholic bishops of Latin America.[29] They point out that the violations of human rights that this doctrine precipitates are the result of "unjust economic structures, maldistribution of land and wealth, lack of effective social participation by the poor, and the pervasiveness of an ideology of national security which subjugates all rights of the person to the expediency of the State."[30] This methodology guarantees the survival of the present order against all hostilities and pressures.

The comparison of magisterial theology to national security ideology does not rest on those land, wealth, or economic interests which are clearly

[26]John XXIII, "Pacem in terris," *The Gospel of Peace and Justice*, no. 41.

[27]United States Bishops, "One in Christ Jesus: A Pastoral Response to the Concerns of Women for Church and Society," *Origins* 19 (April 5, 1990) 717–40.

[28]Peter J. Henriot, "Our Best Kept Secret: Looking toward 1991," *Center Focus* 87 (November 1988) 4.

[29]III General Conference of Latin American Bishops, *Puebla Conclusions* (Washington, D.C.: National Conference of Catholic Bishops, 1979) no. 49.

[30]Brian Smith, "Churches and Human Rights in Latin America: Recent Trends on the Subcontinent," *Churches in Politics in Latin America*, ed. Daniel H. Levine (Beverly Hills, Sage Publications, 1981) 156.

visible in the political realm. Nor does it rest on the brutality of the methods used to deny rights in national security states, though Boff has pointed out the deleterious effects that denunciation and margination can bring to dissenters within the Church.[31] The comparison rests upon the subjugation of rights and the tightly limited decision-making process which are sanctioned by religious claims and used for the protection of power.

Two further characteristics of national security doctrine are instructive of this comparison. When the security of structures is overvalued, there is a concomitant tendency to confuse the *status quo* ("what is") with something essential ("what must be").

> Frequently, protecting essential rules is confused with maintaining the status quo, chiefly by the action of interested groups who view any change or tendency to change as a threat to basic rules, even calling these changes subversive. Since national security regimes have generally lost touch with a large part of their social base, they easily become victims of such a confusion.[32]

Finally, in the situation of national security, conflict is seen as a constant threat which must be avoided. In dictatorships this leads to an ever-widening circle of enemies who are never beyond suspicion and constantly victimized.[33]

This brief description of the characteristics of the excesses of national security suggests that what is created in such countries, as is created today in the Church, is a serious difference of opinion—not about the cause of injustice but about the very existence of injustice. What some, notably the Church, call "serious abuses of human rights," the practitioners of the doctrine of national security describe as the strategy necessary to protect essential values of life, liberty, and Christianity. The calls to desist, which the Church continues to issue to such governments, are perceived, one may suggest, as tantamount to proposals of national destruction. Protecting the state is an end which excuses brutal but necessary means.

Similarly, the suggestion of human rights violations in the Church is not argued on the level of cause but on the level of existence. The Church, according to this reasoning, is not violating rights or unjustly excluding participation, but obediently following the command or at least plan of Christ. Appeals for change clearly must be denied in order to faithfully maintain Christ's own design for the Church. This has been described as an ideological blindness and it afflicts most notably those who have decision-making

---

[31]Boff, *Charism and Power*, 37.
[32]Robert Calvo, "The Church and the Doctrine of National Security," *Churches and Politics in Latin America*, 150.
[33]Ibid.

authority within the Church, but also those who offer blind obedience to that authority.[34]

The perception of unjust conditions in the Church is further similar to national security conditions because both may produce a serious impasse. The victims of an abusive state are in many senses powerless to bring about the very changes that they envision. Peaceful means of education and organization are frequently difficult or even impossible. Viable means of peaceful change are not contained within existent political structures, in fact are banned or completely eliminated. Finally, people may resort to violence, attempting to overthrow the government by revolution. Clearly the structures of Roman Catholicism are in no way as menacing or dangerous. But avenues of change are equally limited when power is held in the hands of the few.

Conclusion: Pressure for Change

Today, some national security states have changed dramatically because of internal and external forces which could not be controlled. Suffice it to say that the Church may yet experience the effects of similar forces. The Church is subject to the many influences of the times and in many ways shaped by forces it cannot control. Yves Congar, in looking back on the period of Vatican II reform, noted the rapid and in some ways unexpected changes that occurred in society and which tremendously influenced the Church in ways that were not anticipated by the council.[35] Today, in a similar way, cultural norms and expectations within societies which accept and enjoy a degree of personal freedom, increase peoples' unwillingness to accept decisions and disciplines which are considered arbitrary. Resistance to the perception of authoritarianism within the Church is itself becoming an example of an external pressure to change.

Boff proposes some internal rays of hope that may brighten an otherwise bleak picture of the prospects of fashioning a socially just Church for the future. Primarily the gospel itself is an ongoing challenge to every form of social injustice. Reading the signs of the time and casting the light of the gospel on injustice is not simply something that the Church does for the benefit of political or economic structures. The gospel, and the very image of authority as service that Jesus proposed, is a standard of judgment against which all the structures within the Church of Christ must be measured.[36]

---

[34]Gregory Baum, "Structures of Sin," *The Logic of Solidarity*, 110.

[35]Yves Congar, "A Last Look at the Council," *Vatican II Revisited by Those Who Were There*, 351.

[36]Boff, *Charism and Power*, 43–46.

Additionally, the very social teaching of the Church itself reflects back upon it, at every level, with the potential to cause internal conflict within the Church's own consciousness. Again, the value of what is and has been taught by the Church, which in 1991 celebrated one hundred years of modern social teaching, cannot be underestimated. The social teaching of Roman Catholicism has been repeated and enhanced in a systematic fashion, creating an authoritative and inspiring tradition of analysis, concern, and challenge. As it is appropriated at the local level and people become aware of Catholic social teaching (what Peter Henriot calls "our best kept secret") a sharper awareness of the characteristics of injustice in general leads to a sharper perception of injustices within the ecclesial community. People ask questions:

> The radical understanding of social justice and the ethical critique of institutions found in recent papal and episcopal documents make Catholics ask questions about the justice of ecclesiastical institutions.[37]

This is the sense of "internal contradictions within the ecclesiastical consciousness itself" to which Boff refers.[38]

It is in this context of external and internal forces which are pressures toward the creation of justice within the Church that I propose to assess the contribution of canon law. Having stated clearly my conviction that the law is by no means the source of injustice in the Church, though frequently a rationale for injustice, I will propose some ways in which canon law is a strength in the pursuit of justice and some ways in which it is a weakness. My initial point was that both the current law and the current understanding of social ministry have been greatly influenced by Vatican II. I will consider, then, the significance of the postconciliar content of the revised Code of Canon Law, as well as some intangible qualities which might be called the spirit or mentality of the law.

III. Canon Law

Canon law is a practical guide to life in the Church. Some behavioral link to moral theology has been and continues to be emphasized.[39] Without diminishing the priority of theology over law, the association of law with ecclesiology is perhaps more accurate today.[40] Canon law delineates

---

[37]Baum, *The Logic of Solidarity*, 110.

[38]Boff, *Charism and Power*, 43.

[39]See Ladislas Orsy, S.J., "Moral Theology and Canon Law: The Quest for a Sound Relationship," *Theological Studies* 50 (1989) 151–67.

[40]Bertram Griffin, "The Parish and Lay Ministry," *Chicago Studies* 23 (1984) 45.

precisely the structure and structures of the Church. The value of the law may be seen in its simplicity, its affinity to concrete situations, its capacity to express the ideal within the life of the Church without eliminating the real and ordinary. There has been within recent history and up to today a certain aversion to law and especially legalism, the absolutizing of the role of the law and the reduction of Church life to Church law. However, leaving aside the worst centralizing features of the Code of 1917, and recognizing all reasonable limitations, law is a necessary feature of an organic community desiring order and harmony.[41]

The Spirit of the Law

It would be minimalistic, however, to reduce the law to nothing more than a necessary evil. But, as John Paul II expressed it, law should remain within a certain hierarchy in which its place is rightfully subordinated to higher virtues and realities:

> It is sufficiently clear that the purpose of the Code is not in any way to replace faith, grace, charisms, and above all charity in the life of the Church or of Christ's faithful. On the contrary, the Code rather looks toward the achievement of order in the ecclesial society, such that while attributing a primacy to love, grace and the charisms, it facilitates at the same time an orderly development in the life both of the ecclesial society and the individual persons who belong to it.[42]

During the interim of revision that occurred between the council and the promulgation of the Code, Pope Paul VI gave a great deal of impetus to the effort of re-visioning the law.[43] In particular he stressed two relationships which are necessary to understand not just the content of the law, but the spirit of the law. One is the bond between law and justice, the other between law and equity.

Canon law should be an expression of justice and a means for administering justice in the Church. The following quotation shows the similarity between the sense of social justice in the Church, expressed in terms of peace and human rights, and Paul VI's understanding of justice protected by the law:

> [Rather] justice is that which brings peace to others. There is no true peace except in justice. And true justice is not to be found in a legislation that is imposed by one or another group because of its strong position in society.

[41]See Orsy, "Moral Theology and Canon Law," 153, and also Boff, *Charism and Power*, 77.
[42]"Sacrae Disciplinae Leges," xiii.
[43]Francis G. Morrisey, O.M.I., "The Spirit of Canon Law and the Teaching of Paul VI," *Readings, Cases, Materials in Canon Law,* ed. Jordan F. Hite and others (Collegeville, Minn: The Liturgical Press, 1980) 19–31.

It is found, on the contrary, in the concern for assuring even better protection for natural rights.[44]

And this justice and the protection of rights, Paul VI explained, would be identified with flexibility rather than rigidity and would not be achieved in legalism. The law must not appear to dominate every detail of Church life. "It will appear rather as but one facet of that life: an important one, indeed, but also one which serves the life of the communion as such and leaves to the individual believer the freedom and responsibility needed in building up the body of Christ."[45]

The relationship of law to justice was strong in Paul VI's mind and so was the notion of equity, that is "justice tempered with the sweetness of mercy." When law is applied to concrete situations it is to be done with equity. "Equity takes the form of mildness, mercy and pastoral charity and seeks not a rigid application of law but the true welfare of the faithful."[46]

The spirit of the law, tied as it is to justice and equity, is in many ways intangible. It is the tone and vision of what law can be and should be in the Church. It is distinct but not separate from the sum of the canons. Clearly it should be expressed in the totality of laws. The spirit of the law, according to both John XXIII and Paul VI, was to be guided by the spirit of Vatican II. Justice and equity, as described by Paul VI, were to replace the trademarks of preconciliar law—rigorism and legalism.

We may view the spirit of the law as contributive to the effort of creating justice within the Church. It communicates ideals commensurate with the Church's overall commitment to social justice and human dignity. It was expressed in the principles which governed the revision process and attempted to keep the revision on course with Vatican II.[47] Determining and safeguarding the rights of individuals within the community was prominent within the principles, creating a substantial difference between the two Codes. The articulation of basic rights, we will see when considering the content of the current Code, is a major strength that canon law may contribute to shaping the future of the Church.

A final more or less intangible characteristic of the Code of Canon Law comes from Vatican II and should continue to shape the Church of the future. It is the way that the Code was reordered to manifest the teaching of conciliar decrees. Book 2 of the Code is called "The People of God" and it introduces the common status of all Christ's faithful before mentioning the clergy and before the hierarchical constitution of the Church

---

[44]As quoted in Morrisey, *Readings, Cases, Materials in Canon Law*, 20.
[45]Ibid., 21.
[46]Ibid., 22.
[47]See *Code and Commentary*, 6.

is described. This may appear a small matter, but it is in fact following the lead of *Lumen gentium,* imaging the Church as above all the people of God. Within the Code, as within the consciousness of the Church itself, is a disconsonant realization, however nascent it may yet remain, that before the Church is hierarchical it is a community of radically equal believers.[48]

The spirit of the law should be a primary factor in teaching the law. I dare to say that in the two major institutions where law is taught in Canada and the United States today, this is the case. Canon law is not presented as a set of answers to every conceivable pastoral situation. It is not presented as the sum total of the canons in the Code. The most valuable asset of a canonical education is a way of thinking, a way of thinking which is absorbed, as it were, by studying the clarity and order of the law itself and the underlying values which it seeks to protect. One need only point to the work of the Canon Law Society of America for an example. Its prolific efforts on behalf of the best possible revision and now the best possible understanding of the Code embody that comprehension of the law which far transcends legalism while seeking the road to justice.

The Content of the Code

The spirit of the law is distinct from the collection of laws which is the Code of Canon Law. As mentioned above, the Code contains the legal formulation of many of the very problems that the Roman Catholic Church is experiencing today. The Code, after all, is nothing more than an expression of current magisterial theology and doctrine. I have noted that the single line of canon 1024, which excludes women from sacred orders, speaks volumes about sexual discrimination within the Roman Church. Commentators point out that this canon is not surprising since the magisterium has not changed its positions and canon law is itself subject to the magisterium.[49] Others have drawn attention to the fact that the revised Code had the effect of legislating answers to controversial theological, pastoral, and canonical issues. For some people, undoubtedly, the appearance of the Code in 1983 signaled the end of the discussion, the resolution of disagreements, the happy return to legal stability.[50] There is no denying this mentality in the Church and the subsequent use it makes of the law. This view, however, ignores important innovations which are equally part of the content of the Code.

[48]See Thomas J. Green, "Persons and Structures in the Church," 24–94.

[49]See *Code and Commentary,* 141. "Although the interpretation of this canon is traditional and clear, the literature on this canon during the revision process exceeds the total amount of literature on all the other canons on orders," 723.

[50]Thomas J. Green, "The Revised Code of Canon Law," 617–52.

There are a substantial number of canons in the Code which deal explicitly with the rights people enjoy as members of the Church. Before delineating the obligations and rights[51] of members based on their state of life, the Code articulates in sixteen entirely new canons the rights common to all Christians. Canon 208, following *Lumen gentium* no. 32, establishes that before all else, and by virtue of baptism, there is a genuine equality of dignity among all Christ's faithful. This is really a new idea. It is a departure from a long tradition, still operative in many ways, which views the laity as unequal to the clergy.[52] Inequality goes back as far as Gratian and therefore has influenced the Church for almost nine hundred years!

Baptismal equality is followed by a series of common rights which include, among others, the right of members to make their needs known, to express their views, and to communicate them to others (canon 212). Christ's faithful enjoy the rights of association (canon 215), collaboration in the mission of the Church (canon 216) and Christian education (canon 217). They are free to do research and to express their ideas in the areas called "sacred sciences" (canon 218). Each person has the right to his or her good reputation (canon 220).

These rights are new and the way that they are phrased reflects the tension that their introduction causes within the traditionally stratified ecclesiology of the Roman Church. They are couched in cautionary language which portrays a hesitant tone. The expression of a right is almost always accompanied by a phrase such as "each according to his or her own condition," or "provided it is in accord with church teaching," and "with due allegiance to the magisterium of the church." The excessive use of qualifiers is daunting. Despite this, one may take some encouragement from the fact that John Paul II, in his rather brief Apostolic Constitution promulgating the Code of 1983, drew specific attention to the need to define and safeguard the rights of the faithful in a Code of Canon Law.

The biggest difficulty with these and any rights is the question of how they are to be defended if and when they are violated. Canon 221.1 says that "the Christian faithful can legitimately vindicate and defend the rights which they enjoy in the Church before a competent ecclesiastical court." This is clearly an ideal and not a reality in the Church today. Bringing this canon to life is fraught with difficulties. On a practical level ecclesiastical tribunals are almost exclusively marriage tribunals. More fundamental problems are the fact that cases which involve bishops must be heard in Rome,

---

[51] A rather interesting philosophical discussion, which is reflected in the Code, marks the difference between "rights and obligations" and "obligations and rights." See James H. Provost, *Code and Commentary*, 137–38.

[52] *Code and Commentary*, 140.

and, within a hierarchical Church, one is more often than not seeking justice from the very persons who are part of the injustice.

Many canonists have pointed to this serious flaw in the law and to the resultant perception of the Church which it engenders. James Coriden expresses the link between unprotected rights and an unjust Church:

> Rights which are declared but undefended are a mockery; when the claims cannot be vindicated, the rights are useless. Any society which fails to provide remedies for wrongs, reasonably adequate and available mechanisms for the redress of grievances, ways to insist on the basic claims which are constitutionally asserted, is not a just society. For those very reasons our Church is perceived by many of its members, as well as outside observers, to be an unjust Church.[53]

The ideal of recognizing the rights of Church members is a significant addition to the Code of Canon Law. The ideal, however, must yet become a reality in order for the Church to be an institution that values and safeguards the rights it proclaims and the persons who enjoy them. Only then will the common perception of the Church begin to change.

Following sixteen initial canons containing common rights, there are eight new canons which deal with the rights and capacities of the laity. These canons are more significant for what they don't say than for what they do say. The Code of 1917, by way of example, in one of only two canons dealing with the laity, prohibited lay persons from wearing ecclesiastical garb! There is nothing so condescending here. If the initial canons on rights may be interpreted as a beginning and first attempt at expressing rights within the Church, these canons may be perceived similarly as the preliminary effort to imagine that the laity have some actual functions and a collaborative role in the Church.

Three of these canons which should be mentioned deal with the laity having "official positions" within the Church. Lay members of the Church may be assigned to ecclesiastical offices and serve as advisors (canon 228), they may receive a mandate to teach the "sacred sciences" (canon 229), and they may have employment within the Church (canon 231). Lay employees are entitled to a decent remuneration which, according to canon 231, includes their pension, social security, and health benefits. Certainly, this is progress, but there is one regressive canon in this section. It is that law (canon 230) which prohibits women from being installed in the ministries of lector and acolyte. Since the Code of 1983 progressed greatly from the Code of 1917 in treating laymen and laywomen equally, this canon has been seen

---

[53]James Coriden, "A Challenge: Make the Rights Real," 3, and also, *Code and Commentary*, 153–55.

as a setback to the effort to eliminate sexual discrimination. The equality that was described in canon 208 is violated in canon 230, evidence that the Church has a long road ahead in regards to living out its very own ideals.

Another dichotomy that may be seen in the canons on the laity is the difference between secular and sacred arenas of activity. Following Vatican II, there is a tendency to see the "temporal order" as the rightful place of the laity and their mission is to renew it. An overemphasis on this distinction leads to the vision that the world and the Church are two separate realities. It also leads to the idea, contrary to the social teaching of the Church, that the cultic, sacramental, or liturgical functions of the Church, exercised by the clergy, are the Church's proper activities.[54] While previously mentioned canons open up the concept of ecclesial ministry to the laity, there remains a problematic concept of "inside-outside" ministry.

A final important addition to the content of the Code is some new canons which specifically recommend the promotion of social justice and reflect conciliar and postconciliar developments.[55] The laity are to promote social justice (canon 222.2), the clergy are to foster peace and harmony based on justice (canon 287), pastors are to use their homily "to foster works which promote the spirit of the Gospel, including its relevance to social justice" (canon 528). Canon 747.2 upholds the Church's right to teach "even in respect to the social order" and canon 768.2 says that those who preach should "explain to the faithful the teaching of the magisterium of the church concerning the dignity and freedom of the human person."

All of these canons recognize that social justice is a newly understood part of the Church's mission. Again, they do tend to be the expression of an ideal. They are exhortative by nature, which is to say that like many canons in the code, they would be difficult, near impossible, to enforce.

We have already seen that canon 231 expresses an individual's right to a decent remuneration in Church employment. A corresponding canon, canon 1286, states the obligation of ecclesiastical administrators to pay employees a just and decent wage. This is to be done in accord with "church principles in the employment of workers." Clearly, it is the intention of this canon to apply the Church's own teaching to its own institutions. The Church as an economic agent has long been accused of inconsistency between teaching and practice in the treatment of workers. The United States bishops' pastoral letter, *Economic Justice for All,*[56] took up this question (nos.

[54]See Avery Dulles, "Vatican II and the Church's Purpose," 349, for agreement, and *Catholic Social Teaching: Our Best Kept Secret,* 20, for a different view.

[55]See Terence T. Grant, "Social Justice in the 1983 Code of Canon Law: An Examination of Selected Canons," *The Jurist* 49 (1989) 112–45, for details.

[56]United States Bishops, *Economic Justice for All: Pastoral Letter on Catholic Social Teaching and the U.S. Economy* (Washington, D.C.: National Conference of Catholic Bishops, 1986).

347–58) in detail. More equitable salaries must be addressed, as well as the rights of workers to organize and the promotion of equality between women and men in wages and the availability of good jobs.

Conclusion

I have suggested that the creation of justice within the Church itself is a necessary component for the twenty-first century. Justice within ecclesial structures must go hand-in-hand with the body of social teaching that the Church celebrated in 1991. The theory is in place, beginning at least with Vatican II and written in volumes of documentation in the past twenty-five years. The emphasis for the future must be the transformation of old ways of thinking into new ways of acting.

Can canon law contribute anything to the pursuit of social justice by the Church and in the Church? There is certainly within the spirit of the law and, to a limited extent, within the content of the law, ideas which are supportive of this effort. That is to say, those who desire to build justice into the Church would find in the law some strengths which would justify their efforts. The ideas of justice and equity, the image of the Church as the people of God, the initial efforts to articulate and safeguard the rights of members, and commitment to social justice as part of the mission of the Church are present in the Code. There is not enough there to legislate or in any way force the Church to observe justice or respect the human rights that Boff and others consider violated. But these ideas are present in the Code however exhortative they may yet remain.

In the commitment to justice within the Church, the Code reflects hesitant steps toward change and inclusion. This is the greatest weakness in the limited attempt to put into practice what is preached. Over and over, commentators have to remind readers that this is just a beginning. Effective actions, new strategies, are needed to test and perfect this tentative commitment. As Boff points out, "It is not new ideas but new and different practices (supported by theory) that will modify ecclesial reality. These modifications in turn open the way for a corresponding theory, leading to a new reading of the Gospel and tradition."[57] This is the project that ought to lead us into the twenty-first century.

[57] Boff, *Charism and Power,* 44.

Chapter 10

Encyclical Social Teaching since Vatican II:
Contradiction or Coherence?

Michael J. Schuck

In a 1981 address marking the ninetieth anniversary of Pope Leo XIII's social encyclical *Rerum novarum,* John Coleman posed the following question. Given the "massive sea change" in philosophical and theological concepts effected at the Second Vatican Council, in what sense (if any) does encyclical social teaching constitute a coherent unity of thought?[1]

This is a good question. Social thought of any kind must be internally coherent to be credible. The social theories of John Rawls and Alasdair McIntyre engage us, for example, because they offer coherent arguments over which we can profitably debate. Now, on the occasion of *Rerum novarum*'s centenary observance, it would do well to ask again: do the papal encyclicals communicate a coherent social teaching?

Encyclical commentators disagree. Noting shifts in the letters' sources, methods, and conclusions over time, some conclude that papal teachings do not cohere. As one commentator insists, encyclical teaching is

> . . . an uncritical eclecticism of unrelated parts or an opportunistic syncretism of unrelated parts, artificially put together and polished in accordance with the interests of the Church as a political instrument for the power of the papacy.[2]

Others assume some sort of coherence but largely overlook the issue, focusing instead on the letters' specific topics.

From discussions directly treating and affirmatively answering the coherence question, two solutions have emerged. The first can be called the "natural law" theory of encyclical coherence. This is exemplified in Roger

[1]John A. Coleman, "Development of Church Social Teaching," *Readings in Moral Theology No. 5: Official Catholic Social Teaching,* eds. Charles E. Curran and Richard A. McCormick (New York: Paulist Press, 1986) 176.

[2]Remark of Alfred Diamant, quoted in Coleman, "Church Social Teaching," 345.

Charles' *The Social Teaching of Vatican II: Its Origin and Development* (Oxford: Plater Publications, 1982).

Citing Vatican II's *Dignitatis humanae,* Charles believes papal thought unites around the moral theory of natural law. "God's eternal law, objective and universal," writes Charles, constitutes the "ultimate and objective ethical norm" of moral life. Possessing a nature "created by God," human beings can discern eternal law through natural law. This latter law provides general moral principles which abide in and guide conscience (the "proximate and subjective ethical norm"). Humans grasp the full implications of these principles through historical experience, assisted by God's "divine positive law" (Ten Commandments, teachings of Christ, and precepts of the Roman Catholic Church). In Charles' view, all encyclicals use natural law as a base for developing further teachings specific to political, family, and economic relations in society.[3]

The second solution to the coherence question can be called the "human dignity" theory. This approach is represented in David Hollenbach's *Claims in Conflict: Retrieving and Renewing the Catholic Human Rights Tradition* (New York: Paulist Press, 1979). "The thread that ties all these [papal, conciliar, synodal] documents together," says Hollenbach, "is their common concern for the protection of the dignity of the human person." Human dignity connotes an understanding of human life as transcendental, a valuation anchored in Genesis 1:26: "Let us make man in our image and likeness." According to Hollenbach, popes since Leo XIII have articulated an expanding list of human rights as conditions for the societal protection of human dignity.[4]

Close analysis of the papal letters sustains neither the natural law nor human dignity theories of encyclical coherence. However, it would be precipitous to conclude that encyclical social teaching is thereby incoherent. This paper argues that papal thought coheres around a communitarian understanding of social ethics. This understanding is rooted in a shared—though variegated—communitarian theology of God, society, and the person. From this theology the popes have generated a cluster of persistent social recommendations and judgments reflecting a communitarian perspective. Space does not permit a complete analysis of encyclical coherence in terms of both its general theological-ethical claims and particular social recommendations and judgments. Such analysis is available elsewhere.[5] In-

---

[3]On eternal law, see Roger Charles, *The Social Teaching of Vatican II: Its Origin and Development* (Oxford: Plater Publications, 1982) 9, 12. On natural law see 86.

[4]See David Hollenbach, *Claims in Conflict: Retrieving and Renewing the Catholic Human Rights Tradition* (New York: Paulist Press, 1979) 42, 103.

[5]See Michael J. Schuck, *That They Be One: The Social Teachings of the Papal Encyclicals 1740–1989* (Washington D.C.: Georgetown University Press, 1991).

stead, this paper surveys the theological and ethical roots of encyclical communitarianism.

This overview is based on a study of all the papal letters, not just the seven or eight conventionally designated "social" encyclicals. Two factors make this approach necessary. First, reading the entire corpus reveals the broad patterns of papal theology which frame encyclical social teaching. Second, incorporating all the texts allows the seventy-seven letters written before Leo XIII to resurface—a retrieval which helps answer the question of encyclical coherence.

Three broad patterns of papal theology are evident across the 250 years of papal encyclicals writing. The first pattern occurs in the seventy-seven encyclicals written during the pontificates of Benedict XIV (1740–1758), Clement XIII (1758–1769), Clement XIV (1769–1774), Pius VI (1775–1799), Pius VII (1800–1823), Leo XII (1823–1829), Pius VIII (1829–1830), Gregory XVI (1831–1846), and Pius IX (1846–1878).[6] In this "pre-Leonine period," a literary device commonly employed to convey key themes of Christian faith is the pastoral metaphor of a shepherd and his flock. Though other images also appear, the popes' frequent use of the sheepfold metaphor gives the pre-Leonine period discussion of God, society, and the person a distinct character.

When Pius IX says in *Exultavit cor Nostrum*, 3, that "all our hopes must be placed in God alone," the typical pre-Leonine period referent is Christ the Good Shepherd. The source for this image is John 10:1-31, where an analogy is drawn between a shepherd's care for his flock and Jesus' readiness to teach and die for humanity. Correspondingly, the popes represent society as a pasture. Like a pasture, society provides nourishment and protection for the flock. But Benedict XIV warns in *Ubi primum* that pastures also contain "trackless places," "ravening wolves," and evil men "in the clothing of sheep." Society, then, must be approached very circumspectly.

The papal perspective on the person is also influenced by the sheepfold metaphor. Characteristic of pastoral literature in general, the popes value the human qualities of memory, simplicity, and obedience. Memory is considered a key medium of Christian faith. In *Cum summi*, 4–5, Clement XIV asks clergy and laity to retain the "magificent heritage" of Christ's teaching and faithfully "cling to the footsteps of our ancestors." At the same time, the popes stress the moral virtues of simplicity and obedience through frequent emphasis on the imitation of Christ and the analogy between lambs and the laity.

[6]On the beginning of the encyclical genre of papal communication, see Paul Nau, *Une Source Doctrinale: Les Encycliques* (Paris: Les éditions du Cedre, 1952) 42, n. 1, and Sean O'Riordan, "The Teaching of the Papal Social Encyclicals as a Source and Norm of Moral Theology: A Historical and Analytical Survey," *Studia Moralia* 14 (1976) 140.

A different pattern of papal theology crystallizes during the pontificates of Leo XIII (1878–1903), Pius X (1903–1914), Benedict XV (1914–1922), Pius XI (1922–1939), and Pius XII (1939–1958). Through new attention to medieval theologian-philosopher Thomas Aquinas, the 185 "Leonine period" encyclicals shift the dominant interpretive image of Christian faith from the sheepfold metaphor to the metaphor of cosmological design.

This shift is reflected in the popes' lessened emphasis on God as Good Shepherd and increased use of the metaphor of God as designer of the universe. Evident throughout the Leonine period letters, this change mirrors the new papal interest in Aquinas' theological vision of God as rational creator, sustainer, and fulfiller of all things. The recovery of Aquinas also affects the popes' attitude toward society. Confident in what Pius XI's *Quadragesimo anno*, 43, calls God's "universal teleological order," the popes drop their predecessors' reticent attitude toward society and begin exploring the "God-embedded purposes" of all social relations and institutions.

As the crown of God's created order, human beings participate in the divine "curve of destiny" by exercising the powers of reason and freedom. According to Leo XIII in *Libertas*, 5, these capacities of the "naturally Christian soul" are possessed by everyone. But sin impairs these powers, making necessary the added supernatural tenets of Christian faith and morals. These tenets aid, but do not replace, natural reason and freedom. Faith and reason, morality and freedom cannot conflict, insists Pius XI in *Rappresentanti in terra*, 28, because "both come from God, who cannot contradict Himself."

The most recent change in papal theology occurs in the twenty-two encyclicals of John XXIII (1958–1963), Paul VI (1963–1978), and John Paul II (1978–). Bolstered by theological developments at the Second Vatican Council, the "post-Leonine period" popes communicate the themes of Christian faith less through the cosmological metaphor than the metaphor of dialogical journey. Here, the image of God as fellow traveler displaces the earlier shepherd and designer metaphors. In *Ecclesiam suam*, 19, Paul VI explains how "the method employed by God in revealing himself to men," is a "two-way relationship" initiated by God "through Christ in the Holy Spirit."

The dialogical journey metaphor also encourages a distinct perspective on society. Unlike an ominous pasture or teleological structure, society is the necessary, historically changing context for God's conversational pilgrimage with humanity. The redemptive message of the Holy Spirit is "constantly carried out," says John Paul II in *Dominum et vivificantem*, 59, within the physical and social "history of the world."

Some post-Leonine period discussions of the person evidence this new sensitivity to experience and context; others show continued commitment to the Leonine period focus on universal principles derived from human reason and nature. For example, the popes fluctuate between a postconciliar notion of faith as the response of one's whole being to the experience of God's self-revelation and the earlier Leonine period approach which defines faith as an intellectual ascent to divinely revealed truths. Likewise, the basis of morality is sometimes located in an affective experience of moral value (especially the value of human solidarity). At other times it is rooted in rational comprehension of natural law and faithful attachment to God's divine positive law.

The patterns of papal theology have clearly changed over the past 250 years. The popes' pastoral, cosmological, and dialogical metaphors have produced different images of God, society, and the person. These images have helped shape distinct—and in some cases, contradictory—social teachings.[7] Yet at another level the patterns are linked. The shepherd's ingathering, the creator's unified work, the traveler's dialogic fellowship: each image expresses the divine will that humans—like God—seek, build, and sustain community life. An oft-repeated scriptural passage in the papal encyclicals is Jesus' John 17:11 prayer to the Father "that they may be one, even as we are one."

At the same time, the popes' different models of society (ominous pasture, structure of divine purposes, historical context for divine-human dialogue) mutually express the idea that God's will is mediated through society. In this characteristically Roman Catholic perspective, "there is no realm whatsoever outside the dominion of . . . God."[8] Thus, the conditions of society are always a moral and religious concern.

With regards to the human person, whether one concentrates on the human capacity to loyally retain traditions, intellectually grasp universal principles, or affectively experience solidarity, each approach accents the communal character of human existence. With this typically Roman Catholic focus on the "social constitution of human existence," the "idea of a discretely autonomous individual self all but disappears."[9]

The popes' distinct yet unified theologies shape a communitarian ethic. But like their theologies, the communitarian ethic is imaged in several different ways.

The pre-Leonine period popes construct a "territorial" communitarian ethic. It is territorial in that the popes focus exclusively on reforming social ideas and practices within Roman Catholic countries and regions. The ethic

---

[7]Some of the reversals in papal social teaching are the moral assessments of participatory democracy, Church-state relations, religious freedom, the labor movement, and Christian-Jewish relations.

[8]Monika Hellwig, *Understanding Catholicism* (New York: Paulist Press, 1981) 185.

[9]Roger Haight, *Dynamics of Theology* (New York: Paulist Press, 1990) 4.

is communitarian by virtue of the texts' descriptions of the person and society. In the pre-Leonine period letters the human self is embedded in the traditions of the community. One acquires a sense of identity and purpose by exercising one's communal functions and obligations. Society is construed as a hierarchically organized community of mutual aid where people with customarily acknowledged roles and powers work together, deferentially, for the preservation of the whole.

The Leonine period popes present a "cosmological" communitarian ethic. Here, the communal character of self and society is grounded in the universal design of nature, not the exigencies of living in a sheepfold. Human identity and purpose are still located in communal functions and obligations, but the basis of this view shifts from territorial customs to universal nature. Society is still envisioned as a hierarchically organized community of mutual service, but now justified on universal, not local, grounds.

The post-Leonine period popes offer what can be called an "affective" communitarian ethic. In this approach the communitarian self and society are founded on affective experience, not on the requirements of sheepfold survival or the universal design of nature. Still community-dependent, human identity and purpose is linked to an affective "we-feeling" and "role-feeling" which emerges from one's historical experience of human solidarity and social significance.[10] In the post-Leonine period letters, the character of society as a community of mutual aid is less a product of territorial loyalties or cosmological nature than what Roberto Unger calls the "political realization of the ideal of sympathy."[11]

On one level the popes' patterns of ethical reflection are distinct, on another level they are linked. Whether rooted in territorial custom, cosmological nature, or affective sentiment, the popes uniformly define the human person by the totality of its relations with other selves. In this, the encyclicals share a communitarian perspective on the human person unlike the Enlightenment-inspired notion of the self as a "radically unencumbered," autonomous "chooser of ends."[12] Similarly, society—whether construed territorially, cosmologically, or affectively—is a community of mutuality, a "koinonia." As such, the popes perennially decry the Enlightenment image of society as an artificial contract between autonomous individuals "undertaken for self-interested rather than fraternal reasons."[13]

[10]David B. Clark, "The Concept of Community: A Re-examination," *The Sociological Review* 21 (August 1973) 404.

[11]Roberto Mangabeira Unger, *Knowledge and Politics* (New York: The Free Press, 1975) 221.

[12]Allen E. Buchanan, "Assessing the Communitarian Critique of Liberalism," *Ethics* 99 (July 1989) 98.

[13]Raymond Plant, "Community: Concept, Conception, and Ideology," *Politics and Society* 8 (1978) 98.

From the standpoint of general theological-ethical claims, then, papal social teaching is not incoherent. Its coherence, however, lies in a shared use of neither the natural law moral theory nor the concept of human dignity. Natural law moral theory is not utilized throughout the papal encyclical literature. The pre-Leonine period letters make no appeal to this theory. The post-Leonine period letters use it, but not exclusively. Only the Leonine period letters unequivocally employ the moral theory of natural law.

Likewise, the concept of human dignity is not used throughout the encyclicals. Pre-Leonine period letters make no reference to this concept. Though Leo XIII, Pius X, and Benedict XV acknowledge the elevated status of human beings as the *imago dei,* this is not a concept around which their social teaching revolves. The incidence of the term "human dignity" increases in the letters of Pius XI and Pius XII, but it does not acquire the status of a virtually free-standing moral concept until the post-Leonine period.

Though a full investigation of encyclical coherence requires analysis of the popes' specific social recommendations and judgments, this overview indicates how papal social teaching coheres around a communitarian theology of God, society, and the person. From this theology, the popes have framed a social ethic unified around understandings of the person as "embedded" in community and society as a "mutuality of service." Recognizing that different, even contradictory, teachings have appeared over 250 years of encyclical writing does not detract from the fact that the letters cohere around a communitarian understanding of social ethics.

Introduction to Women in the Church

Women in the Church

Rosemary Broughton

"The joys and the hopes, the griefs and the sorrows of those of this age, especially those who are poor or in any way afflicted, these are the joys and hopes, the griefs and anxieties of the followers of Christ." Thus begins the document of Vatican II which explores the meaning of the Church in the Modern World, in a genre called a "pastoral constitution." For those of us who were young in 1965, these were heady words, a proclamation of and from a Church that seemed marked with new vitality. But maybe it was ourselves who were marked with vitality; those of us who were brinking on our existential moment, when—as Bernard Longergan later spoke of it—we find out for ourselves that it is up to ourselves to decide for ourselves what to make of ourselves.

Those opening words affect us yet. Yet now they are words of the heart as well, heard with the mellowness and burden of maturity, with a more sober view of the ecclesial future.

In the first article, "Women of Vatican II: Recovering a Dangerous Memory," Carmel McEnroy traces for us the experiences of the twenty-three women who were invited to the third session of the council in 1964. For both the men and women at the council, their presence gave a new, though marginal, flavor. From the vantage pont of the nineties, their narrations evoke memories of "aggiornamento" and give the post-Vatican II baptized members of the Church a factual base for further pursuit. Hopefully, this article is a foretaste of further work in this Vatican II arena by Carmel McEnroy.

Mary Ellen Sheehan continues the reflection on women in the Church in her article "North American Roman Catholic Bishops and Women's Equality in the Church: A Reflection on Post-Vatican II Developments."

She notes the fact that "Vatican II has changed irreversibly our ecclesial consciousness through its challenge to understand Church more widely, to own our own baptismal commitment and membership more profoundly, and to actualize that ownership more concretely."

The guiding question of her writing here is: how are our North American bishops exercising their self-proclaimed prophetic and teaching office concerning justice and women?

After reviewing the cultural and theological views voiced by both Canadian and United States bishops in the years since Vatican Council II, Sheehan identifies lingering issues. In the search for justice and gender equality in the Church, these issues focus on the fruitful use of social analysis, the living relationship between democratic values and hierarchical structures, the search for an adequate ecclesial concept of personal gender relationships, the sign value and signifying potential of women, and the consonance of episcopal practice with proclamation.

In this last decade of the century, it is hard to escape the questions of the "pastoral constitution" of the Roman Catholic Church. Time has changed our horizons; birth and death have weaved themselves into our expectations.

Like the Cross of Jesus, the life of women in the Church is the source, for many of us, of our sorrows and griefs. In the transparency of the Cross, the grace given in the life of women is the wellspring as well of our hope and of joy.

Chapter 11

Women of Vatican II:
Recovering a Dangerous Memory

Carmel McEnroy, R.S.M.

What's so exciting or daring about inviting twenty-three women as silent spectators to a gathering of some three thousand men? Nothing really—until one specifies that the event is an ecumenical council of the Roman Catholic Church, and that never before in its history have women been present at one of its councils, although they have always constituted more than half of humanity and of Church membership.

It was sensational news in 1964 when fifteen women appeared at the third session of Vatican II (this was later expanded to twenty-three before the end of the fourth session in 1965), but their presence has been conveniently minimized, trivialized, or omitted from most conciliar scholarship.

Twenty five years later, when there is a tendency in hierarchical circles to retreat from the frontiers opened up at the council and to ignore the demands of women for more active participation in their Church, it is well to recall Paul VI's courageous action and to recover this dangerous, subversive memory. For it is not well known, even among renowned feminist scholars, that there were *any women* present at the council.

Paul VI dared to break an ancient taboo by inviting a small but significant group of women auditors to the council as a symbolic presence, despite curial opposition. In fact, the Pope was disappointed when no women were on the first list of lay auditors a year earlier.

Carmelite Donal Lamont, an Irish bishop in Rhodesia at the time, told me that "it would be an egregious error to think that bishops came to the council determined to keep women out. We were all formed in the straightjacket mentality of Vatican I," he said. "With no previous experience of women's involvement in Church structures, it never occurred to us that they should be there. However, under the guidance of the Spirit, a new awakening took place—like spring coming to the Arctic, thawing the barque of Peter out of its ice-locked moorings. Many of us welcomed new possibilities and exclaimed, 'thank God our time is now.' Women's coming was part of these 'signs of the times.' " I might add that the women themselves did not expect to be there either, and they welcomed the invitation as a great privilege and responsibility.

As we celebrate the twenty-fifth anniversary of the council's closing, I wish to bring to light some memories of the most prominent of the first Council Mothers in history. My findings are based on personal conversations and exchange of letters and phone calls with several of the auditors or with people who knew those now deceased, as well as written sources by and about them. Let me highlight a few points through three questions: (1) Who were the women and why were they invited? (2) How did they experience the council? (3) What difference did their presence make?

I. Who were they and why were they invited?

The twenty-three officially invited female auditors came from fourteen different countries. Thirteen were laywomen, and ten belonged to religious communities. They were women known to bishops and recommended by them because of their high national or international profile. The auditors admit that they were not at the cutting edge in terms of feminist issues, such as advocating women's ordination, which was first raised by the Swiss lawyer, Dr. Gertrud Heinzelmann, and other members of St. Joan's Alliance before the council in 1962.

Three auditors were from the United States: Mary Luke Tobin, Catherine McCarthy, and Claudia Feddish. Mary Luke Tobin was Superior General of the Sisters of Loretto from Nerinx, Kentucky, and the newly elected president of the Conference of Major Superiors of Women Religious. Tobin was halfway across the Atlantic on her way to Rome, "just to see what was happening," she says, when she received a shipboard call from a *New York Times* reporter asking how she felt about being invited as an auditor. That was the first she heard of it. Catherine McCarthy of San Francisco (originally a Bostonian) was invited in her capacity as president of the National Council of Catholic Women. Claudia Feddish of Uniontown, Pennsylvania, Superior General of the Basilian Sisters of Saint Macrina, belonged to the Byzantine rite, an order with Sisters behind the Iron Curtain.

Spanish Pilar Bellosillo was president of the World Union of Catholic Women's Organizations (WUCWO), representing about thirty-six million women. Her hairdresser was the first to tell her of her appointment—he had read it in the morning paper!

Australian Rosemary Goldie was executive secretary of COPECIAL (The Permanent Committee for International Congresses of the Lay Apostolate) and had worked within Vatican City since 1958. Paul VI, the former Cardinal Montini, knew her from her work on the laity and referred to her in an audience as "our co-worker." Goldie says, "I was there. It would have been hard not to invite me."

French Marie Louise Monnet was also known to Paul VI as the founder of MIAMSI (International Movement for the Apostolate in the Independent Milieux). She was the very first woman to enter the council on September 21, 1964—even ahead of the president of WUCWO. Her friends tell an amusing story about how that came about. Paul VI greeted Monnet in an audience given to MIAMSI. She thanked the Pope for his willingness to invite her as an auditor. She knew that several French bishops had nominated her, although no official list was yet published. What could the Pope do but let MIAMSI in on a secret—its president was indeed on his list. Next day Monnet made her grand entry to St. Peter's. Archbishop Hurley of Durban publicly acknowledged her presence: "Flowers have at last bloomed in our land!"

French Suzanne Guillemin, superior general of the Daughters of Charity of St. Vincent de Paul, internationally based in five continents, was an obvious choice for an auditor. She was already pioneering in the Sister Formation Movement and led the Daughters of Charity in the revolutionary act of modifying their habit in September 1964, replacing the familiar coronet with a simple blue veil—an action that merited comment even from the French Prime Minister, Charles de Gaulle: "Changing the coronet of the *filles de la Charité?* Well, one might as well propose changing the French flag!"

Italian Constantina Baldinucci was superior general of the Sisters of Maria Bambina (the Child Mary) and president of the Italian Sisters' Union. She was well known to Cardinal Montini in Milan. When Paul VI was elected, he cabled Baldinucci saying he would remain the congregation's cardinal protector and asking that four Sisters come to take care of his Vatican apartment.

French Sabine De Valon, superior general of the Religious of the Sacred Heart, was known in the Sacred Congregation for Religious. She hailed women's role in the council as "moving from the waiting room into the living room." Italian Alda Miceli represented Secular Institutes, a new phenomenon for many bishops at the time.

Mexican Luz Marie Alvarez-Icaza and her husband were the only married couple invited as such. They had founded the Christian Family Movement, were parents of twelve children (later expanded to fourteen), and had done international research on the family in thirty-six countries prior to Vatican II.

Two Italian war widows, Ida Grillo and Amalia De Montezemolo, were invited as an eloquent symbolic condemnation of war and the hope for lasting peace. Other women came from Lebanon, Egypt, Ukraine, Uruguay,

Argentina, Germany, Holland, and Czechoslovakia. The international selection gave public recognition to the phenomenal involvement of women on a world scale in activities now recognized as the Church's mission.

II. How did they experience the council?

The women were romanticized, ignored, trivialized, and finally taken seriously for their worthwhile contribution as *periti* in their own right, "experts in life," as Paul VI called them. They were initially invited to "sessions of interest to women." Since they could not imagine what might not be of interest to them, they were determined to miss out on nothing.

Many bishops stopped by the tribune of St. Andrew to the right of the main altar to greet them, either out of genuine interest or sheer curiosity. Half jokingly, a bearded archbishop exclaimed that hitherto the one place he felt safe was in the hallowed male enclave of St. Peter's, but now the women invaded even that. Pilar Bellosillo recalls an elderly bishop covering his eyes each time the women passed by on the way to receive Communion at the daily conciliar Mass.

Mary Luke Tobin recalls her first day at the council. Martin Work led her to the coffee bar and introduced her to several bishops. Next day a separate bar was set up for the auditors. They called it "Bar-NONE" to distinguish it from the episcopal "Bar-Jonah" and "Bar-abbas." Apparently, some bishops found it too close for comfort to be rubbing shoulders with women over coffee. This segregation, while not fully observed, was regrettable because it narrowed the women's opportunities for communicating their ideas. Often what was spoken at the coffee bar got voiced in the aula. Paul VI said the women were to be "auditores" (listeners) in the aula but "locutores" (speakers) everywhere else.

What was it like being an auditor at the council? Pilar Bellosillo remembers: "There was so much light. I often lay awake at night trying to process it all." She remembers the utter shock and pain of bishops from her native Spain during discussions on Religious Liberty. "These were the days of Franco's dictatorship," she says, "and the consequences of a Declaration on Religious Freedom were traumatizing to insular-minded Catholics."

When asked for a spontaneous image of Vatican II, Rosemary Goldie replies: "A tidal wave or a great mountain coming over me; it was exhilarating!" Goldie was already living at international level for several years. She was directly involved, though unofficially, in conciliar preparations. "We were much better prepared than most bishops," she says. "We had a sense of the world-church."

Alda Miceli describes her experience as "a prolonged retreat, but much deeper and more long lasting. It marked me for life." Several women highlight the ecumenical exchange, especially the frequent lunches with the Brothers of Taizé, where topics raised in the aula were picked up and continued. There was also the first official women's ecumenical meeting at Vicarello in October 1965. It brought together about thirty Protestant, Orthodox, Anglican, and Roman Catholic women from fourteen countries—sisters, deaconesses, theologians, leaders of lay organizations, and auditors from the council. Among them were two future presidents of the World Council of Churches—American Dr. Cynthia Wedel and Swiss Dr. Marga Buhrig. They made joint recommendations about women's inclusion in ministry. Most importantly, women of different religious denominations got together and talked. Age-old barriers came down. New and lasting bridges were built.

Collaboration was a new experience for most of the women—collaboration on an ecumenical level, between laity and bishops, between laity and religious, and even among religious communities. They imbibed the spirit and inductive method of the conciliar commissions and brought them back to their respective organizations. "Bishops were consulting the laity about situations in their lives about which there was as yet no official teaching," says Pilar Bellosillo. "That was new and exciting. We experienced for the first time that *we were the Church.*"

Women discovered each other and their common concerns. The foundation for a worldwide, ecumenical women's movement was laid. They began to join hands across the world, to weave a web of solidarity that will eventually entangle oppressive and destructive powers.

Before passing on to the actual involvement of the female auditors at the council, I want to include remarks from Canadian journalist Bonnie Brennan. They capture some of the same general attitudes exhibited toward the conciliar women. Bonnie Brennan and a layman, Bernard Daly, were there as part of the bishops' staff entrusted with the task of informing Canadian Catholics about the council through the radio and press. Brennan was there only for the third and fourth sessions, 1964 and 1965.

Guest passes to the working sessions were available to bishops for important guests and were usually issued to visiting priests. During the fourth session, Daly asked the bishops if they could get him a visitor's pass. About twelve Canadian bishops sent a request to Cardinal Felice's office, requesting two passes—one for Mr. Bernard Daly and the other for Miss Bonnie Brennan. The passes were issued for a week or two to "Reverendissimo Sacerdotal Bernard Daly and Reverendissimo Sacerdotal Bonnie Brennan, i.e., Father Bernard Daly and Father Bonnie Brennan."

They both entered the aula next Monday morning and sat with the lay auditors. On the second morning, the guard at the tribunal challenged Brennan's pass. One of the Canadian bishops argued with him and insisted on sending back the two passes so that Cardinal Felice could clear up the matter. Brennan and Daly were given seats in the special guests' area until coffee break. Archbishop Krol then told them they could stay for the rest of the morning, but their passes had been revoked because no journalists were permitted to attend the sessions.

Brennan explains how the press focused on the "novelty" factor of a woman having been issued a pass as "Father" and then having been asked to leave. False stories began to grow and spread. Some said she was disguised as a priest—wore a cassock; another said she had hidden in the church overnight. Brennan demythologizes the incident and explains that *both* passes were revoked because both were *journalists*.

Brennan says that as a woman journalist, she didn't feel treated any better or worse than male journalists by bishops, *periti,* or Vatican clerics. In fact, she found much less male chauvinism among the clergy than among the male population of Rome or the press corps. She found some "paternalism" among the clergy, but then she was twenty-nine and thirty years of age at the time and far from home. She appreciated the kindness and fatherliness shown to her. It's only looking back from the 1980s that she began to see it as a form of paternalism. She reminded me of the importance of being realistic about the time period of the 1960s and not to judge it by 1990s measuring tapes.

III. What difference did the women make?

Their most direct involvement in shaping future Church teaching took place in the commissions and subcommissions that wrote the documents. Their inclusion on such commissions was determined by the prefects, which accounts for their glaring absence from the commission for *Perfectae Caritatis* (on Religious Life). Bernard Häring recounts Cardinal Antoniutti's historical remark: "You may try again at the fourth Vatican Council."

Thanks to Cardinal Prefect Emilio Guano and Coordinating Secretary Bernard Häring, women played a significant role as full voting members in the mixed commission for *Gaudium et spes* (The Church in the Modern World). Excerpts from Häring's letter to me in 1988 give firsthand behind-the-scenes information. Cardinal Bea had asked for further representation from Eastern European and Third World countries, so the numbers were increased. Häring recounts his conversation with Guano. H: "This step, important as it is, does not change much, since fifty-five percent of world Catholics have no representation whatever." G: "What do you mean?" H: "The world of women. I think we should get them into our commission if they have no place even in the commission for the religious, although they are approximately eighty percent of the religious." G: "Whom would you like to invite?" Looking at the prepared list headed by Rosemary Goldie, Guano approved, adding a few more names.

Häring invited Goldie, Tobin, Bellosillo, Guillemin, Monnet, and Vendrik to the two-week working session on Schema 13 at Ariccia (January 21–February 6, 1965), and they all came. Proud of his achievement, he explains:

> Maybe not even Guano knew what had entitled me to invite these gracious ladies. Cardinal Ottaviani—considered almost blind—saw them of course. He made no trouble. He did not inquire how it came to this surprising presence, and nobody had the courage to tell them they should not be there. So, in a very relaxed atmosphere, they participated just as the men did, talked frankly, and were listened to. This in the doctrinal, mixed commission for the major document *Gaudium et spes,* was something quite different from being "auditrices," listening women. The ladies in the commission made excellent contributions in preparing the text and in understanding a little bit better the world today.

Other women participated in the ten subcommissions that reworked the text when it was being discussed in the aula during the last session. All the other documents were, as Canadian Bishop Alexander Carter of Sault Ste. Marie said, "conceived in the original sin of clericalism," although women and laymen gave input on some later drafts. One of the changes the women effected in *Apostolicam Actuositatem* (on the Lay Apostolate) was to get rid of the separate roles of women and men specified in the first draft. Their rationale was that since all women in the Roman Catholic Church are lay, whatever applies to laity applies equally to women and men. The fact that there are so few specific references to women in the conciliar documents was deliberate and significant on the part of the auditors. The essential foundations were laid in terms of the basic equality of all in Christ Jesus (Gal 3:28, cited in LG 32), the creation of humankind as man and woman in God's image (GS 12), plus a clear condemnation of any discrimination in the fundamental rights of persons by reason of sex, race, etc. (GS 29, LG 32).

This formed the basis for Goldie's response to French Archbishop Claude Dupuy's question, "Should the council speak about women?" After consultation with Pilar Bellosillo and the other women, Goldie replied with three points: (1) Since society is made up of men and women, the importance of this for the Church's mission in the world today must be recognized. (2) Some aspects concerning women more directly should be addressed but as part of the larger human concerns and never as separate problems. (3) All rigid limitations or speaking of women poetically and therefore unrealistically (comparing them to flowers, etc.) should be avoided.

Presumably, the female auditors were on a par with their male counterparts, but old prejudices prevailed when it came to speaking in the aula. Laymen spoke on six different occasions in St. Peter's, while women were denied this equal opportunity, despite two petitions to the pope from the joint group of auditors. They were told that it was considered premature for a woman's voice to be heard in St. Peter's. Alda Miceli quips that it was not until the 1971 synod that the bishops were sufficiently mature to hear women speak.

Needless to say, the ambiguity of woman's place was not resolved by the council's end. This was clearly manifested in the closing ceremony on December 8, 1965, when women were singled out as a separate category to which a special message was addressed, side by side with rulers, intellectuals, scientists, artists, the poor, sick and suffering, workers, and youth. The women would have preferred a symbolic inclusion in all the other categories.

The council Fathers' well-intentioned gesture demonstrated their own confusion between idealizing women, thereby perpetuating the burden of pedestalism, and acknowledging the equality which the women sought so hard to establish. The gesture mixed romanticism and prophetic challenge. The message made women the custodians of peace and virtue in the world, while giving them ammunition for their own liberation. They were told that "the Church is proud to have glorified and liberated woman . . . to have brought into relief her basic equality with man. But the hour is coming, in fact has come, when the vocation of woman is being achieved in its fullness, the hour in which woman acquires in the world an influence, an effect, and a power never hitherto achieved." This is ecclesial dynamite, now forgotten. We need to retrieve it, regardless of the dangerous consequences in challenging the hierarchical Church to implement its own teaching.

IV. Conclusion

The presence of twenty-three officially invited female auditors at Vatican II was a modest beginning twenty-six years ago. Paul VI's symbolic gesture recognized that women can no longer be left out of the decision-making body of the Roman Catholic Church. The women took to heart the papal mandate to bring the world to the council and the council to the world. They were proud of their bishops and Pope and supported them in implementing their response to the "signs of the times."

It is high time now, on the threshold of the third millennium, to revisit Vatican II and then to move forward, carrying the conciliar torch to its logical conclusion—the complete elimination of *all* discrimination in the

Church and the renovation and integration of Peter's barque from stem to stern. Then the Church, as a prophetic example of the equality of all in Christ Jesus, can more credibly critique society.

Chapter 12

Roman Catholic Bishops on Women's Equality:
Some Post-Vatican II Developments

Mary Ellen Sheehan, I.H.M.

One of the extraordinary features of the Second Vatican Council is the strength with which it reinstated the Church's commitment to establishing justice in our times as a striking sign of God's realm among us. One of the extraordinary features of our recent cultural experience is the strength with which the movement for establishing women's equality has emerged world wide. Roman Catholic reflection, deeply affected by both movements, is undergoing currently a renewal that is pushing at all the known boundaries of theology and pastoral practice.[1] In this development it is important to note that many North American bishops have also engaged in the interface of Vatican II justice concerns and the women's movement as can be seen in statements and pastoral letters they have published over the last two decades.

This article focuses on some of these episcopal writings asking the questions: How are the bishops exercising their prophetic and teaching office concerning justice and women? Are there any signs in their proclamations of transformational theology and practice which establish *in fact* the equality of women? The study centers on the bishops, not because they are solely

---

[1]See, for example, the following works and their bibliographies: James Coriden, ed., *Sexism and Church Law: Equal Rights and Affirmative Action* (New York: Paulist Press, 1977); Elisabeth Schüssler Fiorenza, *Bread not Stone* (Boston: Beacon Press, 1984); Mary Jo Weaver, *New Catholic Women: A Contemporary Challenge to Traditional Religious Authority* (New York: Harper and Row, 1985); Joanne Wolski Conn, ed., *Women's Spirituality: Resources for Christian Development* (New York: Paulist Press, 1986); the essays in *Horizons* 14 (Fall 1987); Rosemary Radford Ruether, "Christian Quest for Redemptive Community," *Cross Currents* 27 (Spring 1988) 3–16; Anne E. Carr, *Transforming Grace: Christian Tradition and Women's Experience* (San Francisco: Harper and Row, 1988).

responsible for the transformational imperative of Vatican II and not because they can speak authentically about women's experience of injustice, but because of a theologically based pragmatic realism. The theology of episcopal office, including its notion of jurisdictional power, makes bishops powerful brokers of Vatican II's conversion agenda. By definition, they *have* to be involved in the praxis goals of the council and thus must engage actively the question of women's equality.

A complete analysis of all the bishops' statements cannot be offered here. Looking at some statements from both the Canadian and United States bishops, however, can provide some insight into whether or not the bishops' reflections hold any promise for widening the basis of theological reasoning and practice regarding our Church's tradition on women. As well, attention to such texts can identify some of the tensive areas between emerging feminist thought and the bishops' current theological reflection.

I. The General Character of Recent Episcopal Statements on Women

Since 1971, Canadian bishops have issued about fourteen public statements on women and United States bishops have published over twenty. The statements include interventions at Roman synods, pastoral letters in local dioceses, reports of national level committees on Women in Church and Society, conferences, public addresses, and media interviews. As well, using a consultative process similar to the one employed in developing two other recent national pastoral letters on Peace and on the Economy, the United States bishops are currently involved in developing a national level pastoral letter.

The first draft of this proposed letter, *Partners in the Mystery of Redemption: A Pastoral Response to Women's Concerns for Church and Society,* received considerable evaluation after its publication in 1988.[2] The second draft, *One in Christ Jesus: A Pastoral Response to the Concerns of Women for Church and Society,* in circulation since April 1990, was tabled by the bishops in November 1990, due to a high level of dissatisfaction arising in various quarters and for various reasons.[3] It remains to be seen whether or not the bishops' commitment to develop this pastoral letter will be successful.

---

[2]See, for example, "Comments on the First Draft of the NCCB Pastoral Letter: Partners in the Mystery of Redemption," issued by *The Center of Concern* (Washington, D.C.: June 1988).

[3]Besides various reactions from groups in the United States, the bishops received a warning from authorities in Rome not to publish the Letter. As well, they were divided themselves on the merits of the second draft. See, for example, Archbishop Rembert G. Weakland, "Herald of Hope: A Pastoral on Women," *The Catholic Herald of Milwaukee* (May 10, 1990).

II. Some Recent Statements by Canadian Bishops

For the Canadian bishops it is important to start with the intervention of George Cardinal Flahiff of Winnipeg at the 1971 Synod in Rome. In preparation for the Synod with its twofold theme of the *Ministerial Priesthood* and *Justice in the World,* the bishops dialogued with women on recommendations formulated from women's groups in the Archdiocese of Edmonton. Among other requests, the women asked that all discrimination against women be removed from Canon Law, that women be given equal rights in the Church, that women be admitted to ordination, that the clergy be taught to respect the inherent dignity of women in all domains, and that there be greater solidarity with women working outside the home, especially those suffering injustice.[4] During their plenary assembly in 1971, the bishops agreed to raise the issue of women in the Church and society at the Synod in Rome.

Representing the bishops, Cardinal Flahiff addressed the synod assembly briefly and unambiguously. He stated that the Church must reexamine the scriptural and historical arguments preventing the admission of women to public ministry. As well, the Church must eliminate all passages in the Code of Canon Law that reflect the position of the natural inferiority of women to men. He noted Vatican II's "categorical statements against all discrimination against women in the Church" and the fact that many find "that no notable effort has been made to implement this teaching. . . ."[5] Toward changing this situation, he posed two questions:

> Given the growing recognition both in law and in fact of the equality of women with men and the recognition likewise of the injustice of all discrimination against women, should we raise or should we not raise the question whether women too are to have a place in the sacred ministries of the Church as they exist or as they are developing? With the emergence of new forms of ministries, under the direction of the Holy Spirit, to serve a society that is developing so rapidly, can we foresee or at least allow for ministries for women that are even better adapted than the traditional ones to their nature, their gifts, their competence both in the society and in the church of the modern world of which *Gaudium et spes* spoke so eloquently?[6]

[4]As reported by Bishop Remi J. De Roo in "Women in the Church: Challenge for the Future," a public address given in Washington, D.C., October 12, 1986. Available on tape from Time Consultants, Washington, D.C.

[5]George Cardinal Flahiff, "Address to the Synod of Bishops in Rome," October 14, 1980, *Origins* 10 (1980–1981) 295.

[6]Ibid., 296.

As a practical step, he urged the immediate establishment of a gender-mixed Papal Commission to study the question of the ministries of women in the Church, observing that

> despite a centuries old social tradition against a ministry of women in the church, we are convinced that the signs of the times (and one of those signs is that already many women perform many pastoral services and with great success) strongly urge a study at least both of the present situation and of the possibilities for the future.[7]

Flahiff believed that unless such a study was begun at once, the bishops could indeed find themselves "behind the course of events."[8]

The Canadian bishops continued their proclamation on equality for women at the 1980 Roman Synod on the Family. Bishop Robert Lebel of Valleyfield, Quebec, told the Synod assembly that it is

> out of fidelity to the Word of God that the church ought to recognize as positive the modern feminist movement. It is a question, as a whole, of progress within civilization and it is one more step in the coming of the kingdom.[9]

Lebel warned that the Church, rather than lagging behind, should be boldly prophetic in word and action in promoting women's liberation. The situation of the oppression of women, both in society and in the Church, is a sinful one that must be denounced and corrected. Lebel pointed out as unreasonable and sexist, for instance, the current practice of prohibiting females from altar service. Bishops, he cautioned, should spare themselves the embarrassment of having to defend such unreasonable regulations. But it is not enough to condemn sexism. Women must become co-responsible for the broader pastoral activities of the Church, including participation in planning and decision-making.[10] Bishops are called not to obscure the Word of God by reticence but rather to proclaim it by welcoming the ministry of women as an opportunity for the Church.[11]

The 1983 Roman Synod on Reconciliation became the occasion for the Canadian bishops to express themselves even more strongly on the question of women in the Church. In his intervention, Archbishop Louis-Albert

[7]Ibid.

[8]Ibid.

[9]Bishop Robert Lebel, "Address to the Synod of Bishops in Rome," October 14, 1980, *Origins* 10 (1980–1981) 302.

[10]This point was no doubt influenced by the results of a survey conducted by the Canadian Catholic Conference in 1978 on women in Church positions. For some results of this study, see *Origins* 8 (1978–1979) 714–15, margin notes.

[11]Lebel, "Address to the Synod of Bishops in Rome," 302.

Vachon of Quebec City recalled that the Church has indeed been prophetic in its recent teachings on justice. He warned, however, that

> these appeals of the church to the world for the advancement of the status of women are on the point of losing all impact unless the recognition of women as full menbers becomes simultaneously a reality within the church itself.[12]

Reconciliation promotes a new humanity in Christ. It is a path toward realizing "an egalitarian partnership between men and women for the coming of the Kingdom and the growth of humanity."[13]

Vachon made two further points. First, he insisted on the necessity for men and women to listen to each other deeply and openly in order to grasp the reality and pervasiveness of sexism in society and the Church. In particular, he asked his brother bishops of the universal Church "to recognize the ravages of sexism and our own male appropriation of church institutions and numerous aspects of the christian life [including language]" and to overcome archaic but still operative negative conceptions of women which prevent genuine relationships of equality. Second, he called all to be opened anew to the Spirit of God for individual and collective conversion so that we can "discover what we must change in order to bring about the recognition of women as having the same full membership status as men."[14]

As a practical step, Vachon advocated "organized structures for dialogue" at all levels of Church life to implement "new bonds of equality between men and women in the church."[15] Flahiff's 1971 recommendation for a Vatican level commission was thus broadened to embrace every area and level of Church life in order to produce concrete results in favor of establishing women's equality.

In 1984 Bishop Bernard Hubert of Saint-Jean-Longueuil issued a diocesan pastoral letter, *Une Complémentarité Réciproque*, where he insisted that no one, and especially not priests, can be indifferent to the question of women in the Church and society. Even at the risk of conflict, the issue "must be brought to the forefront of the Christian community."[16] Pastors are crucial in this process and Hubert warns them neither to trivialize nor to be neutral. Instead they must proclaim and teach actively the social and

---

[12]Archbishop Louis-Albert Vachon, "Address to the Synod of Bishops in Rome," October 3, 1983, *Origins* 13 (1983–1984) 335.

[13]Ibid.

[14]Ibid.

[15]Ibid.

[16]Bishop Bernard Hubert, "Complementing One Another: A Pastoral Letter on the Status of Women to the People of the Diocese of Saint-Jean-Longueuil," December 7, 1984. English translation by Alexander Farrell and Antoinette Kinlough.

theological foundations for change regarding the status of women in the Church and society.

Hubert legitimates the centrality of the question of women theologically. The struggle to eliminate the sin of sexism is a moral imperative. Jesus laid claim to the equality of each person as made in God's own image. There is no relation of inequality, no servitude, no domination, no exploitation in the Trinity. The full equality of women and men made real concretely is *required* as the sign of God's own life among us. The renewed ecclesiology of Vatican II stresses fundamental equality as a characteristic of the assembly of believers. Differences of gifts and functions are not meant to lead to a structure of superiority of one function over another.

In this context, Hubert says that the issue of women's ordination is not immediately solvable, resting as it does on further theological reflection and universal Church recognition. But he also asserts that

> the more women transmit their experiences of life to the Christian community and share it with the members of the Church as a whole, the more the teaching of the magisterium will be enriched by that which constitutes the contemporary experience of faith.[17]

Thus, while acknowledging current teaching which excludes women from ordained ministry, Hubert clearly signals pastoral practice as a source for challenging that teaching.

Acknowledging the conflict and ambiguity inherent in the process toward genuine mutuality in the Church, Hubert proclaims a comprehensive ecclesiology that includes struggle. Human struggle is not exempt from "the sin which feeds injustice and exploitation," but neither "is it without the grace to further the Kingdom. . . . " Vatican II has called the whole people of God to unceasing renewal. "Fortunately," Hubert recalls, " . . . the Church has all the freedom it needs to call itself into question again and again. Through all the changes of this world, it seeks and finds its Savior."[18]

In 1986 Bishop Remi De Roo of Victoria addressed a conference on *Women in the Church* in which he argued from a theological and pastoral view of Vatican II similar to that of Bishop Hubert.[19] But he made two additional points worth highlighting here, namely, the need for in depth social analysis of sexism and the need to invoke a renewed pneumatology in favor of realizing the equality of women in the Church today. The value-laden, historically conditioned assumptions of a patriarchal Church, a du-

---

[17]Ibid.
[18]Ibid.
[19]De Roo, "Women in the Church: Challenge for the Future."

alistic anthropology, a dichotomized private and public ethics, and reductionistic thinking need to be exposed by in depth social analysis if the blocks to theological and pastoral reconstruction are to be removed. De Roo acknowledged his indebtedness to contemporary feminist scholars, particularly Elisabeth Schüssler Fiorenza and Rosemary Radford Ruether, for this critical awareness and further asserted that the feminist movement represents the ultimate challenge in contemporary thought by its exposure of the domination and misuse of power inherent in the patriarchal model of social and ecclesial organization.

Like Hubert, De Roo sees the need to construct an alternate worldview by recovery of the broader theological tradition to undergird the discipleship of equals. He emphasizes the creative presence of the Holy Spirit of God. Real assent to the Holy Spirit, De Roo asserts, would be a humbling but revitalizing experience for the Church, one that would indeed lead to the elimination of gender as an attribute for determining fitness for public ministry. De Roo observes that despite official limitations to the exercise of ministry by women in the Church, the trend toward more and more participation of women in Church processes and ministries continues. In challenge to the current practice of excluding women from ordination, De Roo asks: Is not the Church's credibility being irreparably harmed? Are not ecumenical initiatives being adversely affected? Is not true justice being blocked? In fact, may it not be a time for the entire Church to experience and to test the possible call from the Spirit to women for ordination?

De Roo appears to be more open and exploratory than closed and decided, more oriented toward the future than toward the past, and more confident than not in the presence and gifts of the Holy Spirit in the whole Church. But he recalled that in the present we are a long way from a genuine converted consciousness on women's full equality. He asks for bridge-building and for concrete commitment to struggle for the large-scale cultural reversals implied in the demise of patriarchy and the establishment of the full equality of women in the Church and society.

At the 1987 Roman Synod on the Laity, Archbishop James M. Hayes of Halifax noted the urgency of the theme.

> We must work together as God's people—laity and clergy together—along with the members of other Christian churches and communions and in cooperation with all persons who are striving to build a better world. God calls us to have done with violence, injustice and discrimination, and to weed them out of the field of human history. We must endeavor together to respond to the life-threatening questions of our time: the search for peace, the awesome potential of biogenetics, the massive suffering imposed on the poor by international debt and the displacement of people, the challenge of a secular culture, etc., . . . lay Christians are also necessary to assure the authenticity

and vitality of the church's witness—to struggle against the forces of division, injustice and exclusion within the church.[20]

Making a concrete proposal to this end, Hayes asked for the accredited admission of laity, religious, and clergy to all future Synods.

Even more far-reaching was Hayes' request to move toward a comprehensive "synodal process," a proposal advanced by the Canadian Bishops at the Extraordinary Synod on Vatican II in 1985.[21] If indeed the Church is *communio,* then there is the need for constant dialogue among the members, even when there are difficulties, for "where real consultation and participation occur the Holy Spirit leads us through a kind of conversion"[22] that renews the dynamism and direction of the Church's mission.

At the same Synod Archbishop Jean-Guy Hamelin of Rouyn-Noranda, Quebec, struck a chord of urgency regarding women, stating that the very credibility of the Church as witness is at stake if the equality of women is not established in representation and decision-making, in access to pastoral responsibilities, and in the removal of all institutionalized inequality in canon law. The issue of ordaining women must be pursued, he said, particularly since "the reasoning used so far to explain the reservation of sacred orders to men has not seemed convincing, especially not to young people."[23]

In prophetic sounding words, Hamelin warned his fellow bishops to be challenged deeply by feminist developments and to adjust in mind-set, language, and practice. The women's movement, he emphasized, "is not a passing fad. . . . " The establishment in fact of the full equality of women in the Church "is essential to the sign value of the church as sacrament and to the witness which the church is commanded to bear."[24] While claiming that discernment is needed in the women's movement, Hamelin nevertheless recalled that it was identified as "a sign of the times" by Pope John XXIII.

This theme of the women's movement as serious and as "a sign of the times" is expressed in the Canadian bishops' 1989 pastoral message on implementing inclusive language in the daily life of the Church.[25] The bishops

[20]Archbishop James M. Hayes, "Address to the Synod of Bishops," October 9, 1987, *Origins* 17 (1987–1988) 343.

[21]On the Synod proposal, see "Witness of Hope and Truth: Synodal Orientations," the Intervention of Bishop Bernard Hubert, November 26, 1985, in *Twenty Years Later* (Ottawa: Canadian Conference of Catholic Bishops, 1986).

[22]Hayes, "Address to the Synod of Bishops," 344.

[23]Bishop Jean-Guy Hamelin, "Address to the Synod of Bishops," October 9, 1987, *Origins* 17 (1987–1988) 347.

[24]Ibid.

[25]Pastoral Team of the Canadian Conference of Catholic Bishops, "To Speak as a Christian Community," *Origins* 19 (1989) 257–60.

call for two levels of implementing inclusive language. The first is long-term, the collaborative work of scholars to transform biblical and liturgical texts. The second is immediate, actions to be taken now in the home, at social gatherings, in work places; in parish bulletins, liturgy and preaching; and in their own episcopal communications.

The bishops teach that the use of inclusive language is related integrally to the Church's own ministry of reconciliation, one which calls for redressing the wrongs of history against women. If language has been a cause of the exclusion and suppression of women, it can equally be an instrument of correction on the way toward establishing the fundamental equality, dignity, and inclusion of women in fact. In no sense can language be taken as neutral or innocent, even if many still believe it to be so.

Also in 1989, resulting from an extensive consultative process with over twenty women scholars, practitioners, and educators, the Quebec Bishops' Assembly published a challenging statement on violence against women.[26] The statement provides a clear and disturbing reflection on the extent of verbal, physical, psychological, sexual, and conjugal violence against women and its heretofore legitimization in theological as well as social theory. It was written to sensitize priests, agencies, and pastoral workers to the issue; to present a social and theological analysis of its depth causes; and to identify immediate action to be undertaken in the Church. What is at stake here, the authors proclaim, is the very reality of our commitment to the liberating mission of Jesus Christ.

III. Some Recent Statements by the United States Bishops

Over the same stretch of time, the United States bishops have also issued statements on women in the Church and society. Besides work by the National Conference of Catholic Bishops,[27] there have been over twelve diocesan pastoral letters. While there are differences between the Canadian

---

[26]"Violence en Héritage: Réflexion pastorale sur la violence conjugale." (Montreal: Comité des affaires sociales de l'assemblée des évêques du Quebec, 1989). English translation available.

[27]Since 1972, the National Conference of Catholic Bishops has had several special committees on women's issues. For some idea of this history, see the following NCCB reports: "Theological Reflections on the Ordination of Women," *Origins* 2 (1972–1973) 437–38, 443; "Dialogue on Women in the Church: Interim Report," *Origins* 11 (1981–1982) 82–91; "Dialogue on Women in the Church: Second Report," *Origins* 12 (1982–1983) 1–9; "Toward an Expanded Dialogue with Women: Report of Bishop Michael McAuliffe," *Origins* 12 (1982–1983) 422–24. McAuliffe's report led to the establishment of the current NCCB Committee charged with developing the national level pastoral letter referred to earlier in this paper.

and United States bishops' statements,[28] there are also some parallel theological and pastoral reflections, as a consideration of some of them will show.

In a 1980 pastoral letter, Archbishop Raymond Hunthausen of Seattle set forth both theological and pastoral reflections for overcoming discrimination against women based on gender. Change will occur, he teaches, when we realize that salvation is liberative and for all on equal terms, when we see that the maleness of Jesus is not the primary significance of the incarnation, and when we accept that we must continually seek and live in a Church that is whole, just, and moving toward full incarnation of God's love. Hunthausen urged the implementation of some nine actions in his diocese, including the elimination of sexist language and imagery from diocesan and parish publications, equal access for women to theological and pastoral education according to their capacities, and the active recruitment of qualified women to exercise a wide range of pastoral ministries in the diocese.[29]

Also in 1980, Archbishop Peter Gerety of Newark issued a pastoral letter reflecting at length on biblical, historical, and theological foundations for establishing the equality of women in the Church. Stressing themes similar to Hunthausen's, Gerety urgently called the people of his diocese to see the equality of women in the Church as a moral issue, a matter of justice. While upholding the present position of the Church on the exclusion of women from ordination, he says that women "justly expect admission to all ministries and office permitted to them by the church." He calls for the "speedy integration of women" into ministries that are presently open to them and for the elimination of all traces of discrimination between men and women.[30]

Two Minnesota bishops, Bishop Victor Balke of Crookston and Bishop Raymond Lucker of New Ulm, issued a joint pastoral letter in 1981. They situate their reflections within a Christian humanism that calls for a gospel-based commitment to the dignity and equality of all persons leading to changes in structures, customs, institutions, and relationships for the good of all. Balke and Lucker are very direct in naming the evil of sexism.

[28]The Canadian synod statements have been stronger than the United States ones. There are more diocesan level pastoral letters among the United States bishops and also more concrete strategies and actions indicated than in the Canadian bishops' statements. Like the United States bishops, the Quebec bishops are far more engaged in active consultative processes with women in their dioceses than their English-speaking counterparts in the rest of Canada. The United States bishops are engaged in trying to develop a national level pastoral letter, something which the Canadian bishops have not undertaken to date.

[29]Archbishop Raymond G. Hunthausen, "Pastoral Statement on Women," April 30, 1980, Archdiocese of Seattle.

[30]Archbishop Peter Gerety, "Women in the Church," *Origins* 10 (1980–1981) 582–88.

Sexism, directly opposed to Christian humanism and feminism, is the errone-
ous belief or conviction or attitude that one sex, female or male, is superior
to the other in the very order of creation or by the very nature of things.
When anyone believes that men are inherently superior to women or that
women are inherently superior to men, then he or she is guilty of sexism.
Sexism is a moral and social evil. It is not the truth of the biological, sociological or psychological sciences, nor is it the truth of the Gospel. Sexism is
a lie. It is a grievous sin, diminished in its gravity only by indeliberate ignorance or by pathological fear.[31]

By contrast, the bishops teach, was Jesus' attitude and practice of relating
to women. Jesus "neither demeaned them nor divinized them—two extreme and inhuman ways of relating to women (ways women have historically experienced)" both of which have prevented women "from being full
participants, equal to men, in the human enterprise."[32]

As a way to overcome individual and structural sexism, these bishops
propose a thorough examination of conscience. As for individual sexist attitudes, their questions include: Do I ever make disparaging remarks about
women or react approvingly when others make such remarks? Do I stereotype women in any way or approve—even by silence—of statements that
do stereotype them? Do I willingly listen to women when they speak about
their status in the Church and in society? Does it bother me when others
speak of God as maternal as well as paternal?

In regard to structural sexism, the bishops ask: Do my diocese and/or
parish and school pay a just salary to women employees, a salary equal to
men in similar positions? Does my diocese and/or parish provide a known
and approachable forum for women to speak on issues especially relevant
to them? Does my diocese and/or parish use inclusive language in its publications and communications and in the liturgy wherever possible? The
bishops proclaim the need to change attitudes and practices as a matter of
justice and a measure of our fidelity to the gospel.[33]

In 1982 Bishop Matthew Clark of Rochester, New York, published a
pastoral letter that reflects at length on women's painful experiences of exclusion and oppression and their tragic consequences for all in the Church.
He offers a lengthy theological reflection on women's history and call to
ministry in the Church, and he calls for all to enter the way of conversion
and reconciliation to overcome sexism against women. He calls too for the

---

[31]Bishop Victor Balke and Bishop Raymond Lucker, "Male and Female God Created
Them," *Origins* 11 (1981–1982) 334.
[32]Ibid., 336.
[33]Ibid., 336–37.

inclusion of women in the Church as prophets, teachers, and preachers of the gospel as well as leaders in pastoral care and governance.[34]

Like Bishops Balke and Lucker, Clark concludes his letter with a series of challenging observations and calls for action. He offers eight reflections on discriminatory attitudes toward women, and he calls for repentance over the past, conversion regarding the present, and committed perseverence against the temptation to quit or otherwise withdraw from the concrete process of realizing women's full equality in the Church. He outlines twelve action steps toward a reconstructed future including: the full admission of qualified women to all ministries not requiring ordination; scholarships for women to study at the local seminary and other institutions; continuing research by theologians and biblical scholars on all questions related to the issues of women; the use of inclusive language; the continuing education of priests on women in the Church, sexism and clericalism, and team ministry.[35]

Unique to the United States bishops, as mentioned above, is their decision to develop a national level pastoral letter on women in the Church and society whose origins, history, and present status are too long to deal with adequately within the scope and purpose of this paper. The strongest point about this endeavor thus far is its commitment to a consultative process, however conflicting its results may have been and may continue to be. Such a process at least makes evident the extent and seriousness of the problem.

Cardinal Bernardin, Archbishop of Chicago, for instance, recently said to his brother bishops:

> The difficulties we have encountered and continue to experience with our pastoral letter on *women's concerns* are a sign of the unrest and alienation affecting many women, even as some support the more traditional roles of women. In any case, the issue of ordination and jurisdiction, or the exercise of authority, as they relate to the ministry will not simply go away by *fiat*. The feminist movement impacts the church. How can the church, in light of its constitution and mission, best address *the aspirations of women?* There is no doubt that we must.[36]

While the Cardinal still asserts that the concerns are *women's* rather than the Church's and that they are about the *aspirations of women* rather than about *concrete matters of injustice,* his words do show recognition of the fact

---

[34]Bishop Matthew Clark, "American Catholic Women: Persistent Questions, Faithful Witness," *Origins* 12 (1982–1983) 273–86.

[35]Ibid., 285–86.

[36]Cardinal Bernardin, "Address at the U.S. Bishops' Third Special Assembly," June 26, 1989, *Origins* 20 (1990) 147. Italics mine.

that the issues cannot be ignored by reason of the Church's own proclamations on eliminating all forms of injustice, including those that are gender-based.

At the same time, the bishops have not yet embraced the work of some of the most serious and creative Roman Catholic feminist theologians, a fact borne out by theological weaknesses in the two drafts of the document appearing to date. Issues already well analyzed by their women theologian consultants back in the early 1980s (patriarchy, power, the need for deep systemic analysis, the misuse of such notions as *complementarity* and *mutuality,* placing the burden on women by naming the issues as *women's*) continue to plague the letter. As well, it seems that the bishops have chosen to tread lightly, and maybe even retreat, in the face of cautions by the Bishop of Rome and other like-minded theologians regarding the letter and its consultative process.

It remains to be seen whether the bishops will stay with the process of writing a national level pastoral letter or whether they will abandon the project because it is too controversial. What is certain is that the process itself, as difficult as it might be and as long as it might take, offers the occasion for a truly *opportune time* to stay with the historical struggle of establishing *in fact* the full equality of women in the Church and society.

IV. Summary Reflections

This review of some North American Roman Catholic bishops' statements on issues related to women in the Church and society has shown that the bishops have engaged the prophetic and teaching character of their episcopal office, to some degree at least, by denouncing sexism and proclaiming the equality of women. For the most part, their statements use a reflective methodology concentrated on recovering some liberative aspects of the biblical and theological tradition. Some also show signs of welcoming contemporary thought on gender equality, and many are full of concrete suggestions to redress and overcome the evil consequences of entrenched sexism.

On public record, the bishops have acknowledged the women's movement as a positive and permanent feature of our contemporary consciousness. They have condemned sexism as a moral and social evil and they have advocated an egalitarian partnership of men and women in the Church. They have argued theologically that women are indeed fitting signs of God in history, fully equal to men, and further that their full membership in the Church in theory and in practice is necesary for the truthfulness of the Church itself as a credible prophetic witness to the liberating love of God as given to us in Jesus Christ and the Holy Spirit.

The bishops have spoken of new bonds of equality, thus admitting to the inequality that is in the Church, and they have acknowledged their own need for deep conversion, as well as calling all in the Church to such change. They have reminded themselves and all other members of the Church that while human struggle is not without sin neither is it without grace to further God's reign in establishing gender equality.

At the same time, the bishops' statements raise issues that will continue to nag at the edges, or perhaps even at the center, of Church authority. The bishops have not yet engaged in depth social analysis on the links of sexism with patriarchal power, especially as it is at work in the Church. They have not firmly committed themselves to removing institutionally the stones—ignoring or silencing women's voices, denying or minimizing their basic human rights, blaming or holding them responsible usually for domestic violence, repressing or excluding their gifts for ministry—which block women from full life in the Christian community. They have not yet been sufficiently critical of the notion of *complementarity* which more often than not is taken to mean *equal but separate* than a genuine *egalitarian partnership*. They have not yet drawn the full consequences, both with respect to the pervasive use of male images for God and to proper relationality in the Church, of proclaiming that women are indeed made in God's image, and not in any derived or secondary sense as the tradition has taught so successfully. They have not yet come to the conclusions implied in teaching that women are indeed not only *proper but necessary signs* of God's fullness among us. They have not yet exercised their own responsibilities in realms where they are unique decision-makers regarding teaching and practice that discriminate against women (worship, equal access to ministry and to theological and pastoral education, finances, just employment, etc.).

The bishops' statements show them revisiting the Christian tradition and invoking some forgotten strands that hold some promise for a more comprehensive, liberative, and inclusive theological reflection and pastoral practice. It seems likely, however, that the gap between proclamation and practice will continue to haunt the bishops for some time to come since there is a long way to go yet in understanding and admitting to how gender relations are experienced, constituted, and controlled in the Church.

It is no time to withdraw or to try to maintain the old order, although several bishops these days seem so inclined. The Church, as Bishop Hubert put it, has to continue to exercise its freedom and trust in calling itself into question as it seeks to bear witness in the struggle for the eradication of sexism and the establishment of the full equality of women. The global transformation of consciousness regarding the full and equal inclusion of women in the Church and society has just begun. Linked with other liberation movements of our planet, it is *the* call of our era.

Chapter 13

Marriage and Divorce Twenty-Five Years after Vatican II

William P. Roberts

Celebrating the Second Vatican Council twenty-five years after its closing could not be complete without reflecting on an important area of Church life very much affected by the thinking of the bishops of that council, namely, marriage. This chapter will reflect on how the council changed our understanding of marriage. It will then proceed to trace some of the implications this perspective has for our approach to marriage and divorce. It will also point out some of the unresolved questions this new understanding raises.

I. A New Understanding of Marriage

The 1917 Code of Canon Law had defined marriage as a contract by which each of the couple "gives and accepts a perpetual and exclusive right over the body for acts which are of themselves suitable for the generation of children."[1] The Code went on to say that every valid contract of marriage between baptized persons was by that very fact a sacrament.[2] The primary end of marriage is the procreation and education of children, while the secondary end is "mutual help and the allaying of concupiscence."[3]

At the Second Vatican Council, the official Church description of marriage underwent some drastic changes. Instead of referring to marriage as a contract, the council speaks of it as a covenant in which the couple mutually bestow the gift of themselves to each other, and form a lasting and intimate partnership of married life and love.[4] Nor is there any mention of "primary" and "secondary" ends.

[1]Canon 1012, and canon 1081, no. 2.
[2]Canon 1012, no. 2.
[3]Canon 1013, no. 1.
[4]*Gaudium et spes*, no. 48.

172

This enhanced understanding of marriage has opened the door to a deeper spirituality of marriage that embraces the entirety of one's marital life. It is a spirituality that calls for a total effort on the part of spouses to give of themselves to one another, with all of the dyings and risings that are entailed. It challenges a couple not only to fidelity in the sexual area of their life, but to a faithfulness to the commitment ever to create a more intimate marital partnership of life and love.

This Vatican II perspective on marriage, however, has also given rise to many, as yet, unresolved questions. Under the 1917 Code of Canon Law's view of marriage, it was relatively simple to determine what were the requirements to enter a valid marital contract. Sexual potency, proper canonical form, and proper consent to exhange mutually the rights over one's body for acts of sexual intercourse open to procreation, were not too difficult for lawyers to measure. But discerning what level of maturity and self-giving are required in order to enter a marital covenant in which both pledge to give of the gift of themselves to each other in an intimate partnership of marital life and love is a far more complex matter.

II. Marriage as Sacrament

In light of the theology of Vatican II, there have been two important developments in our understanding of Christian marriage as a sacrament. First, we have come to see that it is inadequate to speak merely—or primarily—of the wedding ceremony as the sacrament of marriage.

The wedding ceremony should mark the *beginning* of the couple's life-long experience of marriage as a sacrament. Through their giving of themselves to each other in an intimate partnership of marital life and love, and through their doing this in light of their faith and love of Jesus Christ, the couple minister this sacrament to each other for the duration of their married life. More precisely, they become sacrament to each other in the context of their unique marital relationship. They become sign to each other of Christ's nurturing love and concern, not only in the sense that they manifest in their love the kind of love that Christ has for them, but also in the deeper sense that through their presence and their love and concern for each other, Christ communicates his redemptive and transforming presence, love, and concern.

The wife and husband are, as the Roman Catholic Church has perennially maintained, the true ministers of the sacrament of matrimony. But their ministering does not end at the close of the wedding ceremony. That liturgical celebration marks the beginning of their mutual marital ministry.

The second development in regard to the theological understanding of the sacrament of marriage is the move away from perceiving every valid marriage between two baptized Christians as being automatically (or "by that very fact") a sacrament.[5]

A sacrament ("a sign instituted by Christ to give grace") is a visible manifestation to those with Christian faith of the presence and redemptive action of the crucified and risen Christ. Through the sacramental action of the ecclesial community that we call Church ("the people of God"), Christ acts now in a way that transforms and enriches those who participate in the sacrament.

In order for marriage to be experienced as a sacrament, more, then, is necessary than the mere fact that one was baptized at some past moment in one's life. If Christian sacraments are for the baptized, must it not be asked what one's baptism means to one? Does one still adhere to her/his baptismal commitment? If Christian sacraments only speak to those with Christian faith, must it not also be asked whether one still believes in that Christian faith? Who is Jesus Christ for that person? Does the individual have any personal relationship with Christ? What degree of Christian faith and commitment is minimally required for marriage to be a Christian sacrament?

If in the sacrament of marriage, the visible manifestation of Christ's redemptive action is the intimate partnership of marital life and love that the couple share together, then, what is the minimal degree of love and marital partnership and sharing that is required in order for a particular marriage to be a sacrament? What happens if that minimal degree of intimacy was once present in a marriage, and then is irrevocably lost? Does the "marriage" still remain a sacrament, even when everything that is ordinarily associated with the idea of marriage is forever gone from the relationship?

These are some of the questions that flow from a contemporary understanding of sacrament and of marriage. These queries will not go away. It is of paramount importance that they be addressed until they are suitably resolved.

III. Marriage Preparation

The enhanced understanding of marriage and the deeper appreciation of what is involved for marriage to be experienced as a sacrament by Christian couples have obvious implications for marital preparation. Most dioceses have already seen great steps taken in improving the quality of programs for future married couples. The old "Cana Conference" model has in large

---

[5]See, for example, Theodore Mackin, S.J., "How to Understand the Sacrament of Marriage," *Commitment to Partnership: Explorations of the Theology of Marriage,* ed. William P. Roberts (New York: Paulist Press, 1987) 34–60.

part been either expanded or replaced by programs that include not only instruction, but also self-inventories, discussions with married couples, and retreat-like weekends. While these new programs are clearly a move in the right direction, many feel they do not go far enough and that new creative approaches are still needed.[6]

This is not the place to provide a complete outline of the elements that need to be present in a post-Vatican II marriage preparation program. It must suffice here to underscore the need for adequate preparation for three significant dimensions of marriage for a Christian couple: creating intimacy, entering into a genuine marital partnership, and living marriage as a sacrament of Christ's love.

First, a couple need preparation for entering into an intimate communion with one another. A beginning step in this preparation is *assessment*. The couple should be helped to assess what present gifts and future potential they have for creating an intimate marital relationship with each other. They need to assess to what degree they possess and/or do not possess three of the essential elements involved in forming an intimate marriage: the desire for intimacy, the ability and generosity to give of oneself to the other, and communication skills.

How high on their list of priorities is intimacy in marriage? Is it of equal priority for both of them? How much are they willing to sacrifice in order to achieve this priority?

Are they each capable of giving of the gift of self to the other? How generous are they in sharing their time? Are they capable and willing to expend the psychic energy necessary to be present to one another in a full way, that is, not just physically, but also emotionally and spiritually?

How well are they able to communicate with each other their plans and schedules, their ideas and feelings, their hopes and fears? Are both communicating with the same degree of openness? Are they mutually satisfied with the level of communication they have so far achieved? What areas need improvement?

Facing honestly these kinds of questions will enable a couple to discover how suitable they are for one another in terms of creating intimacy in marriage. If they find they are not suitable, they can be helped to decide to go their separate ways. If they are basically suitable, but discover deficiencies, they can be guided by a pastoral minister, a wise and experienced married couple, or by a professional counsellor on how to improve in these areas.

The second dimension of marriage that needs to be addressed in a preparation program is that marriage is a *partnership* of life and love. After gener-

[6]One such approach is proposed by JoAnn Heaney-Hunter in her as yet unpublished paper presented at the Vatican II Conference on September 28, 1990, entitled "Continuing the Journey of Faith: Using the RCIA as a Model for Marriage Preparation."

ations and generations in which patriarchal marriages have dominated the scene, it ought not be assumed that everyone is willing and able to enter a relationship in which both the female and male accept each other on equal footing. A couple before marriage need to evaluate their attitudes toward the opposite gender. Do they really believe that marriage is a partnership in which both the woman and the man together are co-heads of the household? Do they believe that tasks ought not be assigned according to gender stereotypes, but rather shared on the basis of mutual interests, talents, and fairness? Are there any ways in which their present relationship manifests sexist biases? If so, what are they willing to do to overcome these?

Finally, a good preparation program ought to help the couple appreciate the sacramental dimension of Christian marriage, and how ready and willing they are to experience this sacramentality in their own marriage. This issue makes each partner confront the meaning of her/his baptismal life and Christian faith, and to determine to what degree their Christian commitment has influenced the history of their relationship thus far, and what are the possibilities of it shaping their future marriage as a lived sign of Christ's love.

IV. The Wedding Ceremony

Since the Second Vatican Council the wedding ceremony has undergone a number of liturgical changes that have made it more intelligible and have allowed greater participation on the part of those attending. Much, however, still needs to be done so that the wedding liturgy can better reflect a post-Vatican II theology of marriage.[7] The following are a few of the ways in which this can be done.

(1) The Roman Church holds that the ministers of the sacrament of marriage are the couple. If this is so—and I deeply believe it is—then the wedding ceremony, in which the couple begin their sacramental life together, ought to reflect this reality, so that it is obvious to all in attendance. This means that the couple—not the priest or deacon—ought to have "center stage." They ought to face the congregation, and have microphones, so that they can be heard. They ought to be so prepared so as to pronounce their marital commitment without being coached. They also ought to be allowed a leadership role in the prayers.

The priest or deacon is there to be a witness and to assist the couple. He should limit himself to those roles that are assigned him by canon law, and not act as if he is the minister of the sacrament. Accordingly, he should

---

[7]For a number of good insights in this regard, see *Alternative Futures for Worship,* vol. 5, Christian Marriage, ed. Bernard Cooke (Collegeville, Minn.: The Liturgical Press, 1987).

locate himself off to the side, so as not to obscure the central position of the bride and groom.

(2) If marriage truly is a partnership, then this needs to be reflected in the readings and the prayers. All sexist language and patriarchal views of marriage and gender stereotypes should be assiduously avoided. The prayers and blessings should bring out the equal status of the bride and groom, and their mutually shared responsibilities. Other vestiges of the patriarchal past would also best be avoided, such as the veiling of the bride and the "giving away" of the bride by one male to another.

(3) The sacrament of matrimony ought to be linked to the couple's baptism and confirmation. This could be done by including a renewal of the Christian commitment made in baptism and confirmed in confirmation. However, a much more positive and theologically enriched formula of renewal of baptismal commitment should be developed than the rather impoverished alternatives presently available. Having made such a renewal of the baptismal commitment, the couple can then make clear that they are choosing each other in Christian marriage as a way of living out more fully their baptismal life.

(4) The formula of the Christian wedding vows is in dire need of a complete overhaul. As I have suggested elsewhere, a non-believer could recite either option of the present formula without any qualms of conscience.[8] Neither option contains any reference at all to Christian belief or to the Christian dimension of marital living. If we really do believe that the marriage of Christians is a sacrament of Christ's love, ought not this reality be referred to in the marriage vows? Could not the marital commitment be worded in a way that includes the pledge to live, work, and relate in a truly Christian way, not only toward one another, but as a couple toward the wider human community? Could not mention be made of the couple's commitment to further through their marriage the reign of God in their home and on the face of this earth?

V. Interfaith Marriages

The past quarter of a century has seen a pronounced increase in the number of interfaith marriages among Catholics. At least four factors have contributed to this increase: The Vatican Council's new attitude of openness to other denominations and other religions, less discouragement and greater acceptance of interfaith marriages, a larger number of Catholics attending public schools and universities as well as a greater number of persons from

---

[8]See William P. Roberts, *Encounters with Christ* (Mahwah, N.J.: Paulist Press, 1985) 240.

other denominations and religions attending Catholic educational institutions, and increased sharing in prayer and ministerial projects with persons of other faiths.

One of the things that has changed in regard to marriages between Catholics and those of other religions or denominations is the terminology. The very general term "mixed marriage" has given way to the more specific term "interfaith marriage." Some have called for even more specific language. Michael Lawler speaks of "ecumenical marriages," by which he means marriages between two Christians of different confessions in which "both parties are faithful to their religious duties."[9] Elsewhere my wife and I have distinguished three kinds of interfaith marriages: interreligion, interdenominational, and intradenominational.[10] This last type refers to marriages between persons of the same denomination, but with very pronounced (possibly irreconcilable) differences in their faith and their religious practices. While such marriages have not in the past been considered under the category of "interfaith" marriages, we believe they should be, since they can sometimes pose more serious problems than many interdenominational marriages.

While marriages between Christians of different denominational confessions can obviously pose difficulties, they can also become an important part of the ecumenical movement. If such couples can share a great deal of their common faith and love of Christ, and their commitment to the gospel, they can learn to appreciate each other's tradition, and in that context better understand and work out the differences. Such ecumenism on the family level can serve as an inspiration to the wider Christian community in the effort to break down prejudices and foster unity.

Marriages between Christians and persons belonging to other world religions involve, of course, even more pronounced differences. Again, however, such couples can get in touch with what they have in common in terms of their faith in God, and in terms of their heritage. So, for example, in the Jewish-Christian marriage, both can share the Jewish heritage they hold in common, as well as their regard for Jesus as a good and holy Jew, and a prophetic teacher and healer. Against that backdrop they can then respect their differences. Success in this regard contributes to the fruitfulness of the ongoing dialogue between Jews and Christians. *Mutatis mutandis,* similar parallels can be made in marriages between Christians and persons of other religions.

Progress has been made in the past twenty-five years in the effort to respect the consciences and sensitivities of both parties in interfaith marri-

---

[9]See his latest book, *Ecumenical Marriage* (Mystic, Conn.: Twenty-Third, 1990).

[10]See Challon O'Hearn Roberts and William P. Roberts, *Partners in Intimacy: Living Christian Marriage Today* (Mahwah, N.J.: Paulist Press, 1988) ch. 9.

ages. Issues, such as the following, keep begging for further resolution: intercommunion in marriages between Christians of differing denominations; how strictly to insist on canonical form as a condition for validity of the marriage; the need to require the Catholic party to promise to do all in her/his power to bring the children up as Catholics.

VI. Consummating the Marriage

According to the 1917 Code of Canon Law, a valid marriage is consummated when "there has taken place between the parties the conjugal act to which the matrimonial contract is by nature ordained and by which husband and wife are made one flesh."[11] The notion of a consummated marriage became very important on the pastoral level and in the marriage tribunals because the one kind of marriage that the Roman Catholic Church has held as absolutely indissoluble is a valid sacramental marriage that has been consummated.[12]

The 1917 Code definition of consummation made sense in the context of that Code's definition of marriage.[13] If one's understanding of marriage is focused on each other's right over the body for acts of sexual intercourse that are open to procreation, then it is logical to conclude that such a contract is consummated by the first act of intercourse after the wedding ceremony.

Once, however, we accept the post-Vatican II era's description of marriage as an intimate partnership of life and love, the doors are swung wide open to deep questioning regarding when and how marriages are consummated. The first level of questioning has to do with what kind of an act of sexual intercourse is necessary to consummate an intimate marital love relationship. How could such a relationship be consummated by an act of intercourse that was done without love, or with disregard for the spouse, or by violent force against the spouse's wishes (marital rape)? The 1983 Code partially addressed this question by adding a qualification that was lacking in the previous code. A marriage is consummated, it states, by an act of sexual intercourse that is performed in a human manner (*modo humano*).[14] What is left unclear is exactly what is required for an act of sexual intercourse to be performed in a "human manner."

The second level of questioning probes more deeply. Can any single act of sexual intercourse consummate an intimate partnership of life and love? Is not the forming of such a relationship a longer and more complex

[11]Canon 1015, no. 1.
[12]1917 Code, canon 1118; 1983 Code, canon 1141.
[13]As cited in the beginning of this chapter.
[14]Canon 1061, no. 1.

process? At what point can a marriage, understood this way, be said to be consummated? What are the criteria for making such a determination?[15]

VII. Marital Sexual Morality

Again, the understanding of marriage reflected in the old code was the controlling factor in the determination of what was to be considered moral or immoral in regard to sexual behavior in marriage. Since marriage was seen as the exchange of rights over each other's bodies for acts of intercourse that were open to procreation, marital morality focused on three responsibilities.

First, there was the obligation to "render the debt," as the old moral manuals put it. This referred to the "duty" that the spouse had to respond to the other's request for sexual intercourse. The second moral mandate was to avoid adultery. The third was to refrain from any genital activity that was not performed in such a way as to be conducive in itself for procreation. Thus, any form of artificial contraception and any male orgasm outside the act of sexual intercourse were seen to be against the "natural law."

Once, however, marriage is perceived as a covenant of intimate partnership in which the couples give the gift of themselves to one another, sexual intercourse is perceived in an entirely different light. It is meant to be the most physically intimate expression of the emotional and spiritual intimacy that exists between the couple in their total life together. To the degree in which sexual intercourse reflects this intimacy, it can, in turn, nurture it. It is incumbent on the couple, then, to act in such a way in their lives as to foster this emotional and spiritual intimacy. It is also incumbent on them to approach sexual intercourse with the kind of mutual respect, sensitivity, and love that is necessary if intercourse is to foster intimacy in their total relationship.

In this context, restricting the moral mandate to one of "rendering the debt" is seriously inadequate. A marriage is in deep trouble when sexual relations have been reduced to that.

In light of this renewed understanding of marriage, it is also inadequate to speak of marital fidelity in terms of merely avoiding adultery. Instead, marital fidelity takes on the much richer meaning of being faithful to the commitment of growing in marital intimacy in all of its dimensions, including the sexual. It means being faithful to the romance.

The third aspect of the older approach to marital sexual morality is also seen in a new light when situated in the Vatican Council's understanding

[15]For a brief treatment of this question, see Bernard Cooke, "Indissolubility: Guiding Ideal or Existential Reality," *Commitment to Partnership*, 72–73.

of marriage as an intimate partnership of life and love. In the older approach what was "natural" in marital genital expression was determined primarily in terms of the biological. But if sexual intercourse is a symbolic expression of the couple's total gift of themselves to each other, then it is important to consider the nature of that entire reality in all of its dimensions: emotional, psychological, spiritual, and relational, as well as the physical. For the Christian couple, what is appropriate or inappropriate in the sexual expression of love must also be evaluated in terms of how it is meant to be a sacramental expression of Christ's self-gift and love of the couple.

VIII. The Annulment Process

The shift in the understanding of marriage since Vatican II has had deep effects in our understanding of the grounds for annulment.[16] When marriage was perceived primarily as the mutual exchange of rights to each other's bodies for acts of sexual intercourse that are open to procreation, then the principal grounds for declaring Church marriages invalid were the lack of free consent and the inability to perform the act of sexual intercourse. Once, however, we think of marriage along the lines of Vatican II, the grounds for annulment become much broader. The couple must have the will and the capability not only to engage in the physical act of sexual intercourse, but must also possess the personal qualities necessary for entering into a lifelong intimate partnership of life and love.

IX. Indissolubility

The Catholic Church continues to be committed to the permanency of marriage as taught by Jesus and upheld through the centuries by the Catholic tradition. What has come to the fore in the past twenty-five years, however, is increased questioning regarding the meaning of Jesus' teaching and regarding how indissolubility is to be understood.[17]

In regard to how Jesus' teaching on divorce and remarriage is to be interpreted there are at least two areas of questions. First, Jesus enunciates his prohibition against divorce without any distinction between marriages among people who are baptized and those who are not, or between marriages that are consummated and those that are not consummated. What,

[16]For an excellent treatment of this topic, see Lawrence G. Wrenn, *Annulments* (Washington, D.C.: Canon Law Society of America, 1983).

[17]See, for example, Cooke, "Indissolubility," *Commitment to Partnership*. Also, Theodore Mackin, S.J., "The International Theological Commission and Indissolubility," *Divorce and Remarriage: Religious and Psychological Perspectives*, ed. William P. Roberts (Kansas City, Mo.: Sheed and Ward, 1990).

then, is the basis for the distinctions made by Church teaching whereby only sacramental and consummated marriages are "absolutely indissoluble"? If exceptions can be made for non-sacramental or non-consummated marriages, why can they not be made for sacramental and consummated marriages?

Second, one of the versions of Jesus' divorce sayings appears in the context of the Sermon on the Mount. Here Jesus proclaims prophetic ideals that humans must strive for, but cannot perfectly achieve in the context of sinful humanity. Accordingly, the Church has never insisted that we follow Jesus' prohibition against oaths (Matt 5:33-37), or that we always fulfill the directive, "Give to anyone who asks you, and if anyone wants to borrow, do not turn away" (Matt 5:42).[18] If we recognize that these sayings are examples of prophetic proclamations of ideals that Jesus challenges us to strive to attain as best we can, but are not laws in the strict sense, on what basis do we interpret the divorce sayings of Jesus as laws that admit of no exceptions?

In regard to indissolubility, a principal question that needs to be addressed is this: is indissolubility an ontological reality or a moral mandate? In other words, does the statement, "what God has united, human beings must not divide" mean that humans are incapable of dissolving marriages, or does it mean that they ought not to do so?

The Roman Catholic Church of the Latin Rite has traditionally held that it is impossible to end a consummated sacramental marriage. Even if everything has irrevocably gone out of a marital relationship that is ordinarily associated with marriage, intimacy, or partnership, there remains, the official position claims, the marital bond. So, even in the case of a couple whose sacramental and consummated marriage ended in bitter divorce twenty years ago, and who have neither seen nor heard from each other since, there still exists the marriage bond. Hence, such a couple are bound to their marriage to one another and are prevented from entering another marriage until one of them dies.

The question raised in regard to this position is what precisely is the nature of this marital bond that is supposed to continue to exist even when all marital love and communication have ceased? What could this bond be that exists over and above the relationship, and independent of it?

X. Conclusion

The bishops at the Second Vatican Council spoke of marriage in a new and refreshing way. Anyone who is happily married can much more easily

---

[18]Scripture quotations are taken from the *New Jerusalem Bible.*

identify their marital experience with the thinking of Vatican II than with that of the 1917 Code.

This renewed perception laid the foundation for the developments that have taken place over the past quarter of a century in both the fields of theology and Canon Law in regard to marriage. Is it too bold to hope that in the next twenty-five years we as a Church may be empowered to address in a Spirit-filled way some of the unresolved questions these developments have raised?

Introduction to Catholic Higher Education

Catholic Education

James L. Heft, S.M.

In the two sessions on Catholic higher education, six papers were presented: "The Role of Philosophy in Priestly Formation" by Lawrence F. Hundersmarck, chair of the Department of Philosophy and Religious Studies at Pace University; "Catholic Schooling in America" by Michael J. Guerra, executive director of the NCEA Secondary Schools Department; "American Catholic Higher Education since Vatican II" by William P. Leahy, S.J., assistant professor of history at Marquette University; "The Role of Women in Catholic Higher Education since Vatican II" by Alice Gallin, O.S.U., executive director of the Association of Catholic Colleges and Universities; "Is There a Borderline between Church and Culture?" by William M. Shea, chair of the Department of Theology at St. Louis University; and "The Catholic University and Academic Freedom" by James L. Heft, S.M., provost of the University of Dayton.

Abridged versions of the papers by Heft and Shea follow.

Chapter 14

The Catholic University
and Academic Freedom

James L. Heft, S.M.

After studying the debate of theologians on the limits and forms of dissent, several commentators have come in recent years to the conclusion that if light is to be shed upon this debate, a broader context needs first to be established. Thus, these commentators frequently highlight the nature of religious tradition, the *sensus fidelium,* the meaning and the proper limits of the magisterium, and so on.[1]

I suggest that, in a similar way, any discussion of academic freedom in a Catholic university may be better understood by attending first to a broader context. If we grasp more clearly what a Catholic university ought to be, we should then be able to understand the essential role that academic freedom plays within its life.

The recently released document from the Congregation for the Doctrine of the Faith, *Ex Corde Ecclesiae,* following *verbatim* a 1973 statement produced by the International Federation of Catholic Universities, states that there are four "essential characteristics of a Catholic university as 'Catholic':"

> (1) a Christian inspiration not only of individuals but of the university community as such; (2) a continuing reflection in the light of Catholic faith upon the growing treasury of human knowledge, to which it seeks to contribute by its own research; (3) fidelity to the Christian message as it comes to us through the Church; (4) an institutional commitment to the service of the people of God and of the human family in their pilgrimage to the transcendent goal which gives meaning to life (par. 13).

These four themes underscore the need for a community of individuals inspired by the gospel, describe human knowledge as continuously grow-

[1] See my "The Response Catholics Owe to Non-Infallible Teaching," *Raising the Torch of Good News,* ed. Bernard Prusak, Proceedings of the College Theology Society (1986) 105–26.

186

ing and state that Catholic scholars ought to contribute to that growth, and indicate that the gospel message, which emanates from the Church, orients the university community to the service of the people of God who are on pilgrimage—that is, on their way, searching and reaching for God.

Compare this vision of what makes a university Catholic to the description provided in 1960 by the president of St. John's University in Jamaica, New York, as he addressed his faculty senate:

> The University is committed to Catholicism and, since the great majority of the students are Catholic, the tone of the lectures certainly should be Catholic. The content of the texts should be Catholic, or at least they should not run, in any way, contrary to Catholicism. . . . St. John's University is committed to pure Thomism as a system of philosophy. . . . It is the handmaid of the Catholic theology which we teach. . . . Whatever is said in any course may not, in any way, contravene pure Thomism or Catholic Theology.[2]

In 1960, most presidents of most Catholic universities in the United States would have described the Catholicity of their university in much the same way. But today, few philosophy departments continue to teach "pure Thomism as a system of philosophy." In a recent article on Ph.D. programs in Catholic theology, Thomas O'Meara of Notre Dame mentions that there are no strong programs and faculties in the thought of Thomas Aquinas.[3] Of course, dramatic changes have taken place in Catholic higher education through the increasing number, religious diversity and influence of lay faculty and administrators, the new modes of governance, and the widespread acceptance of academic professionalism.

More has changed than just physical circumstance, however. Since 1960, we have gone through far-reaching and dramatic changes in the very way that we understand Catholicism. The Catholic world, if you will, has changed, but we are only now becoming aware of the new situation we are in. The late Walker Percy described well in one of his essays this moment of delayed recognition. "There is a lag," he wrote, "between the end of an age and the discovery of the end. The denizens of such a time are like the cartoon cat that runs off a cliff and for a while is suspended, still running, in mid-air but sooner or later looks down and sees there is nothing under him." The old synthesis—the classical way of thinking, as Bernard Lonergan described it, the pure system of Thomism as the president of St. John's wanted it—has almost everywhere vanished, and we are at present in the process of building a new way of perceiving the Catholic identity of our educational institutions.

[2]Cited by David O'Brien, "The Church and Catholic Education," *Horizons* 17 (1990) 16.
[3]See "Doctoral Programs in Theology at U.S. Catholic Universities," *America* (February 3, 1990) 80.

The new Catholic identity will need to include a pluralism that emphasizes relation, not relativism; will need to encourage a hermeneutics of retrieval as well as one of suspicion; will need to learn from culture as well as to critique it. Catholic intellectuals need to think through the pluralism that exists not only about them, but within them. As theologian and student of American culture William Shea put it recently:

> [T]he actual pluralism of our actual personal and communal life is not adequately comprehended in the two terms church and culture, nor is pluralism's meaning to be confined to the obvious and shallow sense of the variety of options available in our intellectual and spiritual consumer society. The point is that we ourselves are plural. Figuring out what constitutes the plurality is a genuine intellectual problem; and learning to cope with pluralism is one of the chief objectives of higher education.[4]

In calling for a dialogue between faith and culture, between Christian belief and science, between the Catholic intellectual tradition and professional education, *Ex Corde Ecclesiae* ensures that the Catholic university of the future will be neither monolithic nor monochrome, nor ever achieve its goals through any form of monologue. A certain pluralism will be a constant characteristic of true Catholic universities in the future.

Realizing that the age of tidy synthesis is over, how might we now describe the characteristics of a Catholic university? The characteristics I would name are these. A Catholic university should be, above all, a community of scholars, the majority of whom draw upon Catholicism as integral to their scholarship.[5] At the heart of a university is its faculty, and not only the faculty of theology and philosophy, though these should play an especially important role, but also those who are scientists and engineers and lawyers and business people. At a Catholic university, faculty from every discipline need to be willing to explore together the ethical and religious dimensions and ramifications of their disciplines.

Catholic identity should not be housed primarily in the presence and activities of the Campus Ministry staff, as important as these are. Nor should the responsibility for articulating Catholic identity be placed upon only the administration of a university, while the faculty devotes itself to generating ideas and conducting debates. I am not here minimizing the importance of liturgy well done and pastoral services readily available, nor am I suggesting that administrators should play an insignificant role in setting an intellectual and religious tone for an institution's academic life, and, of

---

[4]See Shea in this volume.
[5]See W. Burkhardt, "Intellectual and Catholic? Or Catholic Intellectual?" *America* (May 6, 1989) 421.

course, in making critically important decisions about the distribution of funds within an institution. But all these efforts must be in conjunction with those of a faculty willing to enter wholeheartedly into the exploration of issues that will inevitably cross disciplinary boundaries.

While some of our faculty would like to become more familiar with other disciplines in an effort to deepen and broaden their grasp of their own discipline, few of them actually do so. Their hesitancy is based not only on their own perceived lack of competency to do such interdisciplinary exploration, but also on the lack of an institutional incentive. In too many of our institutions, faculty are penalized when they focus on anything other than their specialty. This is especially the case for those teaching on the graduate level. At this level, we sometimes witness the sad spectacle of faculty who are more loyal to their own discipline and professional societies than they are to their students. We need faculty whose dedication to their students is demonstrated by their efforts not only to stay abreast of current developments in their disciplines, but also to contribute to the development of their discipline.

Catholic universities need to explore more than the ethical dimensions of their disciplines. Faculty members need to explore and develop the whole Catholic intellectual tradition. There are many ways to describe that tradition. Suffice it here to say that it presupposes an historical awareness, a sense of the importance of ritual and symbol, an openness to intuition and wonder, and a celebration of art and drama. Without these sensibilities, the intellectual life runs the risk of reducing itself to the merely cognitive, to that which is instrumentally rational, and to that which can be proven empirically. Were we to describe the Catholic intellectual tradition in theological terms, we would speak of sacramentality, the importance of tradition, the centrality of the community, and the complementarity of faith and reason. Were we to speak of it in philosophical terms, we should speak of analogical thinking, the natural law tradition, the centrality of the idea of character, and of the importance of the virtues.

If a Catholic university gathers scholars who are committed to an intellectual tradition characterized by comprehensiveness, sacramental sensibility, fidelity to the gospel, and concern for moral commitment, then how should academic freedom function in such a university? *Ex Corde Ecclesiae* states that every Catholic university, as a university, "possesses that institutional autonomy necessary to perform its functions effectively and guarantees its members academic freedom, so long as the rights of the individual person and of the community are preserved within the confines of the truth and the common good" (par. 12).

The 1979 papal constitution, "Sapientia Christiana," established rules for ecclesial institutions teaching only specifically Church-approved courses of study. In such ecclesial institutions, bishops are permitted by Church law to intervene directly. *Ex Corde Ecclesiae* is written for institutions which operate under predominantly lay boards of trustees and in whose internal governance, as the document states in paragraph 28, bishops do not enter. Thus, institutional autonomy is preserved. Other possible external threats to institutional autonomy, such as the federal government, sponsored research monies, accrediting agencies, parents, and alumni, are not mentioned in the document.

What might *Ex Corde Ecclesiae* mean when it states that it recognizes "the academic freedom of scholars in each discipline in accordance with its own principles and proper methods, and within the confines of the truth and the common good" (par. 29)? Is such an understanding of academic freedom the same as that which is commonly defended in academic circles in our country? The common understanding of it in this country has been greatly influenced by the AAUP: academic freedom, in current usage, "denotes the freedom of professionally qualified teachers, first, to pursue their scholarly investigations without interference; second, to publish the results of their research and reflection; and third, to teach according to their own convictions, provided that they remain in the area of their competence and present the alternative positions with sufficient attention and fairness. Many statements on academic freedom add that in cases of dispute, the competence and professional conduct of the teacher should be assessed by experts chosen from among academic colleagues or peers."[6] Proponents of this definition also typically stress that any limitation of academic freedom is injurious to the academic standing of the college or university.

Much of what the AAUP stated in 1915 concerning academic competence is valuable and should be adopted: for example, that in dealing with controversial matters professors should set forth divergent opinions without suppression or innuendo and remember that their business is not to provide the students with ready-made conclusions, but to train them to think for themselves; professors should aim at education and not indoctrination. Moreover, the AAUP has developed procedures for due process drawn from the American legal culture and, before that, from the common law tradition. Such procedural principles include:

> the strong presumption of innocence until there is clear and overwhelming proof of guilt; the right to confront one's accusers and cross question them; the right to have issues heard and tried by a jury of one's peers; the right of access to records concerning oneself kept by public authority; the right to insist on the terms of a duly concluded contract, even against employers

[6]Avery Dulles, "The Teaching Mission of the Church and Academic Freedom," *America* (April 21, 1990).

or superiors; the right to have conflicts tried by the norms of properly promulgated and publicly accessible laws and regulations; the right to hear judgment given and explained; and the right of appeal.[7]

Many of these elements of due process have been woven into the document drawn up to deal with conflicts that may arise between the American bishops and theologians, but have yet to find their ways sufficiently into the heritage of Roman law. Roman law, however, has not been completely bereft of elements of due process. For example, the Fourth Lateran Council (1215), when setting down the process of "accusation" and "inquisition" by bishops stated: "He who is the object of an inquiry should be present at the process, and, unless absent through contumacy, should have the various headings of the inquiry explained to him, so as to allow him the possibility of defending himself; as well, he is to be informed not only of what the various witnesses have accused him but also of the names of those witnesses."[8] Obviously, these few conciliar elements of due process have frequently not been followed.

In our own century, there are problems with Catholic universities adopting, without question, the interpretation of academic freedom proposed by the AAUP. The AAUP itself has recognized on several occasions that its idea of academic freedom raises serious questions for Church-related institutions. In 1915, the AAUP stated that such institutions do not accept freedom of inquiry or of teaching, and do not have as their purpose to advance knowledge by "unrestricted research and unfettered discussion of impartial investigations, but rather to subsidize the promotion of the opinions held by persons usually not of a scholar's calling." In other words, the AAUP judged then that "true academic freedom" was not possible in Church-related institutions. In 1940, the AAUP again warned that Church-related institutions, when hiring a professor, should out of fairness state explicitly the limits that exist on academic freedom. In 1982, it stated further that a "college or university is a marketplace of ideas, and it cannot fulfill its purpose of transmitting, evaluating, and extending knowledge if it requires conformity with any orthodoxy of content or method." And finally, in 1988, a report of the AAUP stated that any requirement of doctrinal fidelity in essence conflicts with the definition of an institution of higher learning.

The Vatican document speaks of academic freedom "within the con-

---

[7]See Monika Hellwig, "American Culture: Reciprocity with Catholic Vision, Values and Community," *The Catholic Church and American Culture,* ed. Cassian Yuhaus, C.P. (Mahwah, N.J.: Paulist Press, 1990) 67–68.

[8]Canon 8, "De inquisitionibus;" see Leonard E. O'Boyle, O.P., "Theologians and the Magisterium," *Doctrine and Life* 32:4 (1982) 251.

fines of truth and the common good." While any commonly agreed upon interpretation of this qualification of academic freedom seems not yet to exist, we can get some insight into its possible meaning by considering what academic freedom should mean for Catholic theologians. For theology to be Catholic, it must root itself in the history and experience of an historical religious community. As Richard McCormick writes:

> The facts (truths) that found and energize the believing community and influence its moral behavior are not like data from other disciplines. They concern God's nature, intentions, and actions as experienced and interpreted by a historical religious community. To reject such a context (catholic) is to misunderstand either theology and/or its Catholic specification."[9]

In a lecture on "Academic Freedom" given at the University of Dayton in January 1988, Charles Curran presented three "safeguards" to academic freedom: (1) discussion and mutual criticism by peers; (2) the right of bishops to point out errors and ambiguities of a theology of particular theologians; and (3) competency, which for the Catholic theologian requires that he or she theologize within and not against dogma.

It should be noted, however, that the second and third safeguards are not formulated by theologians alone, but ultimately by the Church as a whole, through the special ministry of the bishops. Many bishops are not professional theologians, yet they play a key role in judging what constitutes dogma. These last two safeguards would likely appear to the secular academy as mechanisms that include more than merely peer review, and therefore would be rejected as inconsistent with true academic freedom. What all this means is that academic freedom for theologians in particular will operate in a Catholic university in ways that can only appear to be different from, if not perhaps alien to, the way it is understood to operate by the secular academy.[10]

While Catholic theologians must enjoy "unrestricted research and unfettered discussion of impartial investigations," they will, if they wish to remain Catholic, conduct their research and engage in discussions that will illuminate, evaluate, enhance, and deepen Catholic dogma. Within that context, theologians draw upon a rich and living source of truth to which they add their own insights.

What should be done about professors of theology who no longer accept what McCormick describes as the "Catholic context?" First of all, they

---

[9]Richard McCormick, "The Search for Truth in the Catholic Context," *America* (November 8, 1986).

[10]See, for example, Douglas Laycock and Susan E. Waelbroeck, "Academic Freedom and the Free Exercise of Religion," *Texas Law Review* 66:7 (June 1988), which criticizes Curran's notion of academic freedom as not consistent with the AAUP understanding.

should realize that it is not for them to define officially what is Catholic. Second, as long as such professors follow the rules of competency described above, continue to respect the mission of the university, they may remain as members of the faculty as individuals who then would contribute to a dialogue with Roman Catholicism on the very point at which they differ from it. As Raymond Schroth puts it:

> In general practice it (academic freedom) means that no professor, who in the judgment of the scholarly community, otherwise meets the criteria for academic excellence—in scholarship, teaching and academic citizenship—should lose his [her] job because of his [her] ideas. Period. If his [her] ideas disturb the peace of the community and threaten to destroy its public image, the university will have to protect its image in other ways. It can insist that a professor distinguish his [her] position from Church teaching, choose which courses he [she] teaches, meet his [her] arguments with better ones; but it shouldn't fire him [her].[11]

A Catholic university needs to respect tenure if it is to be a university. At the same time, a Catholic university needs to hire a faculty that truly supports its special mission, a mission that includes much more than theological research and teaching. If scholars at a Catholic university are to bring faith and culture into constant fruitful dialogue, then all of the disciplines need to participate in that discussion. When the scholarly discourse and academic curriculum of a Catholic university is shaped by a concern for wholeness, for historical and sacramental sensibility, and for ethical reflection and moral commitment, the difference between the ethos of a Catholic university and a state university becomes palpable.

Elsewhere I have attempted to describe a Catholic university as an "open circle,"[12] that is, sufficiently circumscribed to constitute a community of discourse, but open enough to welcome others with different perspectives. There is therefore a need on a Catholic campus for students and faculty from other religious traditions, precisely to keep the dialogue more honest and open. And there is also the need on many campuses, an ever more important one at the present time, for a conscious commitment to finding, keeping, and developing the Catholic scholars who make the circle both Catholic and open.

Of course some people (parents, wealthy benefactors, administrators, and even students) still think that the only points of view permissible on a Catholic campus should be those which support Catholicism. Such people

---

[11]Raymond Schroth, "Tough Choices on Campus," *Commonweal* 113 (March 28, 1986) 170–75.

[12]See my "Academic Freedom and the Catholic University" *Theology and the University,* ed. John Apcsynski, Proceedings of the College Theology Society (1990) 233ff.

do not understand the nature of a university. They need to be reminded that the Latin word *campus*

> means field. It designates the arena where armies settled disputes with lance and sword. College campuses exist in part to render such incivility obsolete. The vigorous exchange of ideas by the open minded in the university setting is the way to reconcile our differences. That is why colleges have campuses, open forums for discussion and clash of ideas.[13]

At this point in the history of Catholic higher education, however, the discussions and clash of ideas should be aimed at contributing to, among other things, the development of the Catholic intellectual tradition.

In the last analysis, no simple formula exists that provides a clearly delineated way for a Catholic university to preserve both its religious identity, which it must do if it is to remain Catholic, and its academic character, which it must do if it is to be truly a university. While particular challenges posed by academic freedom in the Catholic university can be met, the process will often require both a reverence for our tradition and a commitment to its enhancement. Bishops and theologians will need to work together more effectively, and theologians, in our country, will have to work harder at avoiding what Walter Burkhardt recently described as their "intramural internecine hostility." Perhaps the biggest immediate challenge is the deepening within the faculties of Catholic universities of a fuller grasp and appreciation of the Catholic intellectual tradition as it touches upon all the disciplines. In this broader context, that is, in the context of a community of scholarly discourse that draws upon and enriches the Catholic intellectual tradition, academic freedom will be a safeguard and not a threat.

---

[13]McCormick, "The Search for Truth."

Chapter 15

Catholic Higher Education and the Englightenment:
On Borderlines and Roots

William M. Shea

It seems evident that the task of the scholar and the university is the creative appropriation of a tradition in a new context. The documents of the Church and recent commentators use the image of "borderline" to indicate the place and role of Catholic higher education. That image indicates well enough that the task of Catholic higher education is the mediation of the Catholic tradition. But let me turn to another aspect of the image of the borderline. Modern culture, or, in its broadest sense, the Enlightenment, is not only to be pictured on the other side of a borderline, but as a "root." Catholic higher education has two roots, both of which are its own, one the Church and one the culture.[1] The Enlightenment is also the heritage of Catholic higher education.

Let me begin with a quotation that cautions against my assertion. These are the words of the distinguished Catholic philosopher, J. M. Cameron, at the University of Dayton more than a decade ago:

> There is a serious threat to the freedom of the Catholic university. It comes, not from Rome, from the Curia, from bishops, but from the dominant culture of Western society, filled with a hatred of life and of human virtue, lost in a maze of ephemeral intellectual fashions. (This is not the whole truth about Western society, but it is the aspect of it which we are tempted to forget.)

[1]And it speaks to three publics like David Tracy's theolgian: the Church, the academy, the public; see David Tracy, *The Analogical Imagination: Christian Theology and the Culture of Pluralism* (New York: Crossroad, 1981) 3–46. On the public task of Catholic higher education, see W. M. Shea, "Beyond Tolerance: Pluralism and Catholic Higher Education," *Theology and the University,* ed. J. Apczynski (Lanham, Md.: University Press of America, 1990) 255–72; and David O'Brien, "The Church and Catholic High Education," *Horizons* 17 (1990) 7–29.

I think we—Catholics engaged in higher education—owe it to our society to challenge it in the sharpest possible way, to draw from the rich resources open to us—the prophetic tradition, the theological tradition, the words of the Gospel—words of warning and consolation.[2]

Professor Cameron is not only eloquent, he is correct. I cannot help but think of abortion clinics wherein human life seems no more than means to an end, to be eliminated for "higher goals," whether political or personal. I do not want to forget what Cameron warns me to remember.

But some of his rhetoric and argument remind one of the Church-culture dichotomy of the anti-modernist period of Catholicism, another era and another argument. The borderline seems a division, between those who know the truth and try to live it and those who do neither. Is that picture of the Church and the Enlightenment helpful and illuminating? That is the question. I do not find it so.

Let us ask how in practice we have adjusted to the Enlightenment. If we Catholics now accept and practice historical and literary methods in biblical studies, if we now approve and foster democratic politics and liberal political values, if our educational system now embraces freedom of inquiry and communication, if we favor religious freedom and are reconciled without regret to religious pluralism, if we preach from the highest pulpit the right of nations to self-determination—and all these convictions are indigenous to the historical process called the Enlightenment and all of them opposed by the Church in the past—then is not the war with the Enlightenment over? And if the war is over, then what is our relationship to the Enlightenment now? We should deplore its crimes, as we should those of the Christian Churches, but it may be a mistake to speak of it as if the Enlightenment were another community than our own, as if there is a culture "out there" beyond a borderline.

If we are to draw on our Catholic heritage to evaluate the culture, are we not also to draw on the authentic values of the Enlightenment to evaluate the Church? In addition to the Catholic rush to evaluate modernity by Catholic norms, are there pertinent and legitimate norms derived from modern experience to evaluate the Church—without disguising them as "gospel norms"? Have feminists, Jews, secular humanists, and the original Enlightenment figures such as Hume, Voltaire, Montesquieu, Kant, said nothing of independent value, nothing that "must be heard" within the Church and for the Church?

Richard J. Neuhaus, former Lutheran pastor and now a Roman Catholic, has made the case for over twenty years that the "secular society" must

---

[2] J. M. Cameron, "Academic Freedom in the Catholic University" (printed University of Dayton lecture, September 14, 1978).

not be allowed to set the agenda for the Church and that the Church must set the agenda for the society. The Church, so far as I can make out from his writings, has little to learn, no criticism to answer, from the culture in which it lives.[3] In my view the Enlightenment has much to say about and to the Church. The Second Vatican Council is unintelligible unless it is construed as a response to a world that left the Church behind and for good reason. While the Church has the message of salvation to preach to modern culture, modern culture has hard-won lessons to communicate to the Church. And Catholic higher education is the place in which the Enlightenment has been and must continue to be recovered as our heritage.[4]

In other words, then, just what are the *vetera* and the *novum?* Are there two heritages, two roots, and not one? This is an existential question for the Church, the university, and the individual. If I (we) must create a future, out of what are we to make it? What is my past, how many pasts, *vetera,* do I have? Do I have a past which teaches me things the Church has not, in addition to the things the Church has taught me? We have come to the point at which we say without feeling peculiar: these two traditions are mine.

We must render suspect the received divisions into the canonized opponents, the Enlightenment and the Catholic Church. We have to question such expressions as "borderline." The place of Catholic higher education in relation to the culture must be clarified. The literature typically gives us this picture: Catholic higher education examines, assesses, intellectually purifies the culture outside the Church for the sake of the Church. Or it mediates to that culture the results of its retrieval of the Catholic intellectual tradition. The images are attractive—they appear throughout recent official documentation from both Church and Catholic higher

[3]Richard J. Neuhaus, *The Catholic Moment: The Paradox of the Church in the Postmodern World* (San Francisco: Harper and Row, 1987); also, with Peter Berger, *Against the World for the World: The Hartford Appeal and the Future of Religion* (New York: Seabury Press, 1976).

[4]For example, the Land O' Lakes statement of 1967 is unequivocal in its acceptance of the AAUP principle: "The Catholic university today must be a university in the full modern sense of the word, with a strong commitment to and concern for academic excellence. To perform its teaching and research functions effectively the Catholic university must have a true autonomy and academic freedom in the face of authority of whatever kind, lay or clerical, external to the academic community itself." This seems to me to be a classic statement of the Enlightenment root of Catholic higher education. The text can be found in *The Catholic University: A Modern Appraisal,* ed. N. G. McCluskey (Notre Dame, Ind.: University of Notre Dame Press, 1970). A case might be made that later Church documents reveal the Land O' Lakes statement to be the aberration. In 1979 *Sapientia Christiana* conditioned that commitment with the requirement for a canonical mission for theology/religions teachers, and the new Code of Canon Law in 1983 mentions a "mandate" for theologians in Canon 812. There are in the Document of the Congregation on Christian Education several instances in which the recognition of academic freedom is carefully, but not specifically, modified.

education leaders. As attractive and, indeed, illuminating as they undoubtedly are, they are also inadequate to all that Catholic higher education actually does.

The mediating conversation between Church and culture is not primarily with those outside and for those within. The conversation is within and about ourselves and our dual rootage in the history and culture of the West, not only ancient and medieval but modern and contemporary. The image of the dialogue between faith and culture is accurate only if it is realized that the dialogue is first and foremost my dialogue with my traditions. My traditions embrace not only the line that runs from the four Gospels to the present Catholic Church, but the line that runs from Haran through Sinai and Jamnia to present-day rabbinic Judaism and the fate of Israel, and again, the line that runs from Adam through Babel and the nations of the *Goyim* to my brothers and sisters in the Golden Temple of Amritsar, and to my brothers and sisters who shout for joy at the sight of the Ka'bah. Proximately, my intellectual tradition includes that modern Western culture forged largely without the aid of and often with the opposition of our Church. In this sense neither I nor Catholic higher education belongs solely to the Church; the Catholic university is as well an educational institution of the human community with responsibility for the traditions of that community.

We must deal with our Enlightenment heritage in exactly the same way we deal with our Catholic heritage, *in oratione obliqua et in oratione recta*, by historical scholarship and creative engagement, by the hermeneutics of retrieval and not only of suspicion. On the Enlightenment side, as on the Catholic side, there are things to be undone and repented of, but on both sides there are things to be celebrated and appropriated. The issue now, it seems to me, is the critical engagement of the Church as well as of the Enlightenment, suspicion of them both and not just of one, retrieval of them both and not just of one.[5] The Catholic university is the best example of the dual rootedness of contemporary Catholic life, and is the place where the complicated interrelation of the roots can be worked out intellectually.

That task is manifestly not a matter of educating students and prepar-

---

[5]See William Portier, "The Mission of a Catholic College," *Theology and the University*, ed. J. Apczynski, 237–54, on the question whether the Enlightenment represents a radical break with the past in regard to freedom of inquiry. In the typical Enlightenment view, Christianity, especially the Roman Catholic Church, presents an anti-human ideology inherently opposed to Enlightenment humanism. Although there is data to support the accusation, it is not all the data there are, and some Enlightenment figures chose to ignore the other. To repeat the remark of David Tracy in *Plurality and Ambiguity: Hermeneutics, Religion, and Hope* (San Francisco: Harper and Row, 1987), there is not tradition, the Enlightenement included, that is not morally ambiguous.

ing them for life in the real world (as we teachers love to think we are doing), but rather a question of educating ourselves who are already the real
world, discovering ourselves in that real world, what kind of world it is,
and how we are to be at once responsible and critical citizens of both society and Church. Our *real* world is in fact the ecclesial world, the American
cultural world, the Western world, the human world; we are in it, it is ours,
not in the sense of lost and conquered territory but as a common heritage.

Catholic higher education's struggle over the past twenty-five years, if
I read the literature aright, has been about Catholic higher education's identity as higher learning (professionalization, specialization, "excellence"),
and it has also been about Catholic higher education's identity as Catholic.
Essentially the second has been an argument over whether loyalty to a tradition need be dogmatic and uncritical, specifically whether the Catholic
university could house argument and conversation about the most basic
religious issues and serious disagreement about them.[6] In the course of this
discussion—now a generation old and continuing—Catholic higher education might have surrendered its Catholic identity. It seems to me that the
vigor of the Association of Catholic Colleges and Universities, for one thing,
is proof that it has not. Some may argue that Catholic higher education
has quit or is in danger of quitting its Catholic identity.[7] But my experience
confirms my reading. I have spent some time on a dozen Catholic campuses in the past few years, and the difference from my own university is
palpable. Catholic higher education has refused to allow a separation of religion from the rest of life and academic life from the service of the Church
and the community.

But the struggle over educational excellence and Catholic identity reflects
the explicit dual commitment of Catholic education, to live in the Christian story and to do so dialectically. We not only sing and enact the story,

---

[6]See James Heft, "Academic Freedom and the Catholic University," *Theology and the Uni-
versity*, ed. J. Apcyznski, 207–37; and George A. Kelly, ed., *Why Should a Catholic University
Survive?* (New York: St. John's University Press, 1973); Neil G. McCluskey, S.J., ed., *The
Catholic University: A Modern Appraisal* (Notre Dame, Ind.: University of Notre Dame Press,
1970). For a view from within the controversy, see the essays by Peter O'Reilly and Rosemary
Lauer on St. John's University, *Continuum* 4 (Summer 1966) 223–52.

[7]See George A. Kelly, *Why Should a Catholic University Survive?;* David O'Brien warns about
losing a sharp sense of Catholic identity in his *Horizons* essay. Colleges in New York took down
their crucifixes in order to qualify for state funds; a few Catholic colleges gave up their Catholic identity entirely, among them Manhattanville College. But it may also be true that Catholic colleges curtail their academic interest in the name of Catholic identity, at least in the sense
that their devotion to traditional Catholic communitarian values exceeds their devotion to
academic excellence. A soon to be released DePaul University study shows that academic excellence is not a priority of some United States Catholic colleges in the view of students, faculty,
and administrators.

but reflect on it. We question it: What does it really mean? Need it be purified? How are we to live with it and in it? To what does it lead us? Has it been subject to distortion? Has it served oppression? Who sings and acts it with authority? Catholic higher education is a home of dialectical reason, of the *logos*, but also of the story, the *mythos*, and not one without the other. There seems to me very little chance that Catholic higher education will now make the same mistake as the Enlightenment, namely, reject the story as an illusion and replace it with a now discredited "Story of Reason," signalled so neatly in Harvard's motto, *Veritas*, wherein truth has been deftly amputated from Harvard's original *Veritas pro Christo et ecclesia*.

University is the *locus* of analysis and dialectical examination of ecclesiological, political, and cosmogonic myths. Romanticism, a counter-revolution against the original Enlightenment's attempt to eliminate myth, attempted a restoration of myth on the grounds of intuition; its Catholic cousin, Integralism, despite its claims to logical coherence, defended the Catholic myth on the basis of dogmatic faith, another version of intuitionism; their opponents, the Modernists, hankering after modernization through demythologization, wanted religious commitment to rest on the Romantic intuition.[8]

But commitment resting on Romantic intuition is not enough, any more than Enlightenment reason is enough. Commitment, at a certain stage in the life and development of a community and an individual, must be joined by self-criticism. It has been so joined in Catholic higher education, and this is a reason for the *religious* trouble into which Catholic higher education occasionally falls. Let me suggest a parallel. William Bennett, former Secretary of Education, wanted from American Higher Education a commitment without criticism, and perhaps some Catholic leaders and scholars want from Catholic higher education a commitment without criticism also. Bennett wanted a blank check on the classics of the West, and perhaps some Catholics want one on the magisterium.[9] But the modern uni-

---

[8]On the variety of American Catholic adjustments and reactions to American culture, see Patrick Carey's introductory essay to his collection of texts, *American Catholic Religious Thought: The Shaping of a Theological and Social Tradition* (Mahwah, N.J.: Paulist Press, 1987), and his essay "American Catholicism and the Enlightenment Ethos," a paper read to the Woodrow Wilson Center (April 1990), and to appear in a volume of papers entitled *Knowledge and Belief in America*, ed. Michael J. Lacey and myself (Cambridge University Press). See also the typology outlined by David O'Brien, including Romantic Catholicism, in his *Public Catholicism* (New York: Macmillan, 1989). On the Catholic modernist crisis of the turn of the twentieth century and its Integralist component, see Gabriel Daly, *Transcendence and Immanence: A Study in Catholic Modernism and Integralism* (London: Clarendon Press, 1980), and Lester Kurtz, *The Politics of Heresy* (Los Angeles: University of California Press, 1986).

[9]See William J. Bennett, "To Reclaim a Legacy" (Washington, D.C.: National Endowment for the Humanities, 1984); W. Shea, "John Dewey and the Crisis of the Canon," *The American Journal of Education* 97 (May 1989) 289–311; and "From Classicism to Method:

versity, while it may be the grandchild of the medieval university, is the direct offspring of the Enlightenment.[10] Its metier, when it is at its (Platonic?) best, is dialectical criticism. The university, Catholic or otherwise, may have no unquestionable assumptions and commitments, no ideologies or dogmas beyond question, argument, and conversation. Neither of its roots can escape research, interpretation, history, and dialectic, and both need constant creative transposition.

The culture you live in, then, is Catholic but much else besides, and it is *all* yours and not just its Catholic aspects. In other words, while you are Catholic, that is not the only thing you are. Second, you are one type of Catholic and that is not the only type of Catholic there is. In fact, if you are like myself, you may be several of the other types. The culture on the other side of that imagined borderline is *our* culture. The Church on this side of our imagined borderline is itself a truly remarkable plurality that needs mediation, and not a simple unity that needs only reiteration. Thus, press it a bit and the image of the borderline yields to an educational task far more complex than appears in the usual rhetoric, my own included.[11]

The pluralism of our individual and communal life is not adequately comprehended in the two terms Church and culture. The point is that we ourselves are plural. Figuring out what constitutes the plurality is a genuine intellectual problem; and learning to cope with pluralism is one of the chief objectives of higher education. We inherit both the culture of the Enlightenment and the culture of the Church. Like Matthew and Luke, we are not explained by Mark alone, but also by Q.

John Dewey and Bernard Lonergan," *American Journal of Education* 98 (May 1990). For the conservative interpretation of current tensions in the Catholic Church, see George A. Kelly, *The Crisis of Authority* (Chicago: Regnery Co., 1982).

[10]See "The Mission of Holy Cross," a paper prepared by a faculty committee under the chairmanship of David O'Brien. In it we read: "An American Catholic liberal arts college shares much with any other American liberal arts college: a commitment to standards of open, critical inquiry which derive from the Enlightenment, to tolerance born of insight into the plural and ambiguous character of societies and of history, and to an intellectual and moral community which affirms freedom of inquiry, of speech, and of religion. Holy Cross thus in large part accepts the institutional structures and assumptions about knowledge and inquiry that are honored in any Western college or university" (8). This is an interesting confirmation of my "two source theory."

[11]W. M. Shea, "Beyond Tolerance," *Theology and the University.*

Part III
The Church after Vatican II

Introduction to the Liturgy

Liturgical Renewal

Philip J. Murnion

It is not possible to summarize liturgical renewal in a few paragraphs. Rather, I will offer but a few reflections on renewal.

First, while the renewed forms of all the rites, which stress intelligibility and participation, have the potential of revolutionizing such basic matters as where we locate the presence of God, how we establish and foster relationship with God through the mystery of Christ and in the community of the Church, and what are to be the relationships between the people of God and the clergy, nonetheless the new form still lives in old (sometimes hand-me-down) wineskins. The members of the Church, laity and clergy alike, still retain much of the preconciliar paradigm as their basic orientation to ecclesiology and liturgy. God's presence not only is "out there" for many of us (and perhaps at least sometimes for most of us), but in recent years we are in danger of pushing God farther out into deistic distance from the human condition. This can be as true of the transcendentalists who derogate from the value of human processes as for the immanentists who make the sacred so familiar and homely that any self-respecting God must be more awe-inspiring than that. The mystery of God's presence in the community as well as in the Communion is yet to be adequately and reliably expressed in Mass and sacraments, in the words and music, the postures and gestures, the symbols and space of the participants. We seem to be halfway there and with little consensual effort to stay the path of renewal begun in the council.

Second, since the Scriptures are at the heart of the renewal as living Word of God and as the language of the exchange between God and the assembly, it makes a difference how well-versed we are in this language and how well-served we have been in the translations we have been provided. The just-being-completed revised translations of the lectionary are evidence that our first vernacular lectionary, in its use of familiar language, often lacked the ability to express the Word of God in all its power. Furthermore, it was the contention of one of the conference papers that the abridgement of the psalms used in the liturgy often eliminated the "lament" expressions, those verses which touched the agony of our relationship with God, something any language of prayer needs if it is to be authentic. But aside from the biblical words we are given, the power of the liturgy depends on our familiarity with these words. In recent years, the Bible has become much more familiar to Catholics in general and to the thousands who have participated in Scripture courses, study groups, and prayer groups in particular. Nonetheless, much greater familiarity will be necessary for the liturgy to be truly our discourse with God, for God's words to be our words.

Third, the liturgy is located in the Church, the Church that defines the relationships among its members—laity, religious, clergy, hierarchy—and its relationships with the wider world in all its actions and policies. Both sets of relationships are in transition. Internally, along the male-female, lay-clerical, individual-communal, and hierarchical-collegial axes relationships are not clear or consensual. Externally, where the Church community is located along the cultural-countercultural and the social-political continua remains to be worked out. The ambiguity and tensions in these relationships seriously affect the quality of the public, corporate worship we call liturgy.

We can take some pride in the fact that the Catholic Church in the United States, with probably the most diverse membership, has been as forthright and energetic in pursuing renewal as any Church. Furthermore, the members of the Church have taken on the new forms of worship with general enthusiasm. The challenge is to complete the full reform of which the initial stages are as much promise as fulfillment.

In the conference session, attention focused on the rite of reconciliation because two of the four papers offered views on this rite. The papers fostered lively discussion on the individual rite of reconciliation and on how to make it as fully an occasion of grace, as much of an ecclesial and spiritual experience as possible, one in which confessor and penitent stand under the same cross with equal need of salvation and jointly celebrate the mercy of God. The paper that follows offers a valuable analysis of and helpful proposals for the reform.

Chapter 16

Sin, Penance, and Reconciliation in the Postconciliar Church

Francis J. Buckley, S.J.

Many people say that Christians today have *lost a sense of sin*. They point to the rising rate of divorce, of pregnancy outside marriage, of abortion, of drug use, of pornography, of terrorism, of suicide. Not only do people perpetrate these horrors; they boast of them. They call what is bad good and openly flaunt it as a desirable life style—or death style. We are so bombarded by different moral standards that all boundary lines seem to have become fuzzy and unfocused.

Sin does not grate on us like fingernails scraping a chalkboard or assault us like a whiff of raw sewage. We grow accustomed to it like tasteless tomatoes or squeaky hinges or leaky faucets, like the background noise of city traffic or the presence of smog or lead in the air, as part of the environment in which we live and move and have our being. We take sin for granted and adjust to it.

We have swung so far away from the distorted image of a vengeful God always watching to punish us if we slip, that now God is pictured as a benign and doting grandparent who smiles at our temper tantrums and lets us grow up to be little dictators. The parables of Jesus about eternal punishment seem to many to be rhetorical exaggerations, hardly to be taken seriously. Surely God will be able to find some excuse for our faults, just as we do ourselves. This is quite like the line of argument used by the serpent in the Garden of Eden: "God told you that you would die if you ate the fruit of this tree? Oh no, you won't die. God must have been mistaken when God said that. Or perhaps you did not understand God correctly. Or maybe God is jealous and does not really want you to be happy. Try it. You'll like it."

When finally our eyes are opened and we do think of sin as destroying or threatening a relationship with God, it is usually someone else's relationship, not our own. It is so much easier to spot injustice or malice in someone else's attitudes or behavior, to spot a speck in their eyes while overlooking the two-by-four in our own. Who would be so foolish as to jeopardize a relationship with God? Both Peter and Judas said, "Not I, Lord! Don't blame me."

On the other hand, people today all over the world are far more aware of the sinfulness of racism, whether in America or South Africa or Sri Lanka. We are more sensitive to the exploitation and abuse of women and children and minority ethnic groups. We are more alert to senseless biases against the aged or handicapped. We have felt moral revulsion at the genocides carried out in our century in Germany, Poland, Russia, Turkey, Yugoslavia, Cambodia. We are appalled at religious wars in Lebanon, Northern Ireland, Nigeria, and the Sudan, where religion is often used as a cloak for economic or political self-interest. We are shocked at the pollution of our environment and the tragic waste of our resources on costly weapons systems instead of food, clothes, and shelter for the burgeoning population of the world.

We have modern novels with no heroes, modern plays with no plot, modern music with no melody or harmony, modern art with no shape or beauty, modern philosophy with no meaning. Our artists thus express symbolically the confusion, discord, depression, and despair which plague us from without and tear us asunder from within. We are all too conscious of evil, demonic forces beyond our understanding or control. *In fact, we have not lost but deepened our sense of sin.*

We have become sensitive to sin on three levels—*micro, macro,* and *cosmic.* The New Rite of Penance (225–28) provides an examination of conscience on the *micro level,* focusing on "what *I* have done or failed to do." Have I broken the commandments of God or the Church? Or better, have I deepened my response to God? Have I deepened my relationships?

There is also a *macro level*—social sin in which biases, prejudice, greed, resentment, fear, lust, anger, impatience, racial or ethnic or national pride are built into political, social, and economic structures. Examination of social conscience usually looks at "what *we* have done or failed to do."

Have we been sensitive to social injustices, to the homeless who are mentally disturbed and unable to care for themselves, to the illegal aliens who are afraid to return home and are often exploited here, to pastors and church administrators who refuse to pay a living wage or let workers organize into unions despite the clear teaching of the Church, to the AIDS victims who are virtually banished from jobs and schools, to unwed mothers who are pressured into marriage or abortion? What have we done, not just as individuals, but in *groups,* to care for the victims—and even more importantly, to remove the causes of social injustices and sins? Do we elect legislators who will work against what the Pope calls "the senseless and immoral arms race,'' who will resist the liquor lobby, who will vote against funding abortion? Do we help Mothers Against Drunk Drivers, Alcoholics Anonymous, the Sanctuary movement, bilingual education?

In the groups which we belong to—unions, country clubs, political parties—are we guilty of any social sins in the way we treat one another? Are there factions or cliques which damage the common good? Are there any biases or vices or fear or pride built into the rules or bylaws or customs? What can we do about that individually or with other members of the group? What can our group do to fight against social sin and injustice in the broader society around us? Are we doing enough?

There is also a *cosmic level* of sin which pervades everything—our sluggishness in resisting evil, our reluctance to do good, our bland optimism that everything will work out okay, our pessimistic suspicion that whatever we do will make no difference anyway, a feeling that it is useless to fight city hall or the Mafia or drug dealers or drunk drivers or the insurance companies or the government of South Africa or China or Cambodia since the environment is being destroyed and the economy is out of control and politicians will never have the courage to sacrifice their own personal interests for the sake of the common good, and even if such politicians did exist they would never get nominated and we could never vote for them. We do not today have the energy or passion for good because our parents or teachers or friends did not love us as they should have, and so our response to God inevitably has been doomed to fall short of what it should be. The serpent in the Garden of Eden in Genesis has grown into the great red dragon of the Apocalypse and it is threatening to swallow us all.

This pervasive presence of evil sapping courage and hope is a form of sin which is cumulative and transcends the personal responsibility of any one individual. We all are responsible for giving in to it, we all are affected by it, we all must struggle against it, not relying on our own power but relying on God's promises to come and help us make this a better world. It is good to examine our consciences to see if we have yielded to it—and to listen to what God says about it and how God invites us to overcome it in and through the Church.

I. Reconciliation

There are several levels of reconciliation, just as there are levels of sin. *On the micro level* of the individual, after we have looked into our hearts and recognized the personal sins there, we repent and ask God to forgive and heal us. This is usually done in individual confession with absolution. Most penitents confess only their own personal sins, rarely mentioning social sin, occasionally asking for help with cosmic sin.

On the macro level social sin is brought to awareness very effectively by communal penance services with or without absolution. It is important for us to become aware how the Church is damaged not only by individual sins, but also by sinful structures which compromise our apostolate directly and indirectly. For example, racism or ethnic pride can directly weaken our preaching of the gospel if we demand that everyone adopt Western European Catholicism as the only legitimate form of the Church. Some priests in our country removed all statues and vigil lights from the Church, keeping Hispanics from feeling at home. Some bishops refused to allow charismatic prayer groups in their dioceses. Indirectly the witness of the Church to God's preferential option for the poor is weakened if the Church talks a lot about social justice but does not put it into action. That is why the Synods of 1971 and 1977 said that action on behalf of social justice is an essential element of the gospel.

The Constitution on the Sacred Liturgy of Vatican II (no. 27) states that communal celebration involving active participation of the people is to be preferred in all sacraments to a more private and individual celebration. In the sacrament of reconciliation, communal celebration calls attention to the presence and role of the Church as the community hurt by sin and healing sin.

In communal penance services, communal singing, the proclamation of God's Word, a homily, an examination of conscience, a communal penance, a rich symbolism of community (joined hands, imposition of hands, tracing of a cross on the forehead, ashes, water, incense, burning a list of sins, a knotted rope cut or burned or dissolved, candles, sign of peace, solemn blessing, alms) highlight the communal nature of sin and forgiveness and reparation, and foster an appreciation of Church as a family of sinners who are grateful for being forgiven and who pledge to help one another remain faithful to the God who has welcomed us home. We are reminded of our responsibility to work together in the power of the Spirit to repair the damage done by our sins and to make the Church more attractive by our love.

On the cosmic level communal penance services can make us more aware of the cumulative effects of original sin on us personally and on society, so that we rely more deliberately on God's healing strength and ask God to set us free from the bonds of past sins so that we can more joyously celebrate our liberation.

II. The Theology Underlying the New Rite of Penance

There seems to be a cycle in the history of penance to move from the medicinal model (Jesus and Paul) to juridical ("public penance") to medicinal (Irish monks) to juridical (scholastics and Trent) to medicinal today.[1] This may be due to a constant tendency of all institutions to codify charisms, to embody piety in law. The charism then reappears spontaneously in a new form not covered by law. The motivation for codification is good: to stress the importance of piety; but the result is often stifling. Certainly this has been the experience with penance in the Church. Ladislas Orsy, S.J.,[2] Dionisio Borobio,[3] and the Introduction accompanying the New Rite[4] all try to reemphasize the medicinal dimension. But priests still generally operate according to the judicial model; this creates tensions. It is one reason why so many of them feel inadequately trained. This emerged in a recent survey of bishops, clergy, and laity.[5]

The role of the fundamental option in the spiritual life, touching both sin and reconciliation, is readily recognized by American Catholics. Sin is not seen primarily as a pattern of behavior, but as the underlying attitude. Reconciliation then demands a change of heart, a rearrangement of priorities which will affect behavior. This ties in closely with the shift from the juridical model, which is concerned with externals, to the medicinal model, in which the focus is interior healing. This also flows from the biblical emphasis on covenant. Sin is infidelity to our covenant relationship to God and the community. Both God and covenant community call us to conversion and help us to a change of heart.

Gradually the term "reconciliation" seems to be replacing "confession" or "penance" as the preferred term for the sacrament. This indicates that people are recovering the insight that God plays the primary role in the process of healing, and that renewal of our relationship with God (recon-

---

[1]F. J. Buckley, S.J., "Healing and Reconciliation in the Gospel according to Luke," *Tripod* 52 (August 1989) 31–37, rpt. in *Emmanuel* 96:2 (March 1990) 74–80; "Tradition and the Traditions," *Emmanuel* 96:2 (January 1990) 14–21; "Punishment and Penance in a Changing World and Society," *Theology Confronts a Changing World*, ed. Thomas M. McFadden, Annual Publication of the College Theology Society (Mystic, Conn.: Twenty-Third Publications, 1977) 243–45.

[2]"The Sacrament of Penance: Problem Areas and Disputed Questions," *Proceedings of the Canon Law Society of America* (1986).

[3]"The Tridentine Model of Confession in its Historical Context," *Concilium* (1987) 22, 27–29, 32.

[4]Secs. 1, 4, 5, 6, 7, 10, 11, 18. Cf. also "Report of the CTSA Committee on the Renewal of the Sacrament of Penance," *Catholic Theological Society of America* (1975) 15, 25, 32; F. J. Buckley, S.J., "Recent Developments in the Sacrament of Penance," *Communio* 1 (Spring 1974) 84–88; "Punishment and Penance," *Theology Confronts a Changing World*, 234–36, 240–43, 246–54.

[5]"Sin and Reconciliation in the United States Today: Report on a Survey Conducted by the National Conference of Catholic Bishops," *Living Light* (Fall 1990). The official report on the survey appeared in *Origins* 19:38 (February 22, 1990) 613–24.

ciliation) is more important than the acts of the penitent (penance and confession), though these remain important.

The shift to the interior is also reflected in the fact that central concern in the sacraments has moved from validity to fruitfulness, from *ex opere operato* to *ex opere operantis*. This was a healthy development, focusing on the ultimate purpose of the sacraments, spiritual growth and union with God. It also was directly intended by the Constitution on the Liturgy (no. 11). This development is quite congenial to American pragmatism, to our proclivity to tinker with what we do to do it better.

III. Shifts in Traditional Piety

After Vatican II, the Bible replaced rote prayers like the rosary, litanies, and novenas. Its prominence in the Liturgy of the Word at Mass accelerated a pre-existing trend to Bible study. Scripture also became prominent in penitential services, charismatic meetings, basic communities, Renew, the retreat movement, and other movements. Television and radio evangelists became very popular among Catholics, reinforcing interest in the Bible.

People became more, not less, active in liturgical and personal piety. This was the primary goal of the liturgical reform of Vatican II (*Sacrosanctum Concilium,* nos. 10, 11, 14). Popular movements also abounded, in which people assumed more responsibility apart from the liturgy.

The Eucharist became more central in piety, not simply to be adored in Benediction, but to be eaten as spiritual food in Communion, uniting the communicant to both the community and to God. Physical symbols were rediscovered as leading to spiritual effects. People came to appreciate the presence of Christ in the ministers, in the Scripture readings, in the entire community as well as in the Eucharistic species (*Sacrosanctum Concilium,* no. 7).

Interest in spirituality has blossomed. Sessions on the spiritual life at religious education congresses are sellouts. More and more people are getting spiritual directors. Retreats, long and short, are becoming more popular. Books on prayer are best sellers. This reflects broader cultural trends: fascination with forms of Eastern mysticism, with Native American religion which celebrates harmony with the cosmos, with new prayer forms. This is also connected to a deeper sense of incarnation and sacramentality, to a desire to encounter God in others, in dialogue, in touch, in community, and in persons who represent that community.

These trends heightened expectations of more personal involvement in reconciliation, which were not met in the routine celebration of the sacrament in Rite I (individual confession and absolution).

Some priests wanted to confine the sacrament to mortal sins and even suggested to penitents that they were wasting their time with trivia, thus driving penitents away. As numbers declined, hours for confession were rescheduled to meet the convenience of the priests, not the people.

The healing aspects stressed in the renewal of the sacrament were not brought out by confessors in celebrating Rite I: half of them do not adapt penances to the sins, needs, and circumstances of penitents; more than half never or rarely discuss formation of conscience or the nature of sin.

Official Church teaching before, during, and after Vatican II had begun to stress social sin, and occasionally cosmic sin. Individual confession was not well adapted to highlight this, but penitential services were very effective in heightening awareness of these other forms of sin. This was a growth in piety based on fidelity to the magisterium. If it found its expression in communal penance celebrations, why not attribute this development to the work of the Holy Spirit? This new sensitivity to social sin and the need for God's healing may be a change as significant as the move from public to private penance fourteen hundred years ago.

IV. Deeper, More Realistic Sense of Sin

Not all sin is mortal; in the past mortal sin was trivialized by calling trifles mortal sins (breaking laws of fast and abstinence, skipping prime when praying the Divine Office). People today have a more accurate sense of mortal sin as totally destroying their relationship with God; experience tells them that this has not happened, so they are aware that forgiveness does not demand confession by species and number.

Personal sin does not loom so large in the consciousness of the faithful as it does to some of the bishops. The effects of original sin and social sin seem more important consciously and subconsciously to the laity. They are aware of a certain sluggishness in their spiritual life and massive evils beyond any individual's control. They sense the need of God's healing grace to set them free. But these phenomena are rarely confronted in Rite I. People do not feel personally responsible for such sinfulness and consider Rite I to deal with personal responsibility. They do, however, feel somehow responsible for social sin (they explicitly mention that they have received better catechesis on this)—and that is why they attend communal penance services (Rites II and III) in such large numbers, though penitents are still only a fragment of the whole Church.

In Rite I the fundamental question seems to be, "Am I living up to my ideals?" In Rites II and III the fundamental question becomes, "Are my ideals those of the gospel?" Other questions follow: "Are others suffering because of what I have done or failed to do? Are others suffering because of what other people do? What is my responsibility toward those who suffer and those who exploit them?" These questions show moral progress.

We have a deeper appreciation of other means of forgiveness such as: prayer, the Eucharist, alms (acts of charity to others), fasting (self-control), attempts to repair damage; prayer groups and basic communities, which provide opportunities to discuss challenges; spiritual direction and private retreats; communal reconciliation services; the sacrament for the sick; healing Masses.[6] Past experience alienated many—some felt rushed, or wondered why others took so long, were annoyed with distractions instead of entering into a deep examination of conscience, disappointed with insensitive confessors, plagued with false guilt, confessing sins and expressing sorrow by rote.

V. How to Retain the Best of the Past

We can provide a better catechesis on sin and redemption.

There is confusion about the moral teaching of the Church—what the Church actually teaches and what type of assent must be given. Some people assume that what is statistically normal is morally good.

The redemptive death of Jesus should awaken us to the destructive nature of sin as attempted deicide, as an attempt to get rid of the true God to substitute a false god—less demanding and threatening to the status quo. Against that backdrop the passion also reveals the generous mercy of God, Jesus' sacrificial gift of himself to touch our hearts.

The gospels portray Jesus as sent to set people free from hunger, poverty, ignorance, prejudice, loneliness, and disease precisely because all of these have a relationship to sin and symbolize the effects of sin. The Church continues this liberating and healing mission of Christ in many ways, but addresses sin and repair of the damage done by sin most particularly through the sacrament of penance and reconciliation.

The dominant American culture favors superficiality, individualism, quick fixes, scapegoating, and irresponsibility. But shirking responsibility is in fact responding "No" to God—and it has consequences on the spiritual life of oneself and others. At Mass we ask God to forgive the evil we did and the good we failed to do. Yet more than half the priests rarely or never preach about sin or the formation of conscience.

Even though the laity say they have a strong sense of sin and that they have had better catechesis on how sin affects their relationship with God

---

[6] "Report of the CTSA Committee," *Catholic Theological Society of America,* 9. For a bibliography on this, see Felix Funke, "Survey of Published Writings on Confession over the Past Ten Years," *Concilium* 61, 129 ff.

and the Church and human society, the media consistently fail to show any sinful dimension of the all-pervasive cultural evils (drugs, violence, terrorism, poverty, disease, prejudice). What is worse, priests rarely preach on the social and ecclesial dimensions of sin (usually only at celebrations of Rite II or III in Advent and Lent—which are attended only by a small fragment of the parish). Priests need more training to preach effectively on the ecclesial dimensions of sin and penance, helping people to realize that the entire Church is wounded by each sin and that the entire Church prays for the conversion of sinners. Parish bulletins could be used to catechize about the sacrament, making clear the connection between sinful social structures and the sacrament of reconciliation. It is important for people to realize that the sacrament liberates from the personal consequences of sin and also from the broader consequences which they feel so uneasy about.

We can provide a better catechesis on the value of frequent confession, apart from obligation.

Such a catechesis must build on experience. It cannot substitute for experience. Therefore, it will be successful only after the clergy have been retrained so that people experience confession as prayerful, healing, fruitful.

Most penitents do not think they need the sacrament; they feel that other means of forgiveness are open to them. Insistence on the necessity of the sacrament will therefore fall on deaf ears. This may indeed be a sign of moral maturity on their part: they are forming their consciences, then deciding for themselves. They have discovered what most helps them encounter the merciful God who welcomes, forgives, and heals them.

People should be encouraged to confess because they want to, not because they have to. In fact, people who have really destroyed their spiritual life through mortal sin and later repent invariably want to confess, regardless of any law compelling them to do so. In reality any such law may be descriptive rather than prescriptive.

For centuries sacramental absolution was received rarely in the Church. The reason for more frequent confession was not some law, but the experience of the people that this helped spiritual growth. Hence the vital questions are: "How can the sacrament be made more attractive? How can it be connected to people's deep hunger for contact with God, for spiritual healing and growth?"

We can train most priests to be good confessors.

Surely one key element in making the sacrament more attractive is to improve the skills of the confessors. In this sacrament the conversation is the sign. It embodies the sacramentality, especially in Rite I, the very Rite whose use has declined. Homilies and pastoral letters will not suffice. They will not reverse the trend until people experience the healing, forgiving, reconciling ministry of Jesus through the words of the priests. If people are deeply touched in the sacrament, they will return more often—and tell others to come.[7]

Not all priests have a charism to hear confessions fruitfully, using all the dynamics of Rite I. But even those who do have the charism need more training to be good confessors. Seminaries have not properly prepared them to celebrate forgiveness in such a way that the sacrament is made attractive and spiritually helpful, an encounter with the friendly and healing Savior.

We can make better use of communal penance celebrations.

Rite II, communal celebration with individual absolution, could combine the individual contact of Rite I with communal elements to highlight the communal nature of sin, forgiveness, reparation, and an appreciation of the Church as family. It can be particularly effective in calling attention to the role of the Church as the community hurt by sin and healing sin. This type of public gathering provides opportunities to heighten awareness even of individual sin, its causes and its effects on the individual and the community through the use of contemporary media—posters, photographs, slides, films, tapes, videocassettes. These cannot be used in Rite I. Rite II is well-attended in some parishes, attracting twenty-five percent of the parish. It is well-adapted to family reconciliation if the whole family attends. It seems to work best with small groups—retreats, school classes, children.

The response of the faithful to Rite III, general absolution, was positive and spontaneous, very like the response to the vernacular in the Eucharist. It was a genuinely popular religiosity, like that of novenas and Charismatic renewal. As many as thirty-three percent of some parishes attended this devotional form of penance. It broke the routine characteristic of Rite I and was popular with all age groups (especially the elderly and young), liberals and conservatives, from mentally handicapped to highly intelligent. In fact this rite brought many back to the sacraments. It has been especially helpful to the fearful, scrupulous, and embarrassed.

Sacramental celebrations with general absolution—Rite III—improve people's sense of the Church as a community of sinners who have been redeemed; already partly holy though not yet perfect. We are not alone in sin, but God loves us all—and asks us to accept one another as sinners trying to struggle against evil. God's mercy deserves to be celebrated communally.

[7]"Children and God: Communion, Confession, Confirmation," *Corpus* (1970); *"I Confess"—The Sacrament of Penance Today* (Notre Dame, Ind.: Ave Maria Press, 1972); *Reconciling* (Notre Dame, Ind.: Ave Maria Press, 1981).

Rite III provides an opportunity for a lengthy examination of conscience (and indirectly formation of conscience), especially on sins often overlooked by those who frequent Rite I: social sins like racism, economic injustice, institutionalized violence; general sinfulness, which is the experience of the effects of original sin; and the power of sin which leads to dehumanization and alienation. People want to be challenged by the gospel and have their social consciences stretched. Rite I does not usually stretch social conscience; Rite III does.

Even more interesting, the more frequently Rite III is celebrated, the more frequently people return to Rite I, individual confession and absolution. The reason may well be that in Rite III the people rediscover the ecclesial dimension of sin and the role of the Church in reconciliation. They become less satisfied with other means of reconciliation and desire the more personal sacramental sign of Rite I.

Many priests prefer Rite III as being more like the way Jesus treated people; not so juridical, complicated, and forbidding. This is in fact a return to the discipline of the early Church.[8] General absolution also provides an opportunity for priests to forgive who do not relate well to people in Rite I. Their celebration of the sacrament becomes fruitful as well as valid.

We can adapt the celebration of reconciliation to American culture.

Many people whose native language is not English find it hard to confess. Many from countries with a shortage of priests have no habit of frequent confession. Different ethnic groups—Anglos, Blacks, Hispanics, Filipinos, Vietnamese relate to the sacrament differently. They have different expectations and different customs. A simple, rapid touch may be very effective for some groups, especially in a public setting—e.g., Jesus with public sinners like the woman caught in adultery, the paralytics, lepers, Zacchaeus; Mother Teresa with crowds; the pope on tours. Hispanics are often content with the barest form of the sacrament, treasuring the briefest personal contact with the priest as a sign of God's personal concern. What for Anglos would be a truncated, mechanical ritual has profound meaning for them. This factor must be taken into account, since Hispanics will soon be at least forty percent of all Catholics in our country.

Another broader and perhaps more important cultural issue emerged from the recent survey on reconciliation: the massive misunderstanding among many bishops of the reasons for the drop in confessions. They thought people were staying away because they had lost a sense of sin, were confused about morality, and disagreed with Church teaching. The laity

---

[8]Ladislas Orsy, S.J., "General Absolution: New Law, Old Traditions, Some Questions," *Theological Studies* 45 (1984) 681–82.

ranked those reasons quite low; the real reasons were awareness of other means of forgiveness and bad experiences with confession in the past.

Many bishops thought people were not very interested in spiritual growth through the sacrament; the laity in fact ranked this quite high. This confusion among many bishops about what the people really want and value points to a serious need of bishops to listen to more laity and get to know them better. Otherwise two subcultures, clerical and lay, will develop in the Church in the United States, as it has in Europe.

In interpreting the canons which deal with Rite III, general absolution, not all bishops recognize that there are many occasions when too few priests are available for the proper celebrations of Rites I or II, which involve individual confession. If these confessions are not to be reduced to rote recitations of sin with little or no time for personal advice, they cannot average less than three minutes. If three hundred persons assemble, then ten priests would need an average of ninety minutes apiece, just to hear the confessions adequately, not counting time for the hymns, Scripture readings, and homily. This would make the penitential celebrations too long to be attractive in our culture.[9]

The bishops of the United States were within their canonical rights to decide that the "long time," *diu*, a person would have to remain in mortal sin without the opportunity to confess (to qualify for general absolution) would be one month.[10] But the minority of bishops who opposed that norm felt that it does not take the state of mortal sin seriously enough. They were right. St. Alphonsus Liguori thought that *diu* for remaining in mortal sin would be twenty-four hours, certainly not one month.[11] American Catholics are much closer to the spiritual sensitivity of St. Alphonsus.

[9]Buckley, "Recent Developments," *Communio* 1 (Spring 1974) 94–95.

[10]"The National Conference of Catholic Bishops and the bishops of the province of Iowa and of Region 9 (Iowa, Nebraska, Kansas, and Missouri) have determined that Form 3 should be used only on the condition that individual confession and absolution would not be available to penitents within one month after Form 3 is celebrated." Most Reverend William Bullock, "Reconciled in Christ," *Origins* 19:38 (February 22, 1990) 626; cf. also "The Sacrament of Penance: Guidelines for Illinois Dioceses," *Origins* 18:34 (February 2, 1989) 559; "Discussion of General Absolution at Collegeville," *Origins* 18:8 (July 7, 1988) 120–21.

[11]In *De Sacramento Paenitentiae*, sec. 490, he cites Suarez, Viva, Renzi, and Fagundez as interpreting *diu* as less than two to three days, and then adds, "It seems to me hard for one who is in mortal sin to remain without absolution for even one day." Vermeersch in *Theologia Moralis* 3 (Gregorian University Press, third ed.) sec. 588, says that one is excused from integrity by the inconvenience of not remaining in the state of grace for even one day, and goes on to cite Viva: "It is a very grave inconvenience to lack *diu* the sacramental grace of forgiveness of sins and the help of grace to avoid sin in the future, as well as the grace of the Eucharist, especially because contrition is difficult for a sinner remaining long in the state of mortal sin." Cf. also Buckley, "Punishment and Penance," *Theology Confronts a Changing World*, 251–52, 255.

Bishop Carlos Sevilla suggests that deaneries or parish clusters gather to celebrate communal penance with a bishop. This would heighten appreciation of the involvement of the universal Church. It would also bring bishops closer to the people for something other than the biennial celebration of confirmation. Another advantage is that the bishop could judge on the spot whether to provide general absolution.

Chapter 17

Regeneration and the Spiritual Power of the Laity

Joe Holland

Introduction

Somehow over the centuries the evangelical and sacramental charisms of ordained leadership and intentional communities, both institutional charisms *within* the community of Jesus' disciples, were partially disfigured by the imposition of two alien forms from pagan religions, namely the clerical and religious states—both defined as separate and spiritually higher subcultures *above* the laity. In this disfiguration of Jesus' community, most Christians came to understand themselves as outsiders to the evangelical and sacramental sphere, not truly holy like clergy or religious, and hence only clients or consumers of religious energy from these higher states. I believe the presently profound technological and spiritual crisis of late modern culture (a crisis which I have addressed elsewhere[1]) is in fact rooted in this disfiguration of Christian energy. Consequently, according to this analysis, the Catholic turn to the laity as the *ecclesial source* of spiritual energy is a great healing step for the Western Church and for Western culture. In this essay, I will focus on the distortion of clericalism in relation to the laity, since elsewhere I have addressed the late modern crisis of "religious life."[2]

I. The Rise of Pagan Clericalism

The idea of a religious or clerical elite caste is as old as human civilization. The high classical empires began with urban-based pagan king-warrior-priests who learned how to dominate various tribes around their cities, or-

[1]See my various essays on this theme available from The Warwick Institute, 257 Warwick Ave., South Orange, N.J. 07079 U.S.A.
[2]See my essay, "The Transformation of Religious Life at the Birth of a Postmodern Era of Lay Spirituality," also available from The Warwick Institute.

ganize them into worship at their temples, conscript their labor, and take from them heavy taxes.

One of the ways by which these king-warrior-priests justified their seizure of power was to say that their sphere of activities was sacred, while all else was profane. Profane in its Latin roots comes from *pro fanum* meaning "outside the temple." Thus what the pagan priests did in the temple was called sacred or religious, but what other people did outside the temple was called profane (or later secular).

As the early civilizations developed, the originally ruling king-warrior-priests eventually let others do their military work for them. Then it was not long before a separate military caste of warrior-nobles developed. Since the warrior-nobles now had the weapons, they turned the tables on the priests, took the kingship from them, and converted the priests into their ideological servants. Now the palace was separated from the temple. As a result of this priestly loss of kingly power, a tendency rose up and remained among priestly groups in all civilizations to resent those in society who held the highest power, in place of themselves.

So there has always been in human history this hidden and resentful clerical wish to regain control of all society. This is the first clerical temptation. To some degree it triumphed in Europe during the Middle Ages when bishoprics and monasteries became major centers of economic and military power.

But when such triumph was not feasible, priestly groups have been tempted to compensate for their absence of political and military power by puffing up their religious importance and by holding themselves religiously above others. This is the second clerical temptation. It was that way in Israel when Jesus came on the scene.

Yet the roots of the biblical tradition were always uneasy with the sacred/profane distinction. Recall that Yahweh originally did not want Israel to build a temple, for fear it would become like the pagan nations. Later, after the Temple had been built and become corrupt, King Josiah held the equivalent of Israel's Vatican II liturgical reform of the Temple. But the prophet Jeremiah warned that liturgical reform of the Temple alone was a shallow and even dangerous thing,

> Put not your trust in the deceitful words, "This is the temple of the Lord! The temple of the Lord! The temple of the Lord!" (Jer 7:4).

Because Israel narrowed its religious consciousness to "churchy" things and so became idolatrous, Yahweh had foreign armies destroy the Temple and send the people in the bitter suffering of exile, as Jeremiah had foretold. Still later, Jesus warned of the same danger, and the destruction of the second Jewish Temple soon followed.

II. The Lay Teaching of Jesus

Jesus did not present himself in Israel as a priest. Apparently he was not born into one of the priestly families (like his cousin John), nor did he wear priests' robes. He severely criticized those religious leaders who made a public display of special titles, flowing robes, seats of honor, etc. Rather, Jesus presented himself as a lay person—a teacher or rabbi yes, but in Israel the rabbinic teacher was lay.

To be still more careful that his followers not succumb to the clerical temptation, Jesus insisted that they should not call any of their leaders by the titles of rabbi, teacher, or even father. Thus in the Gospel according to Matthew, we read,

> As to you, avoid the title, "Rabbi." One among you is the teacher, the rest are learners. Do not call anyone on earth your father. Only one is your father, the One in heaven. Avoid being called teachers. Only one is your teacher, the Messiah (Matt 23:8-10).

Right after that in Matthew's Gospel comes Jesus' strongest denunciation of the religious leaders for setting themselves above the people. By contrast, Jesus' own teaching stressed that ordinary people are the salt of the earth, the light of the world, a holy nation, a priestly people, as indeed the Hebrew Scriptures had taught of the ordinary people of the *laos* of Israel.

The word that the translators of the Hebrew Scriptures into Greek had used to describe this chosen, holy, royal, and priestly people was *laos*, from which we derive our term "laity." The word "laity" thus means God's own chosen, holy, royal, and priestly people. The words religious and priestly are generally not used in the New Testament apart from laity, because they are contained in the laity.

III. Lay Character of the Early Church

When Christianity was separated from the synagogue, this idea of the chosenness, holiness, royalness, and priestliness of the *laos* (i.e., laity) was applied by Jesus' followers to the gathering of Jesus' disciples, which we call the "Church." They understood themselves as a holy nation, a priestly people. In that sense the word laity is simply an interchangeable term for the word Church.

How often have I been told by well-intentioned people that we should eliminate the word "laity," because it is so demeaning. Just the opposite! We need to eliminate the word "clergy" to rediscover the spiritual depth of the word "laity."

There were many offices and charisms in the early lay gathering of Jesus' disciples—especially the episcopate, the presbyterate, and the diaconate, as well as prophets, healers, etc. These were charismatic offices with real power—for example the *episcopos* or bishop was the real leader of the community of disciples, with real authority, though he was forbidden by Jesus from lording this authority over the community or from making himself seem important.

In addition, there was no thought that for religious reasons such lay leaders of the lay community would not be married. The witness of celibacy was treasured within the early Christian community, but it was not seen as a requirement for a special clerical or religious caste. Rather, it was to be found where the Spirit willed it—randomly within the full community of disciples. In fact, the presumption for the episcopal leaders of the community was just the opposite, namely that they would be married. So in the New Testament, we read,

> A bishop must be married only once . . . keeping his own children under control . . . for if a man does not know how to manage his own house, how can he take care of the Church of God (1 Tim 3:2-5).

This quote, if nothing else, should make it clear to us that the gospel has no place for the religious-secular distinction, which is historically based on the non-evangelical view that the sexual realm is somehow below the holy. In the Western tradition, such disparaging of human sexuality is a legacy not of Jesus, but of Plato.

Thus it was that Peter, the first bishop of Rome, was married, and Jesus visited the home of his mother-in-law. For centuries the Christians of Rome fondly celebrated the feast day of Petronilla (i.e., little female Peter), reportedly Peter's daughter, as one of their favorite saints.

Thus important Church offices and charisms were all understood as within the laity, not outside or above them. There was no special dress, or honor, or title for these people. In the apostolic Church, Peter had no title but Peter, John no title but John, etc. There were no holinesses nor eminences, nor most reverends, right reverends, very reverends, nor even unadorned reverends. Indeed John and the others would have been embarrassed by anyone who used such terms, and probably would have become angry at them for so threatening the gospel.

In the fundamental biblical sense, to distinguish by levels of honor, or by the holiness of states in life, the laity from the clergy, or even levels within clergy, or later so to distinguish "religious" from "seculars," or even "religious priests" from "secular priests," is a great blocking of the evangelical good news. There were of course the titles "sister" and "brother," but not for "professed religious"—rather for all in the gathering of disciples.

In this way, following Jesus' instructions, the apostolic Church made sure that all the disciples knew that the spiritual power of the gospel was their personal power and their personal responsibility. If some individuals did not feel sure of that power, it was only because they had not yet received the special gift of the Spirit, which is boldness. But that was solved by praying over them and asking the Spirit to come upon them with the gift of boldness. Thus lay boldness rather than clerical honor was the loving power of the early community of disciples.

IV. Subsequent Confusions and Healing Reforms

Later, with the appropriation of Roman imperial administrative forms of pagan religion, the word "clergy" was introduced into the Christian vocabulary and then counterposed to the word "laity." Bishops and presbyters were granted special social privileges by imperial Roman law, as had been the case with imperial pagan priests before. Eventually many of these "clergy," and especially the bishops among them, would be corrupted by the political power and financial wealth given to them in the late Roman Empire.

In reaction to this early clerical corruption of the leaders of the gathering of Jesus' disciples, a movement of reform grew up. This was the originally lay movement of the desert fathers, which later grew into monasticism. Some lay disciples abandoned the corruption of the urban Church of the Roman cities (which was forgetting the Cross) and went out to the desert, as Israel and Jesus had done before them. Over time, their reform had an enormous influence on the urban Church, such that a tradition developed in the Eastern Church that it was better to chose one's bishop from these reforming lay disciples in the desert, rather than from the often compromised urban clergy.

Over time, however, as monasteries grew wealthy and powerful, lay monks also wished to be clericalized, such that today monasticism appears to us as a clerical rather than lay movement. Yet even the prayer of the hours, which we consider a clerical or religious prayer, was originally a Jewish lay prayer, taken over from the synagogue where a minion of lay people, often elderly retired men, gathered throughout the day to pray the psalms of David.

Still later, with the rise of the medieval commercial cities, when monasticism lost much of its original spiritual power, new lay movements of renewal again developed to teach us the original vision of the gospel. Perhaps the most dramatic of these was the Franciscan movement.

Approximately eight hundred years ago, a young lay man named Giovanni Francesco Bernadone ("Saint Francis") gathered around himself some other lay people and originally called their little band the "brothers of the lower class," or on other occasions "the men of penance from Assisi." Today, in our typical obscuring of the biblical vision, we make Francis' followers sound "religified"—meaning something strange and distant from everyday Christians. Instead of the clear and simple translation of his group's name as "brothers of the lower class," we now use the Latinization, "friars minor." (*Menores,* from which comes the Latinization "minor," was the class term used in Francis' time to name the lower class of the poor.)

When even Francis' movement was forced to become religified and clericalized, he still turned to those who still knew themselves as lay to create what others would later call the "Third Order." The term "order" comes from imperial Roman administrative language, and means in effect a social class. Thus a lay third order would mean the third class down the social (or in this case spiritual) ladder. In that sense an "order" at the bottom of the spiritual ladder is paradoxically truest to Francis' deeply evangelical sense that the first shall be last and the last first. But Francis never called this group a third order, only "the brothers (and sisters) of penance"—one of the very names he had given to his original group in Assisi.

As we can now see, a central issue of reform for the Church today is the choice between these two alternatives.

The Imperial Clericalist Model

This is an elite clerical caste (adopted from pagan imperial religions) which is then portrayed as above the community of lay Christians, in effect suppressing the evangelical power of the laity. This model began with the imperial domestification of Christianity and intensified with the economic and military power of bishoprics and monasteries in the Middle Ages.

The Apostolic Lay Model

This is the original model of a lay community containing within it various charismatic offices, including the ministry of the ordained. This model allows the boldness of the Holy Spirit to come forth amidst the full lay community of Jesus' disciples, as we remember together that we are all empowered by and responsible for the love of the gospel.

When the lay rootedness of the entire Church is rediscovered, then the *laos* vastly increases its evangelical energy. But when this lay-rootedness is confused and forgotten by clericalism, then the *laos* is diminished in its evangelical energy. When the community of disciples allows this lay spiritual energy to weaken, its mission grows weak. When this lay-rooted energy is strengthened, then the community's mission grows strong.

We are once again at a crossroads in the Western Church. It appears that, in the new transition from a modern print-based culture to a post-modern electronic culture, the false power of clericalism is again fading. But the death of clericalism is not the same as the death of the ministry of ordained bishops, presbyters, and deacons, nor is the end of a higher "religious state in life" the end of evangelical intentional communities. To unleash the full power of these these offices and communities as servants of the spiritual boldness of the *laos,* it is necessary first to cast aside this clericalism and religiosity. But is this happening?

V. Various Present Tendencies

So far, in our present cultural transition, it seems that we have many distinct tendencies flowing among us all at once—some creative, some destructive, many ambiguous.

Neo-Clericalism

One dangerous tendency is a neo-clericalism—the attempt to protect fading cleric status and even to expand its false power. In some ways the power of neo-clericalism seems to be growing, but it may be simply the swan song of a dying form.

Lay Professionalism

A second dangerous tendency is to think that professionalization of lay ministries will solve the problem of the clerical crisis. We should welcome and clearly need countless more lay ministers, including ones who are well-prepared professionally. The danger here is not with lay ministries themselves, nor with professional training, but with a new temptation to replace a clerical hierarchical class with a professional bureaucratic class, and still not to turn in a fundamental way to the spiritual power of the broad lay roots of the *laos.*

Lay Privatization

A third dangerous tendency is deepening spiritual privatization—a spiritual renewal which turns the *laos* inward only toward Church activities, or points it outward but only in terms of ethics. The problem here is not the Church activities or ethics per se, but the failure to understand the sacred character of society in its family life and work life, in its science and technology, in its economics, politics, and culture—indeed in the sacred character of the entire universe—and to see these as mediators of the fundamental disclosure of the Word of God.

Two ambiguous but potentially creative tendencies, I believe, are both the reforms among many religious orders to link themselves with the laity, and the birth of new lay movements of renewal.

Religious-Lay Bonding Projects

These are to be praised for looking to the laity. In some cases, however, I have the impression that at least the language of bonding projects places the particular charism of the religious order in a more central position than the lay-oriented gospel of Jesus Christ. Thus sometimes literature invites lay people to join the religious in the institute's charism, rather than asking them through the institute's charism to serve the gospel of Jesus—into which laity have already been baptized. Wherever this danger is present, there would be a turn to lay energy, but only to protect the religious temptation.[3] On the other hand, the new association of traditional religious with laity offers the possibility for deep transformation of the communities themselves.

New Lay Movements

These are rich new examples of earlier waves of lay-inspired renewals of the community of Jesus' disciples. Some examples are Opus Dei, charismatic covenant communities, Communion and Liberation, etc. Such movements may be the great hope of the future of Catholicism. But presently sometimes such movements paradoxically appear to support a clericalist view of Church linked not to the normative vision of the New Testament, but to the imperial/medieval clerical distortions. Wherever this danger is present, a lay movement would be drawing on the rich treasury of lay energy, but then orienting it to serve the clerical temptation.

Small Communities

Finally, there are countless hopeful signs that many of Jesus' lay disciples, organized into small communities of the household church, are recovering the boldness of the Holy Spirit to share the good news with the full community of disciples, with family and friends, and with all the earth. This good news which Jesus brought tells us that as laity, indeed as humans, we are made in the female and male images of God, and that our spiritual creativity flows from the communion in us of those two divine images.

---

[3]Perhaps the most important United States experiment in this area is Maryknoll Lay Missioners. The Scarbor Foreign Mission Society in Canada has a similar and important project which, though smaller than the Maryknoll one, is marked by greater community integration.

VI. Problems of the Lay Side

In pointing to the laity, I do not wish to suggest that the laity are some magic utopian solution just waiting to end the interrelated crises of Western culture and the Western Church. Quite the contrary. For if Western culture is in crisis, then the laity are a central part of that crisis.

My own experience suggests that the laity will be drawn into their full-blown vocation, communion, and mission only slowly, and perhaps kicking and screaming in protest along the way—much like an addict being forced into a recovery program. Addicts do not wish to face their accountability for the spiritual power within them. They do not wish to admit that their own image is the image of God. Neither do any of us. Thus it is also with the Catholic laity.

Recall that when Moses, in response to God's command and power, led the children of Israel out of their slavery in Egypt, the children of Israel did not thank Moses. Rather they complained to him,

> Why did you do this to us? Why did you bring us out of Egypt? Did we not tell you this in Egypt, when we said, "Leave us alone, let us serve the Egyptians?" (Exod 14:11-12)

So will it be, I believe, with the laity's acceptance of evangelical power and mission. Its birthing may occur only in anger and protest—perhaps as a wife sometimes curses her husband when the muscular contractions of childbirth reach their peak. "Why did you do this to me," the laity may bitterly lash out at those Church leaders and staff, as well as other lay leaders, who truly confront them with the terror of their spiritual power.

By the way, this spiritual power comes not first from our being Christian, but from our humanity. The image of God in us is not first the Christian image, but the human image. That image has been wounded by sin, but not destroyed. The purpose of the gospel is not to substitute for our human spiritual power, but to heal it and to make it even more powerful.

But it appears so much easier for lay persons to let bishops, priests, deacons, religious sisters and brothers, and even lay ministers, take exclusive responsibility for spiritual power. Then these roles can be described as "religious vocations." For, just as Jesus warned against, the laity will happily reward these folks with long religious or professional titles, the first seats in holy places, awe and respect for their religious offices, and generous financial donations. The laity will say, "How different these religious people are from us—how much holier, or how much more intelligent, or how much more professional, in sum how superior!"

But the sad secret of such praise and respect is that laity thereby free themselves from their own terrifying responsibility for spiritual power. Laity thereby pretend that their everyday life is really not religious, and that only certain places and certain people are religious (of course not our places and not ourselves). Laity will thereby claim to be free from accountability for the despiritualization of society, for social injustice, and for ecologically destroying the earth.

This is why Jesus reserved his strongest anger not for sexual sinners like an adulteress or prostitute, nor for those like tax collectors or rich merchants who lusted after money, nor even for imperial oppressors like Pontius Pilate who seized such unjust human power over life and death. No, as we remember from the Gospels, Jesus' greatest anger was for those religious leaders who believed that religious energy was centered in themselves and in their states in life—above the ordinary people. For these, Jesus said, the severest sentence will be given (Mark 12:40). Jesus knew that we would so easily surrender our spiritual power to a religious caste as a way of avoiding the terror of our God-given spiritual responsibility.

Conclusion

In this essay it has been my goal to remember how the teaching of Jesus about the spiritual power of the laity provides energy for the community of Jesus' disciples to heal persons, communities, and the entire earth.

In its history Western Catholicism has been a rich carrier of evangelical and sacramental energy. But if Western Catholicism now fears for its future and tries to protect its dwindling institutional resources according to a neo-clerical (or neo-religious) strategy, then—as Jesus taught us—in trying to save its life, Western Catholicism could well lose it. But if Western Catholicism is willing to risk its future with the laity, then—as Jesus taught us—in giving up clerical or religious security, it will gain fresh lay life.

Such a spiritual lay opening by Western Catholicism would, I believe, also draw to the Western Church the life-bearing energies of non-Western cultural traditions—so much more aware than Europeans or European Americans of the spiritual power of the laity. I would also propose that such new lay-rooted spiritual energy could prove—in ways we have yet to imagine—an important part of healing the deep pathologies of Western culture.

Come Holy Spirit,
send forth your Spirit,
and we shall be recreated,
and you shall renew the face of the earth.

Chapter 18

The Rise of Lay Ministry
in the Years since Vatican II

Zeni Fox

Introduction

Persons old enough to remember the preconciliar Church will be aware of a significant change in the past twenty-five years. Whereas once clerical black and the subdued browns, greys, blacks, and white of the habits of vowed religious defined all of those in leadership roles in our parishes and institutions, today fewer priests, sisters, and brothers, plus many, many more lay ministers, make it seem as if we have moved from the era of black and white into that of technicolor. At parish staff meetings, at liturgical celebrations, at professional Church meetings on the diocesan and national levels, we realize that the Church looks less monochromatic, and that a diversity of lifestyles is vividly expressed in the rainbow of colors. What has caused this change, and what does it mean for the Catholic Church in the United States today?

The story of the emergence of lay ministry in this period traces its official beginnings to the documents of the council. Cultural trends and the movement of the Spirit in the Church also are factors contributing to this change. This paper will reflect on these factors, in an effort to understand what has created this phenomenon. It will also assess the challenge which this presents for the Church and its ministers at this time. In order to do this it will analyze the development of lay ministry within the Church community,[1] in the broadest sense of that term, and will look at a microcosm

---

[1]Lay ministry in the world or the marketplace is an important topic frequently discussed in the Church today, but goes beyond the confines of this paper. A good introduction to the topic is Robert L. Kinast, *Caring for Society: A Theological Interpretation of Lay Ministry* (Chicago: The Thomas More Press, 1985).

of lay ministry, ecclesial ministry[2] (professionally prepared lay people employed full-time in ministry), to further define the issues we face as a Church.

I. The Parish in 1990

One way to glimpse the "explosion of lay ministry"[3] is to look at the contemporary parish. The Notre Dame Study of Catholic Parish Life undertook a complex sociometric analysis of who provides leadership in parishes. They found that leaders included pastors, paid staff composed of clergy, vowed religious and laity, and volunteers.[4] In the total sample, three out of every ten parishes included lay persons on their pastoral ministry staffs. In addition, a broad range of volunteers minister in parishes, and many of these are among the leaders of the parish.[5] This picture fits the ideal presented by the Bishops' Committee on the Parish:

> Among the specifically defined roles, those of pastor and priest remain central. . . . But there are many other pastoral roles as well: roles assigned to the restored permanent diaconate; to the director of parish catechesis; to the Eucharistic minister, lector, and music leader; to those in education ministry; and to those responsible for developing the parish's social ministry. . . .[6]

The Bishops add that these specifically defined roles "exist to enable all parishioners to work toward this building of community."[7] The new Code of Canon Law reinforces this perspective, stating that all members of the parish have a responsibility for the life and action of the parish.[8] Cultural trends in the United States, emphasizing participation and voluntary effort would reinforce this theological vision.

However, the average parishioner does not need sociological surveys and official statements to be aware of this explosion of lay ministry. The bulletin informs her; its masthead often lists the names of the clergy, the D.R.E., the music director, the youth minister, etc. Announcements about meetings of catechetical ministers and liturgical ministers and diaconal ministers

---

[2]Although not widely used, this term is useful; it was introduced by the American bishops in the pastoral letter, *Called and Gifted: The American Catholic Laity* (Washington, D.C.: United States Catholic Conference, 1980) 6.

[3]Robert J. Hater, *The Ministry Explosion: A New Awareness of Every Christian's Call to Minister* (Dubuque, Iowa: Wm. C. Brown, 1979).

[4]Report No. 9, "Parish Life among the Leaders" (Notre Dame, Ind.: University of Notre Dame, 1986) esp. 1–2.

[5]Ibid., 6.

[7]*The Parish: A People, A Mission, A Structure* (Washington, D.C.: 1980) 8.

[7]Ibid.

[8]*The Code of Canon Law in English Translation*, Canon Law Society of Great Britain and Ireland (London: Collins, 1983) 95.

abound. The entrance procession at Sunday liturgy reminds him; lectors and Eucharistic ministers and adult acolytes process in with the priest. The diocesan paper contains notices of ministry training programs, many generic and of two or three years duration,[9] as well as others focused on a particular ministerial function. Posters announce multitudes of area and national convocations of ministers.

What has brought us to today?

II. Vatican Council II

The first document approved by the Council Fathers was the Constitution on the Sacred Liturgy. It contains a vision of Church which will lead to the birth of today's communities, in which lay ministry is a dominant factor.

In the Constitution, the great importance of the liturgy in the life of the Church is stressed: "The liturgy is the summit toward which the activity of the Church is directed; at the same time it is the fountain from which all her power flows" (art. 10). Furthermore, the liturgy is seen as "the outstanding means by which the faithful can . . . manifest . . . the real nature of the true Church" (art. 2). At liturgy, we are most what we are: the Church. And, in order to *be* Church, to manifest the true nature of the Church, it is essential that laity take an active role. For this reason, the Fathers state:

> Mother Church earnestly desires that all the faithful be led to that full, conscious and active participation in liturgical celebrations which is demanded by the very nature of the liturgy. Such participation by the Christian people as "a chosen race, a royal priesthood, a holy nation, a purchased people" (1 Pet. 1:9; cf. 2:4-5) is their right and duty by reason of their baptism (art. 14).

Jungmann has called this summons to active participation the refrain of the Constitution, noting that it recurs at fifteen other places in the document.[10] And, since the liturgy manifests the nature of the Church, since all the power of the Church flows out from this central action of the community, the document heralds a model of the Church in which all members are invited

---

[9]Cf. *Preparing Laity for Ministry*, National Conference of Catholic Bishops (Washington, D.C.: United States Catholic Conference, 1986), which indicates that the great majority of United States dioceses offer such programs.

[10]Josef Andreas Jungmann, "Constitution on the Sacred Liturgy," *Commentary on the Documents of Vatican II*, vol. 1, ed. Herbert Vorgrimler (New York: Herder and Herder, 1967) 17. See also Bernard Häring, *Road to Renewal* (Montreal: Palm Publishers, 1966) 120–21, for a similar evaluation of the importance of this stress on the laity at the council.

to be active. Indeed, all are reminded that participation is their right and duty, derived from their baptism.

Whereas all are called to participate actively, some of the laity are designated as having particular official functions to perform:

> Servers, readers, commentators, and members of the choir also exercise a genuine liturgical function. They ought, therefore, to discharge their offices with the sincere piety and decorum demanded by so exalted a ministry . . . (art. 29).

In light of future developments, the use of the word ministry in this context is significant. It is clear that these designated ministries complement the active participation of all the faithful, and of the presider as well.

In 1972, in his apostolic letter *Ministeria Quaedam*, Paul VI expanded this concept when he declared that, "Ministries may be committed to lay Christians." In doing so, he refers back to the principle of active participation of all the faithful at liturgical celebrations, and to the idea of different orders and ministries in the worshipping community.[11] He mandated that official rites of installation be prepared for the ministries of lector and acolyte. To this day, these are the only ministries which may be received in this official fashion.[12]

The theme of ministries is continued in the Dogmatic Constitution on the Church, which stresses that it is Christ who "continually distributes in His body, that is, in the Church, gifts of ministries through which, by His own power, we serve each other unto salvation . . . " (art. 7). Furthermore, Christ bestows charismatic gifts freely in the Church, "among the faithful of every rank" so that they may be "fit and ready to undertake the various tasks or offices" for the good of the community (art. 12). Pastors are called upon to recognize the charismatic gifts given to the laity (art. 30). The laity's share in the priestly, prophetic, and kingly functions of Christ is affirmed but their activity is directed especially toward temporal affairs (art. 31). However, citing the example of the laity who labored with Paul, the Fathers declare that the "laity can also be called in various ways to a more direct form of cooperation in the apostolate of the hierarchy . . . (and) deputed . . . to exercise certain church functions for a spiritual purpose" (art. 33). In fact, pastors are encouraged to "confidently assign duties

---

[11] *Vatican Council II: The Conciliar and Post Conciliar Documents,* ed. Austin Flannery (Northport, N.Y.: Costello Publishing Company, 1984) 428–29.

[12] In light of the fact that very few adults minister in these roles, yet many do so in other roles, this represents something of an anomaly. This idea is explored by David Power, *Gifts that Differ: Lay Ministries Established and Unestablished* (New York: Pueblo Publishing Co., 1980) ch 1.

to (the laity) in the service of the Church, allowing (them) freedom and room for action" (art. 37).

Many of these same themes are continued in the Decree on the Apostolate of the Laity. The stress throughout the decree is on the laity's role in the temporal order. However, article 22 states: "Deserving of special honor and commendation in the Church are those lay people, single or married, who devote themselves and their professional skill either permanently or temporarily, to the service of associations and their activities." The article notes that the number of such persons is increasing, and that pastors should be certain that the demands of justice, equity, and charity should be met "particularly as regards proper support for them and their families." In addition, they should be sure these lay people "enjoy the necessary formation, spiritual consolation, and incentive."

In this overview of some aspects of the teaching of the council, the ideas which have influenced the emergence of lay ministry as we know it in the Church today have been highlighted. It would also be possible to examine other teachings in the same documents which are less positive toward lay ministry, but in the confines of this paper that is not possible. Since an explosion of lay ministry has occurred, it would seem that the teachings which affirm this have been heard by many.

III. The Emergence of Lay Ministry

In the period immediately after the council, Catholics experienced a tremendous amount of change in their Church. Perhaps felt first by most people was change in the liturgy, change designed to effect the more active participation of all the faithful. An aspect of this was a new emphasis on the roles of the servers, readers, commentators, and members of the choir, called for as described above. The phrase "the people of God" was heard everywhere, and the affirmation of many was "we are the Church." Understandings and practices were changing together, as the Church in the United States, probably helped by cultural predilections, adapted structurally and attitudinally.

In the theological community, the kinds of investigations which first explored many of the positions subsequently taken at the council continued to be made by Scripture scholars, ecclesiologists, historians, and dogmaticians. New understandings of ministry continued to emerge. For example the *Concilium* series devoted several volumes to various aspects of this topic, and theologians of different disciplines, such as Raymond Brown, Bernard Cooke, Andre Lemaire, Yves Congar, David Power, Edward Schillebeeckx, and Thomas O'Meara, made significant contributions to the study.

These developments began to affect the Church at the grass-roots level, as can be seen by examining the entries in the *Catholic Periodical Index* for the decade of the 70s. Early in the decade, all references to ministry in popular journals and newspapers refer to priestly ministry or to Protestant ministers. From 1974 to 1978, references begin to reflect a broader understanding: hospital ministry, youth ministry, prison ministry, campus ministry, and family ministry are all emerging. In these ministries, laity and priests worked together. By the end of the decade, a new popular magazine, *Ministries,* was launched, books such as *Parish Ministry Resources* were published, and a new heading appeared in the periodical guide—lay ministry.

An aspect of this development was a significant increase in the number of lay people employed on parish staffs. The late 60s saw the first D.R.E.s and the mid-70s the first youth ministers, two roles which continue to be important today. Writing in this period, Maria Harris linked the new use of the word ministry to the newly designated directors of religious education and the calling of their work, ministry. Her interpretation is that: "Plainly and simply, ministry is the doing of that work formerly allowed only to the ordained: ministry is priestly activity."[13] The sociologist, John Coleman, concurs in this judgment, noting that ministry "has come to be a pervasive catch phrase in Catholic circles of religious professionals (other than priests) just within the last decade." Furthermore, he comments on the fact that it has become "a motivational symbol" for this group, and functions as part of a whole vision of Church shaping their practice and, through them, that of many Church members.[14]

An action by the bishops of the United States during this decade indicates their response to these developments. In 1977, the former Committee on the Lay Apostolate was renamed The Bishops' Committee on the Laity. "The new name reflected the expansion of the Committee's pastoral concerns, moving beyond that of organizations and movements, although including them, to the new emerging lay ministries. . . ."[15]

IV. Who Are the Lay Ministers?

Lay ministers include a significant number of persons who are employed by the Church, and many, many more who serve as volunteers. The Notre Dame Study gives some information about those volunteers who are leaders in their parishes, but the wide range of men and women of all ages who

---

[13]*The DRE Book: Questions and Strategies for Parish Personnel* (New York: Paulist Press, 1976) 186, 188.

[14]"The Future of Ministry," *America* (March 28, 1981) 243.

[15]"Introduction: To Build and Be Church," *Gifts,* Bishops' Committee on the Laity (Washington, D.C.: United States Catholic Conference, 1983) 2.

serve in a great variety of roles has not been studied. However, some studies have been undertaken of laity who are employed by the Church.[16] Because in some sense they serve as a microcosm of the whole body of lay ministers, a profile of these ecclesial ministers will be offered. A study by the author will be used.[17]

The great majority of the ecclesial ministers are women, about eighty percent. The overwhelming majority, ninety-seven percent, are white , although response variations may have slightly affected this statistic. The average age is in the 36–40 category; lay ministers, therefore, are younger than the average priest or vowed religious. Two-thirds are married, most with dependent children. For almost half of the respondents, the salary earned as a lay minister provides supplementary income for the family. As a group, lay ministers are more educated than the average American, but less so than clergy and religious. Over twenty-five percent hold a master's degree, with another ten percent enrolled in a degree program. However, the most common credential is a diocesan certificate, held by fifty percent of the group, with an additional ten percent studying in a certificate program. The role of dioceses in preparing and legitimating lay ministers is clear.

Before being hired by the parish, sixty percent of the lay ministers served as volunteers in ministry, and another ten percent had been priests, seminarians, or vowed religious. Clearly, the charisms of many lay ministers were first tested by the community, before designation to a ministerial role. Over half are employed in the area of religious education, with another almost twenty-five percent serving in the area of youth ministry. This pattern of ministerial effort focused significantly on children and youth is consistent with American Catholics' expectations of their parishes, and is probably influenced by cultural priorities.[18] Other roles filled by lay persons include director of liturgy, pastoral minister, and director of social concerns.

---

[16]Some studies include: Sr. Ann Patrick Conrad and Joseph Shields (Washington, D.C.: CARA, 1982); Thomas P. Walters, *National Profile of Professional Religious Education Coordinators/Directors* (Washington, D.C.: National Conference of Diocesan Directors, 1983) and an update in *Momentum* (1989); Marian Schwab, "Career Lay Ministers," *Today's Parish* (October 1987).

[17]Zenobia V. Fox, "A Post-Vatican II Phenomenon: Lay Ministries: A Critical Three-Dimensional Study (unpub. Ph.D. diss., Fordham University, 1986) 147–247. All statistics given will be from this study, unless otherwise indicated. The population was all persons employed in parishes in ministry positions, in nine dioceses throughout the country, drawn from mailing lists supplied by diocesan offices. When this article was prepared for publication, the comprehensive study of ecclesial ministers, *New Parish Ministers,* Philip J. Murnion, et. al. (New York: National Pastoral Life Center, 1992) had not yet been published.

[18]See, for example, *Notre Dame Study of Catholic Parish Life,* Report No. 8, "Parish Organizations: People's Needs, Parish Services and Leadership." Nancy Hennessy Cooney, in an article, "The Job Market," in the newsletter of the National Association for Lay Ministry (Spring

In recent years, an additional role for lay ministers has been added, that of pastoral administrator of a parish. Usually, these lay persons serve in parishes where there is no resident priest, although at times resident pastors have chosen to delegate administration to another member of the parish team. Vowed religious or deacons are more often serving in this role; the numbers have been increasing throughout the 1980s.[19] While this is a significant trend which bears theological study, the numbers involved are still very small, and the parishes in which these ministers serve tend to be small and isolated. Therefore, the effect on the total Church community is not now as significant as is that of the great mass of volunteer and employed ministers in parishes throughout the country.

V. How Do Lay Ministers Understand Their Role?

The lay ministers' self-understanding is of significance for this analysis, both because it shows that they have internalized the teachings of Vatican II, and because their roles give them significant influence with children, youth, and volunteer ministers. As Coleman noted, these laity view what they do as *ministry*. When asked to choose a word to describe their church work, sixty percent chose ministry, another thirteen percent a word associated with Church mission (vocation, discipleship, apostolate). In a country in which the designation ''profession'' is prized, only ten percent chose this. In keeping with this designation, respondents understand their role as flowing from their baptism. Asked what gives them the authority for their work in the Church, baptism was ranked highest, with professional training and competence significantly lower. Vocation, being hired, a mandate from priest or community, and commissioning, other possible choices, all ranked much lower still. Furthermore, the lay ministers overwhelmingly believe that they have been given a charism for their work in the Church.

Another dimension of their self-understanding can be discerned in the way they understand the Church. Offered the titles of the models of Church described by Avery Dulles, over fifty percent ranked people of God first, and an additional third ranked body of Christ first. Hence, three-fourths chose images that dominated the Vatican II documents. Furthermore, ninety percent of the lay ministers affirm that collegiality is a desirable goal for the Church, and seventy-five percent of the total sample have personally formed some type of group for shared decision-making in their work. Their shar-

1989), indicates that directors of religious education and youth ministers are the two roles employers most often seek to fill.

[19] Study done by the United States Bishops' Committee on the Liturgy, reported in their July-August 1988 newsletter. An in-depth study of these administrators is offered by Peter Gilmour, *The Emerging Pastor* (Kansas City, Mo.: Sheed and Ward, 1986).

ing in ministry is creating a Church in which there is still more sharing of ministry.

At the council, and in many documents and writings since, the role of the minister as servant has been stressed.[20] Some questions designed to discern the locus of attention of the lay minister point toward their emphasis on service to the people. The praise they value most, the criticism which hurts most, the evaluation most sought, the highest valuing of their work, all are vested, not in the pastor, staff, professional peers, family, or friends, but in those directly served. In addition, when planning their work for any given day or week, "the needs of the people" ranks clearly in first place, with personal faith, job description, the pastor, and diocesan and Church guidelines trailing behind. At least at the level of their ideal selves, the lay ministers are shaping a more lay-centered Church.

Have lay ministers been hired in parishes because of a priest shortage? The participants in this study do not think so. Asked why they are employed in their present position, the need for certain areas of specialization in ministry is ranked first and the recognition of a variety of gifts in the community is ranked second. Significantly lower is the third-ranked reason, a shortage of priests. The emphasis on specialization fits the increasing specialization in all professional fields in the United States. Furthermore, most of these ministers serve in parishes with more than one full-time priest: forty-three percent, two; twenty-one percent, three; and sixty-seven percent, four or more.

In addition, in most instances more than one lay minister is employed. The median number is 2.84; sixty-four percent indicated that two or more lay people were professionally employed, excluding those in the school. While the study did not examine the size of the parish in which they worked, the pattern seems to be more one of expanding the number of persons ministering in a parish rather than simply substituting for the missing priests.

In his analysis of the history of ministry, O'Meara notes a reduction in the diversity of ministries which existed in the early Church, and a centralization of ministry in the persons of the clergy (bishop, priest, deacon) and in their leadership and liturgical roles.[21] The laity involved in ministry today represent a renewed expansion of ministry, both in the very fact of the varied services they offer, and in the way they understand what they do. They do not think of themselves as helping the clergy in clerical work, but as performing functions which rightfully flow from their baptism, which contribute to the building up of the community, and which are somewhat

---

[20]A fine example is As One Who Serves, Bishops' Committee on Priestly Life and Ministry of the National Council of Catholic Bishops (Washington, D.C.: United States Catholic Conference, 1977).

[21]Thomas O'Meara, Theology of Ministry (New York: Paulist Press, 1983) chs. 4, 5.

different from the functions of the priest. Given a list of eighteen ministerial functions, respondents were asked which were essential to their role, and which to a priest's. For themselves, the functions most often noted were teacher, community builder, leader, enabler; for priests, they were Eucharistic celebrant, preacher, community builder, and link with diocesan Church. Respondents were also asked which three of the functions were most important for their own and the priest's roles. By an overwhelming majority, the priest's primary function was designated as Eucharistic celebrant. Lay ministers saw their own principal function to be community builder, with enabler of leaders a very close second. Again, we note here the way in which the sharing in ministry by these laity is ordered toward an expanding involvement of still more laity in ministry. The vision of the council, of all the people of God actively involved in the mission of Jesus, sees some fulfillment in this expansion of ministry.

VI. The Next Twenty-Five Years

Will the expansion of lay ministry continue in the future? The present attitudes of ecclesial ministers hold some clues to the future. First, over a third of them indicate that they plan to stay in professional Church work indefinitely, with another third unsure of how long they plan to stay. In fact, forty-five percent responded that the type of work they did implied a permanent commitment on their part. (However, forty percent said it did not.) Furthermore, seventy-two percent said they would continue as volunteers if they left employed ministry; only three percent said they would not volunteer.

Second, when asked if there were someone they considered a model of what it means to be in their role in the Church, more than half said yes, and more than half of these said this individual is a lay person. The involvement of lay people in ministry can be expected to be an invitation to others to serve also.

Attitudes of college students toward vocational choices is also a factor in predicting the future. Hoge's study of Catholic collegians found that very few young adults are interested in the traditional vocations to priesthood and the vowed life, but that a high percentage of both campus ministry leaders and students in general are very interested in the possibility of both full-time and part-time employment as lay ministers.[22]

Another indicator of the likelihood that laity will continue to be involved in ministry is the fact that so many programs for preparing laity for

---

[22]Dean Hoge, *Future of Catholic Leadership* (Kansas City, Mo.: Sheed and Ward, 1987) 188–90.

ministry are offered, through dioceses and academic institutions. In 1986, 164 such programs were identified; eighty percent of them had been begun between 1976 and 1986.[23] The diocesan programs represent an important step by the institutional Church in the affirmation and support of lay ministry.

If lay ministry is to thrive, the process of clarification about the role of laity in the Church will have to continue. Lay ministers often speak of the many ways in which the message of being "second-best" to priests or vowed religious is communicated to them. This may be why, in ranking ways in which their work situation could be improved, lay ministers ranked the following highest: that my efforts are valued, that my role or function be clarified, and that people think more highly of my role. Ranked significantly lower were items pertaining to receiving more money, more security, or more success. A deepened understanding of what it means to have ministers who believe they are called to their work, and given charisms to perform it, yet who are not priests or vowed religious, is needed by the whole community. The ministers themselves, theologians, bishops, and all the faithful must engage this issue.

However, it can be said that it is likely that for many Catholics the acceptance of lay ministers is growing. Hoge found that for a majority of the college students and adults he surveyed in 1985, replenishing the supply of priests was of less interest than was "restructuring parish leadership to include more deacons, sisters, and laypersons."[24] This may be why the great majority of ecclesial ministers indicate that the pastor has delegated authority to them, and that their authority is accepted to a high degree by fellow staff members, by parish leaders, and by parishioners in general. In addition, they perceive themselves as functioning as leaders in their parishes. It would be fair to say that such views about the authority of the laity in ministry represent a significant change among Catholics, one which can be anticipated to continue in the future.

This analysis has not touched upon important issues for ecclesial ministers such as salary scales and portability of pensions. Nor has it examined an issue such as some security about the possibility of continuing to minister when pastoral leadership changes in the parish or diocese, something which affects both volunteer and employed ministers. For the future, these are important, but the self-report of ecclesial ministers indicates that they are not primary.

[23]Suzanne Elsesser and Eugene Hemrick, "Preparing Laity for Ministry: A Report on Programs in Catholic Dioceses throughout the United States," unpub. summary of the research (1986). See n. 9.

[24]Hoge, *Future of Catholic Leadership*, 24–25.

A final question for the future is one with some significance in a Church which deeply values ritual expression. Should a rite of installation or ordination (perhaps to the diaconate, or some additional yet-to-be-named orders) be established?[25] In my study, forty percent of the respondents answered yes to the question: If there were a rite of installation for laity who do your kind of salaried professional Church work, would you choose it? A cross tabulation with the questions about how long they plan to continue in ministry, and whether they see their work as a permanent commitment, showed that one-fourth answered yes to all three of these questions. This represents a significant proportion of the total group. However, in exploring this issue in conversation with ecclesial ministers, I have noted a real ambivalence. On the one hand, they would deeply value what a ritual would mean to them, personally. But on the other hand, they are concerned about creating a new separation between groups in the Church, about once again narrowing the circumference of the circle of those who minister. The commitment to a vision of the Church in which all are actively engaged seems to be primary.

Conclusion

The ecclesial ministers described in this paper are seen as persons who have interiorized the teachings of Vatican II in such a way that they see themselves as called by baptism, and gifted by the Spirit, to share in the ministry of Jesus. Furthermore, they are actively involved in inviting many others to share in ministry, those who share this same understanding of baptism, of charisms, of ministry. In and through these ministers, a new way of being Church is emerging in the Catholic community today, a way articulated at the Second Vatican Council with the image of the Church as the whole people of God.

[25]O'Meara explores this idea in *Theology of Ministry*, 146–53.

Chapter 19

Regional Differences in Priest Decline in the United States Church

Richard A. Schoenherr
Lawrence A. Young

Our data add to the story of Catholic regionalism in the United States by providing an account of geographic differences in the demographic transition of the clergy. In this chapter, we address four specific aspects of regional variation in access to priestly resources. First, we summarize data concerning regional differences in the projected decline in the number of active diocesan priests. Second, we focus on how regional differences in migration patterns have affected regional differences in declining priest populations. Third, we present regression analysis that suggests that environmental constraints which lie beyond the control of diocesan leaders account for most of the diocesan-level variation in the laity-to-priest ratio. Finally, we look at regional differences that are likely to emerge over the next few decades in the laity-to-priest ratio due to the combined effects of clergy decline and membership growth. To make the analysis comparable to other relevant research, we utilize the same divisions and regions used by the United States Bureau of the Census.

I. Data and Methods

Demographic data were gathered from official archives in a random sample of eighty-six Roman Catholic dioceses. The five-year project was sponsored by the United States Catholic Conference, which greatly facilitated access to sensitive data sources. For each diocese we constructed a population register of diocesan priests (see Shryock, Siegel, and others, 1971). The registers contain full names and complete individual level data for all entrances into and exits out of the population of living priests from 1966 through 1984. For the nineteen-year national register, N = 36,370. Using names in the registers allows us to control for under- and overreporting and to estimate census counts in a consistent fashion regardless of different local methods of recordkeeping.

Names and dates were taken directly from original archival material and were not dependent on the recall of diocesan officials. Our insistence on historically accurate documents during the multiphase data collection campaign and methodically rigorous cleaning procedures during data processing has resulted in a highly accurate register of the population under study. (See Schoenherr and others [1988] and Schoenherr and Young [1990a, 1990b] for definitions of variables and further details on methods.)

Making Population Projections

Population analysts increase the plausibility of their projections by hedging their bets. Instead of making one projection we usually make three, based on optimistic, pessimistic, and moderate assumptions. We prefer to describe each set of assumptions and let the reader make the final judgment.

One basic premise governs all the projections to be presented. We presume that the variation, selection, and retention mechanisms that determined the size and shape of the Catholic priesthood population for the past twenty years will continue unchanged for the next twenty years. With the assumption that only Catholic males who will be celibate will be recruited and retained, we constructed three different projection series.

In brief, our optimistic assumptions are based on the best possible interpretation of the historical data, the pessimistic on the worst possible past scenario, and the moderate on the current trends in the sampled dioceses. The moderate assumptions are designed to produce a projection curve which falls approximately midway between the optimistic and pessimistic models.

The optimistic projection assumes that the relatively high ordinations and net migrations, on the one hand, and low resignations and retirements, on the other, experienced during specific years between 1966 and 1985, will dominate in the future. Furthermore, if any of these events showed consistent trends toward even more optimistic levels in the future than experienced in the past, estimates of their 1990–1994 levels are used.

The pessimistic projection assumes the opposite, namely, the relatively low ordinations and net migrations, and relatively high resignations and retirements that occurred during certain other past years are likely to continue in the years ahead. Similarly, if any of these events showed consistent movement toward more pessimistic levels, estimates of their 1990–1994 levels are used.

The moderate projection or middle-of-the-road model results from assuming that the level of ordinations, net migrations, resignations, and retirements occurring in 1980–1984 will continue more or less unchanged from 1985 until the turn of the century. The assumptions about future death rates are based on life expectancy for white males in the United States produced from national census data; we use the same mortality assumptions for the optimistic, moderate, and pessimistic models. Based on our reading of the data and understanding of the Catholic Church in the United States, we make a few other reasonable adjustments to these assumptions. The modifications are described in Schoenherr and Young (1990a).

An important *caveat:* Our population projections do not predict the future. They are merely forecasts of past trends based on reasonable assumptions. The forecasts in this chapter should be assessed carefully and used wisely.

II. Changes in Regional Population Size, 1966–2005

Figures 1 to 4 show the size of the active diocesan priest populations from 1966 through 1984 and projections to 2005 for the four census divisions of the United States. The graphs in Figures 1 and 2 for dioceses in the Northeast and Northcentral divisions of the country show consistent decline over the historical and projected periods. The other two figures for dioceses in the West and South, however, record decline until about 1975, when population size begins to grow again in the Mountain, East South, and West Southcentral dioceses, and level off in dioceses along the Pacific Coast. In the three growth areas, the upward trend continues until the early 1980s, when it begins to dip down again. The stable trend in the average Pacific Coast diocese continues for the entire ten-year period from 1975 to 1985.

Limiting the focus to the moderate projections, all the graphs forecast steady decline from 1985 to 2005. In the West and South, however, the two divisions of the country where dioceses experienced historical periods of decline followed by periods of growth or stability, the moderate curve is surrounded by broad fan-shaped bands—a sign of inconsistent past trends—making the projections difficult to interpret and less useful for planning purposes. Later analysis in this chapter, though, clarifies the direction and force of trends in Western and Southern states.

Figures 3 and 4 provide a graphic view of population change, while Table 1 gives part of the same information but in raw numbers. The table presents the size of the regional populations for 1966, 1985, and 2005—the beginning and end points of the historical period, and the end of the overall projection period—along with the percent decline under optimistic, moderate, and pessimistic assumptions.

Arithmetic means for the United States as a whole facilitate comparisons. The statistics highlight the cleavage between dioceses in the Northeast and Northcentral divisions, on the one hand, and those in the West

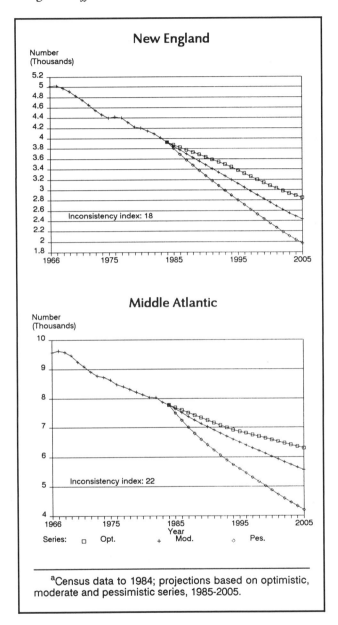

Figure 1. Size of U.S. Diocesan Priest Population: Northeast, 1966–2005[a]

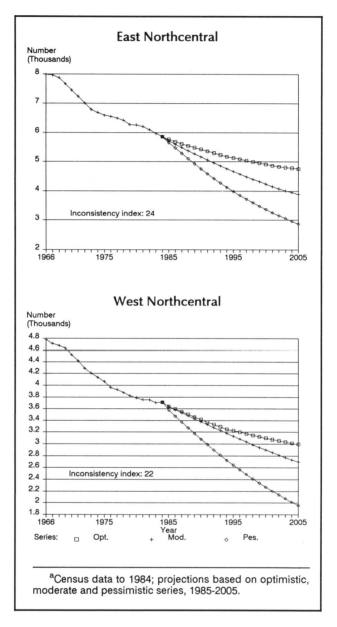

Figure 2. Size of U.S. Diocesan Priest Population: Northcentral, 1966–2005[a]

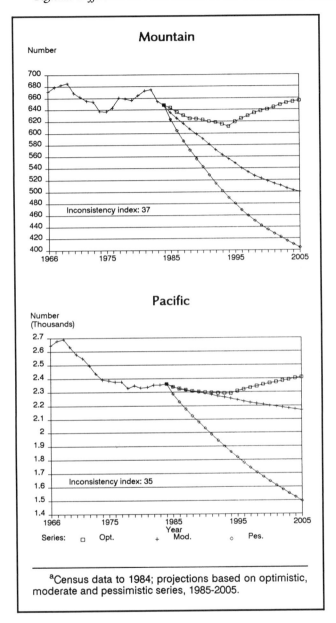

Figure 3. Size of U.S. Diocesan Priest Population: West, 1966–2005[a]

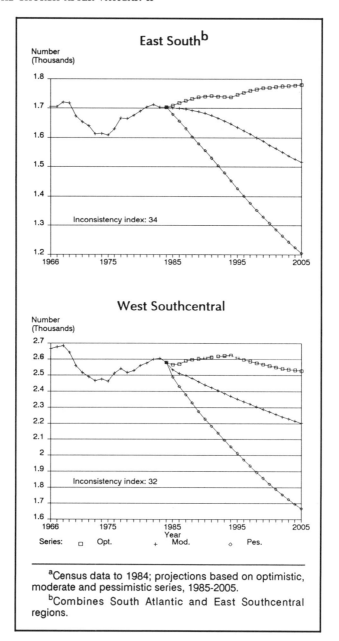

[a]Census data to 1984; projections based on optimistic, moderate and pessimistic series, 1985-2005.

[b]Combines South Atlantic and East Southcentral regions.

Figure 4. Size of U.S. Diocesan Priest Population: South, 1966–2005[a]

Region	1966	1985	Year 2005 Projection Series			Percent Change 1966-2005 Projection Series		
			Opt.	Mod.	Pes.	Opt.	Mod.	Pes.
United States	35,070	28,240	23,040	21,030	16,653	-34	-40	-53
Northeast	14,604	11,518	9,148	7,996	6,163	-37	-45	-58
New England	5,025	3,879	2,849	2,431	1,964	-43	-52	-61
Middle Atlantic	9,579	7,639	6,299	5,565	4,199	-34	-42	-56
Northcentral	12,769	9,418	7,756	6,591	4,831	-39	-48	-62
East Northcentral	7,989	5,748	4,760	3,892	2,874	-40	-51	-64
West Northcentral	4,780	3,670	2,996	2,699	1,957	-37	-44	-59
West	3,319	2,997	3,064	2,666	1,899	-8	-20	-43
Mountain	672	639	655	500	404	-3	-26	-40
Pacific	2,647	2,358	2,409	2,166	1,495	-9	-18	-44
South	4,373	4,305	4,309	3,720	2,872	-1	-15	-34
East South[b]	1,706	1,721	1,781	1,516	1,205	4	-11	-29
West Southcentral	2,667	2,584	2,528	2,204	1,667	-5	-17	-37

[a]Census counts for 1966 and 1985; projections based on optimistic, moderate and pessimistic series for 2005.
[b]Combines South Atlantic and one diocese from the East Southcentral region.

Table 1. Size of U.S. Diocesan Priest Population and Percent Change, 1966–2005; by Year and Region[a]

and South, on the other. Under all three sets of assumptions, the percent decline in numbers of priests is well above the national average in the Northeast and Northcentral divisions and well below the mean in the West and South.

We continue to concentrate on the moderate projections, since the evidence indicates they are the most plausible. Thus percentages in Column 7 show, at the high end of the range, that New England and East Northcentral dioceses will suffer an average loss of over fifty percent of their active clergy between 1966 and 2005. Dioceses in both Southern regions will experience the smallest losses, with an average fifteen percent decline over the four decades.

Under both optimistic and pessimistic assumptions, the picture remains the same. New England and East Northcentral dioceses are again at the high extremes, showing losses of forty percent in an optimistic forecast and over sixty percent in a pessimistic scenario. Similarly, Southern dioceses are at the low extremes; they would lose as little as one percent of their 1966 number of clergy if optimistic assumptions hold true or as much as one third if they approach their pessimistic projections in 2005.

III. Migration

Migration has played a significant role in the demographic transition of the Catholic clergy in some regions and dioceses of the United States. An excess of incardinations over excardinations has a notable impact in stabilizing the change process in certain dioceses. In this section we turn our attention to the impact of migration.

Zero Net Migration

If the clergy decline worsens throughout the world, surplus incardinations as a response to local scarcity may become a contested accommodation to the shortage (Seidler and Meyer, 1989). This consideration prompted us to reexamine our population projections, controlling for net immigration.

One estimate of the real loss of priestly manpower within a country might focus on each autonomous diocese and its ability to recruit and retain its own native clergy. To make such an estimate, we needed to remove the effects of net immigration. Two modifications in the projection procedures were necessary. First, we recalculated the size of the active priest population after removing the number of incardinations in excess of the number of excardinations for each year of the historical period. Then we re-estimated the three projection models, using the same assumptions as before for all other transition events except incardination and excardination. For the al-

Region	1966	1985	2005 Projection Assumption			Percent Difference 1966-2005[b] Projection Assumption		
			Opt.	Mod.	Pes.	Opt.	Mod.	Pes.
United States	35,070	26,736	21,262	19,209	14,906	-39	-45	-57
Northeast	14,604	11,152	8,654	7,629	5,819	-41	-48	-60
New England	5,025	3,733	2,662	2,344	1,879	-47	-53	-63
Middle Atlantic	9,579	7,419	5,992	5,285	3,940	-37	-45	-59
Northcentral	12,769	9,215	7,391	6,344	4,727	-42	-50	-63
East Northcentral	7,989	5,609	4,552	3,751	2,793	-43	-53	-65
West Northcentral	4,780	3,606	2,839	2,593	1,934	-41	-46	-60
West	3,319	2,533	2,456	2,095	1,556	-26	-37	-53
Mountain	672	577	561	468	377	-17	-30	-44
Pacific	2,647	1,956	1,895	1,627	1,179	-28	-39	-55
South	4,373	3,829	3,613	3,178	2,604	-17	-27	-40
East South[c]	1,706	1,543	1,535	1,331	1,076	-10	-22	-37
West Southcentral	2,667	2,286	2,078	1,847	1,528	-22	-31	-43

[a] Census counts for 1966; projections for 1985 and 2005 based on assumption of zero net migration.
[b] Optimistic: ((Col. 3/Col. 1)-1)100; moderate: ((Col. 4/Col. 1)-1)100; pessimistic: ((Col. 5/Col. 1)-1)100.
[c] Combines South Atlantic and one diocese from the East Southcentral region.

Table 2. *Adjusted Size of U.S. Diocesan Priest Population,[a] 1966-2005, and Percent Difference; by Year and Region*

tered projections we assumed that zero net migration would continue throughout the projection period, that is to say, that the number of incardinations would always be balanced by an equal number of excardinations.

Table 2 contains the results of the new projections for the United States as a whole and each census region.[1] If net immigrations were held at zero during the historical period of this study, between 1966 and 1984, the decline in the national diocesan priest population would have been twenty-four percent rather than twenty percent.

Not surprisingly, therefore, the projections adjusted for zero net immigration show considerably greater losses in numbers of priests between 1966 and 2005 than the original projections. The adjusted moderate projection, displayed under "Percent Difference" in the table, reveals that the national population of native diocesan priests would show a drop of forty-five percent between 1966 and 2005. The corresponding figure in Table 1, for native and non-native priests together, shows a loss of forty percent.

The projected size of the native diocesan clergy in 2005, under adjusted moderate assumptions, is just over 19,200. The unadjusted model, which includes excess incardinations, forecasts a diocesan clergy population of some 21,000 as the new century dawns.

An examination of differences across regions reveals, further, that the advantage created by the imbalance of incardinations over excardinations is strong in certain areas but slight in others. For easier comparison, Table 3 presents the adjusted and unadjusted estimates of the percent of decline from 1966 to 2005 based on the moderate assumptions. The table demonstrates that Sunbelt states absorb the vast majority of surplus incardinations.

At the national level, there is a thirteen percent difference between projected decline of native clergy and that of the combined native and incardinated clergy, as the data in the first row of the table show. The national average, however, balances wide extremes. The difference in unadjusted and adjusted projections for Northeastern and Northcentral dioceses is about five percent and the differences for Southern and Western dioceses range from seventy-six percent to one hundred twelve percent.

The advantage gained by excess incardinations in the Mountain area is generally more than three times higher than in the Northeast and Northcentral half of the country. Even so, Mountain dioceses enjoy nowhere near the advantage from incardinations realized in the South and along the West Coast. In the South the advantage is more than fifteen times higher and on the West Coast more than twenty times higher than in the Northeast and Northcentral regions.

[1]The data are presented in the same format as Table 1, which contains the original unadjusted projections.

Region	Percent Decline 1966-2005		Percent Difference[b]
	Unadjusted	Adjusted [a]	
United States	-40.0	-45.2	13.0
Northeast	-45.3	-47.8	5.5
New England	-51.6	-53.0	3.3
Middle Atlantic	-41.9	-44.8	6.9
Northcentral	-48.4	-50.3	3.9
East Northcentral	-51.3	-53.3	3.4
West Northcentral	-43.5	-45.8	5.2
West	-19.7	-36.9	87.3
Mountain	-25.6	-30.4	18.8
Pacific	-18.2	-38.5	111.5
South	-14.9	-27.3	83.2
East South[c]	-11.6	-22.0	89.7
West Southcentral	-17.4	-30.7	76.4

[a]The adjusted assumption projects the decline in native clergy, as defined in the text.

[b]((Col. 2/Col. 1)/Col. 1)100.

[c]Combines South Atlantic and one diocese from the East Southcentral region.

Table 3. Unadjusted and Adjusted Percent Decline in U.S. Diocesan Priest Population, 1966–2005, and Percent Difference; by Region
(Based on moderate assumptions adjusted for zero net migration)

Finally, when the advantages of net immigration are included in the projections, clergy losses in the South and West are notably below the national average, as the first column shows. According to the second column, however, when gains from surplus incardinations are removed, the Sunbelt dioceses, too, have serious problems. Adjusted losses between 1966 and 2005 in that half of the United States would range from twenty-two percent fewer native clergy in Southeastern states to thirty-nine percent fewer native clergy along the Pacific Coast.

Trends and projections based on assumptions of zero net immigration indicate that the shortage of *native* priests does not respect geographic boundaries or favorable climatic conditions.

IV. Explaining Local Variations

A Model Explaining Supply and Demand in Catholic Dioceses

Catholic priests are ordained to serve a community of believers. Among their myriad ministerial tasks is the unique responsibility of presiding at the Eucharistic liturgy or Mass and celebrating the other sacraments. According to extensive recent research on the subject, lay Catholics are welcoming new opportunities to share in the ministry, an emphasis in Catholic parish life encouraged by the Second Vatican Council. Nevertheless, when it comes to the Mass and those sacraments attached to important rites of passage, principally birth, marriage, and death, the vast majority of Catholics want a priest present, not another type of minister (Gilmour, 1986; Leege, 1986; Hoge, 1987).

Concern over the priest shortage takes on poignancy for Catholics because access to the traditional "means of justification" (Troeltsch, 1960) is being threatened. Undoubtedly, the severity of the priest decline should rightly be assessed in terms of the widening laity-to-priest ratio and not just the drop in numbers of priests. Growth in Catholic Church membership continues unabated and, so, many feel the clergy population should definitely be growing, not declining. Therefore, the next step of the analysis considers those conditions that explain variation in the number of Catholics per priest in diocesan churches.

Explaining Local Variation in Laity-to-Priest Ratio

Our regression model was constructed to explain the variance in the 1980 laity-to-priest ratio. All the independent variables tested were likewise measured at the same time point, 1980. Nationally, the "typical" diocese faced a ratio of 1,571 Catholics per active diocesan priest in 1980. This figure is an average of some wide extremes. In Los Angeles, each active priest was matched by almost four thousand church members, for the highest recorded laity-to-priest ratio in our sample. The most advantageous ratio found in our data belongs to the Archdiocese of Little Rock where there were only about five hundred Catholics per active diocesan priest.

Which conditions, among the many tested, have the *strongest* impact on number of church members per priest? We discovered the heaviest influence from three environmental conditions: percent Catholic, percent Hispanic, and percent growth in the Catholic population.

Percent Catholic

The results indicate that the larger the proportion of Catholics to the total population in the diocese, the higher the laity-to-priest ratio, all other relevant conditions being equal. The data demonstrate that if the proportion of Catholics in Diocese A were ten percent higher than in Diocese B, the number of laity per priest would be two hundred higher in A than B.

Percent Hispanic

The higher the proportion of Hispanics in the general population, the higher the laity-to-priest ratio in the diocese. Two dioceses that are identical on all other conditions tested but differ by ten percent in the proportion of the total population that is Hispanic would differ by two hundred in their laity-to-priest ratio. In other words, the laity in dioceses with relatively large Hispanic populations may be systematically underserved because of very high numbers of Catholics per priest. Church members in dioceses with relatively few Hispanics, on the other hand, may find priestly services more available because of low laity-to-priest ratios. This effect from percent Hispanic cannot be explained by other variables in the model, since they have been controlled by statistical techniques.

Catholic Population Growth

Dioceses that experienced a relatively high increase in church membership were likely to have a higher laity-to-priest ratio than dioceses where there was little membership growth. More precisely, a diocese that recorded a ten percent growth in its Catholic population would experience an increase of 150 more Catholics in its laity-to-priest ratio, if all other causal influences were equal. The data show that the demand for priestly services is outstripping the supply of priests in dioceses with rapidly growing church membership.

Two other variables in the model have *moderate* effects on the number of Catholics per priest, namely, the number of religious order priests who reside in the diocese relative to the number of active diocesan priests, and geographic region.

Religious-to-Diocesan-Priest Ratio

Dioceses with larger numbers of religious order priests relative to the size of the diocesan clergy face a higher laity-to-priest ratio than dioceses with smaller concentrations of religious priests. Remember, however, the ratio of Catholics to priest in our study is measured by the number of active diocesan clergy. So the data show that where diocesan clergy face larger numbers of parishioners, religious clergy are present in larger numbers to assist with priestly ministry. In actuality, therefore, a high religious-to-diocesan-priest ratio would increase the laity's access to priestly ministers in the diocese. This finding corrects the initial impression that the combined effects from all conditions tested was to reduce availability of priestly services.

Although some religious priests work exclusively in parish ministry, many others commonly have specialized jobs unique to the traditions of their order or congregation. So, in comparison to active diocesan priests, whose primary duties are parish based, the average religious order priest may be considered a part-time parish minister. (Note, since many religious order priests may actually work full-time in local parishes, our comments stress the influence of conditions *on the average*.) One might conclude, therefore, that, all relevant conditions being equal, in 1980 the average religious priest in the diocese provided priestly services for about 264 Catholic laity.

Region

Notable regional differences in the laity-to-priest ratio are found in the data, which persist even after controlling for differences in relative size and growth of the Catholic population, Hispanic ethnicity, urbanization, affluence, the presence of religious order priests, and recruitment ineffectiveness.

Dioceses along the Pacific Coast and those in West Southcentral states form the most disadvantaged group in terms of the availability of priestly ministers. The laity-to-priest ratio in these dioceses would be much higher than the national average if all causal conditions were the same across the country. Local diocesan churches in East Northcentral, Mountain, and Southeast states form a second group. The number of Catholics per priest in dioceses in this cluster tends to be close to the national mean, all other conditions tested being equal. Dioceses in New England, Middle Atlantic, and West Northcentral states can be grouped together in a third set. Once other conditions are taken into account, dioceses in these regions tend to have laity-to-priest ratios that are notably lower than the average for the country as a whole.

Balancing Supply and Demand

From the model explaining variation in laity-to-priest ratios, once again we discover that the wide variation in the observed data is not primarily the result of local policy or programs but rather of constraints in the environment, which vary in different parts of the country. Without the evidence from the regression model one might conclude that something internal to diocesan organizations creates such large differences across dioceses. The statistical tests demonstrate, however, that over three-fourths of the variance in laity-to-priest ratios is explained not by internal conditions nor by the purposive behavior of people in dioceses but by processes of natural selection, whereby dioceses adjust and adapt to their environments in a fashion that is beyond the control and probably the conscious awareness of organization members.

The data demonstrate that Catholics in the United States do not have equal access to priests mainly because of environmental constraints. Parishes are most likely to be underserved in dioceses with large proportions of Hispanics and relatively large church memberships that are growing rapidly. The same tendency toward sparse priestly service is prevalent in dioceses with relatively high concentrations of affluent and urban populations or that are ineffective in recruiting new priests. The negative impact of these conditions is cumulative such that dioceses characterized by high scores on all the variables would tend to have a very light supply of priestly ministers in the face of very heavy demand. Additionally, parishioners living along the Pacific Coast and in the Southwest are probably the most disadvantaged in the country both before and after taking environmental conditions into account, while those residing in Northeast and West Northcentral states tend to be the most advantaged, especially after considering environmental constraints.

Discussion

Several conclusions may be drawn from the results of testing our causal model. First of all, the advantage that some dioceses enjoy—they have a significantly lower laity-to-priest ratio—is somewhat deceptive since causal conditions account for more than three-fourths of the advantage. Based on the evidence, we can conclude that if ecological conditions identified in the models were suddenly equalized across the country, clergy growth in "advantaged" dioceses would turn into decline, trickling losses would become a steady stream, and low laity-to-priest ratios would climb to nearly the same heights as elsewhere. In "disadvantaged" dioceses the opposite would occur. If identified conditions were equal, extreme high losses in the hardest hit dioceses would be curtailed and the number of Catholics per priest reduced closer to the national average.

The sobering message for dioceses affected by sustained losses in priestly personnel and high laity-to-priest ratios is that the social forces producing higher decline and reducing the availability of priestly ministers are largely environmental conditions outside the control of diocesan leaders. As McKelvey and Aldrich (1983:121) observe, "Thinking that one can control the future is heady stuff." Nonetheless, the view of the population approach to understanding organizational change is that some conditions, principally those that comprise the immediate niche, *are* subject to manipulation by the organization, but that the broader environment is not open to influence.

The descriptive analysis raised the question of why the South and West remained relatively stable with only minimal clergy losses while the priest decline was precipitous in the other half of the nation. The regression analysis in this paper has shown that the priest shortage in the West and South is not substantially different from clergy decline in the rest of the country, once environmental conditions are considered.

V. Laity-to-Priest Ratio, 1975-2005

In the previous section, we argued that while losses in the number of priests represent one way to view the extent of the priest decline, it ignores the impact of the number of parishioners. Our regression analysis has helped explain why Catholics in the United States did not have equal access to priests in 1980, but it says little about future trends in access to priests. In this section, we will present data concerning the laity-to-priest ratio at two different points in time—1975 and 2005. First, however, we address the issue of the growing size of Catholic Church membership during the decades of our study.

Growing Catholic Population

A steady increase in membership has marked the history of the Catholic Church in the United States. During the twentieth century, for example, the number of American Catholics has more than tripled from less than twenty million to over sixty million. Catholicism's share of the total United States population also has increased from under twenty percent to over twenty-five percent during the same period.

Table 4 summarizes data on Church membership for the decades covered by our investigation. The table's first four columns consistently indicate steady growth in the number of Catholics. The last three columns of statistics, however, provide opposing views of the proportion of the United States population represented by Catholics. The Gallup estimates show an increase from twenty-three percent in 1965 to twenty-seven percent in 1985. In contrast, during the same period both the *Official Catholic Directory* and the Glenmary estimates show slow but steady decline in the proportion.

What accounts for these discrepancies?

In a poll, Gallup interviewers ask a national sample of individuals their religious preference along with other questions that permit pollsters to check for consistency. The sources for the numbers provided by the *Official Catholic Directory* and the Glenmary Research Center are contact persons in each diocese. Their estimates would not tend to be based on a scientific diocesan-wide census or sample survey. Actually, some twelve million to fourteen million adult Americans who claim Catholicism as their preferred religion are added to the count of United States Catholics if Gallup's approach is

Year	General[a]	Catholic Number			Pct. of Total U.S. Population		
		Gallup[b]	OCD[c]	Glenmary[d]	Gallup	OCD	Glenmary
	1	2	3	4	5	6	7
Estimates							
1965	194,303	44,138[e]	45,648	--[f]	22.7	23.5	--[f]
1970	205,052	51,715	47,455	44,863[g]	25.2	23.1	21.9
1975	215,973	56,030	48,268	46,183[h]	25.9	22.3	21.4
1980	227,757	61,344	49,865	47,502[i]	26.9	21.9	20.9
1985	239,279	64,341	52,107	49,905[i]	26.9	21.8	20.9
Projections							
1990	250,410	67,334[j]	54,531[k]	52,227	26.9	21.8	20.9
1995	260,138	69,950	56,649	54,255	26.9	21.8	20.9
2000	268,266	72,135	58,419	55,951	26.9	21.8	20.9
2005	275,604	74,109	60,017	57,481	26.9	21.8	20.9

[a] Source: U.S. Bureau of the Census, Current Population Reports, Series P-25, ; for estimates, Nos. 519, 917, 1022; for projections, No. 1018. Figures include Armed Forces overseas.

[b] Source for estimates: Gallup polls; figures cited in Hoge (1987), Table B-1.

[c] Source for estimates: The Official Catholic Directory, 1966, 1971, 1976, 1981, 1986; volumes dated the year of publication contain data for one year prior. Figures exclude eastern rite Catholics but include those under the military ordinariate.

[d] Source for estimates: Johnson et al. (1974), Churches and Church Membership in the United States, 1971; Quinn et al. (1982), Churches and Church Membership in the United States, 1980.

[e] Not available; the figure given is interpolated from 1962 and 1967 data.

[f] Not available.

[g] Not available; the figure given is for 1971.

[h] Not available; the figure given is interpolated from 1971 and 1980 data.

[i] Projected figures for 1985-2005: Col. 1 * Col. 7.

[j] Projected figures for 1990-2005: Col. 1 * Col. 5.

[k] Projected figures for 1990-2005: Col. 1 * Col. 6.

Table 4. Estimates and Projections of U.S. General and Catholic Population, 1965–2005
(Numbers in thousands)

used. For reasons too long to explain here, our analysis of the laity-to-priest ratio is based on the Gallup estimates and projections.

Hispanic Catholics

We believe that Hispanic Catholics constitute a sizeable portion of the "invisible" Church membership not represented in official data. According to the United States Census Bureau, the nation's Hispanic population "has been growing about five times as fast as the rate of the non-Hispanic

Year	Number		Pct. Hispanic in U.S. Catholic Population[c]
	Total [a]	Catholics [b]	
Estimates			
1980	14,458	12,289	20.0
1985	17,322[d]	14,724	22.9
Projections			
1990	20,638[e]	17,542	26.1
1995	22,550	19,168	27.4
2000	25,223	21,440	29.7
2005	28,009[f]	23,808	32.1

[a]Source: for estimates, U.S. Census Bureau Release CB89-158, October 12, 1989; for projections, Current Population Reports, Series P-25, No. 995; includes Armed Forces overseas. Projection data from the middle series.

[b]Col. 1 * 0.85; the USCC estimates that approximately 85 percent of U.S. Hispanics are Catholic (private conversation with Pablo Sedillo).

[c]Column 2 divided by Gallup estimates of U.S. Catholic population (Column 2, Table 9.5).

[d]Interpolated from 1984 and 1986 estimates.

[e]1989 estimate times 102.8; estimated annual rate of growth for 1985-90 is 2.8 percent (see Current Population Reports, Series P-25, No. 995, Table Q).

[f]Interpolated from 2000 and 2010 projections.

Table 5. Estimates and Projections of U.S. Hispanic Population and U.S. Catholic Hispanic Population, and Percent Hispanic in the U.S. Catholic Population; 1980–2005

(Numbers in thousands)

population since 1980" (United States Census Bureau, Release CB89–158). Undoubtedly it is extremely difficult for diocesan officials to improve the accuracy of their estimates of the size of the Catholic population in dioceses with high concentrations of Hispanics. Table 5 gives the United States census estimates and projections of the total Hispanic population, and attempts to provide parallel data on the Catholic Hispanic population. The official projections show that the number of United States Hispanics will almost double from about 14.5 million in 1980 to about twenty-eight million in 2005.

According to United States Catholic Conference estimates, about eighty-five percent of Hispanics are Catholic. Based on that estimate, the number of Catholic Hispanics would almost double from 12.3 million in 1980 to about 23.8 million in 2005.

Estimates and Projections of the Laity-to-Priest Ratio

Table 6 gives national and divisional estimates and projections of the laity-to-diocesan priest ratio, adjusted numbers of priests needed based on a standardized number, along with the corresponding deficit in the priest population if the Church were to maintain the 1975 ratio. When analyzing change over time, it is necessary to establish a standard or point of comparison. Father Robert Sherry, former director of the National Conference of Catholic Bishops' Office of Vocations and Priestly Formation, thinks present concern about availability of the Mass and sacraments may not antedate 1975. So he proposes the 1975 laity-to-priest ratio as a minimum standard for assessing the severity of the priest shortage (Sherry, 1985). His proposal provides a criterion of comparison that is not totally arbitrary so we incorporated it in the analysis. See Schoenherr and Young (1990a) for a more complete discussion of the Sherry Index.

Focusing initially on the row containing national estimates and projections, statistics in Column 3 show that if our moderate projections for the priest population and the Gallup-based projections for the lay population hold true, the laity-to-priest ratio in round numbers will almost double from 1,800 Catholics per active diocesan priest in 1975 to 3,500 in 2005. Suppose, however, the laity-to-priest ratio were to remain constant at the 1975 level of 1,820, in keeping with Sherry's proposed standard. The fourth column reveals that the number of priests needed to maintain the 1975 ratio would have to increase from about thirty-one thousand in 1975 to about forty-one thousand in 2005.

The difference between the number of clergy needed to maintain the 1975 ratio and the number available is the priest deficit (Column 5). According to our moderate projections, there will be about twenty-one thousand active diocesan priests in 2005. To maintain the arbitrary 1975 ratio,

Region	Unadjusted Number				Adjusted Number (Sherry Index)[a]		
	Laity[b]	Priests[c]	Laity/Priest[d]	Priests Needed[e]	Priest Deficit[f]	Deficit Rate[g]
Year: 1975						
Northeast	22,494	13,035	1,726	12,359	676	5.2
Northcentral	16,514	10,655	1,550	9,074	1,581	14.8
West	8,586	3,022	2,841	4,718	-1,696	-56.1
South	8,436	4,072	2,072	4,635	-563	-13.8
National[h]	56,030	30,808	1,820	30,808	0	0
Year: 2005						
Northeast	25,304	7,996	3,165	13,903	-5,907	-73.9
Northcentral	18,005	6,591	2,732	9,893	-3,302	-50.1
West	17,149	2,666	6,432	9,423	-6,757	-253.5
South	15,357	3,720	4,128	8,438	-4,718	-126.8
National[h]	74,109	21,030	3,524	40,419	-19,689	-93.6

[a]Rev. Robert Sherry (1985) suggests the 1975 laity-to-priest ratio as a minimun standard for assessing the severity of the priest shortage.

[b]Source: Gallup (see Table 5) for national data. Divisional data based on the proportion of Catholic population living within division in 1975 and 2005. Proportions derived from the Official Catholic Directory.

1975 divisional estimates:

$$L_{1975} = G_{1975} * D_{1975};$$

where: L_{1975} is 1975 estimate of divisional Catholic lay population; G_{1975} is 1975 Gallup estimate of national Catholic population; and D_{1975} is 1975 Official Catholic Directory estimate of proportion of Catholic population in each division.

2005 divisional projections:

$$L_{2005} = G_{2005} * D_{2005};$$

where: L_{2005} is 2005 estimate of divisional Catholic lay population; G_{2005} is 2005 Gallup projection of national Catholic population; and D_{2005} is 2005 Official Catholic Directory based projection of proportion of Catholic population in each division. In estimating proportions for 2005, divisional and national populations were derived from 1975 and 1985 Official Catholic Directory data based on assumption of geometric population growth (Shryock, Siegel et al., 1971: 378):

$$P_2 = P_0 * (1 + r)^2;$$

where: P_2 is divisional or national Catholic population size in 2005, after two ten-year time periods; P_0 is Official Catholic Directory estimate of initial divisional or national Catholic population in 1985 ; and r is rate of divisional or national population increase during single time period based on Official Catholic Directory estimates of population change between 1975 and 1985.

All numbers are in thousands.

[c]1975 estimates based on census data; 2005 projections based on moderate projections (see Table 1, middle series).

[d]Col 1/Col. 2.

[e]Col. 1/1820: the national 1975 laity-to-priest ratio or Sherry Index.

[f]Col. 4 - Col. 2.

[g]Col. 5/Col. 2.

[h]Because national data include priests from the Archdiocese for the Military Services, U.S.A., the sum or average of divisional data differ slightly from the corresponding national data. National estimates and projections obtained from Schoenherr and Young, Table 9.7 (1990a).

Table 6. National and Divisional Estimates and Projections of U.S. Lay Catholic and Diocesan Priest Populations, Laity-to-Priest Ratio, Adjusted Diocesan Priest Population, and Diocesan Priest Deficit; 1975–2005

however, the Church would need an additional twenty thousand diocesan priests at the beginning of the twenty-first century, though this figure does not take into account the rapid growth of the Hispanic Catholic population.

At the divisional level, the 1975 laity-to-priest ratios ranged from a low of 1,550 in the Northcentral dioceses to a high of over 2,800 in the Western dioceses. The Sherry Index indicates that the average Western diocese already had a significant deficit of diocesan priests in 1975, while the typical Northeast and Northcentral dioceses enjoyed a small surplus of priests.

Our projections indicate that the combined effects of clergy decline and membership growth will lead to significant growth in both the laity-to-priest ratio and the deficit rate of priests in all divisions of the country by 2005. Nevertheless, significant divisional variation will persist. For example, the laity-to-priest ratio ranges from a low of just over twenty-seven hundred in the Northcentral division to a high of over sixty-four hundred in the West. Divisional comparisons demonstrate that the laity-to-priest ratio in the Western division is more than double that in either the Northeast or Northcentral divisions.

The deficit rate shows even more dramatic variation between divisions, ranging from a low of fifty percent in the Northcentral division to a high of over two hundred fifty percent in the West division. The average deficit rate of priests in Western dioceses is five times larger than the deficit rate in the average Northcentral diocese, more than three times larger than the average deficit rate in Northeastern dioceses, and twice as large as the deficit rate for the typical Southern diocese.

The utility of focusing on the laity-to-priest ratio is highlighted by comparing the clergy decline rates in Table 1 with the deficit rates in Table 6. While Table 1 indicates that dioceses in the West and South divisions of the country will suffer the smallest declines in their clergy populations between 1966 and 2005, Table 6 suggests that these same divisions will have the largest deficit of priests given the size of their church membership in 2005. Viewed from this perspective, priests will be a scarce commodity throughout the country, with the greatest needs emerging in those areas with the smallest decline in the absolute number of priests.

VI. Summary

The major findings of this chapter can be summarized as follows:

(1) Significant regional differences have emerged with respect to the projected decline in the number of active diocesan priests. The statistics highlight the cleavage between the Northeast and Northcentral divisions, on

the one hand, and those in the West and South, on the other—with the former suffering significantly more decline than the latter.

(2) Without the gain created by excess incardinations, the decline in the number of active native clergy in the average United States diocese would be even greater. An examination of differences across divisions reveals that sunbelt states in the South and West absorb the vast majority of surplus incardinations. When gains from surplus incardinations are removed, the Sunbelt dioceses, too, have serious problems. Trends and projections based on assumptions of zero net immigration indicate that the shortage of native priests does not respect geographic boundaries or favorable climatic changes.

(3) Most of the diocesan-level variation in the 1980 laity-to-priest ratio can be explained with a set of variables which represent environmental constraints for the diocese. Most prominent among these variables are the percent Catholic, percent Hispanic, and percent growth in the Catholic population. The statistical tests demonstrate that over three-fourths of the variance is explained not by local policies or programs but rather by constraints in the environment, which vary in different parts of the country. That is, Catholics in the United States do not have equal access to priests mainly because of environmental constraints.

(4) While dioceses in the West and South will suffer the smallest declines in their clergy populations between 1966 and 2005, these same dioceses will have the largest deficit of priests given the size of their church membership in 2005. Viewed from this perspective, priests will be a scarce commodity throughout the country, with the greatest needs emerging in those areas with the smallest decline in the absolute number of priests.

REFERENCES

Blau, Peter M. "The comparative study of organizations." *Industrial and Labor Relations Review* 18 (April 1965) 323–38.

Gilmour, Peter. *The Emerging Pastor.* Kansas City, Mo.: Sheed and Ward, 1986.

Hoge, Dean R. *Future of Catholic Leadership: Responses to the Priest Shortage.* Kansas City, Mo.: Sheed and Ward, 1987.

Johnson, Douglas W., Paul R. Picard, and Bernard Quinn. *Churches and Church Membership in the United States.* Washington, D.C.: Glenmary Research Center, 1974.

Kenedy, P. J. *The Official Catholic Directory.* New York: P. J. Kenedy, yearly.

Leege, David C. "Parish life among the leaders." Report No. 9, *Notre Dame study of Catholic parish life.* Notre Dame, Ind.: University of Notre Dame, 1986.

McKelvey, Bill, and Howard Aldrich. "Populations, Natural Selection, and Applied Organizational Science." *Administrative Science Quarterly* 28 (1983) 101–28.

Quinn, Bernard, Herman Anderson, Martin Bradley, Paul Goetting, and Peggy Shriver. *Churches and Church Membership in the United States 1980: An Enumeration by Region, State and County Based on Data Reported by 111 Church Bodies.* Atlanta, Ga.: Glenmary Research Center, 1982.

Schoenherr, Richard A., and Lawrence A. Young. *The Catholic Priest in the United States: Demographic Investigations.* Madison, Wis.: Comparative Religious Organization Studies, 1990a.

————. "Organizational demography and structural change in the Roman Catholic Church." *Structures of Power and Constraint.* Eds. Craig Calhoun, Marshall Meyer, and Richard Schott. New York: Cambridge University Press, 1990b.

Schoenherr, Richard A., Lawrence A. Young, and José Pérez Vilariño. "Demographic Transitions in Religious Organizations: A Comparative Study of Priest Decline in Catholic Dioceses." *The Journal for the Scientific Study of Religion* 27 (1988) 499–523.

Seidler, John, and Katherine Meyer. *Conflict and Change in the Catholic Church.* New Brunswick, N.J.: Rutgers University Press, 1989.

Sherry, Robert. "Shortage? What vocation shortage?" *The Priest* 41 (1985) 29–32.

Shryock, Henry S., Jacob S. Siegel, and others. *The Methods and Materials of Demography* (2 vols). Washington, D.C.: U.S. Government Printing Office, 1971.

Stark, Rodney, and William S. Bainbridge. *The Future of Religion: Secularization, Revival and Cult Formation.* Berkeley: University of California Press, 1985.

Troeltsch, Ernst. *The Social Teaching of the Christian Churches.* New York: Macmillan, 1960.

United States Bureau of the Census. Current Population Reports, Series P-25, No. 519, *Estimates of the Population of the United States, by Age, Sex, and Race: April 1, 1960 to July 1, 1973.* Washington, D.C.: United States Government Printing Office, 1974.

————. Current Population Reports, Series P-25, No. 917, *Preliminary Estimates of the Population of the United States, by Age, Sex, and Race: 1970 to 1981.* Washington, D.C.: United States Government Printing Office, 1982.

————. Current Population Reports, Series P-25, No. 995, *Projections of the Hispanic Population: 1983 to 2080.* Washington, D.C. United States Government Printing Office, 1986.

————. Current Population Reports, Series P-25, No. 1022, *Population Estimates by Age, Sex, and Race: 1980 to 1987.* Washington, D.C.: United States Government Printing Office, 1988.

————. Current Population Reports, Series P-25, No. 1018, *Projections of the Population of the United States, by Age, Sex, and Race: 1988 to 2080.* Washington, D.C.: United States Government Printing Office, 1989.

————. "Hispanic population surpasses 20 million mark." Release CB89-158; Oct. 12. Washington, D.C.: Public Information Office. 1989.

Spirituality

Walter J. Burghardt, S.J.

Unfortunately, the 1990 Washington Conference celebrating the twenty-fifth year since the close of Vatican II did not include a section specifically set aside for spirituality. Not that spirituality was absent from the agenda; it was implicit in papers on the laity and the liturgy, morality and the doctrine of God, biblical studies and women's issues, inculturation and Catholic education, peace and justice.

Still, when not only theology but conciliar documents such as "The Church in the Modern World" focus in large measure on "the call of man and woman to communion with God" (GS 19), it must be admitted that the volume in hand suffers from a lamentable lacuna. In the fiftieth-anniversary volume of *Theological Studies* (1989:676–97), a remarkable article by Sandra M. Schneiders on "Spirituality in the Academy" insisted that "Since Vatican II, both the Catholic and the Protestant Churches have had to contend with an increasing interest in spirituality on the part of their membership; programs designed to foster the lived experience of the spiritual life have multiplied; and the academy is witnessing (not without apprehension) the birth of a new discipline in its midst" (ibid., 676). Schneiders notes Karl Rahner's conviction that "the Christian of the future will be a mystic or he or she will not exist at all" and finds an academic parallel in the conviction of first-rate theologians that "only a theology that is rooted in the spiritual commitment of the theologian and oriented toward praxis will be meaningful in the Church of the future" (ibid., 677).

A conference section on spirituality might have faced up to the difficulty in defining a term that is the title of a twenty-five-volume series, only three volumes of which are devoted to Christianity: *World Spirituality: An Encyclopedic History of the Religious Quest* (1985). It might have delved into spirituality as lived experience and into the academic discipline which studies that experience. It might have revealed the expansion of the term to include non-Christian and even nonreligious spiritual experience. It might have encountered Schneiders' contention that spirituality is not a subdivision of either dogmatic or moral theology, but an autonomous discipline which functions "in partnership and mutuality with theology" (ibid., 689). It would have been fruitful and exciting to investigate spiritual experience in interdisciplinary fashion, as ecumenical, interreligious, and cross-cultural, to see it not only as "interior life" but also embracing other rich dimensions of the human subject—psychological and social, historical and political, bodily and intellectual.

If, as Ernest Becker claimed in a Pulitzer Prize-winning study of the human condition, "The distinctive human problem from time immemorial has been the need to spiritualize human life" (*The Denial of Death*, 1973), future conventions on "the future of the American Church" must focus explicitly on spirituality in the academy and in the arena.

Chapter 20

Gaudium et spes:
Source of Challenge and Hope

Jean Smith Liddell

Why don't Catholics know and practice the rich and respectable traditions of Catholic social teaching? From Leo XIII's Encyclical, *Rerum novarum,* to the United States Bishops' Pastoral Letter, *Economic Justice for All,* the Catholic community has articulated principles for social interaction which express in a "nuts and bolts" kind of way how one lives the Christian life in our times. Following Christ, responding to the commands of Jesus to spread the good news and live as he lived, demands a consistency in all dimensions of human life. Catholic social teaching, in its essence, involves moral decisions which impact economic, political, and social realms. Why don't United States Catholics know the tradition? And why don't they practice it?

The task of communicating the social teachings of the Catholic Church to United States Catholics is not a simple one. According to Kenneth Himes,[1] United States moral theology must learn from liberation theology about the perspective on poverty enfleshed in the experience of the oppressed and the responsible use of power. To answer the question "what does it mean to be a Christian in 1990?" is to raise the issue of the use of power. Rebecca Chopp[2] sees the black Church's experience, base Christian communities, women-Church, and messianic communities of the First World as places where one can speak the word freedom to "the bourgeoisie, [who are] beset with psychic destructiveness, depression, drugs, alcohol, and consumerism." And she sees the possibility of "emancipatory transformation"[3] taking place through these communities. To use Chopp's imagery, it may very well be that United States Catholics need to hear again and receive

---

[1]Kenneth R. Himes, O.F.M., "The U.S. Catholic Contribution to Moral Theology," *New Theology Review* 1 (February 1988) 62.

[2]Rebecca Chopp, *The Power to Speak* (New York: Crossroad, 1989).

[3]Ibid., 7, 127.

this word: freedom. Perhaps theological reflection in the United States is impossible outside of such a dialogue. And once heard and embraced, perhaps then it would be possible to engage United States Catholics in discussions of their social responsibilities that extend beyond their immediate family, neighborhood, community, city, country.

This paper proposes that a new effort to communicate the traditions of Catholic social teaching be made. The theoretical framework for such an undertaking could easily be built with the "praxis" (often referred to as the liberation model) model of contextual theology.[4] The content could easily begin with the reading of *Gaudium et spes*. I would like as well to share two stories of such an endeavor, of experiments in social teaching in which I have participated. The first took place at Saint Xavier College (where I teach) last year as Paul Hazard, professor of philosophy, and I put together a two-day symposium on *Gaudium et spes* for the college faculty, staff, and students. The other endeavor was in the context of a course on the Mission of the Church, in a formation program for lay ministers and deacons for the archdiocese of Chicago. The results of these two efforts convinced me of the fruitfulness of using *Gaudium et spes* as the stimulus for challenging United States Catholics to discover and incorporate Catholic social teachings into their spiritual and professional lives.

I. The Theological Context

In reflecting on the ultimate meaning of the Second Vatican Council, Karl Rahner broke open wide avenues of discovery and challenge. He perceived the power of a new world Church, and the dramatic possibilities for theological development.[5] A paradigmatic shift had taken place, from theology to theologies. Twenty-five years later, the Church is reaping the rewards of this shift. An entire field of theological exploration, the field of "contextual theology," has developed to enable people to "construct" theologies which express their Christian faith in the context of their culture, values, and history.[6] Models for contextual theology have been explored

[4] I am deeply indebted here to the work of Bob Schreiter, C.PP.S., and Stephen Bevans, S.V.D., who teach at Catholic Theological Union in Chicago, where I completed an M.Div. and an M.A. in systematic theology before going to Fordham University to pursue doctoral studies in systematic theology. As a student and now as a faculty member pursuing my own lines of thought, I see the roots of their careful teaching and influence in my own work.

[5] Karl Rahner, "Toward a Fundamental Interpretation of Vatican II," *Theological Studies* 40 (1979) 716–27. This article is a constant reference point for many theologians, in many different fields.

[6] See, for example, Robert J. Schreiter, *Constructing Local Theologies* (New York: Orbis Books, 1985).

and evaluated, especially in the light of the enormous growth of Latin American liberation theology.[7]

Self-conscious reflection on and experimentation with theological methods strikes me as particularly valuable today for teaching and ministry formation efforts. Through these efforts, I have come to see the enormous practical usefulness of the "praxis" model of contextual theology (identified by Stephen Bevans, S.V.D., of Catholic Theological Union, through his reading of liberation theology). This model of theology is an ever-widening circle of interaction between "social reality," analyzed through the disciplines of sociology, history, politics, psychology, economics, and moral principles, and the Christian tradition, the Scriptures, history, and theology of the Church, embraced and embodied in "committed and intelligent action."[8] The analysis of human experience through the richness of the human sciences, common sense and life experience is a gateway for lay people to begin to theologize.[9] It connects their knowledge, experience, and expertise to their spiritual lives in a way that makes it possible for them to articulate their faith. It also opens up the possibilities for "committed and intelligent action," that is for a response to the gospel that is enfleshed in all facets of their lives. This model allows for the introduction of Catholic social teachings as a part of the Christian tradition which deals directly with the day-to-day struggles of the workplace, marketplace, and political arenas.

II. *Gaudium et spes*

The document begins with "the joys and hopes, the griefs and anxieties of the men and women of this age. . . ." These joys and hopes, griefs and anxieties of the human race, the bishops say, belong to the Church as well, to be celebrated, born, endured, and overcome. It was a document of vision.

There is a loss of innocence in the Church of the Second Vatican Council. This document belongs to a Church of the ghettos, of the prisons, of the battlefields, marketplaces, kitchens, and street corners. It is not the product of monasteries and rectories, dark sanctuaries and empty rooms. The

[7]See, for example, Stephen Bevans, "Models of Contextual Theology," *Missiology* 13 (April 1985) 185–202; "A Local Theology in a World Church," *New Theology Review* 1 (February 1988) 72–92; *Models of Contextual Theology* (forthcoming).

[8]Ibid.

[9]Several recent discussions of this perspective can be found in Douglas Hall, *Thinking the Faith* (Minneapolis: Augsburg, 1988); Jack Shea, "Theology at the Grassroots," *Church* 2 (Spring 1986); and Robert Schreiter, "La communité comme théologien," *Spiritus* 28 (May 1987) 147–54.

Church confesses its own sinfulness, its failure to live up to the gospel it preaches, its responsibility for creating doubts in people's minds about the existence of God and the value of the mission of the Church. In the section on atheism they comment:

> Yet believers themselves frequently bear some responsibility for this situation. For, taken as a whole, atheism is not a spontaneous development but stems from a variety of causes, including a critical reaction against religious beliefs, and in places against the Christian religion in particular. Hence believers can have more than a little to do with the birth of atheism. To the extent that they neglect their own training in the faith, or teach erroneous doctrine, or are deficient in their religious, moral, or social life, they must be said to conceal rather than reveal the authentic face of God and religion (n. 19).

The loss of innocence so apparent in the document is reflected in the bishops' awareness of the misery and helplessness of peoples impoverished and oppressed, of the unrelenting threat that nuclear weapons pose to the existence of the human endeavor, civilization, and the planet earth. Squarely facing the almost overwhelming problems of the global community of the 1960s, the bishops' response is one of emphatic hope and encouragement.

The Church of Christ takes her stand in the midst of the anxiety of this age, and does not cease to hope with the utmost confidence. She intends to propose to our age over and over again, in season and out of season, this apostolic message; "Behold, now is the acceptable time" for a change of heart; "behold, now is the day of salvation" (n. 82).

One can recall the Swahili proverb: if it was made by someone, then it can be fixed by someone else. If the structures of human society, culture, politics, and economics are destructive of human life and happiness, then those same structures can be rebuilt anew by the present generation (n. 55).

Even those with a surface interest in Catholicism are vaguely aware that the role of the lay person in the Catholic Church was dramatically changed after the Second Vatican Council. One of the greatest reasons for this change was the new vision of the mission of the Church which comes to light in this document. Facing the almost overwhelming tasks before it, the human race can count on the help—the sweat, blood, and tears—of the Christian community. Catholics are "called to action."

Gaudium et spes defines a Catholic understanding of the human person, the structures of community life, and the nature of Jesus' life and mission. In the sections on particular issues, it addresses marriage and family life, culture, economic concerns, political structures, and the oppressive enormity of the nuclear arms race. I would like to offer two examples of the enormous success of sharing this document with Catholics in settings where they were challenged to reflect and articulate their Christian identity.

Saint Xavier College, Chicago

For the Saint Xavier College community, the commemoration of *Gaudium et spes* began as faculty and students read the document, mined it for its wisdom, and gathered together for a two-day symposium to share their reflections, questions, and insights (December 7 and 8, 1989). Small yellow copies of the document floated around the campus, stuck in piles of books, sitting on desks overloaded with papers. The symposium was the brainchild of Paul Hazard, professor of philosophy, and myself, and we played midwives as we distributed copies, cajoled, and encouraged faculty and staff to read and present papers on the document. A quiet revolution, a small but significant set of conversations took place in hallways, offices, and elevators. "What was the lasting value of this document?" "How could the bishops have understood so well the role of world trade policies in the quest for peace?" "The sexist language is jarring." "The bishops were light-years ahead of their time; their sense of the 'dignity of the human person' is the foundation for a new world order." "There is an elegant simplicity to it." "The vision is timeless."

Eight papers were presented during the symposium by faculty of the college, representing the fields of sociology, economics, history, philosophy, nursing, education, business, and theology.[10] There were two guest speakers who represented dogmatic theology and pastoral ministry.[11] Over the course of the two days, there was plenty of food and lively discussion.

Jobs, bills, college curriculum, acid rain, alienation, evolution, public school education—the topics whirled. Faculty from the Graham School of Management discussed the economic proposals in the document, comments flying, about America's need to be competitive in the world market, to produce products of sound quality. The bishops' call for international cooperation in economic planning was well-received. Sr. Sue Walsh, R.S.M., vice president for Institutional Advancement and Marketing, quoted the passage in the document which states that the human person is "the source, the center, and the purpose of socio-economic life" (n. 63), and drew out implications for the ordinary life of the Saint Xavier College community. Drawn together by a common purpose, the staff, faculty, students, and administration should work together knowing that "a man [or a woman] is more precious for what he [or she] is than for what he [she] has" (n. 35).

The only point of universal agreement among the participants at the symposium was that if the document had been written in 1990, the bishops

---

[10]Maureen Scott, R.S.M., Faisal Rahman, Peter Kirstein, Paul Hazard, Joanne Gruca, Eileen Quinn Knight, Sue Walsh, R.S.M., and Jean Smith Liddell.

[11]John Linnan, C.S.V., associate professor of doctrinal theology, Catholic Theological Union, and Rev. Ray Tillrock, Pastor, St. Barnabas Church, Chicago.

would not have failed to raise concern about the abuses to our environment. Peter Kirstein, professor of history, painted a bleak picture of the real cost of the arms race in his paper, which confirmed the thinking of the participants that the moral implications and actual results of the arms race were devasting for the human community.

In retrospect, it is clear that the symposium was not only a significant event in the history of the college, but was a remarkable success because *Gaudium et spes* is a remarkable document. Enthusiasm and honest pride in the Catholic Church were evident throughout the event.

Ministry Training Program

Gaudium et spes was warmly received by another group of people, extraordinary in themselves. It was my pleasure and privilege to teach a course on the Mission of the Church in a program that trains lay ministers and deacons in the archdiocese of Chicago. Gathered together in one classroom was a collection of folks which represented the Church in all of its diversity. Black, Hispanic, white, male and female, professional, laborer, banker, teacher, cook, well-educated and modestly educated, liberal, conservative, Polish, Haitian, native Chicagoans. United by their commitment to the Christian life and their willingness to minister in the Catholic Church, but somewhat uncomfortable with the theological enterprise, this group came together that first Tuesday evening.

The latter part of the course drew us into discussion of the Second Vatican Council, and in particular, *Gaudium et spes*. The class was divided according to topics in small groups, in which they read, discussed, and presented their views on the various sections of the document. Their self-confidence in theologizing had grown, and their analysis of the documents was exciting and refreshing. One person commented after the course was over, "the Vatican II documents, what a shame they've been hidden for so long. In the hands of the people, what wonderful strides could be made."[12]

The document sparked discussion, disagreement, frustration, and excitement. Several Vietnam veterans were angry that the document contained support for the position of conscientious objectors in war, which had not been communicated to Catholics in the United States at the time. There was unrelenting criticism of the sexist language and perspective. And the idealism of the document in general was pointed out as a weak point by many. But the class experienced and expressed the enthusiasm and pride in being Catholic which had been the result of the symposium at Saint Xavier

[12]Ruth Mendelson, Lay Ministry Training Program participant, Chicago.

College. The consistency of the two responses led me to conclude that there was something of real value occurring, which should be carefully considered.

Conclusion

In the light of these two experiences, it became clear that the use of the "praxis" model for theological reflection was opening up avenues for discovery and renewal within the Catholic community within my purview as a professor of theology. The challenge of Catholic social teaching contained within the teachings of *Gaudium et spes* was received not as an oppressive critique of middle-class lifestyle, which was within the realm of possibility, but spoke to these communities the word of freedom which Rebecca Chopp had anticipated. Why freedom? Perhaps because the ordinary person is accustomed to responsibility, fulfilling job requirements, raising children, taking care of elderly parents, supporting the Church, baking cakes, and coaching baseball teams, and so there may have been a natural willingness to be responsible for a larger community's needs. Perhaps the vision of the document brought out the best in people. Whatever the reasons, the Catholic community should realize the power of this document and draw strength and direction from it.

Part IV

Vatican II in Dialogue

Chapter 21

Twenty-Five Years after Vatican II:
An Orthodox Perspective

Patrick D. Viscuso

The Orthodox Church claims to be the one holy, catholic, and apostolic Church. It is composed of a number of self-governing Churches united by one common faith, communion, and sharing of the sacraments or Mysteries. Each self-governing or autocephalous Church is administered through a synodal structure presided over by a chief hierarch, usually a patriarch, but in some cases an archbishop or metropolitan. The Churches share a common theological, canonical, spiritual, and liturgical tradition, differing mainly in the language of worship and national customs. Many of the chief episcopal sees of the East are of apostolic foundation and in the past occupied eminent places of honor in the ecclesiastical structure of undivided Christendom.

The most prominent sees in the order of ancient primacy are the patriarchates of Constantinople, Alexandria, Antioch, and Jerusalem. The Orthodox believe that Rome should be at the head of the primacy. However, primacy is understood in terms of precedence in honor and love, and in the case of Rome, as first among equals. Ecumenical councils are viewed as inspired by the Holy Spirit and expressing doctrine infallibly. They are seen as a mirror of the Church's structure, which is viewed as a council that is never adjourned and a continuous dwelling place of the Holy Spirit. Only seven such synods are accepted: Nicaea 1 (325), Constantinople 1 (381), Ephesus (431), Chalcedon (451), Constantinople 2 (553), Trullo (692), and Nicaea 2 (787).

The Orthodox Church is composed of the following self-governing Churches: Constantinople, Alexandria, Antioch, Jerusalem, Russia, Romania, Greece, Serbia, Bulgaria, Georgia, Cyprus, Poland, Albania, Czechoslovakia, and St. Catherine's Monastery (Mount Sinai). Immigrants from many of these areas settled in the Western Hemisphere. Since the Russian Orthodox Church had established itself first in the Americas through its Alaskan missions, these bishops administered most Orthodox settlers in the

New World. After the Russian revolution, however, various Old World sees claimed jurisdiction over immigrants coming from their respective countries. At present, the two largest jurisdictions are the Greek Orthodox Archdiocese of North and South America under the patriarchate of Constantinople, and the Orthodox Church in America, formerly the Russian Orthodox Greek Catholic Church in America, which was unilaterally granted self-governing or autocephalous status by the patriarchate of Moscow in 1970.

I. East and West: An Historical Introduction

According to the Second Vatican Council's *Decree on Ecumenism*, Roman Catholics are urged to acquire an accurate knowledge of the historical relations of East and West in order to work effectively for union.[1] Such an understanding should begin with the study of the Byzantine Empire, the Christian Roman Empire of the East. Most historians regard the Byzantine period as beginning with the establishment of Constantinople as capital of the Roman Empire in 330 by the Emperor Constantine the Great, and ending with the fall of the city to the Ottoman Turks in 1453. The term "Byzantine" is derived from the place name, "Byzantium," a small town that existed in the area of the Eastern capital prior to Constantine's foundation. This term was devised and applied to the Empire by modern European historians and was never used by the inhabitants of Eastern Rome. The Byzantines understood themselves to be Romans and their rulers to be in the direct line of the Caesars.

Despite persecution for nearly three centuries under the various pagan rulers of Old Rome, the Church spread in the East through the efforts of the apostles and their successors. Numerous present-day Orthodox sees can claim apostolic foundation. At the end of the fourth century, Christianity became the official state religion of the Roman Empire and a new pattern for Church-state relations developed.

Although the term "Caesaropapism" has been used by certain historians to describe the relations of the Byzantine state with the Church, this relationship is better understood as a "symphony" or cooperation of two authorities, civil and ecclesiastical, in one Christian commonwealth. The emperor acted as the Church's protector in administrative affairs and in this sphere, when the two were in conflict, imperial authority generally prevailed. However, dogma and the sacraments remained outside of the civil authorities' sphere of power. Throughout Byzantine history, every single attempt

---

[1]The English translation of all conciliar documents cited in this study is based on Austin Flannery, ed., *Vatican Council II* (Northport, N.Y.: Constello Publishing Co., 1975); *Decree on Ecumenism*, 14.

of the imperial power to define dogma failed and the emperor was never understood as a priest-king.[2]

The relationship between East and West throughout the Byzantine period is complex and at many points historically controversial. Most scholars believe that estrangement between Latins and Byzantines took place gradually. The most noteworthy events that marked the break were the mutual excommunications of 1054 and the Fourth Crusade of 1204. While many historians see the first as a division that occurred among the upper hierarchy which did not generally affect relationships between Eastern and Western laity and lower clergy, the conquest and sacking of Constantinople by the crusaders is believed to have firmly established the schism on the popular level. Subsequent reunion attempts through the Councils of Lyons (1274) and Ferrara-Florence (1438–1439) were instigated by Byzantine emperors attempting to solicit Western military assistance in the face of a growing Turkish threat, to which the Empire later succumbed. In both cases, the imperial enforcement of union between the two Churches was unsuccessful and eventually repudiated by the overwhelming majority of Byzantine clergy and laity.

After the fall of the Empire, Byzantine Christians became second-class citizens under Ottoman Turkish rule and were highly restricted in the practice of their faith. Nevertheless, many Orthodox Christians of Greece, the Middle East, and parts of Eastern Europe remained steadfast despite hardships and persecution.

The Kievan-Rus were converted to Christianity by Byzantine missionaries during the tenth century. Despite a period of oppression by Islamic invaders, during the fifteenth century Russia overthrew the last vestiges of Mongol Tartar rule and emerged as a defender of Orthodoxy after the fall of Constantinople in 1453. Throughout the nineteenth and early twentieth centuries, the various Orthodox nations of the Balkans liberated themselves from Turkish rule. The Orthodox Churches of these countries aided in such struggles and became closely associated with the national identity of each nation. By the time most Orthodox countries had become free of the Ottomans, the October Revolution brought the Bolsheviks to power and the Orthodox Church within the former Russian Empire was subjected to a terrific and long-lasting persecution. With the Communist takeover of Eastern Europe in the 1940s, this condition became generalized for most Orthodox Churches except for Greece. However, in light of recent developments in Slavic lands, there are signs that the Communist persecution of the Church is coming to an end.

[2]Deno J. Geanakoplos, "Church and State in the Byzantine Empire: A Reconsideration of the Problem of Caesaropapism," *Byzantine East and Latin West: Two Worlds of Christendom in the Middle Ages and Renaissance* (New York: Archon Books, 1976) 55–83.

During the Ottoman period of oppression, Roman Catholic missionaries exploited the weakness of the Orthodox Church. These efforts resulted in the suppression of Byzantine Christianity in some areas of Europe and the creation of Eastern Churches in union with Rome. Many Orthodox derisively termed those who united with Rome, "Uniates." At present, these Eastern Churches include such groups as the Melkites, Ruthenians, Ukrainian Catholics, and others. Among Eastern Catholics, the influence of the predominant Latin Rite has resulted in losses of Byzantine theology, spirituality, and liturgical practices, as well as the adoption of many Western ideas. This process, known as "Latinization," has been exemplified by the introduction of mandatory celibacy among parish clergy, the loss by patriarchs and their synods of self-governance, and the acceptance of liturgical innovations foreign to Byzantine tradition such as stations of the cross, the rosary, indulgences, funeral Masses, spoken Eucharistic celebrations, and many other practices.

Into the nineteenth and twentieth centuries, tension and mutual suspicion existed between the two Churches. Vatican II marked a turning point in the relations of East and West. It initiated what has become known as the "dialogue of love" as well as the present theological dialogue between the two Churches. The dialogue of love may be characterized as an effort to produce an atmosphere conducive to the beginning of theological discussions. This atmosphere consisted of an awakening of the desire and need for a dialogue that had reunion for its purpose. The efforts that produced this awakening were begun by Pope Paul VI and Patriarch Athenagoras of Constantinople through a series of symbolic acts and statements. Among these were reciprocal visits to each other's respective sees, the lifting of the 1054 Anathemas, and the issuance of various statements, which were later collected in the volume, *Tomos Agapes*. After much preparation work, a formal theological dialogue on the international level was initiated in 1980 with the meeting of a mixed theological commission on the island of Rhodes. In the following years, additional meetings took place and agreed statements were produced. In North America, efforts began in 1965 with the foundation of an Orthodox-Roman Catholic Consultation in the United States that has met twice every year since that time and has also issued agreed statements on topics ranging from the Eucharist to the persecution of Christians in Turkey.

II. Vatican II and Eastern Christians

Two documents of the Second Vatican Council are of special concern to Orthodox and Eastern Catholics.

The first is the *Decree on Ecumenism* which includes a section entitled, "The Special Position of the Eastern Churches" (nos. 14–18). This section contains a recognition of the Orthodox Church as possessing "true sacraments, above all—by apostolic succession—the priesthood and the Eucharist, whereby they are still joined to us in closest intimacy." On this basis, the decree allows for "some worship in common (*communicatio in sacris*), given suitable circumstances and the approval of church authority" (no. 15). Elsewhere in the decree (no. 8), "worship in common" is not considered a means of unity, but in fact depends on "the unity of the Church which ought to be expressed" and "the sharing in the means of grace." Consequently, the permission granted for some common worship implies a recognition that the Orthodox are in some way part of the Roman Catholic Church.

The second document is the *Decree on the Catholic Eastern Churches*. This decree may be regarded as the vision that the council set forth for a reunited Church of East and West. Among the many points made in the document, two will be emphasized by this study: the ecclesiological position of the Eastern patriarchates, and the sacrament of matrimony.

According to the decree, the institution of the patriarchate was recognized by the ecumenical councils. In the past, Eastern patriarchs were said to have enjoyed a "precedence of honor" as well as "rights and privileges" that should be restored, but "without prejudice to the inalienable rights of the Roman Pontiff" (see nos. 7–11). The significance of these rights is clarified through an examination of later attempts to put the council's teachings into practice, among the most recent, the newly promulgated *Code of Eastern Canon Law*.

III. The Eastern Code

On June 10, 1972, Pope Paul VI set up the pontifical commission in order to revise Eastern canon law. In the 1974 "Guidelines for the Revision of the Code of Eastern Canon Law" approved by the first plenary assembly of the commission, this revision of the Eastern code was seen as implementing the *aggiornamento* decreed by the Second Vatican Council and as fulfilling the council's mandate in the *Decree on the Catholic Eastern Churches* to safeguard the legal patrimony of the East.[3] According to the guidelines, the sources for the commission's work were "the Apostolic Tradition," "Oriental canonical collections," and "the customary norms common to

[3] *Decree on the Catholic Eastern Churches* 5, 6; Italian, French, and English texts of the guidelines were published in *Nuntia* 3 (1976) 3–24; the English text was reprinted in Frederick R. McManus, "Decrees and Decisions," *The Jurist* 37 (1977) 171–80. In this study, references are made to the latter version.

the Oriental Churches and not fallen into desuetude."[4] The result of the commission's efforts is the present legislation, proposed as a code for all Eastern Catholic Churches based on their common legal tradition and promulgated on October 18, 1990.

The ecumenical character of this code is especially important to the Orthodox Church. The commission was charged with fulfilling a special task entrusted by the Second Vatican Council to the Eastern Catholic Churches, namely, the "special office of promoting the unity of all Christians."[5] In particular, the guidelines for revision state, "due consideration must be given, in the revision of the *CICO* [Codex Iuris Canonici Orientalis], to the *aggiornamento* to which the Orthodox Churches are tending in the hope of an ever greater unity of the *Canon Law of all the Oriental Churches.*"[6] From an Orthodox perspective, the code is significant ecumenically since it represents the vision that Rome has for the Eastern Catholic Churches in union with her, and by extension, Rome's view of her future relations with the Orthodox Church.

IV. Patriarchs and Ecclesiology

The primacy accorded to the Pope of Rome by the code is obviously foreign to the ecclesiological outlook of the Orthodox Church. The code characterizes the holder of the Roman See as the unique successor to St. Peter (*CICO*, 43). As outlined in canons 43 through 54, Rome exercises universal authority over the other four major patriarchates. Canon 51 states that the Roman Pontiff alone convokes, presides over, transfers, suspends, dissolves, and confirms an ecumenical council.

An Orthodox would not be able to accept the assertion that the Roman See acting alone on the basis of her own authority convoked, suspended, transferred, dissolved, or confirmed any of the seven ecumenical councils. This unacceptance is rooted in a different vision of the Church. According to this perspective, the criteria by which a council is recognized as ecumenical ultimately rests on its reception by the Church as the Body of Christ rather than its acceptance by one bishop.

---

[4]McManus, "Decrees," 174.

[5]The Eastern Code will be cited throughout this study as *CICO* (Codex Iuris Canonicis Orientalis). For the Latin text of the draft code, see *Nuntia*, 24–25 (1987); for its English translation, see Francis M. Zayek, Victor J. Pospishil, John D. Faris, Michel Thériault, eds. and trans., *Code of Eastern Canon Law 1986 Draft* (Brooklyn: United States Eastern Catholic Bishops' Consultation, 1987). The English translation of citations from the promulgated code used in this study is based on the latter work.

[6]McManus, "Decrees," 175.

The conflict of these two ecclesiologies is particularly revealed in Title IV (*De Ecclesiis patriarchalibus*) where no mention is made of the apostolic succession of the four ancient patriarchates. In fact, throughout the code, Rome is the only see referred to as apostolic, although it is noted in *CICO*, 48, that the titles "Apostolic See" and "Holy See" refer not only to the Roman Pontiff, but also to the Roman Curia.

The reason for this use of the term "apostolic" lies in the fact that in the code, patriarchal authority is derived from Rome and not from an independent apostolic foundation. According to the code, the Roman Pontiff controls patriarchal appointments and resignations by granting or withholding ecclesiastical communion (*CICO*, 77). Rome also exercises universal ordinary authority in all eparchies:

> The bishop of the Roman Church, in whom resides the office granted in a unique manner to Peter, the first of the apostles, and which is to be transmitted to his successors, is the head of the College of Bishops, Vicar of Christ, and Pastor of the universal Church on earth, and as such, in virtue of his office, he enjoys supreme, full, immediate, and universal ordinary power in the Church, which he can always exercise freely (*CICO*, 43).

This point is also emphasized in *CICO*, 45:

> (1) By virtue of his office, the Roman Pontiff enjoys power not only in the universal Church, but also possesses a primacy of ordinary power over all the eparchies and their groupings, by which the proper, ordinary, and immediate power which the bishops possess in the eparchy committed to their care is indeed both strengthened and safeguarded.

> (2) The Roman Pontiff, in fulfilling the office of supreme Pastor of the Church, is always joined with the other bishops and with the universal Church; however, it is his right to determine according to the needs of the Church the manner, either personal or collegial, of exercising this office.

The relationship of the patriarchs and papacy is discussed specifically in *CICO*, 92:

> The patriarch is to manifest hierarchical communion with the Roman Pontiff, successor of Blessed Peter, through fidelity, veneration, and obedience which are owed to the pastor of the universal Church.

Within this framework, the patriarchs of Constantinople, Antioch, Alexandria, and Jerusalem would be reduced to representatives of the Roman Pontiff that derive their legitimacy, apostolicity, orthodoxy, and jurisdiction from one successor of St. Peter.

V. Marriage

The *Decree on Catholic Eastern Churches* "confirms and approves the ancient discipline concerning the sacraments which exist in the Eastern Churches" (no. 12). The validity of marriages between Orthodox and Catholics in non-Catholic Eastern Churches was recognized with the provision that "the presence of a sacred minister is sufficient, provided the other prescriptions of canon law are observed" (no. 13). The priesthood of the Orthodox Church was recognized as valid elsewhere in the decree. However, the definition of these legal "prescriptions" was not contained in the document. This point is also clarified through an examination of the new Eastern code.

In its treatment of marriage, the code does not rely to any great extent on Byzantine canonical sources. This is most apparent in the definition of matrimony that appears in *CICO, 776*:

> The marriage covenant, established by the Creator and ordered by His laws, by which a man and a woman by an irrevocable personal consent establish between themselves a partnership of the whole life, is by its natural character ordered toward the good of the spouses and the generation and education of offspring.

A comparison of this text with Canon 1055 of the *Codex Iuris Canonici* (1983) reveals the source of the legislation:

> The matrimonial covenant, by which a man and woman establish between themselves a partnership of the whole life, is by its nature ordered toward the good of the spouses and the procreation and education of offspring; this covenant between baptized persons has been raised by Christ the Lord to the dignity of a sacrament.[7]

It is apparent that the *Codex Iuris Canonici* was used as the main source for the Eastern code's most basic canon defining matrimony.

Several ecumenical problems are raised by the use of this definition. The Orthodox Church does not view matrimonial consent as the essential element that establishes the nuptial union. The blessing of the priest is viewed as founding the marriage. Consent is considered a requirement for reception of the sacerdotal blessing. This position is based on Byzantine canonical sources and articulated in the Agreed Statement, *On Mixed Marriages* (May 20, 1970), of the Orthodox-Roman Catholic Consultation in the United States.

---

[7]James A. Coriden, Thomas J. Green, Donald E. Heintschel, *The Code of Canon Law: A Text and Commentary* (New York: Paulist Press, 1985) 740.

Another major issue is raised by the phrases "ordered by His laws" and "by its [the partnership of the whole life] natural character ordered toward the good of the spouses and the generation and education of offspring." "Partnership of the whole life" is a translation of the Latin text, *totius vitae consortium* (*CICO*, 776). This is close to Herennius Modestinus' usage of *consortium omnis vitae*. However, Byzantine canonical definitions of matrimony do not describe this consortium or partnership as structured for the procreation of children. Although certain contemporary Orthodox synodal statements condemn the use of artificial contraception, none of these are held to be binding for the entire Orthodox Church, which has not legislated on this subject.

Another major question is the dissolubility of marital unions. The Eastern code places no restriction on the number of marriages that can be contracted after the successive deaths of spouses:

> The sacramental bond of marriage for a consummated marriage can be dissolved by no human power nor by any cause other than death (*CICO*, 853).

This reiterates the position of the *Codex Iuris Canonici* regarding remarriage after the death of a spouse.[8] Although Byzantine canon law permitted the widowed to remarry, these unions were viewed as concessions made to avoid the more serious consequences of fornication. Fourth marriages were considered an indulgence of licentiousness and prohibited. Second and third unions were subject to penance. The first marriage was maintained as ideal and lawful.

Contemporary Orthodox legislation continues to restrict the number of successive unions to three.[9] A penitential rite is used in the celebration of remarriage.[10] In contrast, the promulgated Eastern code does not place limits on the number of unions for the widowed and consequently fails to take account of an important aspect of Byzantine canon law.

The code also contains major features of the annulment procedure found in the *Codex Iuris Canonici* (1983; *CICO*, 1357–1384). Tribunals headed by judges investigate impugned marriages for impotence and/or defect of consent. Officers of the tribunal include the Defender of the Bond, the Advocates of the parties, and the Promoter of Justice. The tribunals are con-

---

[8]Ibid., 811: "A ratified and consummated marriage cannot be dissolved by any human power or for any reason other than death."

[9]*The Tomos of Union*'s limit of three marriages continues to be in force. For a discussion of the *Tomos*, see Alexander P. Kazhdan and others, *The Oxford Dictionary of Byzantium* (Oxford, 1991) 3:2093.

[10]For an Orthodox text of this service, see N. M. Vaporis, ed., and John von Holzhausen and Michael Gelsinger, trans., *An Orthodox Prayer Book* (Brookline, Mass.: Holy Cross Press, 1977).

cerned with determining whether a marriage was established and granting an annulment if a sacramental marital bond was not formed. In contrast, according to the contemporary marriage legislation of the Orthodox Church as exemplified by the Greek Orthodox Archdiocese of North and South America, spiritual courts presided over by bishops dissolve marriages "contracted legally and in accordance with the sacred canons" by granting ecclesiastical divorces.[11] In addition, the Archdiocese allows "with condescension and according to economy" the remarriage of the innocent party.[12] The difference between granting annulments and ecclesiastical divorces points to deeper disagreements concerning the nature and formation of marriage. Rather than promoting unity, the newly promulgated code highlights a major stumbling block to progress in ecumenical relations.

A final point concerns the marriage of baptized and non-baptized parties. The code allows the local hierarch to grant dispensations for disparity of cult, a diriment impediment (*CICO*, 803, 814, 815). Such dispensations permit the formation of marriage by the exchange of marital consent between non-baptized and baptized persons. These provisions are similar to those provided by the *Codex Iuris Canonici* (1983).[13] In Western canon law, the resulting union is recognized as a valid non-sacramental marriage.[14] The same type of recognition is implied by the *CICO*. In addition, since Eastern Catholics exchange consent during the marriage ceremony, dispensations for such marriages necessarily imply that non-baptized parties may participate in the marital rite and undergo nuptial crowning.

This raises a major theological problem since in the Orthodox Church, the only valid marriages are formed through the rite of crowning, which is regarded as a sacerdotal blessing that establishes sacramental unions. The Orthodox Church does not recognize non-sacramental marriages. The exchange of marital consent is a requirement for the reception of the nuptial blessing, but not an element that forms the nuptial union. According to Orthodox canon law, a non-Christian cannot receive a Mystery or sacrament other than baptism. Hindus, Buddhists, Muslims, and Jews cannot be blessed with marriage crowns in the Orthodox Church.[15] Consequently, non-baptized persons are prevented from validly marrying Orthodox spouses under any circumstances. As is evident, the conflicting treatment of dis-

---

[11]This citation is taken from two Archdiocesan encyclicals, protocol numbers 116 and 206A, respectively dated June 16, 1966, and November 21, 1973, which set forth the grounds allowed for ecclesiastical divorce.

[12]Ibid.

[13]Compare canons 1086, 1125, and 1126 of the *Codex Iuris Canonici* (1983).

[14]Ladislas Örsy, *Marriage in Canon Law: Texts and Comments, Reflections and Questions* (Wilmington, Del.: Michael Glazier, Inc., 1986) 112–13.

[15]Standing Conference of Canonical Orthodox Bishops in America, *Guidelines for Orthodox Christians in Ecumenical Relations* (1973) 20.

parity of cult by the *CICO* and Orthodox canon law reveals and emphasizes the major theological differences between the two Churches concerning the formation of marriage.[16]

Conclusion

The *Decree on Ecumenism* exhorts Roman Catholics to obtain an accurate understanding of Eastern Christianity. A vision of unity between East and West is set forth in the *Decree on Catholic Eastern Churches*.

One of the most recent attempts to implement the basis of this unity is the newly promulgated Code of Eastern Canon Law. The vision of the united Eastern and Western Churches presented by the code is one in which the patriarchs of Constantinople, Alexandria, Antioch, and Jerusalem would derive their legitimacy, apostolicity, orthodoxy, and jurisdiction from Rome. Rome would exercise universal local authority throughout the Eastern Churches. In turn, the hierarchy of the Eastern Catholic Churches would function as representatives of the Apostolic See.

The code's matrimonial legislation is based on Western canonical sources. Consequently, its perspective is heavily influenced by the concerns of the Roman Catholic Church regarding matrimonial consent and the generation of offspring. Major problems are raised by the code's provisions for marriage with non-Christians and annulment.

On the basis of this brief examination, it can be concluded that the major legacy of the Second Vatican Council for the Christian East, the new Eastern code, will emphasize major differences between the Orthodox and Roman Catholic Churches and erect major barriers to the future development of ecumenical relations.

[16]The present study is based on my article dealing with the Eastern Code, "Orthodox-Catholic Unity and the Revised Code of Eastern Canon Law," *The Journal of Ecumenical Studies* (1990).

On Jewish-Christian Dialogue

Krister Stendahl

Two things matter now. Both were highlighted in our section of the Washington Conference. It is time for letting the dialogue spread on the grass-roots level, and, as Sr. Mary Christine Athans, B.V.M., of the College of St. Thomas (St. Paul, Minnesota) made clear in her presentation, such dialogue is not just an "application" of what scholars have worked out. The grass-roots work engenders its own intellectual excitement and personal commitment. It is also indispensable for combatting bigotry. That grass-roots work surely matters now.

The other urgency that emerged strongly and spontaneously in our section was the need for creative theological moves a good way beyond what was done—or perhaps even envisaged—by Vatican II. That council constitutes, of course, a monumental breakthrough in the history of Jewish-Christian relations, not only for Roman Catholics but for the whole of Christendom. The council gave encouragement to many of us Protestants: If Rome can change, why should we be so timid? To be sure, there are parts of the Church—Catholic, Orthodox, and Protestant—where the boldness of Vatican II and the later guidelines are opposed, especially in the Middle East, and under the strain of growing impatience with the present Israeli government's policies toward Palestinians. But I think it is clear that the Church did turn a corner, and there is no way back.

Even so, the theological challenge of the deeper implications of the moves taken by Vatican II is now upon us, as witnessed by three of the papers read in our section. Dr. Donald J. Dietrich of Boston College mapped out the ways in which time-honored patterns of *moral* theology are found insufficient and even counter-productive for counteracting the demonic abuses that are amply found in the Church's relation to Jews through history. Partially quoting Johannes Metz, he affirmed:

> The message for Christian theologians is loud and clear—never again do a theology in such a way that its construction remains unaffected or could remain unaffected by Auschwitz. Merely expressing a sense of reconciliation or a Chris-

tian friendliness toward Jews is cheap and ineffective. What must be sought is a concrete and fundamental revision of the consciousness we have of the God-man relationship both for our interaction with the Jewish people and for our cognizance of the meaning of man.

That is a tall order but Dietrich makes clear that we cannot stop short—stop halfway on the road begun.

Dr. Bernard Prusak of Villanova University demonstrated another facet of the same need for more substantial moves of interpretation. Few systematic theologians seem yet to have grasped or digested the Christological implications of more recent New Testament scholarship *and* as it opens up new ways of understanding the role of Jews and the death of Jews. Old habits of reading Scripture die hard—not least in systematic theologians. The greatest obstacle to new understanding seems to be the pattern of "Law and Gospel" and the most promising approach seems to be that of Edward Schillebeeckx in his *Jesus: An Experiment in Christology* (1979).

The paper I have chosen for this volume goes even more to the core of that theological challenge which is the maturing consequence of the healing insights of John XXIII and his Cardinal Bea. For John Merkle tackles the issue which—it seems to me—is both the most urgent and the most divisive in contemporary Christian thinking, both for Jewish-Christian dialogue and for the future role of the Church as a community among communities in a plural world. Merkle's suggestive model has the advantage of treating Christianity in its Trinitarian fullness without reductionism, without toning down what is particular to Christian self-understanding. Rather, his proposal has recognized that the mystery of faith transcends the models of "zero-sum" thinking, where a positive attitude to the other would somehow deduct from the value of one's own. Or, to put it in a less abstract manner, Merkle suggests a way in which I as a Christian can sing my song to Jesus with abandon—without telling negative things about Judaism.

The thrust of his paper and of our whole session is strong and clear when it calls for fundamental theological renewal and rethinking. It is not only or finally a matter of improved behavior. While anti-Semitism has been called a grave sin in Church pronouncements over the last forty years, it must be uprooted as a *heresy*—a wrong way of thinking. It is perhaps symptomatic that Church history knows many examples where "Judaizing" was branded heretical, but not cases where anti-Judaism was exposed for what it was and is—the heresy of heresies in the Church since it threatens the very root of the Church's existence—as Paul clearly saw when he perceived the self-serving haughtiness of his Gentile converts (Rom 11:11-36).

Chapter 22

Christian Self-Understanding in Light of the New Jewish-Christian Encounter

John C. Merkle

From its earliest days the Christian Church has defined its identity in relation to Judaism and the Jewish people from which it emerged. Unfortunately, for most of its history the Church has misunderstood and misrepresented Judaism and has failed to appreciate the ongoing spiritual vitality of the Jewish people. But recently, in light of a new encounter with Jews and Judaism, a number of Christians, including Church authorities, have been rethinking and reversing the timeworn Christian teaching concerning the Jewish people and their faith. Traditionally, the Christian Churches have taught that the validity of Judaism came to an end with the coming of Christ and the emergence of Christianity. Christian self-understanding was built in large part upon the notion of Christianity having replaced Judaism as the valid pathway to God. But in the last three decades, ever since the Second Vatican Council, leaders in the Catholic Church and other Christian Churches have affirmed the abiding validity of Judaism. Since Christian self-understanding involved the notion that Christianity superseded Judaism, it is clear that this new affirmation necessitates a reevaluation of Christian self-understanding.

The purpose of this paper is to present a few of my ideas that are a part of what I propose as a reconstruction of Christian faith in light of the new Christian-Jewish encounter. But before presenting this reconstruction, I must share a few of my conclusions about Judaism that have forced me to rethink the meaning of Christianity. The idea that Christianity superseded Judaism was accompanied by misinformation about Jews and their religious tradition. It is therefore imperative that we Christians strive for an accurate understanding of Judaism as we seek to reverse our relationship to the Jewish people and thereby enhance our own life of Christian faith.

I. Judaism: God, Torah, and the Covenant of Israel

Judaism may be described as the collective religious tradition of the Jewish people. With its roots in ancient Israelite faith, Judaism has developed from biblical times onward to this very day. As the Jewish people have adapted to numerous historical circumstances in their ancestral land of Israel and around the world, Judaism has become an exceedingly rich and complex tradition. Indeed, like Christianity, it is a tradition comprised of many traditions. Nevertheless, there are common memories, beliefs, practices, and hopes that lend to Judaism a unity within all its diversity. Most of all, what unites the diverse forms of Judaism is the fact that each in its own way represents monotheistic faith, which is expressed by some degree of adherence to the Torah within the context of the covenant of Israel. So a proper understanding of Judaism, which is necessary for a genuine understanding of Christian faith, demands our coming to grips with Jewish views of God, Torah, and covenant peoplehood of Israel.

However diverse the Jewish interpretations of God might be, they are expressions of belief in the one God of Israel, who is also believed to be the Creator and Redeemer of the world. So Jewish monotheism is not simply a matter of believing in one God; it is an expression of faith in the only true God, the Lord of the universe, who transcends the world while being present to it. As such, it is an alternative not only to polytheism, but also to henotheism, pantheism, and any other type of theism one can imagine.

One of the ways by which Christian theologians have attempted to demonstrate the superiority of Christianity to Judaism has been to advocate the idea that the Christian view of God is superior to the Jewish view. It has often been claimed, for example, that Judaism teaches a God of wrath, Christianity a God of love. To be sure, some of the deeds attributed to God in the Jewish Bible (Old Testament) appear, from the Christian perspective at its best, to be less than godly. But such a contrast is obviously unfair. Not only does it fail to acknowledge the fact that in the Jewish Bible God is repeatedly referred to as loving and compassionate; it also ignores the fact that Jewish views of God have developed well beyond those found in ancient Israelite religion. Post-biblical Jewish understandings of God, no less than developed Christian views, call into question some of the Bible's accounts of God's action. The late Rabbi Abraham Heschel, perhaps the foremost Jewish theologian of the twentieth century, claimed that "in the name of God's mercy, we have the right to challenge the harsh statements of the prophets." But if we criticize biblical "passages which seem to be incompatible with our certainty of the compassion of God," Heschel reminds us that "the standards by which those passages are criticized are impressed upon us by the Bible, which is the main factor in ennobling our conscience and endowing us with the sensitivity that rebels against all cruelty."[1]

---

[1]Abraham J. Heschel, *God in Search of Man: A Philosophy of Judaism* (New York: Farrar, Straus, and Cudahy, 1955) 268.

When we read the sages of Israel—whether ancient, medieval, or modern—we discover that what Jews understand about God's love and compassion is every bit as profound as what Christian theologians have usually claimed could be known only through faith in Christ. While believing that Jesus is the incarnation of God's Word, we Christians must acknowledge also that Jesus was an identifiably Jewish man of God. Indeed, when we compare what Judaism teaches about God to what we have learned from the gospel of Christ, we discover that Jesus had a thoroughly Jewish understanding of God and a thoroughly Jewish way of relating to God. The fact that we believe Jesus' relationship to God was uniquely intimate should not lead us to think that he thereby stood apart from the Jewish faith, but rather that he embodied it in a way *par excellence*. The God whom we Christians have come to know through the gospel of Christ is the God of Jewish faith, the Giver of Torah. In the strictest sense of the term, Torah designates the first five books of the Bible. More broadly, it refers to the Jewish Scriptures as a whole, and even to the entire corpus of authoritative Jewish writings. Torah is often thought of by Christians exclusively in terms of law. Yet only a small portion of the Torah deals with legal matters; most of it is comprised of narratives about God's involvement with humanity, particularly with the Jewish people. To live by way of Torah is "to walk in God's ways" (Deut 10:12), which includes observing commandments of the Torah. Many traditional Jews believe that the biblical Torah in its entirety is the inspired Word of God. Others, like Rabbi Heschel, claim that although not every line of the Torah is divinely inspired, the Torah contains the Word of God. In both cases, traditional Jews believe that the Torah is a sign of God's love and, as such, charts a course by which human beings may live in a way that is compatible with divine love.

There is every reason to believe that Jesus himself was a Torah-observant Jew, even if, like other Jewish teachers, he disputed certain standard interpretations of specific laws of the Torah. Yet, since the first century, Christians have preached the gospel of Christ as liberation from the Jewish Torah. Adherence to Torah has been repeatedly portrayed in Christian polemics as legalism, in contrast to faith. Jesus and his gospel have been continually played off against Judaism and its Torah in an attempt to demonstrate the superiority of Christianity. It even became a standard Christian claim that those who still observed the Torah did so because they rejected grace. Such an idea cannot survive a genuine encounter with Judaism and its understanding of Torah. According to traditional Jewish teaching, Torah is God's gracious gift to Israel and the world. So much for the Christian polemic that contrasts grace and Torah! Again, according to Jewish teaching, the law of Torah is primarily the law of love; and love for God and God's creatures is the purpose of living by way of Torah. So much for the antithesis between Torah legalism and gospel love! To read the Jewish sages is to feel the power of the Torah's challenge and the holiness of its ways.

Living by way of Torah is the way Jews remain faithful to their covenant with God which, according to Jewish faith, was initiated by God. But why did God make this covenant with Israel? It is clear from the Torah itself that God created all human beings to live in harmony with God, each other, and the rest of creation. But time and again God's plan for humanity had been frustrated, as depicted in the mythical story of Adam and Eve's fall from paradise. Nevertheless, God did not abandon the original hope, but rather, through Abraham and Sarah, entered into a special covenant with one people for the sake of all peoples: "Through you shall all the families of the earth be blessed" (Gen 12:36). Centuries later this covenant was renewed at Sinai, when the people accepted the commandments of Torah revealed by God to Moses.

It is because of their covenant with God that the Jewish people have considered themselves to be a "chosen people." There is perhaps no concept in Judaism that has been more misunderstood. Contrary to what critics assume, the idea is not meant to imply that Israel is a superior people, has an exclusive relationship with God, or is the only vehicle of God's revelation. Israel's relationship to God is unique not because God favors the Jewish people over other peoples, but because God has charged them with the task of witnessing to God in a unique way: the way of Torah. Israel has been called to be a "a holy people" (Exod 19:6), a people set apart by way of its covenant, in order to inspire other peoples to turn to God. Living in the covenant of Israel is the Jewish way of living in faith, hope, and love.

It is this very same Jewish covenant that for centuries Christians have claimed was abolished and replaced by a new covenant established in and through Jesus Christ. Along with claiming that the Torah has been superseded by the gospel, the Church has attempted to legitimize its identity and mission by portraying itself as the "new Israel" which has displaced the "old Israel" as God's chosen people. In other words, a living people has been relegated to ancient history, and their faith deemed obsolete. But from all we know of the religious vitality of the Jewish people during the last two thousand years, it is absurd to suggest that their covenant is defunct and that they no longer have a positive role to play in history. Moreover, such a claim is immoral, for it "offends so blatantly against observable fact that it carries the temptation to switch from the indicative to the imperative, as witnessed by the whole appalling history of Christian anti-Semitism."[2] For both historical and ethical reasons, then, contemporary

---

[2]Monika K. Hellwig, "Christian Theology and the Covenant of Israel," *Journal of Ecumenical Studies* 7:1 (Winter 1970) 40–41.

Christians must reject the timeworn idea that the Jewish covenant has been replaced by the covenant in Christ and that the Jewish people have been displaced by the Church as the people of God.

When Christians discover that the Jewish understanding of God is infinitely richer than has been depicted in Christian polemics; that the way of Torah bears the fruit of holiness; and that the Jewish people have endured through untold persecutions precisely because of their fidelity to their covenant, then Christians must develop a new theology concerning Judaism: one that recognizes its permanent validity and, therefore, the ongoing role of the Jewish people in history. And this is precisely what has begun to happen in many Christian Churches during the last few decades. But it seems that few Christians realize the profound implications that this new understanding of Judaism has for Christian identity. Since Christian self-understanding has been built largely upon misinformation about Judaism and Jews, this new awareness must inevitably cause a transformation in Christian self-understanding. In what follows, then, I will suggest how a new Christian theology concerning Judaism might challenge and enhance Christian existence. This I will do by focusing on three central categories of Christian theology—God, Christ, and the Church—in the light of the new Christian appreciation for the Jewish understanding of God, the way of Torah, and the significance of the covenant of Israel.

II. Christianity: God, Christ, and the Church

Christianity is, first and foremost, a monotheistic faith. And the one God whom we Christians worship is the Holy One of Israel, the God of our Lord Jesus Christ. Jesus addressed God as "Father" and taught his followers to do the same; so we Christians, who have come to know God by way of Jesus, have followed his example and taken his advice when speaking to (and of) God. The Christian Church was formed in response to God's Word dwelling in Jesus, God's Word spoken by this faithful son of the covenant who, as such, and in a way *par excellence*, was Son of God; so we Christians speak of Jesus as God's incarnate Word, as God's Son. This same Church which began in the bosom of Israel on Pentecost, eventually was fashioned into a Gentile Church when God's Spirit was "poured out" on Gentiles, inspiring them to respond to God in Jesus' name; so we Christians speak to (and of) God by the power of the Spirit, as in the name of the Son. Given these foundations of our faith, these roots of our Church, we Christians have traditionally expressed our monotheism in Trinitarian terms, speaking of the one God as "Father, Son, and Holy Spirit."

The Jewish people knew God as Father long before Jesus of Nazareth preached his gospel. They listened in faith to God's Word in Torah and the prophets centuries before that Word moved the prophet from Nazareth. And long before the Church spoke of God as Spirit, the Jewish people knew of God's presence as Spirit, cleansing and fortifying the human spirit, empowering the people Israel to live by their covenant with God. All this the Jewish people knew from of old, and to this very day still know. But what they have always emphasized is the oneness (unity) of God who relates to them in a variety of creative and redemptive ways.

We Christians are true to the Jewish faith of Jesus, as also to our own Christian tradition when, along with the Jews, we stress the oneness of God. But this does not preclude our speaking of God as triune: "Father, Son, and Holy Spirit." We know that there is but one God and that God possesses inner unity. But, again, given the way we Christians have come to know God, we have learned to speak of God's inner unity in terms of Trinity. Sometimes the way we have articulated this has sounded more like tritheism (belief in three gods) than Trinitarianism, but this is not what our tradition at its best has promoted. And the risk of such a heresy is lessened when we Christians renew and deepen our ties with the Jewish people and learn to value what they have to tell us about God.

The Christian rediscovery of Judaism as a valid and vital faith must inevitably affect the way we think of Jesus as the incarnation of God. Now that we affirm the Torah as God's abiding Word, we who believe that Jesus is the incarnate Word of God must think of him not in opposition to Torah but as its embodiment. Since God is one, God's Word in Christ to Christians could not be contrary to God's Word in Torah to Jews. So just as Jews do not maintain that Torah is the only way of serving God, we Christians will not claim that faith in Jesus is the only valid way of responding to God. Many Christians may assume that it is easier for Jews to relativize the Torah in relation to God than for Christians to do the same with regard to Christ. It would be difficult for most Christians to paraphrase the following statement by Rabbi Heschel, simply substituting the word "Christ" for the word "Torah": "God is greater than his Torah. . . . The Torah is his, but he is not his Torah."[3] But I believe that Christians could paraphrase this statement in the following way without losing what is essential to Christianity: "God is greater than what has been revealed in Christ. Christ is God's, but God is found not only in Christ."

In the name of the one God who transcends all finite realities, Judaism protests the absolutizing of anything finite. It does, nonetheless, recognize particular finite manifestations of the one absolute God. In this sense it is

---

[3]Abraham J. Heschel, "God, Torah, and Israel," *Theology and Church in Times of Change: Essays in Honor of John Coleman Bennett,* eds. Edward LeRoy Long, Jr., and Robert T. Handy (Philadelphia: Westminster Press, 1970) 75, 81.

an incarnational faith—without positing an incarnation in the Christian sense. Like Judaism, Christianity affirms the reality of a transcendent Absolute. By its doctrine of the incarnation, the Church does not—or should not—intend to absolutize a particular manifestation of God, but to keep alive the memory of that divine manifestation on which Christianity is based. If the incarnation is understood as a particular instance of divine involvement in human history—even as the supreme instance—then this understanding is not contrary to the monotheism of Jesus and Judaism. But if the doctrine of the incarnation is understood to mean that Jesus must be considered the only way to God, then Christian monotheism is attenuated or undermined. This is because God alone, not an incarnation of God, is absolute. It is worse to absolutize something which is not a manifestation of God than to absolutize that which is; but God transcends divine manifestations—even a divine incarnation. If we Christians hold such a view we can make theological room for Judaism and other faiths as valid pathways to God, just as Jewish sages have recognized that "holiness is not the monopoly of any particular tradition" and that "conversion to Judaism is no prerequisite for sanctity."[4]

While we Christians should acknowledge that God alone is absolute, we must also affirm the abiding significance of God's incarnation in Christ, by which we have come to know God. And since the Torah is God's Word, we will also affirm its abiding significance. If we who have faith in Christ cherish also the faith of Jesus, we will be grateful that Jews continue to live by way of Torah rather than abandon it for Christianity. And this will not diminish our gratitude for having been granted the opportunity to live in covenant with God through faith in Christ—a way distinct from but not unrelated to the way of Torah. To be sure, the way of Jesus was the way of Torah. But, paradoxically, what God has wrought through Jesus—by inspiriting Gentiles to heed the gospel preached in his name—is a way for Gentiles to know, love, and serve God distinct from the way of Torah.

The God who formed Israel into a people by way of the covenant reached out beyond Israel and called into being a Gentile Church.[5] Surely this was not to make of the Church a "new Israel" that would take the place and usurp the role of the Jewish people. Rather, in accord with the divine prom-

---

[4]Abraham J. Heschel, "No Religion Is an Island," *Union Seminary Quarterly Review* 21:1 (January 1966) 130, 131.

[5]This is a recurrent theme in Paul M. van Buren's *A Theology of the Jewish-Christian Reality* (San Francisco: Harper and Row, 1980, 1983, 1988), a three-volume work that has inspired much of my own reflection on the relationship of the Church to the Jewish people and my own rethinking of Christian teachings vis-à-vis Judaism. The three volumes of *A Theology of the Jewish-Christian Reality* are: *Discerning the Way* (1980), *A Christian Theology of the People Israel* (1983), and *Christ in Context (1988)*.

ise to Abraham, it was to extend the blessings of covenantal life—albeit in a new form—to the Gentiles. We Christians should think of Christianity not as representing a new covenant that supersedes the Jewish covenant but as a new way, coexisting with Judaism, of living in covenant with God. Such a view constitutes radical transformation in Christian self-understanding, but it is closer to the vision of the earliest Christians who, like Jesus, continued to live within the Jewish covenant.

Chapter 23

Christianity and World Religions since Vatican II

Robert Fastiggi

The movements of the Holy Spirit in the history of the Church are sometimes subtle and imperceptible and sometimes overt and manifest. It is a
fitting testimony to the presence of the Spirit that the shortest of all the
documents of Vatican II may eventually prove to be the most significant.
As one participant in the drafting of the Declaration on the Relationship
of the Church to Non-Christian Religions observes: "In the genesis of no
document have I experienced more deeply the interaction of God's design
and the concrete historical process, the dynamism of progress . . . the holy
step forward which closes a period of history yet opens to a less definite
future. . . ."[1]

What we find in this document (usually referred to as *Nostra aetate*) is
an opening of the windows of the Church to the more than two-thirds of
humanity who embrace a religious orientation other than Christianity. While
the original intent was to draft a document which would improve Christian attitudes towards Judaism, it eventually became clear that there was
a need to expand the document to include all non-Christian religions. With
over one-third of the bishops at the council coming from Asia, Africa, and
Oceania,[2] there was a deeply felt impulse to address the relationship of the
Church to the vast numbers of human beings who find spiritual nourishment and moral guidance from the extrabiblical traditions.

A total of six academic sessions held at the September 28–30, 1990,
Washington Conference touched upon issues related to ecumenism and interreligious dialogue. My purpose in this chapter is not to summarize all
of the papers but to sketch in broad detail some of the main issues that

---

[1]Rev. Thomas Stransky, C.S.P., "The Declaration on Non-Christian Religions," *Vatican II, An Interfaith Appraisal,* ed. John Miller (Notre Dame, Ind.: University of Notre Dame
Press, 1966) 336.
[2]Ibid., 337.

emerged in these presentations and discussions. The contributions of specific speakers will be mentioned, but the chief concern is to provide a synthesis of the underlying movements of history, thought, and spirit reflected in the individual papers.

I. Preconciliar Attitudes towards Non-Christian Religions

Prior to Vatican II, the dominant theological tendency was to emphasize the uniqueness and exclusivity of the Christian revelation. Scripture was appealed to as the witness of Jesus as the only Savior (Acts 4:12) with incorporation into the Church through baptism as the only means for salvation (John 3:5). The famous saying of the third-century bishop, Cyprian—*extra ecclesiam nulla salus* (outside the Church there is no salvation)—was solemnly taught at Lateran IV (1215) and the Council of Florence (1442).

Such exclusivism was gradually rendered more flexible by mention of "baptism by desire" at the Council of Trent in the sixteenth century and by the allowance for "invincible ignorance of the true religion" taught by Pope Pius IX in 1854. However, the question remained to be settled whether any positive values were to be found among the non-Christian traditions.

Along with the trend towards exclusivity, Christian theology has always had a countertendency towards universalism and inclusivism. Even within Scripture, there are various passages which can be cited in support of this more expansive view—most notably Genesis 1:26-27 (the creation of humanity in the divine image), John 1:3 (the creation of all things by the divine Logos), Acts 17:22-28 (Paul's speech at the Areopagus), and Romans 1:19-20 (the knowledge of God through creation).

Beyond Scripture, the primary theological impetus for the universalist trend was the desire of patristic writers to absorb the wisdom of Greek and Roman thought. Thus, St. Justin Martyr (ca. 100–165 A.D.) employed the idea of the universal *Logos* as the explanation of the truths to be found among the pagan philosophers. Similar inclusivistic attitudes can be found among theologians like Clement of Alexandria (ca. 150–219), Origen (ca. 185–255), and the fourth-century historian Eusibius who uses the phrase *praeparatio evangelica* (evangelical preparation) in reference to the non-Christian wisdom which provides a philosophical foundation for the Christian faith.

In the medieval period, recognition of truth and wisdom in the writings of Plato and Aristotle was standard for great scholastic authors like Aquinas (1224–1274) and Bonaventure (1221–1274) and for late Gothic authors like Ramon Lull (1232–1316) and Nicholas of Cusa (1401–1464). In the Renaissance period, philosophers like Marsilio Ficino (1433–1499),

Pico della Mirandola (1464–1494), and Augostino Steuco (1497–1548) developed a highly cultivated irenicism in reference not only to Greek and Roman philosophy but towards other religions as well.

In the last century, the objective study of the history of religions has provided Christians with a vast body of religious literature and philosophy which can be appreciated as part of the collective wisdom of humanity. Because of this increased knowledge of the primary sources of religions like Hinduism, Buddhism, and Islam, the stage was set for Vatican II to usher in a new era of interreligious appreciation, dialogue, and cooperation.

II. The Move from Exclusivism to Inclusivism

Vatican II helps to resolve two fundamental theological issues. The first is the soteriological question of the salvation of non-Christians. While Cyprian's dictum that "outside the Church there is no salvation" must be considered as part of the Church's tradition, there still remains the question of what exactly is meant by the Church. At Vatican II, the concept of Church is extended beyond the boundaries of the visible structure of the Catholic faithful in union with the Roman Pontiff. The Church, as the people of God, is also linked to "those, who being baptized, are honored with the name of Christian."[3] This, of course, would mean the Orthodox and the Protestants. However, the council goes still further and recognizes that even non-Christians are related "in various ways to the People of God."[4] Thus, Jews, Muslims, and "those who in shadows and images seek the unknown God"[5] can be considered as members of the Church, understood in this expanded way.

By means of this theological nuance, Vatican II is able to settle the centuries-old soteriological debate over the possibility of salvation for non-Christians. As the council proclaims: "Those also can attain to everlasting salvation who through no fault of their own do not know the Gospel of Christ or His Church, yet sincerely seek God, and moved by grace, strive by their deeds to do His will as it is known to them through the dictates of conscience."[6]

The second major theological issue that Vatican II helps to resolve is whether spiritual truth can be found outside the biblically based religions of Judaism and Christianity. In this regard, the council clearly affirms the

---

[3]*Lumen gentium*, 15. All translations are taken from *The Documents of Vatican II*, ed. Walter Abbott S.J. (Piscataway, N.J.: New Century Publishers, 1966). Subsequent references to the Documents will be made by title and section only.

[4]*Lumen gentium*, 16.

[5]Ibid.

[6]Ibid.

presence of truth and holiness in the non-Christian traditions. We are told that the Church "looks with sincere respect upon those ways of conduct and of life, those rules and teachings which, though differing in many particulars from what she holds and sets forth, nevertheless often reflect a ray of that Truth which enlightens all men."[7]

This passage clearly affirms that some type of divine truth is found within these traditions. It shows a clear rejection of an exclusivistic paradigm which would regard all extrabiblical religions as corrupt, distorted, or demonic. What remains unresolved is whether these non-Christian religions merely reflect a cosmic sense of the divine as articulated in the classical natural law tradition or whether they contain supernatural truths understood as divine revelation proper.

The closest affirmation of divine revelation is found in reference to Hinduism. Here we are told that in Hinduism people "contemplate the divine mystery" (*in Hinduismo homines mysterium divinum scrutantur*).[8] The term "mystery" in connection with God is used only in reference to two other religions of Vatican II. The Jews are said to be linked to the mystery of God's saving design (*iuxta salutare Dei mysterium*),[9] and the bishops are said to be "stewards of the mysteries of God" (*ministri Christi sunt et dispensatores mysterium Dei*).[10] According to Vatican I, supernatural revelation consists in those "mysteries that are hidden in God, which could never be known unless they are revealed by God."[11]

Is it purely accidental that the Fathers of the council chose the phrase *mysterium divinum* in reference to Hinduism? Perhaps it is more providential than accidental. Hinduism appears to express (at least in archetypal form) several mysteries of the Christian faith prior to the time of Jesus. For example, there is an articulation of mysterious plurality in the Godhead within an underlying unity. There is also the archetype of the incarnation in the various avatars of Vishnu. We also discover in the Bhagavad Gita 18:64-65, the idea that the supreme human happiness lies in the loving possession of God (the Beatific Vision). The Gita likewise affirms the doctrine of divine grace as the only means by which humans can achieve intimacy with God (18:56-58).[12]

Even though Vatican II recognizes elements of truth and holiness in non-Christian religions, it is also clear that the council continues to see Chris-

[7] *Nostra aetate*, 2.
[8] Ibid.
[9] *Nostra aetate*, 4.
[10] *Lumen gentium*, 21.
[11] *Dei Filius*, ch. 4, *The Christian Faith in the Doctrinal Documents of the Catholic Church*, eds. J. Neuner and J. Dupuis (New York: Alba House, 1982) 45.
[12] See José Pereira, *Hindu Theology: A Reader* (Garden City, N.Y.: Doubleday, 1976) 33–34.

tianity (and more specifically, Catholicism) as possessing "the all-embracing means" of salvation and the fullness of the means of salvation.[13] We can say, therefore, that the council moves from exclusivism to inclusivism. The Church does not reject the genuine gifts found within other religions; rather, she claims them as her own. While acknowledging that many elements of sanctification exist outside of her visible structure, the Church, nevertheless, states that "these elements . . . possess an inner dynamism towards Catholic unity."[14]

III. Vatican II and the Expanding Ecumenism

The deep movements of the Spirit present at Vatican II are manifested in an expanded view of divine providence and community. In a Church dominated by the Western Latin Rite, there surfaces a renewed appreciation of the riches of the Eastern Catholic Churches. In a Church wounded by over nine hundred years of schism with the Orthodox Churches of the East, there is felt a sisterly affection and a heartfelt yearning for reunion. In a Church crippled by the shattering of Christian unity in the sixteenth century, there is found a humble spirit of repentance and a move towards reconciliation. Finally, in a Church which has been locked within the narrow confines of exclusivism, there emerges an expanded vision of God's revelation which recognizes in the non-Christian religions a reflection of that ray of Truth which enlightens all human beings.

The influence of this expanding ecumenism is visible in the Catholic academic community. More and more Western Catholics are studying the primary sources of Eastern Catholic and Orthodox spirituality and theology. Philip Yevics points out that Western Catholics have much to gain from a consideration of Eastern Christian ideas of "eucharistic ecclesiology" and "*koinonia*. . . . " His suggestion is that Christians begin to embrace the fullness of orthodoxy as giving "right worship" to God. In regard to the more complicated aspects of ecumenism, Yevicks suggests faithfulness to the maxim attributed to the Patriarch Photius of the ninth century: "In that which is essential, unity; in that which is not essential, diversity; in all things, charity."

Catholics are now reading the primary texts of the Protestant reformers with greater sympathy and objectivity. As Gregory Sobolewski demonstrates, contemporary Catholic opinion about Luther has changed "in substance and style from that of previous generations." Twentieth-century Catholic scholars like Otto Pesch, O.P., and Yves Congar have found many genuine

---

[13]*Unitatis redintegratio*, 3.
[14]*Lumen gentium*, 8.

Catholic concerns in the writings of Luther, even if they might question some of his conclusions. Thus, Sobolewski observes that Catholic scholars "who would perpetuate the denial of Luther's religious insight and genuine contributions to Christianity find little hearing in academe."

IV. Catholic-Jewish Relations

One of the great achievements of Vatican II is in the area of the Catholic appreciation of Judaism as a vital religion. In the wake of the horrors of the Holocaust and the long, unfortunate history of Christian anti-Jewish prejudices, Vatican II serves as a reminder that the Jews remain "most dear to God, for God does not repent of the gifts He makes nor of the calls He issues."[15]

In *Nostra aetate,* four main points are made regarding the Church's relationship to the Jews. The first is that the Church recognizes her "spiritual bond" with the Jewish people. This bond is recognized in the common patrimony of "the patriarchs, Moses and the prophets" as well as in the Jewish background of Christ, the Virgin Mary, and the apostles.[16] The mutual understanding between Christians and Jews should, therefore, be fostered by biblical and theological studies as well as by "brotherly dialogues."

The second point is that there cannot be any collective or ancestral blame on the part of Jews for Christ's death. Christ "in His boundless love freely underwent His passion and death" because of the sins of all human beings.[17] From this follows the third point that the Jews of today "should not be presented as repudiated or cursed by God, as if such views followed from the Holy Scriptures." The final point is that the spiritual love commanded by the gospel moves the Church to deplore "the hatred, persecutions and displays of anti-Semitism directed against the Jews at any time from any source."[18]

The impact of these brief statements on the Jewish faith has been significant. As Rev. Michael McGarry, C.S.P., notes "the most significant breakthrough of *Nostra aetate* is its commitment that the Church become a community of dialogue with . . . Jewish brothers and sisters . . . in such a posture, that we have something to learn in addition to having something to say."

Since Vatican II, a number of positive steps have been taken to help foster this spirit of dialogue. Guidelines have come from the Vatican Com-

[15]*Lumen gentium,* 16.
[16]*Nostra aetate,* 4.
[17]Ibid.
[18]Ibid.

mission for Religious Relations with the Jews in 1975 and 1985 on ways for implementing dialogue and "On the Correct Way to Present Jews and Judaism in Preaching and Catechesis in the Roman Catholic Church." Among the themes emphasized are the recognition of the Jewishness of Jesus' teaching, the Jewish origins of Christian liturgy, the "spiritual fecundity" of living Judaism, the impact of the Holocaust, and the religious attachment of the Jewish people to the Land of Israel.

In academic circles, the influence of Vatican II is being felt in many ways. Rabbis and Jewish scholars are often hired as part-time or full-time instructors in Catholic universities and seminaries. Seton Hall University in New Jersey sponsors a graduate program in Judeo-Christian Studies. The imput of Jewish scholars and leaders is solicited in biblical studies, translations, and the formulation of official Catholic positions related to Judaism.

The present pope has been very active in promoting Catholic-Jewish relations through a number of important meetings and addresses. In addition to speaking at Auschwitz in 1979, John Paul II has met with Jewish groups in the United States, West Germany, France, Brazil, Spain, and Australia, as well as in the Jewish synagogue of Rome. In his address to the congregation in Rome, the Pope stated that "the Jewish religion is not 'extrinsic' to us, but in a certain way is 'intrinstic' to our own religion."[19] The pontiff went on to add: "With Judaism therefore we have a relationship which we do not have with any other religion. You are our dearly beloved brothers and, in a certain way, it could be said that you are our elder brothers."[20] While meeting with Jewish leaders in Miami in 1987, John Paul II promised a Catholic document on the Holocaust and anti-Semitism sometime in the future. Although some areas of Catholic-Jewish relations still need to be addressed,[21] it is safe to say that *Nostra aetate* has ushered in a new era of relations between Catholics and Jews. It can only be hoped that dialogue and mutual understanding will grow stronger in the future.

V. Catholic-Muslim Relations

In an effort to heal the deep wounds left by the long and sorry history of Christian-Muslim tensions, Vatican II tries to stress the religious beliefs that Christians and Muslims share in common. In *Lumen gentium*, 16, Muslims are said to be included in the plan of salvation because they acknowledge the Creator. The council recognizes a spiritual bond with the Muslims

[19]Eugene Fischer and Leon Kleniscki, eds. *Pope John Paul II on Jews and Judaism: 1976–1986* (Washington, D.C.: United States Catholic Conference, 1987) 82.

[20]Ibid.

[21]The question of full diplomatic ties between the Vatican and the state of Israel remains unresolved.

who "professing to hold the faith of Abraham, along with us adore the one and merciful God, who on the last day will judge mankind."[22]

In *Nostra aetate,* there is a longer statement of appreciation on Islam. The Church is said to look upon Muslims "with esteem."[23] There is the recognition that Muslims "adore one God, living and enduring, merciful and all-powerful, Maker of heaven and earth" and Speaker to humanity.[24] The followers of Islam are said to "strive to submit wholeheartedly even to [God's] inscrutable decrees, just as did Abraham with whom the Islamic faith is pleased to associate itself."[25] The council notes that although Muslims do not acknowledge Jesus as God, they revere him as a prophet, and they also honor Mary, his virgin mother. Muslims are commended for their belief in the day of judgment, their prizing of the moral life, and their worship of God through "prayer, almsgiving, and fasting."

The council recognizes that "many quarrels and hostilities" have arisen between Christians and Muslims in the course of the centuries. The desire of the Church now is "to forget the past and to strive sincerely for mutual understanding."[26] Thus, Christians and Muslims are called upon to "make common cause of safeguarding and fostering social justice, moral values, peace and freedom."[27]

Since the council, some concrete steps have been taken to foster Christian-Muslim dialogue. In 1964, while the council was still taking place, Pope Paul VI established the Vatican Secretariat for Non-Christians with a special department on the Islamic faith. From this Vatican Secretariat have come two important instructions on Christian-Muslim dialogue.[28] The first appeared in 1969 under the title "Guidelines for a Dialogue between Muslims and Christians." The second instruction came out in 1981 and was called "Orientations for a Dialogue between Christians and Muslims." Both of these documents provide background information on Islam that Christians should know before engaging in dialogue with Muslims. These documents also discuss the nature of dialogue which involves "relationship of persons" and a "willingness to learn from one another."[29] As John Renard notes: "For both Vatican documents, the key concept is an 'open spiri-

---

[22]*Lumen gentium,* 16.

[23]*Nostra aetate,* 3.

[24]Ibid.

[25]Ibid.

[26]Ibid.

[27]Ibid.

[28]Both these instructions are reviewed in John Renard, "Christian-Muslim Dialogue: A Review of Six Post-Vatican II Church-Related Documents," *Journal of Ecumenical Studies* 23:1 (Winter 1986) 69–89.

[29]Ibid., 77

tuality' that allows one to marvel at the work of the Spirit in other religious traditions.''[30]

The Vatican has sponsored several meetings in Europe and in Africa concerning Christian-Muslim relations.[31] These meetings have mostly involved Christians talking with other Christians about attitudes towards Islam. However, there was a meeting that took place in Tripoli, Libya, February 1-5, 1976, that was a true interreligious exchange between Christians and Muslims. A number of resolutions were drawn up at this meeting. One points to the need for Christians and Muslims to honor each other's religion and denounces "all attempts to disparage or discredit the Prophets and Messengers.''[32] This means that Christians should show respect for Muhammad and recognize his importance for the Islamic religion. Another resolution calls upon both parties to end any use of pressure intended toward conversion from one religion to the other. Other recommendations deal with the need to affirm spiritual values over secularism, the need to emphasize belief in God as the foundation for true morality, and the need for Christians and Muslims to work together in efforts to end hunger and racial discrimination and to promote world peace.[33]

As with Judaism, efforts are being made to educate more Christians about the Islamic faith. Catholics, Protestants, and Orthodox Christians have all become more interested in studying Islam in an effort towards understanding and dialogue. The Pontifical Institute for Islamic and Arab Studies in Rome run by the Missionaries of Africa (White Fathers) is a great center of Catholic studies on Islam. A number of Catholic scholars are working towards the development of a Christian theology of Islam which builds upon the work of two great Catholic Islamicists, Miguel Asin Palacios (1871-1944) and Louis Massignon (1883-1962).

José Pereira, for example, believes that Christians can appreciate Islam as a rejection of various forms of heterodox Christianity and a reaffirmation of the fundamental truths of monotheistic and prophetic religion. Christians should read the Qur'an with an eye towards the positive statements it makes regarding the virginity, purity, and preeminence of Mary and the uniquely gifted and exalted status of Jesus. The Qur'an, thus, can be understood as containing fragments and flashes of the divine truths which are more fully revealed in the gospel.

Since Islam is the second largest religion in the world after Christianity, the encouragement of Christian-Muslim dialogue is absolutely necessary.

[30]Ibid., 85.
[31]See Robert B. Sheard, *Interreligious Dialogue in the Catholic Church since Vatican II* (Lewiston, N.Y.: The Edwin Mellen Press, 1987) 102-09.
[32]Ibid., 107.
[33]Ibid., 108.

The Vatican Secretariat for Non-Christians was renamed the Pontifical Council for Interreligious Dialogue in 1988 in part to emphasize the importance of dialogue with other religions. Cardinal Francis Arinze of Nigeria, the current president of the council, has placed special emphasis on Catholic-Muslim relations.[34] In the future, it can only be hoped that these efforts towards dialogue with Muslims will prove fruitful and productive.

VI. Hindu-Christian Dialogue

"Yours is a land of ancient culture, the cradle of great religions, the home of a nation that has sought God with a relentless desire, in deep meditation and silence, and in hymns of fervent prayer."[35] These words, spoken by Pope Paul VI, in Bombay, India, in 1964 represent a decisive turning point in Catholic-Hindu relations. Although the Catholic appreciation of Hinduism can be traced back to the great Jesuit missionary Roberto de Nobili (1577–1656), it has only been in the last several decades that Catholics, on a large scale, have begun to appreciate the spiritual richness and depth of the Hindu tradition.

One aspect of the Hindu-Catholic dialogue has been in the monastic-contemplative dimension. As Wayne Teasdale shows, there have been a number of people since the time of de Nobili who have attempted to develop a Catholic monasticism which reflects the spiritual roots of the Indian subcontinent. Brahmabandab Upadhyay (1861–1907) was a Brahmin convert to Catholicism who not only founded a Catholic ashram (monastery) but also attempted to create a synthesis between the metaphysics of Hindu Vedanta and Catholic theology. Jules Monachin (1895–1957) and Henri Le Saux (1910–1973) were two French priests who established a Catholic ashram named Shantivanam in Tamil Nadu, South India. Bede Griffiths (b. 1906), an English Benedtine monk, took over as superior of Shantivanam in 1968, and continues the effort to promote a Christian spirituality which incorporates important elements of the Hindu tradition.

Another aspect of Hindu-Catholic dialogue is in the realm of systematic theology and metaphysics. This aspect, of course, is not separate from the monastic-contemplative dimension since issues of spirituality and theology are interconnected in both Hinduism and Christianity. Along with Swami Abhishiktananda (a.k.a. Dom Henri le Saux), the leading figure in Hindu-Christian systematics is Raimundo Panikkar, born of a Spanish mother and

---

[34]See "The Importance of Catholic-Moslem Dialogue," *Our Sunday Visitor* (November 25, 1990) 4.

[35]Pope Paul VI, cited in Neuner and Dupuis, *The Christian Faith in the Doctrinal Documents of the Catholic Church,* 294.

a Hindu father. Panikkar is the author of numerous books dealing with Christianity and interreligious dialogue. Among his best known writings are: *The Unknown Christ of Hinduism, The Trinity and the Religious Experience of Mankind,* and *The Intrareligious Dialogue.*

Panikkar is very much a believer in the reality of universal revelation, and he maintains that Christians can deepen their own understanding of Christ and the the divine through a study of Hinduism and Buddhism. However, he does not believe that an appreciation of the wisdom of these other religions should lead to the abandonment of the Christian faith. As Mary Byles points out, Panikkar makes clear "that dialogue and respect for other traditions does not imply watering down one's faith or diluting it into some least common denominator." Panikkar also emphasizes that one need not be spiritually a Semite or intellectually a Westerner in order to be a Christian,[36] and he makes a distinction between Christendom, Christianity, and Christianness. While Panikkar appreciates the need for Church structure and canon law, he places ultimate emphasis on Christianness which for him is the adoption of "a Christlike attitude," an attitude which is not limited to those who are confessional Christians.

The Christian-Hindu encounter continues to develop and take on new aspects. James Redington, S.J., distinguishes between the "first generation" of Hindu-Christian dialogue which emphasized spirituality and systematic theology and a growing "second generation" movement which emphasizes themes of liberation and social transformation. The first generation is embodied in figures like Henri le Saux and Raimundo Panikkar, and the second generation is represented by Asian liberation theologians like Michael Amaladoss and Aloysius Pieris. These "second generation" theologians point out that discussions of dialogue and inculturation can give way to a type of intellectual-spiritual elitism that ignores the horrible reality of poverty in India and elsewhere in Asia. Pieris, for example, calls upon all Asians—Christians, Hindus, and Buddhists alike—to unite the renunciatory poverty of their traditions with the struggle for the liberation of the suffering poor.

The dynamics of Hindu-Christian dialogue have become part of the fabric of Church life. More and more Christians are now interested in various aspects of Hindu thought and practice, be it yoga, Vedanta, or reincarnation. Some Church leaders, though, are cautious about about this growing assimilation and warn about the dangers of syncretism and "New Age" Christianity. Scholars, for their part, realize the complexity and challenge of undertaking a serious study of another tradition while remaining faithful

[36]See Raimundo Panikkar, "The Jordan, the Tiber, and the Ganges: Three Kairological Moments of Christic Self-Consciousness," *The Myth of Christian Uniqueness,* eds. J. Hick and P. Knitter (New York: Orbis Books, 1988) 89–116.

to their own. Francis Clooney, S.J., for example, recognizes that the development of expertise in a non-Christian tradition is sometimes accomplished at the cost of expertise in the Christian tradition. In spite of these difficulties, it still seems imperative that some members of the Church develop an expertise in non-Christian traditions in order to help guide the faith community in the delicate tasks of dialogue and assimilation. In the process of the systematic study of Hinduism, both the scholar and the faithful can be transformed and enriched.

VII. Christian-Buddhist Dialogue

In the generation before Vatican II, it would have seemed unthinkable for Catholic monks and nuns to be spending time living with their counterparts in Buddhist monastic communities. However, in the postconciliar Church not only does such an intermonastic hospitality program exist, it is also carried out with the knowledge and approval of the Vatican.[37] Buddhists have prayed for peace with the Pope in Assisi, Italy. The Dalai Lama has spoken to Catholics at St. Patrick's Cathedral in New York. Monks and nuns have taken courses in Zen meditation. Vatican II seems to have opened the door to the discovery of a profound wisdom and peace present in the tradition known as Buddhism.

Even before the council some Catholics like Thomas Merton had become fascinated with Buddhism, especially Zen Buddhism. By 1959, Merton's interest in Zen was significant enough that he could write to the great Zen Buddhist scholar, D.T. Suzuki: "It seems to me that Zen is the very atmosphere of the Gospels, and the Gospels are bursting with it. It is the proper climate for any monk, no matter what kind of monk he may be."[38] As Jacques Goulet shows, Merton's love of Zen moved him on a journey towards a global ecumenism which recognizes that "we are all moved by the same Spirit present at the core of our being, calling us evermore to beauty, justice, oneness, life, God, Christ, Buddha, Nirvana."

The text of *Nostra aetate* contains only two sentences on Buddhism. However, even in these few lines there is the recognition of a mature and rich tradition. Buddhism "acknowledges the radical insufficiency of this shifting world." It teaches a path by which people "can reach a state of absolute freedom or attain supreme enlightenment by their own efforts or by higher assistance."[39]

---

[37]See James Conner, O.C.S.O., "Western Monasticism Meets East," *The Catholic World* (May/June 1990) 137–43.

[38]W. H. Shannon, ed., *The Hidden Ground of Love: The Letters of Thomas Merton* (New York: Farrar, Strauss, Giroux, 1985) 561.

[39]*Nostra aetate*, 2.

Given the importance of monasticism within the Buddhist tradition, it is not surprising that some of the most significant efforts in Buddhist-Christian dialogue have been undertaken by Christian monastics. Not long after the council, the Vatican asked Benedictines and Cistercians in Europe to form an organization which could promote interreligious dialogue with non-Christian monastic traditions. This request resulted in the formation of A.I.M. (*Aide-Inter-Monasteres*), an organization based in Paris, which sponsors the activities of *Dialogue-Inter-Monasteres*, a group directly involved in interreligious monastic dialogue. The famous Bangkok conference of 1968 at which Merton died was organized under the sponsorship of A.I.M.

In 1977, the North American Board for East-West Dialogue (N.A.B.E.W.D.) was established. Although this organization was orignially a branch of A.I.M., it has become increasingly independent in recent years. The N.A.B.E.W.D. is principally directed by Cistercian monks and Benedictine nuns, and it publishes a regular newsletter out of the Abbey of Gethsemane in Kentucky.[40] This newsletter serves as a valuable resource for those interested in interreligious events, publications, book reviews, and ecclesial statements. Many Catholic bishops of Canada and the United States find the North American Board for East-West Dialogue to be one of the best sources of information on interreligious activities.

One of the most interesting of all activities sponsored by A.I.M. and the N.A.B.E.W.D. is the intermonastic hospitality program which has organized mutual tours and visitations involving Catholic monks and nuns and Japanese and Tibetan Buddhist communities. In some cases, Tibetan Buddhists have spent as long as six months living in Catholic monasteries, and Cistercian and Benedictine monks and nuns have spent the equivalent times staying in Tibetan monasteries in India. As Wayne Teasdale observes: "These contacts have profoundly deepened the existential dialogue between the Church and Buddhism."

In the realm of Catholic spirituality and theology, some very interesting developments are taking place. Roger Corless, a noted Catholic Buddhist scholar, believes there are four important ways in which Christians can benefit from a study of Buddhism: (1) the appreciation of the primacy of experience over dogma; (2) the centrality of meditation, and its necessarily embodied or incarnational character; (3) the Buddhist teaching of Emptiness and its consequences for an Eckhartian *Gelassenheit,* or letting God be God; and (4) the Buddhist ontology of non-duality as a basis for constructing a universal, non-Hellenistic, Christology.

---

[40]This newsletter can be obtained by writing to: Editor, N.A.B.E.W.D., Abbey of Gethsemane, Trappist, KY 40051. A small donation is requested but not required to receive the Bulletin.

John Keenan is another contemporary Christian Buddhist scholar who is doing pioneering work in the development of a Christology based on the teachings of Mahayana Buddhism. Keenan, like Corless, believes that Christian theology should not be confined to the categories of Greek or Western metaphysics. Thus, he attempts "to think the Gospel faith through the terms and themes of Mahayana philosophy." In the development of a Christian Mahayana theology, Keenan believes that there can be a reclaiming of "the ancient Christian tradition of apophatic theology as a valid way for serious doctrinal thinking." In this way, the Buddhist teachings of emptiness and dependent co-arising can lead to an encounter with Christ in relational terms without attempting to define an identifiable essence of either Christ or the divine. As Keenan explains: "It is in his fully and completely human identity that Christ is God. As embodying dependent co-arising, Jesus is empty of essence. As fully conventional, Jesus manifests the ultimacy of God."

VIII. Ecclesial and Pastoral Implications

Although the Vatican has given official approval to interreligious dialogue, it has also been quite cautious and conservative in its approach. On October 15, 1989, the Congregation for the Doctrine of the Faith (C.D.F.) issued a "Letter to the Bishops of the Catholic Church on Some Aspects of Christian Meditation." Since Vatican II, a number of Catholic communities have developed techniques of prayer which bear some affinities with various forms of Hindu and Buddhist meditation. While monks like John Main, Thomas Keating, and Basil Pennington have encouraged a Christian method of meditation known as "centering prayer," there are others who favor techniques like Transcendental Meditation (TM) taken over from Hinduism or various forms of mantras taken over from Buddhism.

It is was with these concerns in mind that the C.D.F. issued its letter. While many Catholics have reacted to the Vatican instruction as being overly cautious or even misleading, others have tried to emphasize that at least the Letter states that various methods of prayer should not "be rejected out of hand simply because they are not Christian."[41] The main theme of the Letter seems to be that Catholics can make use of non-Christian prayer forms "so long as the Christian conception of prayer, its logic and requirements are never obscured" (sec. 16).

Vatican fears of potential syncretism are also manifest in the December 1988 demand for a year of silence on the part of Dominican friar Matthew Fox. Apparently, Fox's version of "Creation Spirituality" is perceived as being too uncritical in its assimilation of wisdom from Native American,

---

[41]"On Christian Meditation," *The Pope Speaks* 35:2 (April/May 1990) 95.

Eco-Feminist, and "Neo-Pagan" sources. Defenders of Fox, however, claim that the Vatican feels threatened because he is challenging the patriarchical, Eurocentric power structure of present Church authority.

Another area of pastoral concern is the catechesis of non-Christian religions. Most Catholic colleges and seminaries now offer (or even require) courses dealing with non-Christian religions. But how are these religions to be understood? Certainly *Nostra aetate* maintains that elements of truth and holiness are to be found in these religions as well as a ray of the divine light. However, the council still leaves open a number of important questions. Do the non-Christian religions reflect supernatural revelation or do they merely embody what is sometimes called "natural revelation"—the knowledge of God reflected in the natural order? If there is a ray of the divine light, how significant is it? Is it merely a faint glimmer or is it a radiant epiphany?

There are still other pastoral implications of interreligious dialogue for the postconciliar Church. Chester Gillis speaks of a "paradigm shift," and P. Joseph Cahill talks of a "new theological grammar" that is developing on world religions since Vatican II. However, as with most changes, there is sometimes a tendency to either retreat back to an earlier paradigm or grammar or to leap ahead to one that has not been fully established. This explains some of the controversy and ferment that is apparent in the present-day Church.

Chester Gillis, for example, points out that even in Catholic universities, it is not unusual to have students from Jewish, Muslim, Hindu, and Buddhist backgrounds mixing with the traditional Christian students. How should teachers prepare students to have personal contact and theological encounters with those of other faiths? Ronald Pachence suggests that we understand meetings with those of other faiths as "sacramental encounters" in which grace can be mediated. Gillis recommends that we move to a more pluralistic theology of religion in which Christianity is understood as but one among a number of valid religious expressions. In this way, Christians can have a true respect for the faith of the other without being judgmental or assuming an air of religious superiority.

IX. Inclusivism or Pluralism?

The theological issue that is now being faced is whether Christians should continue within the inclusivistic model taught by Vatican II or move towards a more pluralistic model in which Christianity is understood as a sure way toward salvation but not the exclusive way toward salvation. This question has spawned one of the most critical theological debates of recent times. On the one side are those who favor the inclusivist model. According to this view, God's universal salvific is understood to include non-Christians as well as Christians, but Christ is still upheld as the universal means of salvation. In other words, non-Christians are saved through the grace of Christ which works in and through their own religious traditions, whether they know it or not.

The inclusivist model has often been associated with the German Catholic theologian Karl Rahner (d. 1984) who served as a "peritus" for the council. Rahner's theology is apparent in *Lumen gentium,* 16, in which the allowance is made for the salvation of non-Christians who respond to divine grace and follow God as known to them "in the dictates of conscience." For Rahner and Vatican II, Christ is the universal Savior and Christianity is the absolute religion which contains the "all-embracing means" of grace. Thus, the grace which is available for all human beings is universally mediated through Christ, the universal Savior. However, as Francis Berna notes, the inclusiveness of all religious truth in Christ "does not necessarily mean explicit Christianity." Since all human beings experience the mystery of transcendence in the "supernatural existential" of the unlimited horizon of being, all human beings also encounter the grace of Christ in the concreteness of their own "historical reality—as Hindu, Buddhist, Muslim, Jew, or animist."[42]

This is the famous Rahnerian theory of "The Anonymous Christian" which has its supporters as well as its critics. While many Christians feel comfortable with Rahner's position, some Christians (and, of course, non-Christians) do not. For example, K. R. Sundararajan, a Hindu, notes that although Rahner's position is to be preferred over Christian exclusivism, it still seems to be based on a "staircase theory" of religion: "Though the more or less situation is better than 'either or,' it may not prove satisfactory, especially for those placed under the 'less' category." Sundararajan realizes that Rahner's theory is a Christian perspective intended for Christians trying to understand non-Christians. However, he points out that within Hinduism it is possible to have an absolute commitment to one spiritual path without the need to "judge others in terms of the 'Absolute claim' of my religion." Is it possible for Christians to embrace such an overtly pluralistic perspective?

In recent years, there have indeed emerged some Christian theologians who argue for a move beyond an inclusivist paradigm to a more pluralistic position. Thinkers like Paul Knitter, Rosemary Ruether, and John Hick insist that it is imperialistic to claim Christian uniqueness and supersessionism. Knitter believes that it is possible to have a firm belief "in the uniqueness

---

[42]Rahner's exposition of these ideas can be found in *Theological Investigations,* vol. 9 (London: Darton, Longman and Todd Ltd., 1972) 146–56.

and universal significance of what God has done in Jesus" without being closed to the uniqueness and universal significance of what "the divine mystery may have revealed through others." As he writes: "In boldly proclaiming that God has indeed been defined in Jesus, Christians will also humbly admit that God has not been confined to Jesus."[43] More recently, Knitter has urged Christians to adopt the primacy of orthopraxis over orthodoxy and develop a liberation theology of religions in which the preferential option for the poor is the universal criterion of soteriological efficacy.[44]

Needless to say, Knitter has not been without his critics. Some have criticized him for undermining missionary efforts.[45] Others argue that his pluralistic paradigm undercuts the very essence of the Christian faith and creates its own imperialism since it leads to the relativizing of all religious claims to absolute truth.[46] Gavin D'Costa is one of the most articulate critics of the pluralist paradigm and defenders of the inclusivist position. D'Costa argues that it is possible to be faithful to the fullness of Christ and the catholicity of the Church while still being open to hearing "the voice of God, through the Spirit, in the testimonies of peoples from other religions."[47] He maintains that a true appreciation of the universal depth and mystery of Christ and the Trinity can open Christians to the presence of the divine in the other religions without abandoning the essential interpretive framework of the Christian faith.

There can be no doubt that D'Costa's position is more in harmony with the explicit teachings of *Lumen gentium* and *Nostra aetate*. Defenders of pluralism, however, maintain that Vatican II should not be seen as the last word on Christianity and world religions. Rather, it is only the opening to a new horizon. Whatever direction this discussion takes, we can be certain that it will not go away. The very nature of the self-identity of the Christian faith is implicated in this important question of inclusivism versus pluralism.

Conclusion

The progress, creativity, and ferment engendered by Vatican II's statements on world religions are a fitting testimony to the presence of the Spirit

[43]Paul Knitter, *No Other Name? A Critical Survey of Christian Attitudes toward the World Religions* (New York: Orbis Books, 1985) 203–04.

[44]See Paul Knitter, "Toward a Liberation Theology of Religions," *The Myth of Christian Uniqueness*, 178–200.

[45]See article by Lucio Brunelli, "Missionaries without Christ?," *30 Days* (March 1989) 56–61.

[46]See Paul Griffiths, "The Uniqueness of Christian Doctrine Defended," *Christian Uniqueness Reconsidered:The Myth of a Pluralistic Theology of Religions*, ed. Gavin D'Costa (New York: Orbis Books, 1990) 157–73.

[47]Gavin D'Costa, "Christ, the Trinity and Religious Plurality," *Christian Uniqueness Reconsidered*, 27.

at the council. When Pope John XXIII invoked the metaphor of opening the windows to let in some fresh air, he was truly being prophetic. There have been so many positive developments in interreligious dialogue in the last twenty-five years that we can speak of *Nostra aetate* as one of the most outstanding achievements of the council. The Church has moved from the closed windows of the ghetto of Catholic exclusivity to the open corridors of dialogue, love, and cooperation with those of the other faiths.

This is not to say that more cannot be done. The Church, as the pilgrim people of God, is always on a journey filled with struggles, trials, and setbacks. However, as we reflect on the last twenty-five years, we need to marvel at the many breakthroughs in dialogue and cooperation that have been achieved. The Holy Spirit has opened so many hearts and minds to the wisdom and grace found within the diverse religions of the world. Since Vatican II, "the joys and the hopes, the griefs and the anxieties"[48] experienced by Christians can now be seen in solidarity with the deepest spiritual aspirations of the rest of humanity. The windows have indeed been opened. Let us pray that the air will remain fresh.

[48]*Gaudium et spes,* 1.

Conclusion

Rembert G. Weakland, O.S.B.

History teaches us that there are certain events that vividly sum up the past, realistically come to terms with the present, and decisively shape the future. For the Catholic Church, for the whole of Christianity, and for all religions in general we would have to say that Vatican Council II was such an event. I added that it was an important event for all religions because of its attitudes toward those religions, a posture that affected even their life and future through its insistence on a new dialogue with them on those points that are held in common.

These pivotal events often seem to come out of nowhere; but we know that often they have been in preparation for years. Ideas begin to germinate and take hold; the event is but the crystallization of those ideas. Certainly that was true of Vatican Council II as well. We Catholics in the United States did not notice that preparation as much, except perhaps in the area of liturgy, but the buildup in Europe, because it had had a livelier dialogue in recent centuries with the Enlightenment and its consequences, was much more evident. Yet, we can say that the event went beyond the preparation and created its own event.

Some events have an immediate impact; for others the results are a bit slower in coming. Strangely enough, one would have to say that Vatican Council II had both an immediate impact and then a slower but more important delayed influence that grew stronger as the years went on. The immediate impact was also felt first in liturgy, but gradually the underlying ecclesiology that effected such a reform began to take hold of the population. Vatican Council II has had an impact on everyone without exception; it has touched scholars, clergy, and the people in the pew. The mind-change that it has demanded has slowly affected everyone.

After twenty-five years one could say that the immediate impact is over and that the slower assimilation is now in operation. It would also be true to say that opposing sides concerning that event have solidified. Much is being written about that council and interpreting it; but less dialogue is taking place around it, since positions seem frozen. These papers show that this trend does not necessarily have to succeed. There can stlll be much dialogue with regard to the documents and with respect to the spirit of Vatican II. Some would like to deny the point of a "spirit" of Vatican Council II, but that would fly in the face of a very clear reality. Vatican Council II did engender a spirit that has not died.

During this period of slower impact articles such as those collected in this book are important. They show all the divergent ways of looking at the event and of gaining inspiration from it. Moreover, the implementation of Vatican Council II has presented its own point of departure for examination. This council has led to many divergent views as to what happened, what was meant by the documents, what is underneath some of them, how they should be implemented. In other words, the very nature of the event and the documents that it produced have had their own very special effect on the subsequent generation as the council was gradually implemented on the official level. It has led to a richness of points of view and arguments that I am sure the original planners never intended. They thought that their words were clear enough and that the implementation would be fairly simple.

Some, unhappy with the official and unofficial implementation, are trying to go back to the texts themselves, as if nothing had happened since, and reinterpret them along new lines, often with the assertion, implied or explicitly stated, that this new interpretation is the only one intended by the council fathers. This kind of revisionist theory is dictated by a certain uneasiness with some of the theories that have been published in the name of the council.

Others have already demonstrated to their own satisfaction that the council did not have time to bring the issues it proposed to their ultimate conclusions and so have taken as their main effort preparing the ground for Vatican Council III. These enormous differences have led to a certain amount of dispute and at times acrimony; but, all in all, they have been helpful and fruitful—as these essays prove.

More than anything else, however, these articles show that Vatican Council II was not an event where the spirit and the initiative would die quickly. Rather, they are proof that the event, even after twenty-five years, is still able to generate much thought and provoke much debate and discussion. In that respect, one could say that—for modern times—it was indeed a very remarkable event. Few documents in today's world survive several decades in their freshness. Vatican Council II has called Catholics to attractive and stimulating insights, to new visions, to greater openness, to deeper awareness of the world around them and in which they live and move and theologize. It has also affected the rest of the religious world and especially the rest of Christianity. In that it could be called an immense success.

What is important, however, is that it succeeds in bringing us all closer to a realization of what it means to be a part of God's kingdom and shows us how that kingdom is being lived out at the end of our century. For Catholics, at least, it is the focal point and guiding principle in their attempt to come to terms with modernity and its implications for our day. Vatican Council II did not have all the answers to today's world, but it posed the right questions and set us on the right path. For Catholics, also, it marks the end of the isolationism that began with the Enlightenment and signals the beginning of a new period of reflection and action, one that takes this world seriously and wishes to work with all those who are partners in trying to make it a better home for the human family.

It has made us all aware of a basic truth that is so needed in our day and in the decades to come: namely, that we, as a human family, share on this earth a more common destiny than we previously ever could have imagined, and that such a destiny demands new ways of thinking and acting among us.

Church Tody   XXii xxv

Obsequium Religiosum   c752 p 13

Laity — Recent trend. p 226—>